Studies in Legal History

Published in association with the American Society for Legal History

Editor: Stanley N. Katz

Volumes in the Series

Frederic William Maitland: A Life *C. H. S. Fifoot*

Impeachment: The Constitutional Problems *Raoul Berger*

The Autobiographical Notes of Charles Evans Hughes
David J. Danelski and Joseph S. Tulchin, eds.

Prosecuting Crime in the Renaissance: England, Germany, France
John H. Langbein

John H. Langbein

PROSECUTING CRIME IN THE RENAISSANCE

ENGLAND, GERMANY, FRANCE

Harvard University Press Cambridge, Massachusetts **1974**

Library of Congress Catalog Card Number 73-81670
SBN 674-71675-2
Printed in the United States of America

ACKNOWLEDGMENTS

Various portions of this book have been read and criticized in earlier drafts by Messrs. Peter Glazebrook and Michael Prichard and Professor Peter Stein of Cambridge University; Professor R. C. van Caenegem of the University of Ghent; Professor John P. Dawson, Miss Edith Henderson, and Professor Lloyd Weinreb of the Harvard Law School; Professor Thomas H. Green of the University of Michigan Law School; Dr. J. S. Cockburn of the University of Maryland; Professor Thomas G. Barnes of the University of California at Berkeley; and my colleagues Professors Charles M. Gray and Max Rheinstein of the University of Chicago Law School. I have taken many points from them. Chapter 3 received a particularly helpful critique from a parliamentary historian, Mr. Leslie Jenkins of Clare Hall, Cambridge. With respect to Chapter 4 I have many debts. Early in my search for archive material I was given my bearings in discussions with Mr. D. E. C. Yale and with Professor G. R. Elton and his student, Mr. Joel Samaha, in Cambridge; with Mr. John Kaye of Queen's College, Oxford; and in correspondence with Professor J. H. Gleason of Pomona College, California. Miss J. M. Kennedy, City and County Archivist at the Norfolk and Norwich Record Office, helped me to use the Norwich archives. Dr. W. Hamilton Bryson of Clare College, Cambridge, simplified my work in the Public Record Office and deciphered any Tudor handwriting which I could not. Other chapters in Part I have benefited from suggestions made in correspondence by Mr. R. F. Hunnisett of the Public Record Office and Miss Elizabeth Melling of the Kent County Record Office. Miss Henderson, curator of the Harvard Law School Treasure Room, greatly facilitated my use of the early English printed literature housed in her care.

Much of the research for Part II of this book was undertaken during a year's stay at the Max-Planck-Institut für Europäische Rechtsgeschichte, Frankfurt am Main. I am indebted to Professor Helmut Coing, the director, and to the deputy director, Dr. Walter Wilhelm, for making the facilities of the institute available to me. Within its walls I found many counselors to help with the Continental materials: Dr. Dieter Grimm,

Professor Gunter Gudian, Dr. Ernst Holthöfer, Herr Hans-Jürgen König, Dr. Klaus Luig, Dr. Heinz Mohnhaupt, Dr. Norbert Reich, and Dr. Armin Wolf. I must especially acknowledge the help of Dr. Gerhard Immel, the institute's specialist in early modern legislation, to whom I had constant resort, and of Frl. Veronika Götz, director of the library, who went to considerable trouble to assemble material for me from collections near and far.

This study is a revision of a Ph.D. thesis submitted to Cambridge University in 1971. Peter Stein, the Regius Professor of Civil Law, acted as my supervisor. He reviewed countless drafts and improved them all. I recall with great obligation the support and encouragement he gave this work.

During the research and writing of this book I had to impose on the good offices of some strategically situated friends, whose help was extended often: Erich and Rosemarie Schanze in Frankfurt, Guy and Julia Whitburn in London, and Peter Handford in Cambridge.

The photographs from the chap-books that appear in Chapter 2 and on the jacket are used with the permission of the trustees of the British Museum.

The award of a Harvard Law School Fellowship in Foreign and Comparative Law sustained me during three years of research. I must thank Professors Arthur T. von Mehren and John P. Dawson of the fellowship committee for their interest and support. Further financial assistance was received from the Committee on General Scholarships of Harvard University, the Foreign Law Program of the University of Chicago Law School, the Research Students' Fund of Trinity Hall, Cambridge, and the National Endowment for the Humanities. The University of Chicago Law School defrayed the extensive secretarial and related costs of preparing the manuscript to become a book.

Further acknowledgments preface the translations in Appendixes B and C.

ABBREVIATIONS

Brunnenmeister	Brunnenmeister, Emil, *Die Quellen der Bambergensis* (Leipzig, 1879)
Dalton	Dalton, Michael, *The Countrey Justice* (London, 1618)
Dawson, *Lay Judges*	Dawson, John P., *A History of Lay Judges* (Cambridge, Mass., 1960)
Dawson, *Oracles*	Dawson, John P., *The Oracles of the Law* (Ann Arbor, 1968)
Esmein	Esmein, Adhémar, *Histoire de la procédure criminelle en France, et spécialement de la procédure inquisitoire depuis le XIIIe siècle jusqu'à nos jours* (Paris, 1882)
Gleason	Gleason, J. H., *The Justices of the Peace in England 1558–1640* (Oxford, 1969)
Güterbock	Güterbock, Carl, *Die Entstehungsgeschichte der Carolina* (Würzburg, 1876)
Holdsworth	Holdsworth, Sir William, *A History of English Law*, 16 vols. (London, 1922–1966)
Imbert	Imbert, Jean, *La pratique judiciaire, tant civile que criminelle . . .* (Cologny, 1615)
Isambert	Isambert, Decrusy and Jourdan, *Recueil général les anciennes lois françaises depuis l'an 420 jusqu'à la révolution de 1789* (Paris, 1823–1833)
Lambarde	Lambard[e], William, *Eirenarcha: or Of the office of the Justices of Peace* (London, 1581)
Lambarde, *Ephemeris & Charges*	*William Lambarde and Local Government: His "Ephemeris" and Twenty-nine Charges to Juries and Commissions*, Conyers Read, ed. (Ithaca, N.Y., 1962)
Norwich Depositions 1549–54	Norfolk and Norwich Record Office: Interrogatories and Depositions, Case 12, Shelf a, Bundle Ia
Putnam, *Early Treatises*	Putnam, Bertha H., *Early Treatises on the Practice of the Justices of the Peace in the Fifteenth and Sixteenth Centuries*, Oxford Studies in Social and Legal History, vol. 7 (Oxford, 1924)
Putnam, *Toronto*	Putnam, Bertha H., "Sixteenth-Century Treatises for Justices of the Peace," *Toronto Law Journal* 7:137–161 (1947)
Radbruch	Radbruch, Gustav, "Zur Einführung in die Carolina," in *Die Peinliche Gerichtsordnung Karls V. von 1532 (Carolina)*, Reclam ed. (Stuttgart, 1949)

Rye	*Depositions Taken before the Mayor and Aldermen of Norwich 1549–1567*, Walter Rye, ed. (Norwich, 1905)
Schmidt, *Carolina*	Schmidt, Eberhard, "Die Carolina," *Zeitschrift der Savigny-Stiftung für Rechtsgeschichte (germanistische Abteilung)* 53: 1–34 (1933)
Schmidt, *Einführung*	Schmidt, Eberhard, *Einführung in die Geschichte der deutschen Strafrechtspflege*, 3rd ed. (Göttingen, 1965)
Schmidt, *Inquisitionsprozess*	Schmidt, Eberhard, *Inquisitionsprozess und Rezeption* (Leipzig, 1940)
Smith, *De Republica*	Smith, Sir Thomas, *De Republica Anglorum* (London, 1583)
Stephen	Stephen, Sir James Fitzjames, *A History of the Criminal Law of England*, 3 vols. (London, 1883)
von Hippel	von Hippel, Robert, *Deutsches Strafrecht* (Berlin, 1925)
von Weber	von Weber, Hellmuth, "Die Peinliche Halsgerichtsordnung Kaiser Karls V.," *Zeitschrift der Savigny-Stiftung für Rechtsgeschichte (germanistische Abteilung)* 77:288–310 (1960)

CONTENTS

INTRODUCTION

Only in the sixteenth century did English criminal process acquire the outline of modern pretrial procedure for cases of serious crime, a formal system of official investigation and evidence-gathering which came to be called preliminary inquiry. It was first provided in a pair of statutes under Queen Mary in the years 1554–1555, which stipulated that justices of the peace should examine suspects and witnesses, transcribe their testimony, and certify the record to the trial court. These features are reminiscent of contemporary Continental inquisitorial procedure, and they have been taken in previous scholarship to represent in some degree a borrowing from Continental models—a reception of Roman law. Because the investigating magistrate was the key figure in Continental *Inquisitionsprozess*, the Marian statutes raise the issue of whether the attempt was being made to introduce into England the institution which lingers today as the *juge d'instruction* in France and the *Ermittlungsrichter* in Germany. The present study contends that it has been error to ascribe the English procedure to Roman-canon influence. English and Continental sources, it is urged, establish that the English development was indigenous and dissociated from Roman-canon practice.

The Continental sources are indispensable to proper understanding of the reception question, but their utility is wider. Comparison with the Continental systems will raise some key questions about the nature and function of the Marian statutes and the underlying movements in contemporary English procedure to which the statutes responded. For it does not suffice simply to disprove reception. If the proponents of reception misread the evidence, they did not invent it. Something strange to the previous course of the common law was indeed happening. That it has not been properly understood may result in a double sense from the prominence of the reception idea, which not only distorted the previous scholarship but also retarded it. Virtually no work has been done on the aspects of sixteenth-century English criminal procedure which are the concern of this book. Yet these were the formative years, from which much survives into our own day. Part of the explanation for the neglect must be the paucity of certain of the sources; but the reception thesis may also have been a deterrent. For when convention has it that our institutions sprang full-grown from a foreign legal system, the inclination is to leave them to foreign legal historians.

The developments which inspired the reception thesis, and which in the result have been obscured by it, were part of a thorough transformation in the administration of the criminal law—as important a reordering as common law criminal procedure has ever known. These changes admitted into our procedure the essential elements of rationalization which the medieval system had avoided, but which could no longer be shunned. More than was the course on the Continent, however, the development in England involved not a supplanting of older institutions by newer, but a recasting and sharpening of function within a framework of institutional continuity. The law of criminal evidence began to form, rationalizing in some measure the arbitrary medieval institution of jury trial. And the prosecutorial function began to crystallize into the rational and efficient institution of the modern law—removed in function (though not for centuries more in form) from the community and officialized, that is, lodged with the magistrates. Like so much else in Tudor England, this transformation marked the passage from the medieval to the modern world. It was an indispensable prerequisite for the criminal procedure of the nation-state.

I should say for the benefit of nonspecialist readers that the statutory summary in Chapter 4 needs only to be browsed. The statutory analysis in Chapter 1, too, is more technical and slower to read than the rest of the book, but is essential to a critical reading of the remainder.

PART I The Marian Statutes

CHAPTER 1 The Statutory Texts

The essential text for the present study, the preliminary inquiry scheme erected by statute in 1555, has a severely contorted history in predecessor legislation. The careful reader cannot be spared the necessarily technical study of those antecedents. Only with a proper awareness of the content and context of the Marian statutes is it safe to venture out to the grander issues of interpretation they invite.

The Marian preliminary inquiry followed an odd route to the statute book. Initially, most of the mechanics were elaborated in a different setting, as a procedure for the bailing of suspected felons by justices of the peace (JPs); then, within a year's time, the system was reenacted to a wider purpose: preliminary inquiry upon committal, when bail had been denied. (Both statutes are set forth in full in Appendix A.)

It will simplify our account of the Marian legislation to recall a few generalities about the magistracy. The JPs were for the most part leading local gentry, appointed by royal commission for each county. The title "justice" appeared in 1360–1361, when by statute the JPs sitting collectively at their "sessions" were given a judicial power to try "all manner of Felonies and Trespasses . . . ."[1] But that act also prescribed nonjudicial duties, harkening back to the JPs' origins as "keepers" of the peace. It empowered them, for example, to deal with vagabonds—comprehending "all those that have been Pillors and Robbers in the Parts beyond the Sea, and be now come again, and go wandering, and will not labour as they were wont in Times past . . . . " Of these the JPs were "to take and arrest all those that they may find by Indictment, or by Suspicion, and put them in Prison; and to take of all them that be [not] of good Fame, where they shall be found, sufficient Surety and Mainprise of their good Behaviour towards the King and his People, and the other duly to punish . . . ."[2]

1. 34 Edw. III c. 1 (1360–61).

2. Id. Translation from the French of pre-Tudor statutes is that of the editors of the *Statutes of the Realm* here and throughout this work. So too are most bracketed interpolations. Footnotes to editors' commentary and citation of conflicting texts have been deleted. (Spelling in the Marian statutes of 1554–1555 has been modernized in Appendix A and throughout.)

The command to take an active role in what we would regard as police business, coupled with the power of summary conviction for lesser matters, is as old as the office. The justices became impartial committing magistrates only in the nineteenth century.[3] During the centuries before the appearance of professional police, individual JPs (and the constables and sheriffs over whom they became ascendant) policed the land. It is the frontier lawman and his posse rather than the Victorian magistrate that is called to mind by an early fifteenth-century statute directing the JPs, upon report of riot, to fetch a sheriff or an undersheriff and to gather "the Power of the County," thence to gallop off to arrest the malefactors.[4] The JPs came routinely to supervise the rudimentary pretrial procedures of the late Middle Ages. They issued warrants of arrest,[5] and in the statute of 1360–1361 they acquired the power to grant bail.[6]

A. THE BAIL STATUTE

The first of the two Marian statutes, "An Act appointing an Order to Justices of Peace for the Bailment of Prisoners," 1 & 2 Philip & Mary c. 13 (1554–1555), commences with the customary Tudor era preamble recounting the evil it proposes to cure. The problem was collusive bailing of suspected felons by unscrupulous justices of the peace. This was not a new concern. As the Preamble recalls, a statute of 1487[7] had denounced the same abuse and had devised a procedure to prevent it. The 1487 statute required that bail thereafter be granted in cases of suspected felony by not less than two justices (previously a single justice had been able to bail);[8] and further, it required that at least one of these justices certify the fact of the bailment, either to his fellow justices at the next general sessions or to the next sitting commission of gaol delivery.[9]

3. J. F. Stephen, *A History of the Criminal Law of England* (London, 1883) I 220–221 [hereafter cited as Stephen].

4. 13 Hen. IV c. 7 (1411).

5. Stephen I 190.

6. Stephen observes, id. at I 233: "When the administration of justice was in its infancy, arrest meant imprisonment without preliminary inquiry till the sheriff held his tourn at least, and, in more serious cases, till the arrival of the [assize] justices, which might be delayed for years, and it was therefore a matter of the utmost importance to be able to obtain a provisional release from custody."

7. 3 Hen. VII c. 3 (1487).

8. 1 Ric. III c. 3 (1483–84).

9. Simultaneously, a duty had been imposed upon sheriffs and other gaolkeepers to report to the gaol deliverers "every prisoner unto them committed for any [felony] . . . ." This presumably intended a further check on the JPs' bailings, since it would disclose all cases of release of prisoners.

It is not immediately obvious why the draftsmen of the statutes of 1487 and 1554–1555 were so concerned with regulating the power of the justices of the peace to bail, that is, the power to release conditionally, when nothing is said of the power of absolute release. Stephen remarks that "as soon as justices of the peace were erected into intermediate judges, charged to decide the question whether there was or was not ground for the detention of a suspected person, they must have acquired, on the one hand, the power of discharge, and on the other, the power of committal." [10] On this assumption it would seem pointless for the statutes of 1487 and 1554–1555 to have hedged in a JP's power to bail, when he could simply have discharged his favorite.

In point of fact, Stephen erred. The JP's power to discharge was not acquired simultaneously with his power to detain, but centuries later. The seventeenth-century authorities treat the point directly. The first edition of Dalton's *The Countrey Justice* explains in 1618 that, "where any Felonie is committed, and one brought before the Justice of Peace upon suspition thereof, though it shall appeare to the Justice, that the prisoner is not guiltie thereof," the justice must nonetheless either commit him to prison or "joyne with some other in the Baylement of him," because "it is not fit that a man once arrested and charged with Felonie (or suspition thereof) should bee delivered by any mans [*sic*] Discretion, without further triall." [11] Sir Matthew Hale's *Pleas of the Crown* is a little clearer about the rule, if not the rationale: "If a person be brought before a Justice, if it appears no Felony be committed, he may discharge him; but if a Felony be committed, though it appears not that the party accused is guilty, yet he cannot discharge him but must commit or bail him." [12] Only persons exercising a commission of gaol delivery, typically the assize judges, could discharge accused felons.[13] The JP had only two options when someone had been accused of undoubted felony. He could jail the accused or bail him. He could not discharge him. Of course, the

10. Stephen I 233.

11. M. Dalton, *The Countrey Justice* (London, 1618) 260 [hereafter cited as Dalton].

12. M. Hale, *Pleas of the Crown: Or, A Methodical Summary* (London, 1678) 98. This edition denounces as "a surreptitious and very faulty Copy," id. at A2, another edition which differs only slightly in the passage quoted: M. Hale, *Pleas of the Crown: Or, A Brife but Full Account* (London, 1678) 85.

13. E. Coke, *The Fourth Part of the Institutes of the Laws of England* (London, 1644) 168: The justices of gaol delivery "may deliver suspects for felony, &c. by Proclamation, against whom there is no sufficient evidence produced to the Great Inquest to indict them, &c., which Justices of Oier and Terminer, or Justices of Peace cannot do."

fact that a release was conditional and not absolute was simply a matter of the legal theory upon which the JP acted. But when there was subsequent default upon the condition, the accused failing to appear for trial, the consequences were different. There was a forfeiture of bond to the crown, the accused was fugitive, and the trial court would have occasion to determine whether the justice had acted properly—whether the offense was bailable by statute, whether the particular bailment was reasonable.[14] This determination had a sanction: the statutes of 1487 and 1554–1555 imposed fines upon JPs who bailed wrongfully. Hence, to regulate the JP's bailing power was to regulate his sole releasing power.[15]

The stated concern of the Marian bail statute of 1554–1555 was to improve the trial court's basis of review of improper bailment. The complaint voiced in the Preamble to the Marian bail statute is that the procedure laid down in the 1487 statute was being evaded:

> [O]ne justice of Peace, in the name of himself and one other of the Justices his companion, not making the said [companion] Justice party nor privy unto the case wherefore the Prisoner should be bailed, hath often times by sinister labor and means set at large the greatest and notablest Offenders, such as be not replevisable by the Laws of this Realm, and yet the rather to hide their affections in that behalf, have signified the cause of their apprehension to be but only for suspicion of Felony, whereby the said Offenders hath escaped unpunished, and do daily . . . .

When a suspect conditionally released defaulted on his obligation to appear and took flight, he put the amateur law enforcement agencies of the time to the awkward business of apprehending him a second time. Were collusive or otherwise wrongful bailing suspected, the court of gaol delivery had as its only check the certificate required by the 1487 statute. The Marian statute calls that insufficient for two reasons. First, the requirement that two JPs certify the bailment had a loophole: it did not

14. "In felony, bail may be admitted where the fact is not notorious and the person not of evil fame." F. Bacon, "A Preparation toward the Union of Laws," in *The Works of Francis Bacon* (J. Spedding et al., eds.) (London, 1861) VII 727, at 740.

15. I owe this point to the insight of Mr. Peter Glazebrook, who also points out that the responsibility of the hundred for the apprehension of perpetrators of felony within the hundred continued until the accused appeared at trial, which helps explain the tenacity of the rule that only a trial court could discharge an accused. See 27 Eliz. I c. 13 (1585), perpetuating and adjusting procedurally the liability in damages of the hundred for failure to answer for the bodies of felons for felony committed within the hundred. See also infra, Chapter 5, note 72.

direct the two justices to act contemporaneously. Devious JPs had learned, in Lambarde's words, "to borrowe one an others name, (as manye yet still doe) and by that meanes defraude the good meanyng of the Statute . . . ."[16] Second, the certificate itself afforded the trial court inadequate basis for determining whether the bailment had been lawful, since it disclosed the "cause of [the suspect's] apprehension to be but only for suspicion of Felony . . . ." As a remedy, the Marian statute instituted its scheme.

To begin with, the act repeats the absolute prohibition of bail in those serious cases enumerated in the Statute of Westminster I (1275).[17] It then provides that where one or more persons have been "arrested for manslaughter or felony or suspicion of manslaughter or felony, being bailable by law," bail shall not be granted "if it be not in open Sessions" save under certain conditions. That is, when not acting in open court, the JPs may bail accused felons only in conformance with the following statutory terms:

(1) Two justices, of whom one is to be "of the quorum," must join in the grant. This repeats the provision of the 1487 act. (The quorum clause of the commission of the peace designated a "select number" of the justices of the county, at least one of whom was obliged to be among those justices who sat at quarter sessions or who exercised various statutory powers to hear and determine out of sessions. "These of the *Quorum*, were wont not without just cause to be chosen, specially for their learning in the laws of the Realme . . . . [This] power to heare and determine [is that] in which part that kinde of learning is most requisite and serviceable."[18])

16. W. Lambard[e], *Eirenarcha: or Of the Office of the Justices of Peace* (London, 1581) 250 (italics in original) [hereafter cited as Lambarde]. The date of the title page is 1581, "but this is clearly old style since Lambarde's preface is: 'From Lincolnes Inne, this 27. day of Januarie: 1581.'" J. H. Gleason, *The Justices of the Peace in England 1558–1640* (Oxford, 1969) 1 n. 2 [hereafter cited as Gleason].

Three later editions of the *Eirenarcha* have also been used for the present work and are cited by date, e.g., "Lambarde (1588 ed.)." The 1588 edition was the first substantial revision by Lambarde himself. The 1591 edition added a commentary on the new form of the commission of the peace which had been introduced in 1590. The 1599 edition was the last substantial revision by Lambarde, although new editions continued to issue until 1619 when Dalton's manual (supra, note 11), based heavily on the *Eirenarcha*, seems to have supplanted it. Throughout the present work the practice is to cite the earliest edition of the *Eirenarcha* in which a particular point appears—usually, therefore, the first edition.

17. 3 Edw. I c. 15 (1275).

18. Lambarde 55–56. Lambarde's cagey language ("wont . . . to be chosen, specially for their learning") hints at the point Professor Gleason has lately docu-

(2) The justices must "be present together at the time of the said Bailment . . . ."[19] Here is the response to the chicanery denounced in the Preamble.

(3) The two justices "shall certify" the bailment "in writing signed or subscribed with their own hands . . . ." The express requirement of writing and signature does not appear in the 1487 statute, and it may have been that the earlier practice was oral report.

(4) The statute directs that the certificate be submitted to "the next general Gaol Delivery"—not, therefore, to the court of quarter sessions, which in theory had concurrent jurisdiction in most cases of felony. Gaol delivery was one of five commissions customarily issued to the assize judges for their semiannual circuits.[20] By the mid-sixteenth century the commission of gaol delivery was rarely issued separately. When the statute speaks of gaol delivery, therefore, it is using a shorthand expression meaning the itinerant royal judges sitting at assizes in their capacity as trial judges for criminal business. The next Parliament's committal statute carried forward this requirement of certification to gaol delivery. It inevitably resulted in a reallocation of felony trial jurisdiction away from the JPs and to the assize judges, a development whose connection to the rest of the scheme will be discussed in Chapter 5.

(5) There then follows the feature which becomes crucial when it is repeated in the committal statute and which is wholly novel to previous bail legislation:

> And that the said Justices or one of them being of the Quorum, when any such Prisoner is brought before them for any Manslaughter or Felony, before any Bailment or Mainprise, shall take the examination

---

mented: that by Elizabethan times the quorum was already far from "select." Gleason 4. The subject of the quorum and its relation to the Marian statutes will be discussed in Chapter 5.

19. There is a proviso to the statute (par. 2) the apparent effect of which is to relieve borough jurisdiction from compliance with the two-justice rule, but not from the examination procedure and the requirement of certification at gaol delivery. This seems to be the meaning of the language saving to the "Cities Boroughs and Towns Corporate . . . authority to let to bail Felons and Prisoners, in such manner and form as they have been heretofore accustomed," while insisting that they "shall take examinations and bonds as is aforesaid, . . . and shall Certify every such Bailments [*sic*] . . . at the next Gaol Delivery . . . ." Observes Stephen, at I 238: "In a great town where there were aldermen or other magistrates by charter, and a considerable population, the danger of collusion would be less than in the country."

20. W. Blackstone, *Commentaries on the Laws of England* (Oxford, 1769) IV 266–268; for earlier authority, see F. Bacon, *The Use of the Law* (London, 1630) 17–26.

> of the said Prisoner and information of them that bring him, of the fact and circumstances thereof, and the same, or as much thereof as shall be material to prove the felony, shall be put in writing before they make the same Bailment, which said examination together with the said Bailment, the said Justices shall certify at the next general Gaol Delivery . . . .

The apparent object of this procedure in the context of bail was to supply the supervising judges at gaol delivery with a means of evaluating the propriety of any bailment. They were now to have documents which would disclose the extent of the evidence against the released man who failed to appear. There would be a basis for review of the JPs' grant of bail.

That at least was the superficial intent of the scheme. The question lurks whether further evidentiary use of the documents thus produced, either in procuring indictment or at trial, was intended. But the statute seems not to have hinted at any wider design. And the absence of a procedure to gather evidence in this way in the case of the suspect not bailed justifies further doubt. The basic function of the system appears to have been deterrent, to prevent unjustified releases; to the extent that it succeeded, it extinguished its own command to create the documentary material. Conversely, it intended the creation of the documents only when the hazard appeared that there might be no defendant present to try. Hence the direct use of the documents was not against the accused but against the JPs, and this purpose is emphasized when the statute goes on to impose a fine for deviation against the JPs at the discretion of the judge of gaol delivery.

Certain features of the provision for examination need to be noticed.

(*a*) Only one justice must participate in the taking of the examinations, although two are needed to bail on the basis of the examinations. But the examiner must be of the quorum.

(*b*) There is no requirement that the accused reply to questions put to him or answer to the charges made against him, although doubtless it would have been improper to bail a suspect who refused to attempt to exculpate himself.

(*c*) There is no suggestion that examination be under oath.

(*d*) There is no affirmative duty upon the JP as examiner to seek witnesses beyond those who "bring" the suspect. That curious word suggests that the draftsman expected that it would be the constable who would produce the accused before the JP. Sir Thomas Smith, writing in 1565, describes the constable as the man who would customarily "bring" suspects (both of felony and misdemeanor) "before a Justice of the peace to be examined."[21] If someone other than the constable[22] were the instigator of the arrest, be he victim or witness, the statute does not by terms require him to accompany the constable and to be examined. On the other hand, the full phrase reads "them that bring him"; the plural implies that it was usual for the arresting officer to be accompanied by complainants or witnesses. Lambarde, writing in 1582 in the first edition of his handbook for constables, says that when a complainant accuses someone of felony, the constable "may arrest the suspected person, and he shall doe well to carrie him to a *Justice* of the Peace togither with him that doth suspect him, to the end that they both may be examined as apperteineth."[23] Moreover, because citizen participation in arresting suspected felons had wider usage at the time,[24] complainant and arresting officer could be one. Nonetheless, the statutory role of the examining JP is passive. The statute requires him to question whoever comes through his doorway, but it does not command him to organize anything more comprehensive.

(*e*) The words "or as much thereof as shall be material to prove the felony" have been regarded as significant when they recur in the committal statute, because of the prosecutorial character of the option thus given the examiner to record not the whole story, but only the portion tending to criminate. In the bail setting the exclusion from such a document of matters exculpatory may not have been particularly prejudicial, since the document was to be prepared only when the circumstances were favorable enough to the accused that the JP was prepared to release

21. [T. Smith,] *De Republica Anglorum* (London, 1583) bk. 2, ch. 22, at 74 [hereafter cited as Smith, *De Republica*].

22. The constable could arrest on his own motion. He had "sufficient cause" to arrest "if the common voice and fame be, that [the person] hath done a felonie . . . ." W. Lambard[e], *The Duties of Constables* (London, 1582) 17–18.

23. Id. at 17.

24. Speaking of the common law responsibilities of the constable of a town, an anonymous sixteenth-century handbook notes: "And yf felons or murderers be in the towne, and the Constable have knowledge thereof, it is hys offyce and duetye to assemble people for to take them." Anonymous, *In This Booke is contayned ye offices of Sheryffes, Bailliffes of liberties, Escheators Constables and Coroners/ & sheweth what every one of them maye do by vertue of theyr offices, drawen out of bokes of the comon lawe & of the Statutes* (London, before 1543) sig. Gii^{v}. Lambarde's constable's manual (supra, note 22), at 11–12, makes a similar point. Speaking of the constable's power to arrest certain suspicious persons and bring them before a JP for surety of peace, he says: "And if anie such officer be not of sufficient strength to do that alone, then may he take meet aid of his neighbours thereto: and they, in such cases, be compellable to helpe and assist him."

him; and especially because the document seems to have lacked any evidentiary function.

(*f*) The statute is ambiguous about the form of the record to be made. It speaks of taking "the examination of the said Prisoner and information of them that bring him," and of putting "the same" in writing, but then by terms directs that only the examination be certified to the court of gaol delivery. Presumably it was mere drafting oversight which excluded mention of the information from the certificate, since it would otherwise have been pointless to direct its transcription. Later practice did advise certification of the information.[25] Lambarde thought the terms interchangeable when carried forward in the committal statute: "They that take the information, or examination (for this Statute doth use both the wordes) . . . ."[26]

(6) The statute goes on to erect a somewhat similar scheme in a different situation: where a coroner's jury has returned an indictment charging murder or manslaughter or accessory to either. The coroner shall "put in writing the effect of the evidence given to the Jury before him being material . . . ." The statute then declares that the justices of the peace as well as the coroner are authorized "to bind all such by Recognizance or Obligation, as do declare anything material to prove [the offense] to appear at the next general Gaol Delivery . . . to give Evidence against the party so indicted at the time of his trial . . . ." When the coroner is the binding officer, he shall certify in writing to the gaol delivery commissioners both his summary of the evidence at the inquest and the recognizances of the persons bound over to give evidence at trial, together with the "inquisition or indictment" of the coroner's jury. When it is the JPs who have bound anyone in such cases, they are to certify each binding over "in like manner as before is said of Bailments and Examination."

This scheme merits study for the light it casts upon the later committal statute. In the normal course of events the key difference between indictment by the coroner's jury and indictment by the grand jury was one of timing. The coroner's jury was convened at the time of the death, inter alia to view the body, and that could happen months before the next sitting of the court of gaol delivery. The ordinary indicting jury in

25. Says Dalton of the two Marian statutes: "And the said Justice or Justices of peace shall certifie at the next generall Gaole delivery, such examination, information, recognizance, and Bailement." Dalton 260.

26. Lambarde 209.

matters of felony would meet at the same assizes as the trial jury; its indictments would go immediately to trial.[27] There was no problem about informing the trial jury of the evidence given to the presenting jury. The same complainants and witnesses remained at hand. But when the trial jury was to act on an indictment taken by a coroner weeks or months before, usually in some other part of the county, there was a problem that we might term management of the prosecution. Some agency was necessary to produce the witnesses again at gaol delivery. This had been the responsibility of the coroner, who bound the witnesses to appear at the trial, and was himself obliged to attend the assizes. It seems that the JPs, who were much more numerous than coroners and of grander social rank,[28] increasingly were taking a hand in these cases anciently the province of the coroners. It is easy to visualize the situation in which a violent death having occurred, the persons involved would repair to the local JP, whose extensive role in the keeping of the peace would have made him a more familiar figure of authority for the populace than the coroner, whose jurisdiction was isolated and sporadic.[29]

There may have occurred a splitting of the coroner's function in orchestrating the subsequent prosecution at trial, with resulting misunderstandings. Sir Thomas Smith, writing in 1565, speaks of the situation in which an indictment (there is no reason to think it was a coroner's)

27. A summary of the procedure at gaol delivery dated July 2, 1586, and believed to be the work either of the clerk of assize or the assize judges on the Western Circuit, says: "so sone [soon] as seven or eight be indycted they be tried." "A declaracion of the course used and nedeful to be used by the judges in the Westerne circuite in the delivery of the gaol and triall of *nisi prius*," transcribed and discussed in *Somerset Assize Orders 1629–1640* (T. G. Barnes, ed.) (Somerset Record Society, 1959) 54.

28. "The Coroner is one chosen . . . of the meaner sort of gentlemen . . . ." Smith, *De Republica* bk. 2, ch. 21, at 72.

29. The JPs may have been encroaching upon the coroner's sphere, but they had not displaced him. In a case of murder committed at Mayfield, Sussex, in 1595 and known to us through an anonymous contemporary pamphlet, the investigation was carried out entirely by the coroner. He interviewed the 5-year-old son of the murdered woman. The child had witnessed the slaying and accused his father of the crime. The coroner sent for and questioned the father. When he claimed an alibi, the coroner sent for some of his workmates, who contradicted him. The coroner then committed him to gaol at Lewes, from which he was subsequently brought to trial, convicted on the evidence of his son, and hanged. Anonymous, *A most horrible & detestable Murther committed by a bloudie minded man upon his owne Wife* (London, 1595). Cf. "The Manner of the killing, and then *burning of* Jone Dilworth" in Anonymous, *Two horrible and inhumane Murders done in Lincolneshire, by two Husbands upon their Wives . . .* (London, 1607) (italics in original). (The culprit confessed to the coroner and was apparently not examined by a JP; he was tried, convicted and hanged.)

fails for want of prosecution. "For though a man be endicted, yet if when he come to the arainement, there be no man to pursue further, nor no evidence of witnesse or other triall and *indices* against him, he is without difficultie acquited." [30] Smith mentioned the example to illustrate the independence of trial from indictment, but the fact that he chose the case of the bungled prosecution to exemplify that general dichotomy may imply that it was a problem of some currency and concern. The Marian statute may be attempting to coordinate the two officers' roles, to bring the separated strands of a divided investigation together again at the trial court, by requiring each—JP and coroner—to certify his part in such cases. We note that the coroner alone is to certify a summary of the evidence given before his jury, together with the recognizances he has taken binding over to testify at trial those persons whose evidence he thinks material; and that the JPs alone are to certify any bindings over they have made. The point of the measure, therefore, was to facilitate coordination of the subsequent proceedings by the gaol delivery commissioners. It shared with the bail measure the function of informing the supervisory central officers at gaol delivery. It diverged from the bail scheme in the crucial respect that its direct purpose was the building of the case for trial against the accused.

The coroner procedure in the first Marian statute represents something of a mid-passage between the bail procedure and the full-scale preliminary inquiry of the second Marian statute. It is not preliminary. It follows formal indictment. Still, it is very close to the inquiry we shall understand in the second Marian statute: the participation in an organized manner of the local officers in building the case against the accused in a procedure involving transcription of the testimony of accusing witnesses and its certification to the disposing court.

B. THE COMMITTAL STATUTE

The next Parliament extended the bail scheme by "An Act to take the examination of Prisoners suspected of Manslaughter or Felony," 2 & 3 Philip & Mary c. 10 (1555).

The Preamble recites the enactment of the bail statute, describes the examination there required, and continues with the lament that "the

30. Smith, *De Republica* bk. 2, ch. 23, at 76 (italics in original).

said Act doth not extend to such Prisoners as shall be brought before any Justices of Peace for Manslaughter or Felony, and by such Justice shall be committed to Ward for the suspicion of such Manslaughter or Felony, and not bailed, in which case examination of such Prisoner, and of such as shall bring him, is as necessary or rather more, than where such Prisoner shall be let to Bail . . . ." Neither the Preamble nor the body of the statute explains why the examination is "necessary" when the accused is gaoled until trial. That mystery, especially the question of what subsequent use the draftsman intended should be made of the written examination, is the subject of Chapter 2.

The whole of the procedure for examining accused felons the statute prescribes in a single sentence:

> [F]rom henceforth such Justices or Justice before whom any person shall be brought for Manslaughter or Felony, or for suspicion thereof, before he or they shall commit or send such Prisoner to Ward, shall take the examination of such Prisoner, and information of those that bring him, of the fact and circumstance thereof, and the same or as much thereof as shall be material to prove the Felony shall [be] put in writing, within two days after the said examination, and the same shall certify in such manner and form and at such time as they should and ought to do if such Prisoner so committed or sent to Ward had been bailed or let to Mainprise, upon such pain as in the said former Act is limited and appointed for not taking or not certifying such examinations as in the said former Act is expressed.

A second paragraph, requiring the JPs to bind over witnesses to appear at the trial, is based not on the bail provisions of the former act, but on the procedure there devised for the JPs' involvement with coroners' inquests:

> And Be it further enacted, That the said Justices shall have authority by this Act to bind all such by Recognizance or Obligation, as do declare anything material to prove the said Manslaughter or Felony, against such Prisoner as shall be so committed to ward, to appear at the next general Gaol Delivery . . . to give evidence against the party; And that the said Justices shall certify the said Bonds taken before them, in like manner as they should and ought to certify the Bonds mentioned in the said former Act, upon the pain as in the said former Act is mentioned . . . .

Because this terse little statute became the basis of the English pretrial process, we need to pause over some of its detail.

(1) There is an alternation, not particularly well articulated, between the duties assigned to a single JP and those to more than one. It will be recalled that the bail statute required that two justices join in the bailing, although only one needed actually to examine the accused and his "bringers." If a lone justice had examined, it had been directed that he be of the quorum. The committal statute discontinues the quorum requirement; unlike the decision to bail, the decision to commit could be made by any justice, including one not of the quorum. Any justice might therefore examine. The committal statute preserves an option for more than one justice to join in examinations and bindings-over-to-testify, but the entire procedure could be operated by any single justice. Indeed, not only did the committal statute decline to extend the quorum requirement to committal examinations, it seems to have contributed to the debasement and functional demise of the very institution of the quorum of the peace, a point we shall develop in Chapter 5.

(2) The procedure here, as in the bail statute, concerns only felony and manslaughter, not treason and not misdemeanor.

(3) No obligation is expressed that the accused respond to the questions put to him. This omission parallels that in the bail statute but is more significant here, because without the prospect of bail being held before him, the accused has less inducement to speak voluntarily in exculpation.

(4) The statute does not require that the accused or the witnesses be examined under oath. This omission, which also characterized the bail statute, and the diverging practice among Elizabethan JPs on administering oath despite the silence of the statute, will interest us in our consideration of the possible evidentiary import of the Marian examination document.

(5) Again following the bail statute, no duty is imposed on the JPs to seek out and examine witnesses of likely importance. The act by terms requires only that record be made of the information given by the "bringers," and that those of the bringers who have volunteered material testimony be bound over to repeat it at gaol delivery.[31]

(6) A most remarkable feature of the act, which did not occur in the examination provisions of the bail statute, is that the examining JP

31. Stephen thought it "remarkable that the word 'witnesses' is not used." Stephen I 219. The point troubled him because he knew that in seventeenth-century and later practice the JPs behaved as though the word "witnesses" had been used (infra, pages 35–36).

need not immediately transcribe the statements of the accused and of the informants; rather, he is instructed to compose the writing "within two days after the said examination." This means that no verbatim deposition was contemplated, of the sort then common to Chancery and Star Chamber interrogatories and to Continental and ecclesiastical practice. The document the JP was to prepare was less a deposition of the examinant than a memorandum of the JP recounting the criminating evidence which led him to gaol the accused. Chapter 2 will contend that this express negation of a requirement of contemporaneous transcription bears importantly on the key question of whether the draftsman contemplated that the examination document would have evidentiary force.

(7) Like the bail statute, the committal statute gives the JP the option of endowing the documents with a prosecutorial cast by recording either the full story "or as much thereof as shall be material to prove the Felony . . . ." This provision illustrates well the pitfalls of derivative draftsmanship—of republishing statutory language in an altered context. We noticed that in the bail context, the option to record only the criminating evidence imported no particular disadvantage to the accused. The document was compiled only where the accused was going to be bailed, as a check on the propriety of the two JPs' action in granting the bailment should the accused take flight. The function of the document was to provide a basis of judgment against the JPs, not the accused. To serve that purpose, the document had at minimum to disclose the grounds of inculpation.

There would, in fact, have been every inducement to the JPs to include matters of exculpation as well: the occasion on which the examination document would be perused would be when the JPs were attempting to justify to the assize judges the reasonableness of the JPs' grant of bail to an accused now turned fugitive. In that context the statute's grant to them of the option to record only the evidence which put *them* (as well as the accused) in jeopardy was sport. It was another way of setting out the minimum which would satisfy the statutory purpose. However, when carried forward to the committal statute, the JP's option of recording only criminating evidence could appear more sinister,[32] especially if the examination might have subsequent evidentiary significance at trial. The possibilities which the language seems to invite for distortion of the record against the accused were perhaps not realized. Lambarde took the phrase

32. Holdsworth's view. W. Holdsworth, *A History of English Law* (London, 1922–1966) IV 529 [hereafter cited as Holdsworth].

to mean simply that the JP was obliged to ascertain that the conduct complained of really amounted to felony before treating someone like an accused felon.[33] His successor, Dalton, counsels in his first edition in 1618 that the exculpatory be included.[34]

(8) Like the bail statute, the committal statute directs each JP to certify to gaol delivery the written examinations of the accused and the bringers, together with the recognizances binding over witnesses to testify. This raises the question of what use was to be made of these documents at the gaol delivery, which in turn puts in question the purpose of the whole scheme. These considerations occupy the next chapter.

(9) Like the bail statute, the committal statute makes no provision for custody or retention of the documents certified to gaol delivery following the session, or indeed even at the session.

(10) Finally there should be noticed, for comparison with the Continental statutes, the curt and laconic drafting. The striking features of the draftsmanship are three. One is brevity. The examination provisions, exclusive of the Preamble, the enacting clause, the sanction for noncompliance, and the second paragraph dealing with the binding over of witnesses, occur in a single sentence of well under two hundred words directing examination, transcription, and certification. Second, the draft is so dense as to be ambiguous, so ambiguous in fact that the fundamental

33. For, whereas it [the committal statute] requireth that the *Justice* of Peace should in taking the examination, make choise of suche things as bee material to prove the offence, it seemeth necessarie that he (being perhappes unskilfull in the lawes of the lande) shoulde bee somewhat instructed what actes those bee, that doe amount to *Manslaughter* or *Felony* me[a]nt within this Statute, & what other acts (though they carie som resemblance . . . of ye same) yet do not reach so far. And hereby he shall ye better know, when to commit ye partie [that] shal be brought before him, & when he shal not need to meddle with him at all.

Lambarde 211 (italics in original). The passage prefaces an analysis of the elements of manslaughter and felony and cross-references to other discussion of specific offenses.

The reference to the need to instruct unlearned laymen should be noticed for its similarity to one of the great themes of the German code of criminal procedure of the sixteenth century (infra, Chapter 8).

34. It seemeth just and right that the Justice of P[eace] who taketh information against a felon, or person suspected of felonie, should take and certifie, as well such information, proofe, and evidence, as goeth to the acquitall or cleering of the prisoner, as such as makes for the K[ing] and against the prisoner; for such information, evidence or proofe taken, and the certifying thereof by the Justice of peace, is onely to informe the King and his Justices of Gaole deliverie, &c. of the truth of the matter.

And Sir *Edw. Coke* (at lent Assizes at Bury *quinto Jacobi)* advised a Coroner that he ought to have done accordingly, (as I have heard.)

Dalton 265 (italics in original).

questions of the purpose of the legislation and the way it was intended to operate are left obscure. Last, the committal statute is slavishly imitative of the bail statute, and this may in part explain its brevity and ambiguity. Had the draftsman started afresh, he would surely have done a better job of expressing the design he had in mind. Although the draftsmanship complicates our understanding of the committal statute in function and operation, it simplifies the job of understanding the origins of the statute, as Chapter 3, treating the parliamentary history, will show.

CHAPTER 2 The Statutory Intent of Marian Preliminary Examination

That the Marian committal statute is a remarkably opaque document should be plain from the preceding chapter. Its ambiguity forces upon us the singular enterprise of this chapter: to ask of a piece of self-declared remedial procedural legislation what relation that legislation was actually intended to bear to the existing procedure. That fundamental question is left open by the 1555 statute, because it neglected to declare what use was to be made of the documents which the JPs were directed to prepare and to transmit to the court of gaol delivery. Two broad questions arise. Did the Marian statute seek to introduce a variety of Roman-canon Inquisitionsprozess, a system rooted in the examination of the accused and accusers? If not, then what was its object?

A. THE DOSSIER?

The Marian committal statute directed the magistrates to administer a procedure characterized by regular interrogation of accused felons and their accusers, recordation of their statements, and certification of that record to the trial court. We shall see that Continental Inquisitionsprozess could be described in substantially similar terms: it was a system of criminal procedure in which the magistrate investigated, principally by interrogation of the accused; reduced the results of his investigation, including the testimony of the accused, to writing; and transmitted this dossier to the final sentencing court for a judgment which was based upon and effectively controlled by the dossier. This parallel has been thought to bear compellingly on the question of the nature and origin of the Marian preliminary inquiry scheme. The Marian statutes have been believed to be the products of "continental ideas" which were "introduced by the legislature" and which "contemplated an inquisitorial examination of the prisoner . . . designed to give . . . the executive some of the advantages against prisoners which were conferred by the inquisitorial procedure of foreign states . . . ."[1]

This chapter contends that it has been fundamentally mistaken to attribute the Marian scheme to Continental models. The Marian committal statute was organizing a function strikingly different. In Continental Inquisitionsprozess the magistrate's investigation established the facts authoritatively. Not only was the magistrate gathering evidence, it became evidence when it entered his dossier. He was the trier-of-fact, in our terminology. In contrast, this chapter will show that it was no part of the intent of the Marian statute to institute a system of written evidence. The Marian draftsman did not contemplate that the examinations he ordered transcribed would have evidentiary force at trial. The statute did not, even implicitly, preclude the use of the written examinations in evidence at jury trial, and we shall see that in various circumstances they came to be so used. But we shall also see that even those restricted situations were afterthoughts of daily practice, neither designed nor facilitated by the statutory text.

The importance of the appearance of formal preliminary procedure under Mary is that it coincides with the transition of the trial jury from a medieval to a modern role. The growing inability of the jury to inform itself was forcing the state to intervene. The issue is what form that intervention was taking. A rigorous reception thesis would argue that the 1555 statute was seeking to erect a system of investigation and collection of deposition evidence which would obsolete the jury, reducing it to a merely formal body whose real decision-making authority would pass to the magistrates by virtue of their control over the preparation of the dossier. The grand jury did undergo a similar sort of functional displacement. Accusation was passing in function to investigating officials, whose work was regularly (although not inevitably) ratified by a ceremonial grand jury proceeding.[2] Perhaps the draftsman intended that the petty jury too be suppressed. We shall see a striking parallel in the German reception of the fifteenth and sixteenth centuries, and we shall have occasion to review Dawson's account of the analogous development in late medieval France: "The thesis I advance is that the active agent in driving out the lay judges in France was the Roman-canonist system

1. Holdsworth IV 528–529.

2. See P. Devlin, *The Criminal Prosecution in England* (London, 1960) 3–9; see infra, Chapter 5, Section B.

of procedure, especially its modes of investigation and proof." [3]

If the Marian draftsman did not intend to substitute written for oral process, his object must have been less drastic. He was tinkering within the ancient procedure, saving for the jurors their decisive role and attempting to aid them by having the JPs investigate crime and organize the prosecution. That is certainly what resulted. The question is whether a grand displacement had been sought, but miscarried. The answer lies in the question with which we began: what use did the draftsman intend for the documents which he commanded the JPs to prepare and to certify to gaol delivery?

In the bail statute the Preamble allowed us the inference that the certificate was to serve as a control on collusive or unjustified bailings. In consequence of this essentially deterrent function, the possibility that the written examination was designed to have an affirmative and evidentiary function is exceedingly remote; to the extent that the statute succeeded in its stated object of deterring unjustified bailings, it cancelled its own contingent command to create the written examination. The likelihood of evidentiary design arises only in the committal statute, where the bail condition on examination was dropped. Examination was transformed in the second act from irregular deterrent to regular affirmative procedure.

In the committal statute, we have noted, the Preamble is satisfied to say merely that examination is "as necessary or rather more," without identifying the necessity. We can isolate three phases to the examination procedure. Step One is the oral examination of the suspect and the bringers. Step Two is the transcription (within two days) of the examinations.[4] Step Three is the certification, that is, the physical transmission to gaol delivery of the written examinations. It is my contention that Steps Two and Three, which so resemble Continental dossier-building, were in fact conceived as minor administrative matters, without the dossier function; and that the crux of the procedure was Step One, the oral examination of the accused and the witnesses.

The predominant purpose of the statute was to institute systematic questioning of the accused and the witnesses. Because determined private

3. J. P. Dawson, *A History of Lay Judges* (Cambridge, Mass., 1960) 68 [hereafter cited as Dawson, *Lay Judges*].

4. It appears to have been implicit that the "information" of the "bringers" was supposed to be transcribed together with the "examination" of the suspect. Regarding the same problem with the language of the bail statute and the interpretation given it by Dalton, see supra, Chapter 1, note 25.

prosecution would not automatically ensue in all cases of serious crime, the Marian committal statute aimed to prod the justice of the peace into assuming the role we would today associate with the public prosecutor. To that end the statute had four identifiable objects. First, it sought to bestir the JP to investigate allegations of serious crime at the time they were first raised, when the circumstances were fresh. Second, it sought to have the JP ensure that the witnesses whose testimony would be necessary to secure conviction would be discovered and obliged to appear to testify at trial. Third, it sought to induce the JP to educate himself in order that in some cases he would be able to supply at the trial the narrative necessary to give the prosecution coherence. Fourth, in difficult cases it aimed to facilitate the work of the assize judge who conducted the trial by providing him an advance summary of the prosecution case. These points are discussed in Section B of this chapter and set in their larger context in Chapter 5. The crucial contention to which we must first turn is the negative one which derives such significance from the contrast with Inquisitionsprozess: that the Marian draftsman did not intend to institute a system of written evidence, and consequently that he did not contemplate that the written committal examinations would have evidentiary force. What supports this contention?

(1) The second paragraph of the committal statute, which sets forth the procedure for binding over witnesses to testify at trial, supplies the clearest indication of the draftsman's disinclination to erect a system of written evidence. The very statute which requires transcription of the statements of witnesses in the preliminary inquiry simultaneously arranges to compel the testimony of those witnesses at public oral jury trial. What the statute calls the "information" of the bringers was not to be recorded in lieu of their oral testimony at trial, but in advance of it and in addition to it. The Marian committal statute thereby diverges sharply from contemporary Continental practice, where the dossier served as the exclusive basis for decision and evidence not written within it would not be received by the final court of judgment.

(2) The astonishing permission to the JP to delay for two days his transcription of the statements of the accused and the witnesses is devastating to the view that the transcript was intended to have evidentiary import. Had the intention been that the examination document go into evidence, we might surely have expected a requirement of immediate transcription. The two-day delay would have diminished the reliability, hence the persuasiveness, of the testimony—and needlessly, for no par-

ticular reason, in the service of no competing consideration. Conceivably the draftsman was allowing time for illiterate justices to find scribes, although recent study of the educational level of the justices makes that seem improbable.[5] There was ample model for a rule of immediate transcription not only in Continental procedure, but also in the examination practice of Chancery and Star Chamber, where written examinations (usually taken on written interrogatories) did have direct evidentiary force. Nonetheless, the Marian committal statute, departing even from its own special model—the Marian bail statute—introduces delayed transcription. I shall suggest in the next section of this chapter why the provision for delay may have been allowed. The present point is its inconsistency with obvious and widely known standards, English and Continental, for the preparation of deposition evidence.

(3) The statute omits any requirement that the examination of witnesses be on oath, another major ground for doubting that the statute intended to give the examination document evidentiary force. The rule at this time was that the accused could speak in his own behalf at trial, but he could not testify on oath. His statements were received unsworn, as were those of the witnesses in his behalf.[6] The opposite was practiced with regard to accusing witnesses. Not only were they allowed to be sworn, they were probably precluded from testifying without being sworn.[7] Moreover, oath was the invariable practice of every English jurisdiction which customarily based decision upon written evidence: Admiralty, Star Chamber, Chancery, the lesser prerogative courts, the

5. See Gleason 83–95. Although Gleason does show that a considerable rise in the educational level of the JPs took place in the generations following the Marian statutes, the level in his base year of 1562 appears inconsistent with widespread illiteracy in the magistracy. Matriculation at a university or an inn of court can be established for 21 of the 56 justices in Kent, 10 of 28 in Worcestershire, 10 of 24 in in Norfolk, 15 of 38 in Somerset, and 12 of 35 in the North Riding of Yorkshire. Id. at 83–84. It seems unlikely that numbers of illiterates were operating in that milieu.

6. Upon triall of Felons before the Justices of Gaole delivery, the said Justices will often heare witnesses and evidence which goeth to the cleering and acquitall of the prisoner, yet they will not take it upon oath; but doe leave such testimonie and evidence to the Jurie, to give credite, or to thinke thereof as they shall see and finde cause.

> *Popham* chiefe Justice (at Cambridge Assises *tempore Eliz.*) committed one to prison, who, upon the tryall of a felon, called out that he could give evidence for the Queene, and when he was sworne, he gave evidence to acquite the offendor.

Dalton 265 (italics in original).

7. Dalton, at 264, cites Coke. See also the routine swearing of accusing witnesses in the passage from Sir Thomas Smith (infra, page 30).

ecclesiastical courts. Further, we know from Lambarde's *Eirenarcha* (1581) that the Marian statute's failure to require oath was no statutory oversight remedied in practice under the guidance of the central authorities. When Lambarde wrote, a generation after the passage of the Marian statute, there was still a debate among the JPs (discussed below) about whether or not to imply a power, or indeed a duty, to examine under oath. No settled practice developed, and implicitly none was sought by the crown through the supervisory powers of its trial commissioners.

(4) The very fact that the statute nowhere proclaimed any design to transform English criminal procedure is a significant indication that it had none. At best it is difficult to conceive why the draftsman would have wanted to conceal his purpose. Moreover, it surely would have been impossible for him to work his secret revolution through lay JPs. We shall see that the reception of Roman-canon criminal procedure in Germany was accomplished through lay magistrates, but it required extensive legislation of great clarity. The key German statute, the *Constitutio Criminalis Carolina* of 1532, has been called a "law primer" (*Rechtsfibel*)[8]—a veritable instructional manual for the guidance of the uninitiated. It is inconceivable that the Marian draftsman thought to work a revolution in criminal procedure through a nonprofessional and nonbureaucratic corps of magistrates with a statute so brief and ambiguous. And he would have been hardpressed to select a more unlikely model for the new order than the previous year's bail reform—a remedy scheme tailored to a highly particular grievance in a minute corner of the indigenous criminal process.

(5) It is important to be aware that the draftsman's failure to assign evidentiary force to the examination document was no tactical measure designed to bypass or subvert established safeguards of common law trial procedure. The mid-sixteenth-century rules of evidence for common law trial were primitive, for reasons connected with the history of the evolution of jury trial itself (a subject to which this study returns in Chapter 5). The law of evidence neither prohibited nor even seriously circumscribed the use of deposition evidence. Depositions elicited through Council investigations were freely admissible—for example, confessions of accomplices and imputations of accusing witnesses who did not appear at trial. The prototype of this sort of thing, the *Throckmorton*[9]

8. Hellmuth von Weber, "Die Peinliche Halsgerichtsordnung Kaiser Karls V.," *Zeitschrift der Savigny-Stiftung für Rechtsgeschichte (germanistische Abteilung)* 77:288, 290 (1960).

9. 1 St. Tr. 869 (1554).

trial, was precisely contemporaneous with the first Marian statute. The nascent law of criminal evidence may have had a tradition of orality, but it had not yet entrenched the rules to implement its bias. There was no counterpart to the long history of common law jealousy which denied the prerogative courts felony jurisdiction.[10] There was, in other words, no established defense against an attempt to legislate for the systematized creation and employment of deposition evidence. Yet the Marian draftsman relinquished the opportunity to institute such a system. Had his model really been Inquisitionsprozess, he manifestly would have done otherwise.

(6) What particularly reinforces the previous point is the sporadic manner in which the written Marian preliminary examination did acquire limited evidentiary force over the decades. The convenience of practice began to suggest and to institute spasmodically what the draftsman had neglected. It does not seem that central direction lurked behind this growth of custom or usage. That is the import of the disagreement among the JPs which continued into Lambarde's time over whether or not to examine witnesses under oath notwithstanding the failure of the statute to direct or to authorize sworn examination. The principal argument which Lambarde, as an advocate of oath, advances is that "if these informers bee examined upon *Oath,* then although it should happen them to die before the Prisoner have his *Triall,* yet their information may bee given in evidence, as a matter of credite, whereas otherwise it wold be of little or no weight at all, & therby offenders shold the easlier escape unpunished." [11]

It is true that the object Lambarde wishes to promote by conducting examination under oath is to enhance the evidentiary force of the transcript. Yet the crown did not intervene through the assize judges[12] to

10. Holdsworth I 486–488.

11. This is Lambarde's argument to the merits. He considers various analogies from other statutes pointing both ways, then offers the example of the deceased "informers" in order to "adde a reason . . . ." Lambarde 210 (italics in original). (The expression becomes in the 1588 edition, at 216, and thereafter, "adde for reason . . . .") The 1588 edition for the first time asserts the support of the central authorities for oath: "I have heard some *Justices* of Assize deliver their minds accordingly . . . ." (italics in original).

12. An interesting sidelight on this point is that one of the few persons known by name to have taken part in the drafting of the Marian statutes, Serjeant Ranulph Cholmeley, was for some years thereafter regularly in the commission of gaol delivery, inter alia for Essex. Essex County Record Office, *Calendar of Essex Assize Files 1559–1714,* citing Public Record Office: Assizes 35/1/3/1 (1559); 35/1/7/8 (1559); 35/2/3/24 (1560); 35/2/5/1 (1560); 35/3/2/1 (1561) (commissions of gaol delivery

insist upon sworn examination, as it would have done had it wished to implement a system of written evidence. Moreover, it is noteworthy that Lambarde proposes to use the written examination in evidence in that contingency which poses the least threat to the oral tradition—where death has stilled the voice of the witness between examination and trial. It would be hard to devise a more exceptional evidentiary use for the written examination. Dalton, writing about two decades after Lambarde's death, mentions another isolated evidentiary usage which had apparently acquired currency in the interval,[13] and he endorses Lambarde's view that accusing examinations should be taken under oath in order to preserve to them evidentiary force. But it is also Dalton who cautions: "And yet the confession of the offendor, upon his examination before the Justice of Peace shall be no conviction of the offendor, except he shall after confesse the same againe upon his tryall or arraignement, or be found guiltie by verdict of twelve men, &c."[14]

Uniformity of practice under the Marian statutes developed slowly, as did the law of evidence itself. By the later seventeenth century the authorities give a fairly consistent picture of how the Marian examinations were used at trial. They were handed to the clerk somewhat in advance, and he made a special "little Note or Callender of them for the ready finding of them out as shall happen."[15] Then "as the Prisoners are upon their severall tryalls, the Clerk that keepeth the Goale [*sic*]

---

designating Cholmeley). Cholmeley died in 1563. *The Records of the Honorable Society of Lincoln's Inn: The Black Books 1422–1586* (London, 1897) I 339, 341. On Cholmeley's role in the parliamentary consideration of the 1554 statute, see infra, page 58. Cholmeley also sat in the 1555 Parliament. *Members of Parliament: Parliaments of England 1213–1702* (London, 1873) I 393.

13. "That Examinations taken by justices of peace in one County, may be (by them) certified into another Countie, and there read and given in evidence against the prisoner." Dalton 264 (citation omitted) This practice is not noticed by Lambarde in his chapter "Of Certifying *Recordes* of the *Sessions* of the Peace, to other Courtes, or Officers." Lambarde 472–477 (italics in original).

14. Dalton 268.

15. T. W., *The Clerk of Assize, Judges-Marshall, and Cryer* (London, 1660) 7. The Webbs seem first to have noticed this little manual as a source describing the conduct of ordinary criminal trials at assizes and sessions. S. & B. Webb, *English Local Government: The Parish and the County* (London, 1906) 296 n. 2, citing the third edition (1681–1682). The first edition (1660) does not treat sessions procedure. The second edition expanded the manual: Anonymous, *The Office of the Clerk of Assize . . . Together with the Office of the Clerk of the Peace* (London, 1676). For a manuscript forerunner of the genre from earlier in the seventeenth century, see "Heere followes the order of the Gaole Deliverye," British Museum Harley Manuscript 1603, fol. 75–78; another, combining the forms for sessions and assizes: British Museum Lansdowne Manuscript 569, fol. 2–24^{v}.

Book, looketh out every examination of every Prisoner as his cause is in hearing, and if it be Evidence for the King, he readeth it to the Jury."[16] The examinations of witnesses ("informations") could also be read "if the Evidence for the King falter in his Testimony to refresh his memory."[17] Sir Matthew Hale's account, bearing the impress of his judicial experience, underscores how exceptionally the depositions of witnesses were used in evidence, and how inconclusive the written examination of the accused might be:[18]

> These examinations and informations . . . may be read in evidence against the prisoner, if the informer be dead, or so sick, that he is not able to travel, and oath thereof made; otherwise not.
>
> But then, 1. Oath must be made either by the justice or coroner, that took them, or the clerk that wrote them, that they are the true substance of what the informer gave in upon oath, and what the prisoner confessed upon his examination.
>
> 2. As to the examination of the prisoner, it must be testified, that he did it freely without any menace, or undue terror imposed upon him; for I have often known the prisoner disown his confession upon his examination, and hath sometimes been acquitted against such his confession; . . . .

It will be noted in Part II that the means by which Inquisitionsprozess overcame the older law in Germany was the development of a procedure which validated a confession uttered in the magistrate's "pretrial" investigation against attempted recantation at "trial."

(7) One practical illustration of an ordinary criminal trial for felony has come down to us from near-Marian times. Sir Thomas Smith's *De Republica Anglorum,* written in 1565, an even decade after the Marian committal statute, contains a hypothetical account of a criminal trial as part of a larger description of English government. Smith's recollections, from which he composed the book, predate 1562 when he left England to become Queen Elizabeth's ambassador to France.[19] Although Smith's

16. T. W., *The Clerk of Assize, Judges-Marshall, and Cryer* (London, 1660) 14.

17. *The Office of the Clerk of Assize . . . Together with the Office of the Clerk of the Peace* (London, 1681–1682) 48. This qualification does not appear in the 1660 edition, at 14, nor in the 1676 edition, at 15.

18. M. Hale, *The History of the Pleas of the Crown* (London, 1736) II 284–285; cf. id. at II 52. (This edition, the first, was published sixty years after Hale's death.)

19. The book is without citations to authority, and in a letter to a friend also written in 1565 Smith explained that he was writing from memory, having no books with him in France. Smith to Walter Haddon, Apr. 6, 1565, transcribed and translated in the Introduction to T. Smith, *De Republica Anglorum* (L. Alston, ed.) (Cambridge,

treatment is itself not free of ambiguity, it does throw light on trial procedure in the years immediately following enactment of the Marian statutes:[20]

> The crier . . . sayth aloude: If any can give evidence, or can saie any thing against the prisoner, let him come nowe, for he standeth upon his deliverance. If no man come in, then the Judge asketh who sent him to prison, who is commonly one of the Justices of peace. He if he be there delivereth up the examination which he tooke of him, and underneath the names of those whom he hath bound to give evidence, although the malefactor hath confessed the crime to the Justice of the peace, and that appeare by his hande and confirmation, the [twelve] men will acquite the prisoner, but they which should give evidence pay their recognizaunce. Howbeit this doth seldome chaunce, except it be in small matters, and where the Justices of peace, who sent the prisoner to the gaole, is [*sic*] away. If they which be bound to give evidence come in, first is read the examination, which the Justice of peace doeth give in: then is heard (if he be there) the man robbed what he can say, being first sworne to say trueth, and after the Constable, and as many as were at the apprehension of the malefactor: and so many as can say any thing being sworn one after an other to say truth. . . .
>
> This is to be understood although it will seeme straunge to all nations that doe use the civill Lawe of the Romane Emperours, that for life and death there is nothing put in writing but the enditement onely. All the rest is doone openlie in the presence of the Judges, the Justices, the enquest, the prisoner, and so manie as will or can come so neare as to heare it, and all depositions and witnesses given aloude, that all men may heare from the mouth of the depositors and witnesses what is saide.

Smith does say that the JP's examination of the accused "first is read," and further, that "depositions" of witnesses may be read aloud to the jury. However, his emphasis upon the orality of the trial proceedings goes beyond the technicality that documents were read to rather than passed to the jury. He tells us that what we have remarked from Dalton and Hale in the seventeenth century pertained as well in the first years after the Marian statutes: although deposition evidence was permissible, it was insufficient. Without oral testimony the jury might acquit the accused, "although the malefactor hath confessed the crime to the Justice of the peace, and that appeare by his hande and confirmation . . . ." Such

1906) xiii–xiv. It will be seen that *De Republica Anglorum* throws some light upon the taking of examination (infra, pages 96–97), as well as upon this matter of the use of written examination at trial.

20. Smith, *De Republica* bk. 2, ch. 23, at 79–80, 81–82.

an acquittal rarely happens, Smith says, save when the JP who committed him is absent. When the JP is present at trial to support and verify the taking of the confession, conviction is likely. The written examination is ancillary to the oral performance of the prosecuting magistrate.

(8) The evidentiary import of the Marian statutory documents receives some reflected light from the state of the sixteenth-century archives. Chapter 4 will treat these sources directly, but one observation may be anticipated: few examination documents have survived from the gaol delivery sessions to which they were certified.[21] The clerks of assize did not retain examinations, although they did save indictments from gaol delivery. Even in the seventeenth century, so-called depositions may have been regularly collected on only one circuit.[22] The reason seems clear. The work of the documents was done when trial got under way. Seldom employed as evidence, serving only a slight function for the assize judges, used mostly by the JPs as reminders for oral testimony, the examinations were discarded after a brief life. The survival of vast quantities of deposition records from the prerogative criminal process throughout the sixteenth century reminds us further of the relation of documentary retention to evidentiary force. Written evidence was not discarded, even in the localized palatinate prerogative courts.[23] Genuine deposition evidence, when such it was, was preserved. JPs' examinations were not.

(9) Finally, the legal literature of the time suggests some negative evidence. In just those sources where one would expect the workings of a system of written evidence to have been set forth, the Marian statutes passed unnoticed.

Because, as Lambarde put it, the JPs were "perhappes unskilful in the lawes of the lande," it had long been found "necessarie that [they] . . . shoulde bee somewhat instructed . . . ."[24] Lambarde's *Eirenarcha* was

21. Occasional examination exemplars do exist, filed among the indictments of the South-Eastern Circuit. E.g., Public Record Office: Assizes 35/1/4/7, 35/1/4/9 (homicide), 35/1/4/12 (theft) (Surrey) (1559); 35/3/4/12 (Sussex) (1561).

22. The collection which survives (North-Eastern Circuit) begins ostensibly in 1613, but only a few of the examinations predate the 1640s. Public Record Office: Assizes 45.

23. E.g., *Pleadings and Depositions in the Duchy Court of Lancaster: Time of Henry VII and Henry VIII* (H. Fishwick, ed.) (Lancashire and Cheshire Record Society, 1896). Criminal matters are prominent in this selection.

24. See supra, Chapter I, note 33, for the full extract and its context.

itself one of several series of JP manuals,[25] the earliest from the first decade of the sixteenth century. Two of the series straddled the Marian statutes, that is, were in print before the statutes and continued to be reissued in the years following them. The earliest was the anonymous *Boke of Justices of peas,* first published about 1506. The *Boke* went through thirty-six known editions, the last in 1580.[26] Twenty-six editions predated the Marian statutes, ten followed them. Fitzherbert's manual first appeared in 1538.[27] Twelve editions are known. Nine predated the Marian statutes, one was dated 1554, two appeared later (1560 and 1566).

Comparison of the pre-Marian and post-Marian editions of both *Boke*[28] and Fitzherbert[29] yields the following result: neither series[30]

25. One of Miss Putnam's major works was the volume which sorted out the various series of JP manuals and traced the influence, especially in Lambarde, of a manuscript of an Inner Temple reading given by Thomas Marowe in 1503. B. H. Putnam, *Early Treatises on the Practice of the Justices of the Peace in the Fifteenth and Sixteenth Centuries* (Oxford Studies in Social and Legal History, vol. 7) (Oxford, 1924) [hereafter cited as Putnam, *Early Treatises*]. She revised the bibliography to take account of later-discovered editions in Putnam, "Sixteenth-Century Treatises for Justices of the Peace," *Toronto Law Journal* 7:137 (1947) [hereafter cited as Putnam, *Toronto*].

The present study is no occasion for a general discussion of the JP manuals, but the reader should have some sense of the progression within the genre. It was not a static form. The second series enlarged upon the first and the third upon the second, both in size and in purpose. Within each series, however, there tended to be little growth. The first series, the anonymous *Boke* (c. 1506 ff.) (infra, note 26), was hardly more than a formulary with a brief appendage of statutory summary, essentially jurisdictional. In the course of thirty-six editions to 1580 there is only slight alteration, hence no recognition of the vast expansion of JP duties and powers in the years 1506–1580. "In fact, the 'Boke' as a whole scarcely deserves the name of a treatise, but is really more like a formula-book, of the same general type as Registrum Brevium." Putnam, *Early Treatises* 12. The second series, Fitzherbert (1538 ff.) (infra, note 27), is perhaps best described as a species of statutory abridgment, an especially characteristic sixteenth-century form. The third series, Lambarde's *Eirenarcha* (1581 ff.) (supra, Chapter 1, note 16) was larger, more inclusive in its sources (although still largely a compendium and explication of statute law), and more didactic in tone.

26. The count of thirty-six is a revised figure in Putnam, *Toronto,* at 143. First edition: Anonymous, *The boke of Justices of peas* (London, 1506?). The title wanders somewhat over the course of successive editions. The last edition in 1580 was known as *The Aucthoritie of al Justices of peace.*

27. The first edition was in French, with the author unnamed: [A. Fitzherbert,] *Loffice et auctoryte des Justyces de peas* (London, 1538). The second edition, in English, appeared in that year: [A. Fitzherbert,] *The newe Boke of Justices of the peas* (London, 1538).

28. I have used five editions of *Boke* (edition numbers per Putnam, *Toronto*): 1 (c. 1506), 11 (c. 1530), 18 (1544), 25 (1556), and 32 (1580). Miss Putnam discusses the various prints and revisions in *Early Treatises* 18–31. She confirms that the editions from 1550 on were little more than reprintings. Yet one significant change

notices the Marian statutes. The statutes constituted so scant a reconstruction of the magistrate's office that the handbooks of office could ignore them. It diminishes the significance of these omissions quite markedly that most of the editions in both series were almost unaltered reprintings. Moreover, when revisions were made, they were probably the work of printers rather than lawyers. Nonetheless, post-Marian editions continued to appear and to meet the test of market acceptability. It does seem that, had the statutes struck contemporaries as mandating a transformation of the JP's role into inquisitor, into compiler of deposition evidence, the books could not have kept their market without textual revisions to take account of the fundamentally changed character of the office. Not until Lambarde's *Eirenarcha* in 1581, however, does a JP manual begin to speak about the requirements of the Marian statutes.

To summarize: despite surface parallels, the Marian and Continental procedures were oriented toward radically different ends. In Roman-canon Inquisitionsprozess, the investigating magistrate compiled an authoritative written dossier recording his examinations of witnesses and accused upon which final judgment was based. The magistrate settled the issues of fact in his dossier. In Germany and France, this procedure had been the agency by which the magistracy effectively removed the power of decision from lay panels at least remotely similar to the English jury. The question arises whether the draftsman of the Marian committal statute of 1555 intended to work a similar displacement in England. The grand jury was already far along in its metamorphosis from a presenting to an indicting body. Effective control of the accusing function was already in the hands of officials. Was the Marian statute designed to work a similar fate upon the petty jury, transferring control over the fact-finding process to the officials by instituting a

---

was made in the 1556 and later editions: the Henrician statute against the Bishop of Rome was omitted. Id. at 31. Notwithstanding the traditionalized character of the contents, fundamental reforms had to be recognized in later editions. The anonymous editor of the 1556 edition adjusted for the papacy, but not for Marian Inquisitionsprozess.

29. I have used six editions of Fitzherbert (edition numbers per Putnam, *Toronto*): 1 (1538), 3 (1538), 4 (1540), 10 (1554), 11 (1560), and 12 (1566). Miss Putnam's account of the several editions appears in *Early Treatises* 14–17. Again she confirms that there is little change from the editions of the 1540s to the end of the series. But again, fundamental change was reflected: the 1554 edition of Fitzherbert, like the 1556 edition of *Boke*, omitted the statute against the Bishop of Rome.

30. Another series of printed literature which overlaps the Marian statutes likewise ignores them: the anonymous peace officer's handbook noted supra, Chapter 1, note 24 (editions from the 1540s to 1573).

system of written evidence? The contrary position which this chapter has asserted rests upon several arguments: (1) that the statute coupled its requirements of examination and transcription to the scheme of binding over witnesses to public oral jury trial, showing its concern with reinforcing rather than subverting the ancient system; (2) that the statute's allowance of a two-day delay in the transcription of the magistrate's examination collides with the basic principles of a system of written evidence; (3) that the statute's failure to stipulate that witnesses be examined under oath likewise reveals the draftsman's disinterest in the evidentiary import of the documents he directed to be created; (4) that the failure of the statute to announce any design to revolutionize English criminal procedure indicates that in fact there was none, since a nonbureaucratized and nonprofessional magistracy would have had to be trained for a new order; (5) that the existing law of criminal evidence was far too primitive to have placed any serious obstacle in the path of a Romanizing draftsman; (6) and (7) that the practice reported by Smith, Lambarde, Dalton, and Hale shows that there developed only peripheral evidentiary use of written examinations; (8) that the examination documents were not preserved in the manner in which deposition evidence characteristically was; and (9) that the two series of JP manuals which straddle the Marian statutes take no account of them, an unlikely omission were a transition to a dossier system of written evidence to be understood and effected among contemporary justices.

B. THE PROSECUTION

If the draftsman was not evoking the dossier, what did he have in mind? I shall show in the next chapter that the Marian statutes were most likely crown legislation. The thesis of the present study is that the Marian statutes represent the decisive step in the crystallization of the public prosecutorial function for cases of serious crime and its allocation to the justices of the peace. Elsewhere in this book there is some effort to explain that development—its relation to changes in the structure of jury trial, its association with the JPs' other duties, and its context amid other alternatives with which the crown experimented in the sixteenth century. The present object is to show how the Marian committal statute sought to facilitate organization of the prosecutorial function.

The essential reform of the Marian scheme was to inject an official or public element into the ongoing system of private prosecution. The aggrieved citizen, generally victim or kin, would continue to prosecute most cases. The committal statute regularized and reinforced this developed pattern through its provision for binding over the accuser and the accusing witnesses. Their role was transformed from option to obligation. On pain of forfeiting their bonds they were now obliged to appear at gaol delivery to give evidence. The citizen who lost his taste for revenge between the crime and the trial, or who was intimidated, or who was loath to make a long journey to the county town for assizes—he was now bound to attend and to give evidence. But what of the case where there were no aggrieved citizens surviving to prosecute, or where their evidence would have to be afforced in order to be sufficient to secure a conviction? The public interest in law enforcement cannot allow such gaps, and the rest of the Marian committal statute was designed to close them.

It has been said that four interconnected objectives could be attributed to the committal statute. The most fundamental, and worst articulated, goal was to induce the JP to take an active role in the invesigation of serious crime in cases which required it. Second, the statute directed the justice to organize from his investigation a case for prosecution at trial, binding over for appearance at trial both the accused and the witnesses whose testimony would be needed to convict him. Third, the statute had the JP prepare himself to assume where necessary the forensic role of prosecutor at trial. Finally, the statute meant to give a small assist to the assize judge, who coordinated the prosecution at trial, by providing him a convenient summary of the prosecution case.

We have emphasized that the second paragraph of the committal statute shows that the culminating concern of the Marian procedure was the discovery and binding over to testify at trial of "all such . . . as do declare anything material to prove the . . . Felony . . . ." Given the persistence and pervasiveness of orality at trial, reinforced in this way by the Marian committal statute itself, what was the point of the prior written examination? I suggest that the examination document was principally intended to buttress the oral performance of the JP at trial. The examination record was to be a sort of file memorandum for the JP—a prompter, like the notes a modern policeman uses to refresh his memory. When in the seventeenth century we begin to have the trial reports from which to observe, it was the JP "who had got up the case [who] was the principal witness against the prisoner, and detailed at length the steps which he had taken to apprehend him." [31] That this was design and not later usage is the inference to be drawn from the otherwise inexplicable provision permitting the JP to delay transcription of the examination of witnesses and accused for two days. The draftsman's concern was to prevent the facts from becoming too stale before they were entered upon the JP's reminder pad. As a result the examination document, in the unusual case in which it would be used in evidence, would often represent not the deposition testimony of the original declarants (witnesses and accused), but of the JP. It could be either, depending upon the form in which it was made. An examination immediatey transcribed in order to be signed[32] by the declarant would have had evidentiary force. However, the draftsman of the committal statute provided for none of that. He expressly authorized delayed transcription and, implicitly thereby, dispensed with any requirement of deponent's signature. Hence the inference that the draftsman's purpose, the legislative intent, was to secure for the JP a proper system of note-taking, in order that he be prepared to supply at gaol delivery the narrative of crime and circumstance which continues to be the role of official testimony today, and which would have been considerably more central in the infancy of rules of evidence such as that against hearsay.

What of the certification requirement, which surely implies that the Marian examination document was meant to have some further purpose? Two objects might well have carried over from the bail statute from which the certification language in the committal statute was derived. First, the written examination provided means for a crude check by the assize judges on the JPs' investigations. When obvious leads had not been followed up, obvious witnesses not summoned and bound, the judges would have had the same check on collusive or incompetent JP practices that had been sought the year before in the bail statute; and consequently, the draftsman may have thought thereby to create the same sort of deterrent to abuse and slovenliness.

Second, it is likely that the coordinating and supervisory function

31. Stephen I 222–223. It should perhaps be mentioned that all the JPs of the county were obliged to attend the assizes and could be fined for default. Before the gaol delivery commenced, the cryer called the roll, proclaiming: "All Justices of the Peace of our Sovereign Lord the King within the County of *L.* answer to your name at the first call, upon pain and perill that may fall thereon." T. W., *The Clerk of Assize, Judges-Marshall, and Cryer* (London, 1660) 3.

32. "If the offendor upon his examination before the Justice of peace, shall confesse the matter, it shall not bee amisse that the offender subscribes his name or marke under such confession made by him." Dalton 260.

which I have attributed to the certification scheme for coroners and JPs in the second part of the bail statute was also present in the committal statute. It will be recalled that the coroner's certificate allowed the assize judges, who managed the prosecution at trial by calling and questioning witnesses and accused, to have a sort of docket memorandum which would permit orchestration of the proceedings. (It should also be recalled that the committal statute took its provisions for binding over and for certification of the recognizances from the coroner-JP procedure.) In the present context the problem the assize judges faced was not the divided investigation split between coroners and JPs, but the complex investigation carried out by one or more JPs. A JP's documentation of his case against an accused permitted the busy judges to see how they should order the trial. There was no need, or reduced need, for them to confer with the committing JP about it. The documents certified would show which witnesses would put in which proofs, so that the judges could summon them in logical sequence.[33] Finally, as far as the recognizances are concerned, it is manifest from the very nature of the binding-over device (and Smith's account confirms it) that the certification of the recognizances gave the judges a basis for fining defaulting witnesses. Closely related is a usage of the examination document suggested by Lambarde, which may or may not have been present in the draftsman's mind: as a basis for impeachment, hence as a deterrent to changes in testimony between preliminary examination and trial.[34]

33. This relatively informal practice is quite difficult to trace. One of the witchcraft pamphlets mentions examinations having been presented to the assize judges, seemingly in advance of trial. Anonymous, *The wonderful discoverie of the witchcrafts of Margaret and Phillip Flower* (London, 1619) sig. G1^{v}. A clearer reference occurs in another lay pamphlet describing the gruesome murder and dismemberment of a curate in Somerset, enginereed by a family of some standing. At the assizes the judge, Chief Baron Tanfield, "having perused their severall examinations, to avoid all partiallity which consanguinity or acquaintance might impose, his Lordshippe alters the whole body of the *Grand Jury*, which were for the most part of the *Westerne* parts of *Summerset-shire;* and therefore in likely-hood of most known acquaintance unto [the principal defendant] who sometimes had beene a *Grand Jury* man himselfe." C. W., *The crying Murther: Contayning the cruell and most horrible Butchery of Mr. Trat, Curate of olde Cleave . . .* (London, 1624) sig. C3^{v}–C4.

The assize judges regularly reviewed bills of indictment drafted by or on behalf of the JPs (and others) before submitting them to the grand jury; see infra, Chapter 5, note 57.

34. The point comes up in the course of Lambarde's discussion of the merit of sworn examination, Lambarde (1588 ed.), at 216 (italics in original): "I have found by experience, that (without such an oath) many informers will speake coldly agaynst a *Felon* before the face of the *Justice* [of Assize], when as they have first made their bargaine with the offendor (or his friends) before the Justice shall heare of the cause." Dalton, at 264, carries forward substantially this passage from Lambarde.

If the committal statute was principally conceived to place upon the JPs the duty to launch appropriate investigation into allegations of felony which seemed to need it, why was that purpose not made clear in the statutory text? Why does the statute by its terms seem to contemplate a passive JP who awaits the appearance of the bringers and remains sedentary upon their departure? I suggest that this failure of articulation in the committal statute was the consequence of the draftsman's penchant for tracking the language of the bail statute. Because the bail statute had an essentially deterrent purpose, intending to prevent releases rather than to institute investigations, the failure to state a duty of comprehensive investigation is wholly understandable. When it was then decided to erect a preliminary inquiry scheme, the draftsman of the second statute gave no thought to the adequacy of the bail statute as his model, forgetting that its purpose, in preventing bailings, had inevitably also been to prevent investigation; and that consequently, the expression of the investigatory role devised for an undesired contingency might have shortcomings.

The committal statute failed to articulate the active prosecutorial role it was instituting because its draftsman thought he could borrow the language of the bail statute as a shortcut. (This point will become clearer in the light of the next chapter's parliamentary history.) The oversight caused no immediate difficulty, no rush to revise the language to make the prosecutorial role more explicit, because the mechanics were adequately set forth and the purpose revealed itself to contemporaries without better labeling. The Marian magistrate-prosecutor was not a wholly novel figure. It will be shown in Chapter 4 that the JPs already had by statute lesser duties which acclimated them to the role of investigating magistrate for felony; and indeed, that they may have assumed that role in advance of the Marian statutes.

To the extent that post-Marian practice is a guide, the active prosecutorial role can be demonstrated to have been understood by the JPs of that day[35]—although not by twentieth-century historians. The tendency

35. Dalton, at 262 (citation omitted), makes quite clear that the JPs were not limited to examining the bringers:

> And if after [committing the accused and binding over the bringers] the said Justice shall heare of any other persons that can informe any materiall thing against the prisoner (to prove the felony whereof he is suspected) the said Justice may grant out his Warrant for such persòns to come before him, and may also take their Information, &c. and may binde them to give in evidence against the prisoner: For every one shalbe admitted to give evidence for the king.

in our literature has been to deem the Marian procedure "inquisitorial," and to assume that that label sufficiently describes the function.[36] Legal historians have neglected to alert political and social historians to the nature and significance of the Marian scheme. Hence the most recent general history of the magistracy[37] gives no mention of the prosecutorial work of the JPs, or indeed of the Marian statutes; and Gleason's illuminating discussion[38] of Lambarde's "Ephemeris" (a principal sixteenth-century source evidencing the prosecutorial work of the justices) emphasizes the range of the magistrates' concerns without identifying the peculiar purpose for which the justices were typically involving themselves.

One supposes that the principal reason that our legal historical literature has so little noticed the prosecutorial role of the justices of the peace is that the State Trials have oriented us to associate prosecutorial duties with the law officers of the crown. It has not been realized that prosecution by the attorney general, although regular enough in the celebrated political trials, had no counterpart in the ordinary criminal procedure. In the sixteenth century ordinary crime was locally, and in the main privately, prosecuted. Indeed, it was because prosecution by ordinary citizens was so prevalent that the Marian system of official prosecution by the JPs could develop with such relative ease. The Marian magistrate was filling the gaps in a system of citizen prosecution. Typically he could limit himself to binding over aggrieved citizens to prosecute in their own causes. Only infrequently would he have to act "as we now expect the upper ranks of the police force to act, undertaking detective work, getting up the case against the accused, and bringing him to justice . . . ."[39]

Some traces have survived of the prosecutorial work of William Lambarde himself. Between 1580 and 1588 Lambarde kept a diary of certain of his activities as a justice of the peace in Kent, which he titled "An Ephemeris of the Certifiable Causes of the Peace."[40] The diary

36. Holdsworth IV 528–529. Stephen, however, a generation earlier, had been more astute. He pointed to the seventeenth-century State Trials in which it had been the JP who "got up the case" and "was the principal witness against the prisoner . . . ." Stephen I 222–223. In the Marian procedure "the magistrate acts the part of a public prosecutor . . . ." Id. at 221. Cf. G. Williams, "The Power to Prosecute," [1955] *Criminal Law Review* 596, 601.

37. E. Moir, *The Justice of the Peace* (Pelican ed., 1969).

38. Gleason 8–15.

39. G. Williams, supra, note 36, at 601.

40. Published in *William Lambarde and Local Government: His "Ephemeris" and Twenty-nine Charges to Juries and Commissions* (C. Read, ed.) (Ithaca, N.Y., 1962) 15–52 [hereafter cited as Lambarde, *Ephemeris & Charges*].

records out-of-sessions activities—in the main, exercises of the magistrate's office which needed to be reported to quarter sessions or to assizes. Gleason has shown that marginalia on the original manuscript indicate that the diary had a checklist function for Lambarde. When all of the matters up to a given point had been certified, so that concerning them Lambarde had no further duty of reporting or of transmitting documents, a line was drawn and an "X" put alongside.[41] Since the Marian statutes imposed a certification requirement, Lambarde's diary has preserved mention of numerous examinations and bailments in cases of felony, together with a run of lesser matters, such as summary orders about alehouse keeping and bastardy and bindings over to keep the peace. Many entries record the disposition of documents, generally their certification to quarter sessions or to assizes.

A series of entries will show the Marian scheme in operation in Lambarde's hands:[42]

> On Christmas day [1580] my father-in-law [also a JP] and I did send Robert Baker of Kemsing to the gaol, upon his confession of the felonious taking of nineteen sheep, and took a recognizance of 20 [pounds] of Richard Kipps of Kemsing to give in evidence, etc., at the next gaol delivery. . . .
>
> John Crook of Edenbridge and Thomas Andrews of Kemsing were bound by us to give evidence, etc., against the said Robert Baker, 23 January [1581].

Baker's Case bears out some of what has been said in this chapter. Although there was a confession, witnesses were bound. One was bound at the time of the committal of the accused. But others were found and bound a month later.

Occasionally one glimpses the prosecutor sifting his evidence:[43]

> 10 *October* [1581] My father-in-law and I took the examination of William Greaves of Gravesend, arrested for suspicion of the felony of thirty sheep [*sic*], and the informations of Simon Gray, Richard Clipsam, and Robert Cole concerning the same, and committed the prisoner and bound Gray and Cole to give in evidence, viz., either of them in 20 [pounds].

For whatever reason, Clipsam's testimony was not wanted at trial.

41. Gleason 10–11 and plate opposite 10.
42. Lambarde, *Ephemeris & Chrages* 19.
43. Id. at 21–22.

The active role of the justices in investigating serious crime, beyond the literal statutory command to examine the bringers, appears in *Heyward's Case:*[44]

23 *February* [1583] Sir Christopher Alleyn and I examined sundry persons at Sevenoaks concerning the suspicion of willful [*sic*] poisoning of William Brightrede by Thomas Heyward and Parnel, his now wife, then wife of the said William. . . .

28 *February* Sir Christopher Alleyn, Mr. John Lennard, and I examined divers other persons concerning the said William Brightrede's death and concerning the like suspicion of poisoning of Joan, late wife of the said Heyward. And we then committed the said Heyward and Parnel to the gaol.

The situation which the Marian draftsman more clearly provided for was the felony freshly committed, with witnesses accompanying the arrested culprit to the JP's door. Here, however, the suspected murders seem to have been committed well in the past. Community suspicion has found its way to some of the JPs, who begin to investigate. Moreover, they are unable to discover any witnesses whose testimony adds anything to the bare suspicion, for they bind over none. Still, they find the suspicion convincing and they commit. It seems that it will be one of these JPs who will speak against the two prisoners at trial, laying before both juries the circumstances of suspicion as the investigation established them.

Lambarde was a figure of great intellectual and literary attainment, and he had been trained as a lawyer at Lincoln's Inn.[45] Most of his contemporaries in the commission of the peace were very much less qualified by natural endowment and by training for the role of investigating prosecutor.[46] How were lay judges to be made into investigators? We shall see that the German Carolina faced the problem squarely. The statute constituted itself an instructional manual. It supplied the lay inquisitor with minute detail for his detective work, describing the circumstances of various crimes likely to give rise to suspicion.[47] The English had a

44. Id. at 27–28.

45. Adequate biographical detail appears in Read's Introduction, id. at 4–12. A recent amateur biography is W. Dunkel, *William Lambarde, Elizabethan Jurist 1536–1601* (New Brunswick, N.J., 1965).

46. Some of Gleason's data on the general and legal educational level of the magistracy in the year 1562 are set out supra in note 5. See generally Gleason 83–95.

47. Carolina Articles 31–45, 48–53. Illustrative: "When the person suspected and accused of the murder was seen in a suspicious manner at the time the murder

problem similar in kind, although not in degree. Laymen had to be instructed, but not in a novel system and not all at once. Novices joining the lay bench could learn from the veterans, a significant minority of whom were lawyers.[48] Nonetheless, the utility of systematic instruction is obvious, and beginning with the 1588 edition Lambarde's *Eirenarcha* begins to speak to "the pointes that may ingender Suspition . . . ."[49] Dalton's version, overwhelmingly based on Lambarde, is easier to reproduce, and a portion is here extracted:[50]

> Now upon the examination of Felons, & other like offendors, these circumstances following are to be considered: . . .
>
> 2 Quality.
>
> His parents, if they were wicked, and given to the same kind of fault.
>
> His abilitie of body; *sc.* if strong & swift, or weake or sickly not like to doe the Act.
>
> His nature, if civill or hastie, wittie and subtill, a quarreller, pilferer, or bloudie minded, &c.
>
> His meanes; if he hath whereon to live, or not.
>
> His trade; for if a man liveth idly or vagrant (*nullam exercens artem nec laborem*) it is a good cause to arrest him upon suspition, if there have beene any felony committed.
>
> His companie; if Ruffians, suspected persons, or his being in companie with any [of] the offendors.
>
> His course of life; *sc.* if a common Alehouse-hanter, or ryottous in dyet, play, or apparrell.
>
> Whether he be of evill fame, or report.
>
> Whether hee hath committed the like offence before; or if he hath had a pardon, or beene acquited, for felonie before; *Nam qui semel est malus, semper presumitur esse malus, in eodem genere mali* [*sic*].
>
> 3 Markes or Signes.

---

occurred with bloody clothes or weapon; or when he has taken, sold, given away, or still retained property of the murder victim . . ." (Article 33: Concerning sufficient indication of a murder committed clandestinely).

48. By the mid-seventeenth century at the latest, the official clerk of the peace and his assistants as well as the professional or quasi-professional clerks retained privately by individual justices relieved many lay magistrates of the more technical side of the work associated with the commission of the peace. See T. G. Barnes, *The Clerk of the Peace in Caroline Somerset* (Leicester, 1961) 9, 11, 22–23, 28, 46–47.

49. Lambarde (1588 ed.) 218. A forerunner: R. Crompton, *Loffice Et aucthoritie de Justices de Peace* (London, 1583) fol. 64^{v}–66.

50. Lambarde worked out an intricate chart of suspicions, (1588 ed.) at 220–221, which is awkward to reproduce. Dalton's version, at 266, retains a trace of the tabular format: the numbered headings (for example "3 Markes or Signes.") appear to the left of the respective lists, linked by a swirl bar. The extract from Dalton rearranges the headings conventionally (italics in original).

If he hath any bloud about him.

If any of the goods stollen, be in his possession.

The change of his countenance, his blushing, looking downewards, silence, trembling.

His answers doubtfull, or repugnant.

If he offered agrement or composition.

The measure of his foote, or horse foote.

The bleeding of the dead bodie in his presence.

If, being charged with the felony, or called theefe, he said nothing, *f. Cor.* 24.

If he bleede; *fatetur facinus, qui Iudicium fugit.*

Many of "these circumstances" have precise analogues in the Carolina, and the tenor of the whole bears a striking resemblance to the Carolina. The parallel between the Carolina and the JP manuals reminds us that one of the fundamental constraints upon a legal system which assigns important roles to laymen is the need to devise modes of instruction to remedy their inexperience. Moreover, already in the sixteenth century the forms which these two legal systems chose were those to which they would long incline in matters of structure: the Germans to comprehensive legislation, the English to lawyer's treatise.

It remains to inquire why the Marian draftsman opted for lay inquisitors, why the investigatory-prosecutorial role was assigned to the JPs. The issue arose as a consequence of the atrophy of the medieval system which had so long permitted England to avoid the investigating magistrate. The tendency for both juries, but especially the jury of accusation, to become passive, hence dependent upon outside agencies to inform them, forced the question which the Marian scheme ultimately resolved. The Marian solution was neither the first nor the only response. The expansion of the prerogative criminal process, both in the growth of the court of Star Chamber and in the frequent intervention of the Privy Council in difficult criminal investigations,[51] was symptomatic of the dissatisfaction with the ancient procedure; so too, in a narrower sense, was the growth of process by information.[52]

51. Instanced infra, Chapter 4, note 23.

52. See Holdsworth IX 236 ff. Another development was the extension of martial law. An unpublished paper by James V. Capua of the University of Chicago History Department identifies "the reign of Mary as the turning point in the history of martial law in England. [The reign first instances the use of] martial law against persons committing acts which did not in fact represent armed insurrection, but rather criminal offenses which under statute were triable by the regular courts of law." Capua, "An Outline of the History of Martial Law in England" (1973) 37

The Marian Statutes

The extraordinary growth of statutory *qui tam* actions is the most revealing of the crown's various experiments, because it shows the length to which the crown was willing to go to avoid the creation of an expensive, centrally directed professional prosecutorial corps. The informer was thought of as a bearer of "[p]ublic opinion and local knowledge,"[53] a figure who had theretofore been harnessed in presentment juries. Since it had become difficult to extract his information, he would be induced by "sufficient incentives"[54] to divulge it on his own motion. The informer action seems never to have been a serious alternative for the run of felonies. The procedure was confined in the main to economic regulation, where it could be foreseen that the offender would be able to pay a fine in which the prosecutor would share. Soon enough the device revealed its capacity for being abused, and under Elizabeth it required regulation.[55]

The Tudor experiment with informer prosecution of regulatory offenses shows in a related sphere the two themes which underlie the Marian solution for investigation and prosecution of felony. Prosecution should be local, to draw upon the knowledge of the community. And it should be cheap, costing the crown as little as possible. There was only one workable alternative to the Marian scheme of prosecution by local lay officials rewarded with honor and authority rather than money: professional prosecution by a centrally organized and paid prosecutorial corps. There is no evidence that the English gave it any thought. The tradition was otherwise, and neither the money nor the personnel were at hand.

That the JPs should be chosen and not some other set of local persons poses no mystery. They had already risen to preeminence over other local peace officers. To have avoided the JPs would have required the creation of a new office. Evidence in Chapter 4 that informal practice among the JPs anticipated and probably suggested the Marian procedure will put the choice of the JPs in its proper light. Both the prosecutorial

---

(footnote omitted). For a remarkable Marian example, cited by Capua, see J. Strype, *Ecclesiastical Memorials* (Oxford, 1822 ed.) III (pt. II) 130–131.

53. M. G. Davies, *The Enforcement of English Apprenticeship 1563–1642* (Cambridge, Mass., 1956) 25.

54. Id.

55. Id. at 63 ff. Archbishop Whitgift in 1584 justified the use of Roman-canon examination in the court of High Commission "because upon the conviction of suche [sectarian] offenders, no pecuniary penaltee is sett downe, whereby the informer (as in other temporal courtes) may bee considered for his charges and paynes: so that suche faultes should ellse be wholly unreformed." J. Strype, *The Life and Acts of John Whitgift* (Oxford, 1822 ed.) I 318.

function and the technique of examination fitted easily into the justices' duties in keeping the peace. The justices were so apt for the prosecutorial office that they appear to have evolved it on their own.

Thus are we able to infer the meaning of that phrase most opaque of all the Marian language: the committal statute's protestation that when an accused felon was not bailed, but gaoled, then "examination of such Prisoner, and of such as shall bring him, is as necessary or rather more . . . ." The necessity which the draftsman felt was to systematize and officialize the prosecutorial function in English law. In language uttered a few years before the Marian statutes, "there lacketh one thing in this realm, that it hath need of; for God's sake make some promoters. There lack promoters, such as were in King Henry the Seventh's days, . . . men to promote . . . all offenders." [56]

To recapitulate: Marian preliminary investigation did not contemplate the systematic collection and employment of written deposition evidence. Writing in the Marian scheme was merely incidental to a process whose crux remained oral. The real purpose of Marian preliminary inquiry was the organization of official prosecution at jury trial. There is still an important reception theory to investigate, and we turn to it in Chapter 4 and beyond. It is the proposition that the examination technique was derived from Roman-canon process. What remains to be considered as reception, therefore, is not the grand design, but a detail; not Inquisitionsprozess, but a technique wrenched from the context of its system.

C. THE PROSECUTING JP IN THE JACOBEAN CHAP-BOOKS

Our picture of the JP in his Marian role has been assembled in the main from Tudor sources. Once our perspective is lengthened to include Jacobean material, the prosecuting JP stands forth with great clarity. For although conventional law reports are still lacking, another variety of narrative evidence has come down to us which depicts the JPs in the exercise of their Marian role. Some dozens of pamphlets have survived, mostly Jacobean but a few earlier, which describe the investigation of particular crimes and tell us in greater or lesser detail about the JPs' conduct of pretrial examination and about the JPs' performance at trial.

56. *Sermons by Hugh Latimer* (G. Corrie, ed.) (Parker Society 1844) I 279 (footnote omitted), cited by Davies (supra, note 53) at 31.

These "chap-books" were written by nonlawyers for sale to the general public, which may help to explain why the genre is unfamiliar to legal historians. The pamphlets are generally anonymous or signed with initials only. A clergyman, "Henry Goodcole, Minister of the Word of God, and . . . continuall Visiter in the Gaole of Newgate," authored two of them,[57] and the severely moralizing tone of the lot hints that clergy may have written some of the unsigned pamphlets as well. One early pamphlet seems to have been produced or instigated by the examining JP.[58]

In the era before newspapers the chap-books held the place of the sensation-mongering element of the modern press. They were almost all published in London and offered for sale there ("to be sold at his shop in the Popes-head Alley, over against the Taverne doore"; "to be sold at Christs Church dore"[59]), even when the events being reported occurred at a distance. Some pamphlets chronicle two or more unrelated crimes.[60] The crimes narrated break down into three somewhat overlapping categories, each having a manifest appeal to sensation-seeking readers: (1) especially gruesome murders, often involving dismemberment or the burning of the corpse; (2) crimes of witchcraft (easily the most numerous); and (3) crimes of betrayal against a spouse or a master. Crimes of sexual perversion, a staple of modern sensationalist literature, are less in evidence in the surviving chap-books.[61] Persons of gentle status appear as culprits and victims in a surprising proportion of the pamphlets, especially in nonwitchcraft cases; perhaps it excited the readership when felony overflowed its normal course within the lower orders. Not infre-

57. H. Goodcole, *The wonderfull discoverie of Elizabeth Sawyer a Witch, late of Edmonton, her conviction and condemnation and Death* (London, 1621); id., *Heavens speedie Hue and Cry sent after Lust and Murther* (London, 1635). (Unless a name or initials are given in the citations in this subchapter, it can be assumed that the author is unknown. Page numbers have been omitted; italics are in the original.)

58. Infra, note 75.

59. *The horrible Murther of a young Boy of three yeres of age, whose Sister had her tongue cut out . . .* (London, 1606); *The most cruell and bloody murther committed by an Inkeepers Wife, called Annis Dell . . .* (London, 1606) (two versions of the same case).

60. E.g., *Two most unnaturall and bloodie Murthers: The one by Maister Caverley, a Yorkeshire Gentleman, practised upon his wife, and committed uppon his two Children, the three and twentie of Aprill 1605. The other, by Mistris Browne, and her servant Peter, upon her husband, who were executed in Lent last past at Bury in Suffolke 1605* (London, 1605).

61. But see *The Arraignement, Judgement, Confession, and Execution of Humfrey Stafford Gentleman* (London, 1607) (convicted of having "used unlawfull company with two Boyes, & had them carnaly knowne").

The crying Murther:

Contayning the cruell and moſt horrible Butcher
of Mr. TRAT, Curate of olde *Cleaue*; who was firſt murther
as he trauailed vpon the high way, then was brought home to his hou
and there was quartered and imboweld: his quarters and bowels being
terwards perboyld and ſalted vp, in a moſt ſtrange and fearefull manner. For this fact
the Iudgement of my Lord chiefe Baron TANFIELD, young *Peter Smethwicke*, A
drew Baker, *Cyrill Auſten*, and *Alice Walker*, were executed this laſt Summer
Aſſizes, the 24. of Iuly, at Stone Gallowes, neere Taunton
in Summerſet-ſhire.

AT LONDON:
Printed by *Edw: Allde* for *Nathaniell Butter.*
1624.

Trat's murder: The culprits are shown disposing of the corpse. This pamphlet is discussed in some detail at the end of Chapter 2.

Two horrible and inhumane Murders done in Lin
colneſhire, by two Husbands vpon their Wiues: the one
ſtrangled his Wife in her ſickeneſſe fiue and twenty yeares ſince, and not reuealed til Nouember laſt:

The other hauing killed his Wife, made a great fire, and burnt her, which fact was done and renealed in Iune
Anno Dom. 1604.

Thomas Caſh. Iohn Dilworth.

Printed at London for Iohn Wright, and are to be ſold at his ſhop at Chriſt church doore. 1607.

Two murderers in action: Several of the chap-books report two or more unrelated crimes, not unlike modern detective magazines ("pulps").

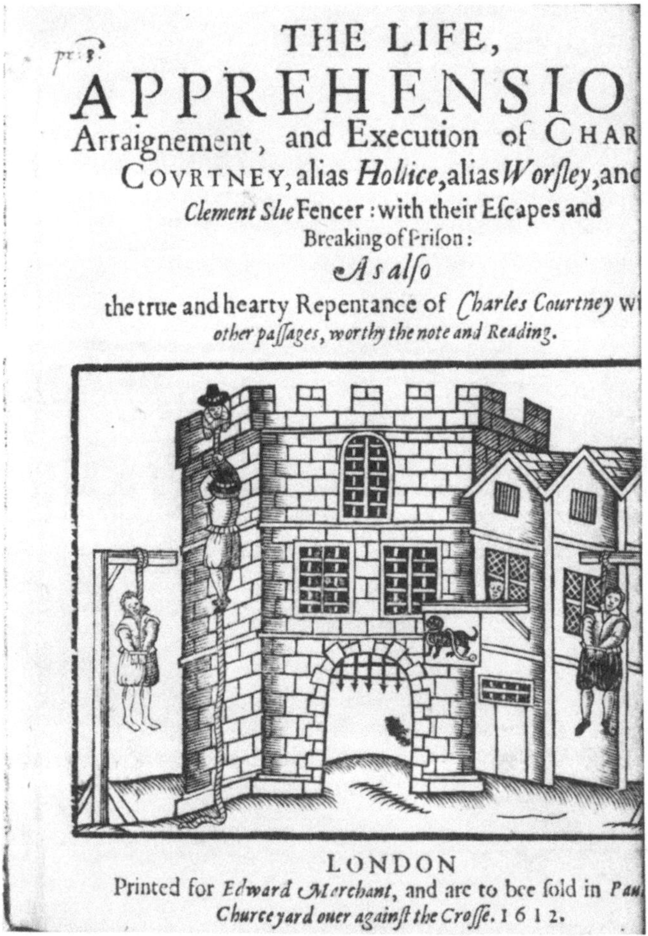

pr: 3.

THE LIFE,
APPREHENSIO
Arraignement, and Execution of CHAR
COVRTNEY, alias *Hollice*, alias *Worsley*, and
Clement Slie Fencer: with their Escapes and
Breaking of Prison:
As also
the true and hearty Repentance of *Charles Courtney* wi
other passages, worthy the note and Reading.

LONDON
Printed for *Edward Merchant*, and are to bee sold in *Pau*
Churceyard ouer against the Crosse. 1612.

Gaolbreak and execution: The synoptic illustration depicts Courtney and a gaolmate attempting to escape in the background, hanged in the foreground.

IF one ſmite another with an Inſtrument of Iron, that hee Dye, hee is a *Murderer*, and the *Murderer* ſhall dye the Death. Or if hee ſmite him with an hand-weapon of wood whereby hee may be ſlayne, if hee dye, hee is a *Murderer*, and the Murderer ſhall dye the Death. *Numb.* 35. *v.* 16.

Countrey-Tom. *Canberry Beſſe.*

he forme of the inſtrument of wood and iron that he uſed to hurt with.

Cover page to Henry Goodcole, *Heavens speedie Hue and Cry sent after Lust and Murther* (London, 1635). The female of the robber pair (shown hanged) would lure victims (represented by the prone corpses beneath the gallows) to isolated spots, where her cohort would club them. Goodcole also wrote the pamphlet account of the case of Elizabeth Sawyer, discussed at pages 49–50.

quently the pamphlets feature crude drawings on the title page; for example, the witch with her demons,[62] the dismembered corpse,[63] or the hanged felons dangling in their nooses.[64]

Timeliness aids sensation; the pamphlets appeared quite rapidly after the events—occasionally even before trial or execution of sentence.[65] The risk of being scooped by a competitor may also have pressured the entrepreneurs of the trade into producing their pamphlets promptly after the events.[66] Their timeliness is a factor which enhances the reliability of the chap-books as a legal historical source. These crimes were not legends embellished over long years of retelling. More important for present purposes, the work of the magistrates is a relatively peripheral aspect of the chap-book scenarios. What really interested the author and his audience, and occasionally did produce exaggeration,[67] was the gore of the crime and the drama of the culprit's downfall. The witchcraft pamphlets, the only ones to have attracted much scholarly attention, have been regularly verified when checked against surviving legal records.[68]

62. *The Apprehension and confession of three notorious Witches . . . (1589)*, reproduced in C. L. Ewen, *Witchcraft and Demonianism* (London, 1933) opposite 169; others are reproduced in A. D. J. Macfarlane, *Witchcraft in Tudor and Stuart England* (Harper Torchbook ed., New York, 1970).

63. C. W., *The crying Murther: Contayning the cruell and most horrible Butchery of Mr. Trat, Curate of olde Cleave . . .* (London, 1624).

64. *The Apprehension and confession of three notorious Witches* (supra, note 62); *The Apprehension, arraignement, and execution of Elizabeth Abbot . . .* (London, 1608); *The Life, Apprehension, Arraignement, and Execution of Charles Courtney . . .* (London, 1612).

65. E.g., the case of Thomas Cash, discussed infra, page 52; the case of Elizabeth James, awaiting execution for murder in Southwark, in *Three Bloodie Murders* (London, 1613).

66. This is a conjecture which the surviving evidence does not quite support. The two versions of the Dell case (supra, note 59) were both printed for one William Firebrand; the second pamphlet was printed for him and a partner, John Wright. Another case described in two surviving pamphlet versions involves a murder committed in 1602, but the second account apparently meant to conceal that it was a decade stale. *The Manner of the Cruel Outrageous Murder of William Storre . . .* (Oxford, 1603); *Three Bloodie Murders* (London, 1613).

67. See the discussion next following of the Dell case. Another suspicious tale: the purported first-person narrative of a contrite gentleman-robber who was executed within hours of attempting to escape gaol. *The Life, Apprehension, Arraignement, and Execution of Charles Courtney . . .* (London, 1612).

68. A careful recent archive study concludes:

> Comparison of indictments and pamphlet accounts [from Elizabethan Essex] supports the general accuracy of both sources. Although there is not always exact overlapping, since each source contains material not found in the other, when they are describing the same event there is little direct contradiction. When there is disagreement, it is on minor matters and supports the

The most useful for present purposes of the chap-book cases is among the least credible. *Dells' Case* (1606)[69] involves the slaying of a 3-year-old boy by an elderly woman, Annis Dell, and her grown son, both of whom were convicted and executed for the murder. There has been considerable exaggeration (if indeed the whole tale is not an outright fabrication). However, in our context a hypothetical magistrate's investigation is nearly as good as a real one, since the hypothetical still typifies the prosecutorial practice of the time as the author understood it.

The victim's body was found in 1602 in a ditch near Hatfield, Hertfordshire, dressed in a fashionable coat. The coat was sent to various market towns in the area and was recognized by a tailor, who had seen the boy wearing it and remembered it because he had intended to copy the design. He had seen the boy being led into the Dells' inn together with a girl child who was perhaps a year older. "The newes of this comming to the eares of Sir *Henry Butler* and one other knight, being both Justices, and both dwelling neere to that place, a warrant was made, by vertue whereof, the said Mother *Dell* and her Sonne were brought before them both, and strictlye examined . . . ." They explained that the two children had been brought to the house by a traveling peddler and his wife, and that both children had departed again with the peddlers. "Upon this their confession, they were were both bound over to appeare and answere at the next Assizes, the Justices hoping ere that time to finde out the actor or actors of that more then [*sic*] monstrous tragedy." New clues did not develop; "yet notwithstanding, they were still bound over from Sise to Sise, almoste for foure yeares . . . ." Then in 1606 there reappeared the little girl whom the tailor had seen accompanying the murdered child to the Dell house. The Dells had abandoned her to die in a "sildome frequented" wood, having first cut out her tongue. She got loose and supposedly went wandering and begging for four years, till one day she chanced to find herself again before the Dell house. This set her to crying, making "extraordinarie noyse" and pointing to the house. Her performance attracted a crowd, which was soon joined by the tailor. He recognized her, whereupon the neighbors hustled her, the tailor, and Annis Dell and her son "before Sir *Henry Butler*, who was the next Justice (and had examined [the Dells] divers times before concerning these Children) . . . ." When the constable told Butler what had just happened, "hee did with greate wisdome and discretion, examine them aparte, one from another." Both denied ever having seen the girl, although "the Taylor did still affyrme it to their faces, that that was the Girle which the Pedler and his wife led into their house long since with the boy." Butler ordered the Dells committed for trial. Then, some little while later by a "mightie miracle" the girl regained her power of speech. Those caring for her "led her againe to the knight before named [Butler, the JP], to whom they told what had happened." He questioned

general impression of accuracy.

Macfarlane (supra, note 62) at 85 (footnote omitted). Cf. W. Notestein, *A History of Witchcraft in England* (Washington, 1911) 346.

69. *The horrible Murther of a young Boy of three yeres of age, whose Sister had her tongue cut out . . .* (London, 1606).

her and elicited all the detail of the murder of her brother and the maiming of herself (the peddler couple had previously robbed and murdered her parents, and had paid the Dells to take her brother and herself).

"To conclude, the Sises being come, an Inditement was prefered against the mother and the sonne, to which inditement they pleaded not guiltie, and put themselves to the ordinarie triall. Whereupon the childe was brought before the Bench, and stood upon the Table betweene the Bench and the Jury. Where after that the foresaid knight had opened some part of this foule offence, the childe was asked diverse of the former questions: to which she answered as before. The taylor likewise was there, who tolde unto the Jurie what he had seene. Then the Jurie was willed to goe togither: but before they went, they did looke into the childes mouth, but could not see so much as the stumpe of a tongue therein. The Jurie staid not long before they returned with their verdite guiltie, whereupon they had sentence of death pronounced against them, and were both hanged at Hartfort, the fourth day of August. 1606."

It is hard to know how much of this story to disbelieve. The girl's sudden tongueless speech is incredible, as is her four years in the wilderness between ages 4 and 8. The tailor also looks somewhat contrived.[70] No matter how much of the scenario was invented, it is likely that the prosecutorial role of the JP in *Dells' Case* is a faithful typification. The author had every incentive to supply maximum verisimilitude to the lesser details of a plot which otherwise turned on a "mightie miracle" and such. The case is attractive for present purposes because it illustrates so clearly the way in which the investigating JP was led to take up a forensic role at trial. Butler "opened some part of this foule offence," that is, he made an opening statement to the jury. And because his star witness was a child who had to be guided in her testimony, he asked her "the former questions"—he reenacted with her before the trial jury the material parts of the out-of-court examination which he had previously conducted.

Fortunately, another pamphlet of undoubted reliability dating from 1621 also evidences the prosecuting JP in both his investigatorial and forensic roles: *The wonderfull discoverie of Elizabeth Sawyer a Witch, late of Edmonton, her conviction and condemnation and Death. . . . Written by Henry Goodcole, Minister of the Word of God, and her continuall Visiter in the Gaole of Newgate.*[71]

70. In the other pamphlet account of this case, the tailor is barely mentioned and Butler's investigations go undescribed. *The most cruell and bloody murther committed by an Inkeepers Wife, called Annis Dell . . .* (London, 1606). Notestein was interested in this pamphlet because an account of a witchcraft case is appended to it. He was unable to confirm any of the events. Notestein (supra, note 68) at 356.

71. (London, 1621). On the reliability of the pamphlet, see Notestein (supra, note 68) at 359.

The pamphlet tells how Elizabeth's doings fell under the suspicious "eye of Mr. *Arthur Robinson,* a worthy Justice of Peace, who dweleth at Totnam [Tottenham] neere to her," and how he prosecuted her to her death. Robinson had long suspected her of witchcraft, as did her neighbors. He sprang into action after "seeing the death of Nurse-children and Cattell, strangely and suddenly to happen." Goodcole's narrative is based on the trial, which he observed. Elizabeth was indicted at the Old Bailey on three counts; she was convicted of one, murdering a neighbor, Agnes Ratcleife, by witch's curse. Agnes had struck a sow of Elizabeth's; Elizabeth "threatened *Agnes Ratcleife,* that it should be a deare blow unto her, which accordingly fell out, and suddenly; for that evening *Agnes Ratcleife* fell very sick, and was extraordinarily vexed, and in a most strange manner in her sickness was tormented . . . ." Agnes lingered for four days, saying to her husband that Elizabeth was occasioning her death. At the trial the husband and the neighbors testified (presumably having been bound over by Robinson to appear—the Reverend Goodcole's narrative does not say). But the jury remained in doubt. "The Foreman of the Jury asked Master *Heneage Finch*[72] Recorder [the presiding judge], his direction and advice, to whom hee Christianlike thus replyed, namely, *Doe in it as God shall put in your hearts."* The JP (Robinson) must have taken the foreman's question as a sign that the jury was at least wavering. He "had often & divers times, upon the complaints of the neighbours against this *Elizabeth Sawyer,* laboriously and carefully examined her . . . ." He had learned from some neighbors that Elizabeth "had a private and strange marke on her body, by which their suspition was confirmed against her, and hee sitting in the Court at that time of her triall, informed the Bench thereof, desiring the Bench to send for women to search her . . . ." Three women were appointed, and duly reported back to the court that they had found a witch's mark.[73] This "gave some insight to the jury," which then convicted her of the murder, for which she was executed.

Robinson's performance exemplifies again the prosecuting JP continuing on from the Marian pretrial investigation to the trial. When he saw his case faltering after his witnesses had testified, he jumped up to add new matter which carried the day.

72. The father of Lord Chancellor Nottingham. The Recorder of London was always a leading lawyer who often advanced to the common law bench. He was sitting under his regular commission of oyer and terminer in a case like this. But the recorder was also a JP. Perhaps it was in that capacity that Finch's predecessor, Sir Henry Montagu, conducted the extensive pretrial investigations in the homicide case of Elizabeth Abbot (1608), which was tried before Sir Edward Coke. "[M]y Lord Chiefe Justice, rising from his seate [at the conclusion of the trial], gave Sir *Henry Mountegue* a worthy commendations [*sic*] for his industry and labor in this case, protesting that since he was acquainted in ye state of such business, he never hears examinations better gathered, a course better shifted, nor a murther stronglier discovered . . . ." *The apprehension, arraignement, and execution of Elizabeth Abbot* . . . (London, 1608). Montagu, however, was the exceptional lawyer-prosecutor, closer to the model of the law officers of the crown than that of the country JP.

73. It is quite clear from the description in the pamphlet that what the women found upon Elizabeth's body was a hemorrhoid.

The chap-books tend to portray the prosecuting JP solely in his investigatorial role, and this is as we should expect. The JP's forensic role was exceptional, and the procedural detail of the trial held no interest for these lay authors and readers. The few Elizabethan pamphlets, which deal mostly with witchcraft, are not so revealing about the work of the JPs (or about much else) as some of the later ones. They commonly string together pretrial examinations with little or no narrative, occasionally appending to the pretrial records some sketchy mention of trial and execution.[74] One of that variety which does portray a determined JP's pretrial investigation is a pamphlet account of the Essex witchcraft outbreak of 1582, believed authored or at least instigated by the examining JP himself, Brian Darcey.[75] The pamphlet purports to reprint Darcey's many examinations, from which it has been fairly observed that he "took particular pains in examining the suspects and his methods included much cajoling and bullying." [76] Toward the end of the century the pamphlets expand beyond witchcraft and become more coherent.[77]

Elizabeth Caldwell (1604),[78] a well-born young woman recently married and living in the county of Chester, attempted with her paramour and a cohort of his to kill her husband by baking him some poison cakes. He survived, but a neighborhood child with whom he shared a cake did not.

> Upon the death of this child, *Elizabeth Caldwell* was apprehended, and brought before three Justices of the peace; namely, Sir *John Savage,* Sir *Thomas Aston,* and maister *Brooke* of *Norton,* where before them she truly confessed all their practises and proceedings from the beginning, even till that day. Upon which confession, [the two accomplices]

74. E.g., *A Detection of damnable driftes, practized by three witches arraigned at Chelmisforde in Essex . . .* (London, 1579).

75. W. W., *A True and just Recorde of the Information, Examination and Confession of all the Witches taken at St. Oses in the countie of Essex* (London, 1582). "The pamphlet is merely a record of examinations. It is dedicated to Justice Darcy; and from slips, where the judge [JP] in describing his action breaks into the first person, it is evident that it was written by the judge himself." Notestein (supra, note 68) at 348.

76. Macfarlane (supra, note 62) at 85.

77. E.g., *A briefe discourse of two most cruell and bloudie murthers, committed bothe in Worcestershire, and bothe happening unhappily in the yeare 1583* (London, 1583); L. B., *The Examination, confession and condemnation of Henry Robson, Fisherman of Rye, who poysoned his wife in the strangest maner that ever hitherto hath bin heard of* (London, 1598) (by introducing rat poison into her vagina).

78. Gilbert Dugdale, *A True Discourse Of the practises of Elizabeth Caldwell . . . . Written by one then present as witness, their owne Country-man, Gilbert Dugdale* (London, 1604).

were apprehended, and brought before the same Justices, and examined as touching the murder, and they very stoutly denied all . . . .

The trial is described only in the result: the paramour refused to plead at the assizes, in order to preserve his property from forfeiture, and was pressed to death. The other accomplice was convicted and executed, as was Elizabeth Caldwell.

Thomas Cash (1607)[79] and a servant girl murdered Cash's first wife some twenty-five years before in Lincolnshire. Cash then jilted the servant girl and married someone else. Now on her deathbed in Shoreditch (London) the servant confessed the murder to her minister. He reported it to the high sheriff of Lincolnshire, who was then in London.

[H]e immediately sent order downe for the apprehending of this *Thomas Cash:* who being apprehended, was had before sir *William Wray* knight, one of the Kings Majesties Justices of the aforesaid countie, who being accompanied at the time when the prisoner was brought with one master *Robert Turret,* fell to examining of the prisoner concerning the fact, who presently confessed it before sir *William Wray* and the foresaid maister *Robert Turret.*

When the pamphleteer wrote, Cash was awaiting trial at the next assizes.

Numerous chap-books[80] chronicle the investigating JPs in witchcraft cases. *Arthur Bill* (1612)[81] is a convenient case to mention because it shows the JPs investigating in a fashion well beyond the Marian statutory minimum of oral examination and transcription. Bill (and others of his family) were put by the JPs to "an experiment that (many thinke) never failes," known as swimming the witch. His limbs were tied and he was thrown into water. When he did not sink, his guilt was clarified. He was convicted at assizes and executed.

Trat's Murder (1624),[82] the last of the Jacobean chap-book cases known to me, is perhaps the most interesting on account of its Sherlock Holmes properties. It portrays a dogged investigation by a pair of Somerset JPs. There is no reason to doubt the tale; the author, one C. W., purports to tell it "according to the best informations he could receive

79. *Two horrible and inhumane Murders done in Lincolneshire, by two Husbands upon their Wives . . .* (London, 1607).

80. Extensively discussed in Notestein (supra, note 68), where, however, no particular note is taken of the legal procedural significance of the activities of the JPs.

81. *The Witches of Northamptonshire . . . who were all executed at Northampton the 22. of July last. 1612* (London, 1612).

82. Supra, notes 33 and 63.

from the Coroner, Jurours, and other worthy persons conscious of all these particulars . . . ." He dedicates the pamphlet to Chief Baron Tanfield, the assize judge, and to the Somerset JPs.

Trat, the victim, described as a B.A. of Magdalen College, Oxford, and a widower, was curate of the vicarage of Old Cleeve. His murder was engineered by Peter Smithwicke (sometimes "Smethwicke"), Junior, the son of a substantial landholder whose own complicity in the crime had not yet been determined when the pamphlet was written. Trat was about to purchase the vicarage from the absentee incumbent, who had acquired it from the Smithwicke family by marriage. The Smithwickes seem to have thought themselves entitled to its return, and wanted its "good annuall profit" back in the family. To prevent the sale, Young Peter Smithwicke arranged for two or three of his servants to waylay Trat and kill him. They dismembered his body, boiled and salted it piecemeal, and buried most of the remains in Trat's home. Further to confuse detection, one of the culprits went riding off across the countryside on the day of the murder dressed in Trat's habit, stopping on occasion to identify himself as Trat. At one point the impersonator "admitted" that he was fleeing, having slain a strange Irishman with whom he fell to brawling in his house. After a fortnight the stench from Trat's house induced a search, where some headless remains of the body were found. The neighbors gave "notice unto Mr. *Thomas Windham* of St. Decoombes, unto Master *Cusse* of Creetch, Justices of Peace in the said County, who with Mr. *John Westcombe* of Haulse, Coroner for the King, came upon their first summons, and taking view of this strange and amazing object, they were much perplext . . . . [T]hey proceeded from thence unto examination of some of the neighbours in that Parish: the Intelligence of whose report might give their eyes some informing light in the mysterie of this businesse. Those examinates ma[d]e it known unto them, that in all likelihood it was Mr. *Trat* their olde Curate that was murthered, there being one of his fingers knowne by a secret marke unto them, and besides, there was a known quarrell betweene Mr. *Smethwickes* company and him . . . which gave some cause of suspition unto them, and that *Alice Walker* besides, servant unto olde M. Smethwicke, had before told some of these Informers, that if the Parson did not come home the sooner, his powdred Beefe would stinke before his coming. These presumptions drew her first of all unto question, and examination before the Justices, who were very sincere and careful in the finding out of this murderous and Butcherly plot. She being tax'd, stoode upon the deniall, but there being great presumptions of her guiltinesse, she was committed unto prison."

Perhaps because of Alice's talk, the JPs were not deceived by reports of the impersonated fugitive Trat. Windham and Cusse searched the Smithwickes' premises, where they found property belonging to Mr. Trat, as well as some further pieces of the parson himself. One of the culprits, Andrew Baker they caught there trying to dispose of "a pot of stinking blood." Another, Cyrill Austin, gave himself away by gossiping about the murder before it was generally known and by clumsily disposing of a bloody handkerchief when it was noticed upon him. The neighbors informed Cusse, the JP, who led an unsuccessful hue and cry to capture him. He was apprehended in Wiltshire, however, where he was examined by another JP and refused to confess. (He was returned to Somerset for trial and convicted with the others.) Young Smithwicke, the apparent mastermind, was convicted on evidence not described, the gist of which was that he had once threatened to cut Trat to pieces and that he had been overly conspicuous in planting his alibi in London on the day of the crime. The grand jury indicted and the trial jury convicted Alice, the two bloodied men Baker and Austin, and Young Smithwicke.

Once again, the JPs had built a successful prosecution case.

CHAPTER 3 The Parliamentary History of the Marian Statutes

It will come as no surprise to students of Tudor legislation that absolutely nothing is known about the drafting process which preceded the introduction of the two Marian bills into Parliament. There is reason to suspect that some sort of *cause célèbre* motivated the bail statute. The malpractice of which the Preamble complains is not the sort that a draftsman conceives in the abstract, and there is no reason to doubt the Preamble's assertion that some JPs had been abusing their power to bail. However, it has not been possible to identify the triggering incident. Nor is that an uncommon outcome, given the state of the Tudor records. We may compare the Statute of Pirates of 1535–1536[1] which ousted civilian procedure from Admiralty criminal jurisdiction. Like the Marian bail statute, its Preamble describes a particularized grievance: that pirates, being a bloodthirsty lot, were killing off the witnesses to their misdeeds, thereby frustrating prosecution for want of the two witnesses required by civilian process. It is unlikely that this situation was merely anticipated; yet a competent search[2] in the somewhat less patchy Admiralty records of the time has failed to reveal the actual event.

Of the draftsman and his preparatory work we have no record. It has sometimes been possible to find earlier drafts and related material in the Henrician State Papers.[3] But the Marian calendar discloses none.[4] Maitland once hinted that Philip of Spain may have brought his lawyer

1. 27 Hen. VIII c. 4 (1535–36); 28 Hen. VIII c. 15 (1536).

2. The current, as yet unpublished, study of the Admiralty by Messrs. David Yale and Michael Prichard. Compare the Statute of Informers, 31 Eliz. I c. 5 (1588–89), studied in M. G. Davies, *The Enforcement of English Apprenticeship: A Study in Applied Mercantilism 1563–1642* (Cambridge, Mass., 1956). "The background of this legislation is unknown." Id. at 66.

3. See, e.g., E. W. Ives, "The Genesis of the Statute of Uses," *English Historical Review* 82:673 (1967).

4. *Calendar of State Papers, Domestic Series: 1547–1580* (R. Lemon, ed.) (London, 1856) 54–71; *Calendar of State Papers, Domestic Series: 1601–1603; with Addenda 1547–1565* (M. A. E. Green, ed.) (London, 1870) 429–440. Also unavailing: *Acts of the Privy Council (New Series): 1552–1554 & 1554–1556* (J. R. Dasent, ed.) (London, 1892) IV and V.

with him[5]—which would be of considerable interest in view of the fact that Philip was later to promulgate one of the major sixteenth-century Continental redactions of Inquisitionsprozess (in the Spanish Netherlands).[6] However, Maitland's remark was inspired by a peripheral source referring to the English sojourn of a Spanish canonist, and none of the documentary sources, Tudor or Hapsburg, suggest that Philip or his suspiciously regarded Spanish entourage involved themselves with aspects of Marian governance not touching religious or foreign policy.[7]

More can be learned about the course of the two bills in the legislature itself, thanks to the journals of the two houses. By way of introduction, it should be remarked that the journals up to and including the Marian years bear no strong resemblance to the modern specimen, much less to Hansard. Debates are not only not transcribed, they are usually not even mentioned.[8] The introduction of a bill, its readings, and the fact of its passage are all that is typically recorded. Generally these monotonous entries reveal only uninformative routine. In the present case we are more fortunate.

5. F. W. Maitland, *English Law and the Renaissance* (Cambridge, 1901) 11–12, 54–55 n. 21.

6. The *ordonnance criminelle* of 1570 (infra, Chapter 6, notes 4 and 5).

7. This conclusion is based upon study of the calendars to the State Papers Domestic and Foreign for the reign, and of the State Papers Spanish. The latter were assembled from the principal Hapsburg archives. *Calendar of State Papers, Domestic Series* (supra, note 4); *Calendar of State Papers, Foreign Series: 1553–1558* (W. Turnbull, ed.) (London, 1861); *Calendar of Letters, Despatches, and State Papers, Relating to the Negotiations between England and Spain, Preserved in the Archives at Vienna, Simancas, Besançon and Brussels: 1554 & 1554–1558* (R. Tyler, ed.) (London, 1949, 1954) XII and XIII.

The Spanish marriage was intensely unpopular in England from the moment it was projected. The House of Commons petitioned against it in advance of the contract. J. A. Froude, *History of England from the Fall of Wolsey to the Defeat of the Spanish Armada* (London, 1870 ed.) VI 123. The English added five clauses to the marriage contract proposed by Charles V. The first: "That no foreigner, under any circumstances, should be admitted to any office in the royal household, in the army, the forts or the fleet." Id. at 135–136. Wyatt's rebellion was launched to the populace on the contention, published in handbills designed to incite uprising, that "the Spaniards were coming to conquer the realm, and calling on loyal Englishmen to rise and resist them." Id. at 152–153. During Philip's residence in England there was continuing friction between his retainers and the natives. A contemporary "reported that the feeling in all classes, high and low, was as bad as possible." Id. at 255, cf. id. at 252–255.

8. E.g., December 31 and again January 2: "Arguments upon the Bill touching the Supremacy." *Journals of the House of Commons* I. (The spelling of journal entries has been modernized throughout this chapter. Page citations have been omitted; both journals are chronological and entries are more easily located by date than by page.)

A. THE BAIL STATUTE

The bail statute was introduced in the House of Lords on November 21, 1554. Second reading was on December 4, on which occasion the bill was ordered engrossed—that is, recopied on parchment. (Because parchment was costly, engrossment was not ordered until it was believed that further substantial textual change in the particular House was unlikely.) The bill was read the third time on December 5 and unanimously passed the next day. This is the uninstructive "legislative history" which is normal to the journals of the period.

The journal of the House of Commons, however, tells a more complex story. Promptly on December 7 the bail bill from the Lords received its first reading in the Commons.[9] Second reading was on December 11. At this point the bill ran into trouble. Annexed to the journal report of second reading is the notation, "Mr. S. *Petre*," which signifies that the bill had been assigned to a committee for revisions too extensive to be worked out on the floor of the House. The member made responsible for the physical custody of the bill, and probably therefore chairman of the committee, was Sir William Petre ("Mr. S[ecretary] *Petre*"). Petre was then principal secretary of state. He was the archetypal crown servant who "served with equal fidelity Henry, Edward, Mary, and Elizabeth."[10]

On December 19 the journal records the unusual entry: "1 *nova.* The Bill for Bailment of Prisoners." Presumably because of objections raised in the debate on December 11, the Petre committee had killed the original bill and substituted a new draft.

9. On December 4, the date of the second reading in the Lords, the Commons journal records the following exceptional entry:

> Mr. Attorney and Mr. Solicitor brought a Bill of divers Names of the upper House, requiring a Number of this House to confer with them for Parliament Matters; which immediately were named, *viz.* The whole Council of this House, and Twenty-one Knights and Burgesses; and sent up to the Lords.

Nothing more is heard of this group, but on December 7 two bills are given first reading in the Commons, both of which have just passed the Lords: "The Bill for Punishments of divers Treasons" and "The Bill for Bailment of Felons by Justices of Peace." These bills touching the criminal law might have been the subject of the meeting on December 4 with the Lords and the law officers of the crown. On the other hand, it would have been unusual for the Commons to appoint a committee to consider bills in advance of their introduction there, especially when the Lords was finding them so untroublesome.

10. *Dictionary of National Biography* XLV 93, at 94. Cf. F. G. Emmison, *Tudor Secretary: Sir William Petre at Court and Home* (London, 1961); on Petre's work on other legislation in the Parliament of 1554–1555, see id. at 183–185.

The new draft failed to put an end to the controversy. This version required seven separate days of debate in the Commons and two further references to committee. First reading was on December 19, second reading on December 22. On that occasion the bill was referred to a committee under "Mr. *Pollard*"—Sir John Pollard, then Speaker of the House.[11] Third reading was on December 24, when the bill was again referred to committee under "Mr. *Cholmeley*"—Ranulph Cholmeley, Recorder of London and (from 1558) serjeant-at-law.[12] Fourth, fifth, and sixth readings took place on December 31 and on January 10 and 12. Only on sixth reading of this nova draft was engrossment ordered. The bill was passed by the Commons on January 14, 1555, then returned to the Lords the same day for both first and second readings. It was read a third time and passed the next day, Lord Stafford[13] dissenting. Dissolution of the Parliament followed a day later, on January 16.

On the crude measure of number of entries in the Commons journal, we should have to say that the bail statute was the most controverted measure before a session of Commons which dealt with, inter alia, the attainder of the Duke of Suffolk; the restitution of Cardinal Pole; the new treason law; and the repeal of "all Statutes, Articles, and Provisions made against the See of *Rome* since the 20th Year of King *Henry* the Eighth . . . ."[14] No bill in this session had so many readings as the bail statute. Most bills had four entries: three readings and passage. The treason bill required two readings in predecessor format, four in nova. The bail bill took two in predecessor, seven in nova. It can be argued that this was a fluke: perhaps the bail bill was last-class freight, always shunted aside by more important matters as it was about to be disposed of. Still, this would defy the norm that uncontroverted matters were dispatched on the minimum, not the maximum, number of readings.

11. *Dictionary of National Biography* XLVI 59–60.

12. *Members of Parliament: Parliaments of England 1213–1702* (London, 1873) I 390; E. Foss, *The Judges of England* (London, 1857) V 413; see supra, Chapter 2, note 12.

This personage is not to be confused with Sir Roger Cholmley, Lord Chief Justice until 1553, who was dismissed upon Mary's accession for having witnessed the will of Edward VI (which had tried to vary the succession in favor of Lady Jane Grey). *Dictionary of National Biography* X 269–270.

13. Henry, first Baron Stafford (1501–1563), who served in the commission of the peace from 1536 to his death, was a minor courtier from Henry VIII's reign to Elizabeth's. To celebrate Mary's accession he published a translation of chapters from a tract of Erasmus on the "brain-sick headiness of the Lutherans." Id. at LIII 450–451.

14. *Journals of the House of Lords* I 491.

Moreover, one of the readings of the bail bill was the sole entry for the day—a rarity, for several readings were customary at each sitting. Indeed, the single-entry phenomenon occurs only one other time in this session, on January 2: "Arguments upon the Bill touching the Supremacy." However, the exclusive reading of the bail statute occurred on December 24, which may have been a sitting affected in duration or importance by Christmas Eve celebrations.

A pair of points of interpretation arise from this parliamentary history. First, it seems that the bill was part of the crown's legislative program. Although its subject matter was criminal administration, it was also supervision and control over the JPs; and this strongly implies that it was a crown measure. Further, when the bill ran into trouble in the Commons, the rescue was supervised by crown placemen of great authority. Finally, the bill survived the press of business at the end of the session to be passed in the Commons two days before dissolution, read twice in the Lords the same day, and both read and passed in the Lords the following day. Crown hands seem to have been guiding it.

Second, we need to ask what was being contested in the apparently long-drawn struggle in Commons. It can be ventured that we are seeing the valiant Commons straining against the importation of the secular inquisition. Yet there is much ground for doubt. Were such the case, it is likely that mention of the contest would have found its way into contemporary chronicles. That a debate raged with such apparent doggedness and yet attracted no notice inclines one to suspect that the subject matter was something fairly petty. We recall that the bail statute was a scheme designed in its mechanics to curb the discretion of the justices of the peace, complete with fines for default. One of the high themes of English history from the mid-fourteenth century on was the nexus between the Commons and the justices. Miss Putnam has described the essential role played by the Commons more than two centuries before the Marian acts in the contest whose outcome raised the local keepers of the peace into justices.[15] A fundamental identity of interest linked the

15. "[I]t was the commons, not the central government, that consistently advocated the increase in the powers of the justices of the peace . . . ." B. Putnam, Introduction, *Proceedings before the Justices of the Peace in the Fourteenth and Fifteenth Centuries* (Ames Foundation) (London, 1938) liii. "If my interpretation is sound, it was the commons, country gentry and the middle classes in the towns, who consistently tried to increase the powers of the justices of the peace, powers that in the Shires were exercised chiefly by the country gentry on the commissions." Id. at lvi.

Commons and justices even then: "the House of Commons, whose membership was largely composed of country gentry and merchants from the towns . . . strongly desired that the commissions be controlled by men of their own kind." [16] This alliance persisted to the Tudor Commons. Gleason's recent study computes that JPs "provided half the members of the Elizabethan House of Commons," and that in Kent in 1584 about half the sitting justices had been elected to the Commons at least once.[17] I suggest that, viewed in the light of this nexus, the nature of the fight in the Commons over a bill disciplining and narrowing the discretion of the justices can be confidently imagined, even though we are unable to reconstruct the rejected first draft or to identify the major alterations made in revision.[18] It seems a good deal more likely that the debate concerned no such great issues as reception and Inquisitionsprozess, but rather the power adjustments between the rulers of the realm and the "rulers of the county." [19] Moreover, the one certainty in the evidence is

16. Dawson, *Lay Judges* 136.

17. Gleason 2, 26.

18. I have examined the so-called "original acts" of both Marian statutes in the House of Lords Record Office. These are the parchments of the acts in the form in which they emerged from the enacting process. It has sometimes been possible to learn about amendments from the cross-outs and interlineations on original acts. See, e.g., F. W. Maitland, "Elizabethan Gleanings," in *Collected Papers* (H. A. L. Fisher, ed.) (Cambridge, 1911) III 157, 185 ff. But not in the present case: the committal statute is a completely clean parchment showing no revision, addition, or deletion. H.L.R.O. Original Act, 2 & 3 Phil. & Mar., no. 13 (1555).

The parchment of the bail statute shows seven interlineations, none of significance. All are additions, mostly of one or two words, amplifying the language previously in place. The only sizable addition is the sentence directing the JPs to certify their recognizances to gaol delivery in connection with coroners' inquests: "And lykewise the said justices shall certifie all and every suche bounde taken before them in lyke maner as before ys said of Bailments and Examination," H.L.R.O. Original Act, 1 & 2 Phil. & Mar., no. 10 (1554–55). It should be mentioned that this parchment is the document ordered engrossed following the sixth reading of the nova draft in the House of Commons. The serious debate had taken place before the transcription to parchment. The amendments inserted subsequently were understandably minor and technical. Mr. Leslie Jenkins has also examined the original act. He tells me that, based upon the presence of six line numbers in the margin, it can be inferred which of the seven amendments originated in which House. The argument is complex, however, and I forgo repeating it because of the insubstantiality of the amendments themselves.

It should also be recorded that session law prints of the Marian statutes reveal no discrepancies from the versions printed in the *Statutes of the Realm* beyond the customary variety in spelling, capitalization, punctuation, and tense. *Anno primo & secundo Philippi & Marie: Actes made at a Parliament begon . . .* (London [Cawood], 1555) fol. xxix–xxx; *Anno secundo & tertio Philippi & Marie: Actes made at a Parliament begon . . .* (London [Cawood], 1555) fol. xxvi^{v}.

19. Maitland's famous phrase. F. W. Maitland, *Justice and Police* (London, 1885) 80. I intend no implication that the statutory sanctions upon the JPs were

that, whatever the system proposed by the crown at the outset, it was rejected and a modification hastily devised. From its very birth, therefore, the Marian scheme has about it an air of the indigenous, of compromise and makeshift.

B. THE COMMITTAL STATUTE

Ten months later the succeeding Parliament enacted the committal statute with the clockwork regularity normal to the legislative process of the time as it has been captured in the journals. The bill was introduced in the House of Commons, not in the Lords where the bail statute had begun. It was first read on November 4, 1555, given a second reading November 7, and given a third reading and passed on November 8. The final two journal entries misdescribe the bill, calling it the "Bill for Bailment of Prisoners" and the "Bill for Bailment and Examination of Prisoners." A bill whose contents were so deficiently known to the recording clerk in the House seems unlikely to have been a subject of very intense debate or interest.

In the Lords, first reading occurred on November 12, second reading on November 16, third reading and passage on November 18.

---

novel. Lambarde collects a dozen in a chapter, "Of the reward, & punishment, of *Justices* of the Peace, for things done, not done, or missedone, out of the Sessions of the Peace." Lambarde 276–281 (italics in original). Most are penalties for failure to intervene against certain threats to the peace. Moreover, "neglect of justices of peace in their duties, in not bringing felons and offenders to punishment, or not certifying recognizances, or not granting the peace, hath had always its due examination and proofs" in the court of Star Chamber. W. Hudson, *A Treatise on the Court of Star Chamber* [temp. Chas. I], printed in *Collectanea Juridica* (F. Hargrave, ed.) (London, 1792) II 64. The predecessor of the Marian bail statute, the 1487 act discussed supra, pages 6–8, itself had imposed a fine upon the JPs for failure to report their bailments to sessions or gaol delivery. 3 Hen. VII c. 3 (1487).

The Marian bail statute, however, constituted a more serious piece of disciplinary legislation than those previously directed against the JPs. It required the JPs to create a written record by which the central authorities could review their actions regularly in an important class of business, which requisite must have struck the JPs as an ominous precedent indeed. This disciplinary character continued for long years to impress itself upon observers as the distinctive element of the bail statute. There is, for instance, Hale's succinct statement: The court of gaol delivery "[m]ay punish those that unduly bail Prisoners, Stat. *de Finibus*, 1 & 2 *Ph.* & *Ma. c.* 13." M. Hale, *Pleas of the Crown: Or, A Methodical Summary* (London, 1678) 158. For an example in which the assize judge in 1661 did fine a JP "for returning only my own hand to the recognizance for bailing, and not my fellow Justice [*sic*] hand with me, who was sick and so absent, and could not joyne (though fine remitted after)" see "Henry Townshend's 'Notes of the office of a Justice of Peace,'

The easy passage of the act creating regularized preliminary inquiry for felony reinforces the view that the Commons opposition to the bail statute had not been to the details of its criminal procedural mechanics, essentially all of which were reenacted in the committal statute.

The confusion of the committal statute with its predecessor by the Commons clerk illuminates how thoroughly dependent the later statute was on the earlier one. I have remarked above on the extent to which the second statute tracks the actual language of the first, and how frequently it repeats the various procedural incidents of the first act. This is a matter of some importance for the reception question in the light of the parliamentary history. The committal statute seems genuinely to be an outgrowth of a procedure originally designed to check bail abuse. The most persuasive reading of the parliamentary history is that the crown in 1554, alarmed by some event no longer known, set out to remedy what it deemed abuse of the bail power by the justices. After considerable strife in the Commons, the crown secured some portion of the reform it had sought—perhaps much of what it sought in procedural mechanics, less in the way of sanctions on the JPs. Then in the interval between Parliaments, there dawned on someone the realization that the scheme just accepted by the Commons could have a far broader applicability than bail. All that needed to be done was to keep right on employing it when bail was denied.[20] In the grand English manner, the figure of the investigating magistrate had stumbled into the common law.

1661–3" (R. D. Hunt, ed.), in *Miscellany II* (Worcestershire Historical Society, 1967) 87–88.

20. I have suggested (supra, pages 18, 19–20, 38) that the awkwardness of the draftsmanship of the committal statute can be explained on the basis that the draftsman thought it necessary merely to extend the investigatory scheme of the bail statute, the sufficiency of which he assumed.

CHAPTER 4 The Origins of Examination by the Magistrates in England

Previous chapters have put forth the view that the Marian statutes did not intend to institute a system of written evidence, and that in consequence, no general adoption of Inquisitionsprozess could have been contemplated. The draftsman conceded the continuity of the petty jury as the trier-of-fact and did not attempt to displace the emergent system of informing the jury through oral evidence at public trial.

It remains open to argument, however, that the Marian statutes represent a more selective reception, a reception in the preliminary process only. The need having become apparent for crown participation in the gathering of evidence for the now-passive trial jury, the Marian draftsman chose as remedy the Continental solution. The English statutes of 1554–1555 were adopting and adapting the Roman-canon institution of the investigating magistrate, which had come to such prominence in the German and French legislation of the 1530s. The English magistrate would not be assembling a dossier upon which to decide the case himself. But in collecting evidence upon which the jury could decide the case, he would emulate the essential technique of his Continental brethren. He would examine the accused and the witnesses. He would interrogate them about the circumstances of the crime. This investigation, we have seen, would enable him to build a case for the jury; it let him discover which witnesses to bind over to testify, and it prepared him to be a witness himself.

The aspect of this argument which is questionable is the matter of origin. Did the English borrow the investigating magistracy from contemporary Roman-canon practice, or did they arrive at it independently? Holdsworth, who attributes many facets of sixteenth-century criminal procedure in both prerogative and common law jurisdictions to "continental ideas," regards the Marian statutes in the same light. The infusion of "continental ideas" in criminal procedure usually came about through judicial practice; Marian preliminary inquiry, however, was "the only one of these changes which was introduced by the legislature."[1] Barnes thinks that "it was Tudor monarchy's unceasing battle against lawlessness that impelled it to borrow this useful weapon from current Continental legal systems."[2] The essence of the argument is that parallelism equals reception. Examination having been a hallmark of Continental procedure, the Marian statutes must have been in imitation.

The present chapter puts forward the opposing view. Section A establishes that for nearly two centuries before the Marian statutes, legislation had been steadily empowering the JPs to examine suspects and witnesses in cases of petty crime. The Marian procedure in cases of felony, it is argued, was an outgrowth of this tradition. Section B continues that point on the basis of the surviving records of the JPs' examination practice. It concludes that the Marian scheme of preliminary inquiry for felony only confirmed and made uniform prior practice among the magistrates.

A. PRE-MARIAN EXAMINATION LEGISLATION

The Tudor era was an epoch of legislation. In "the great outburst of legislation that marks the reign of Henry VIII"[3] the quantity of statute law doubled. England was not in this respect unique. The statute came of age throughout Europe in the sixteenth century, doubtless affected by the newfound capacity of the printing press to make the command operative with an efficiency unthinkable before Gutenberg. The sheer bulk of Tudor legislation gives rise to the suspicion that not all was novel—that matter which had been regulated less formally in former

1. Holdsworth IV 528.

2. T. G. Barnes, "Examination before a Justice in the Seventeenth Century," *Somerset and Dorset Notes and Queries* 27:39, 40 (1955). He continues: "It survives to-day though in a restricted form, in the French *enquete* [*sic*] held by the *juge d'instruction* whose function is that of a refined inquisitor." Plucknett, too, remarked on the parallel to the French. "The effect [of the Marian statutes] was to turn the justice of peace into something between a detective and a *juge d'instruction.*" T. F. T. Plucknett, *A Concise History of the Common Law* (5th ed., London, 1956) 432. Cf. G. Williams, "The Power to Prosecute," [1955] *Criminal Law Review* 596, 601; "Note, An Historical Argument for the Right to Counsel During Police Interrogation," *Yale Law Journal* 73:1000, 1038 (1964); L. W. Levy, *Origins of the Fifth Amendment* (New York, 1968) 35; M. Ploscowe, "The Development of Present-day Criminal Procedures in England and America," *Harvard Law Review* 48:433, 458 (1935).

3. S. E. Thorne, Introduction, *A Discourse upon the Exposicion & Understandinge of Statutes* (San Marino, Calif., 1942) 3.

days was only then being pulled into the statutes. Such was unquestionably the case on the Continent.[4] Stephen inclined to the belief that the Marian preliminary inquiry scheme might have come from such a background:[5]

> Whatever may have been the reason, the fact is certain that no allusion is made to the holding of any sort of preliminary inquiry by justices in any statute passed before the statutes of Philip and Mary . . . . It is probable, however, that from the very earliest times magistrates would make a more or less formal inquiry before they took steps towards the arrest or bail of a suspected person, and it is not at all improbable that the two statutes in question may have given legal sanction to a practice which had grown up without express statutory authority.

While Stephen's instinct was accurate, he was mistaken about the lack of prior statutes. The class of evidence presently to be considered constitutes a massive body of statute law imposing upon the JPs the power and the duty to investigate crime by examination, occasionally preliminary to traditional jury process, more typically incident to summary powers of accusation and trial. Virtually every feature of the Marian procedure can be found in prior legislation addressed to the justices. What was new about the committal statute of 1555 was that it regularized and generalized as a preliminary procedure for felony a practice developed earlier, usually as a dispositive procedure, for petty crime. The pre-Marian statutes commence late in the fourteenth century and are to be found in nearly every reign from the time of Richard II. They overlap, therefore, the formative period of the office of justice of the peace and are wrapped up with its fundamental functional delimitation. They will allow us to suggest that the key procedural features of the Marian statutes had in fact become essential characteristics of the justices' office long before 1554–1555.

When the initial struggle over their establishment in the second

4. This point is developed in Dr. Gerhard Immel's contribution to the forthcoming handbook of European legal history now in preparation by the Max-Planck-Institut für Europäische Rechtsgeschichte.

5. Stephen I 219. Bayne thought so too, citing Stephen: "Although the examination of accused persons in ['preliminary investigations'] was not authorized by law till the middle of the sixteenth century, it is probable that during the whole Tudor period criminals in serious cases were brought in the first instance before justices of the peace, who questioned them and recorded their dispositions [depositions?]." C. G. Bayne, Introduction, *Select Cases in the Council of Henry VII* (Selden Society) (London, 1958) xciii.

quarter of the fourteenth century was past, the JPs emerged with three basic functions in the formal criminal process: the taking of presentment or indictment, the conduct of jury trial, and the power of summary conviction for lesser offenses. What needs to be noticed is that the procedure involved in the justices' summary powers differed radically from their relatively passive role in administering the older jury procedures. It was this "police work" of the justices about which Stephen surmised that it must have compelled them to assume the power to question suspects and witnesses. It is hard to imagine how they could have failed to do so.[6] They would have had the model of conciliar practice to reinforce natural inclination.[7] Still, the vast body of legislation which forms the prehistory of the Marian statutes does not require surmise. In more than thirty statutes predating the reign of Mary the JPs are explicitly commanded to proceed by examination.

1. *The Pre-Marian Statutes*

The importance of earlier legislation to an understanding of the Marian statutes requires that it be set forth in considerable detail. Thirty-one statutes have been numbered chronologically below, to simplify

6. The practice of questioning individuals who may know something about a subject in which one is interested is a palpably efficient way of gathering information. It is also an elementary method, virtually the first which can occur to the mind of the man who requires the information: when in need, ask around. Dawson makes this point in arguing against the reception thesis of the origins of Chancery procedure:

> It is clear at least that long before a separate court of equity had emerged in the light of day, examination of individuals under oath was used as a method of investigation by various agencies of the crown—the King's Bench, Exchequer, Parliament, and certainly the Council. Nor is there any evidence that church court procedures provided a model. A royal government that had come to use juries—twelve-man inquests—on so enormous a scale would surely have had the power to interrogate individuals under oath, and this was an obvious recourse where questioning of individuals might elicit information that crown officers desired.

Dawson, *Lay Judges* 148 (footnotes omitted).

7. What Baldwin calls "inquisitorial examination" (that is, interrogation of individuals under oath) he finds "as early as the reign of Edward II . . ." and regularly thereafter. J. F. Baldwin, *The King's Council in England during the Middle Ages* (Oxford, 1913) 296, 296–301. "[T]he strong insistence at all times upon written evidence" came about because the Council delegated the taking of evidence to "'committees of examination,' as they were called, [which] can be traced to the reign of Edward III." Id. at 300 (footnote omitted). A fourteenth-century exemplar is the "Examination of Gilbert Blount," in *Select Cases before the King's Council* (Selden Society) (Cambridge, Mass., 1918) 33–34. Star Chamber practice followed under the Tudors. Bayne (supra, note 5) at xciv.

The Pre-Marian Statutes

Statute no.	Citation	Year	Subject
1	7 Ric. II c. 5	1383	Vagabonds
2	2 Hen. V c. 4	1414	Laborers
3	2 Hen. VI c. 7	1423	Cordwainers
4	6 Hen. VI c. 3	1427	Wages
5	8 Hen. VI c. 4	1429	Livery
6	8 Hen. VI c. 5	1429	Weights and measures
7	11 Hen. VI c. 8	1433	Weights and measures
8	11 Hen. VI c. 12	1433	Candle manufacture
9	23 Hen. VI c. 12	1444–1445	Laborers
10	3 Edw. IV c. 1	1463	Wool trade
11	3 Edw. IV c. 5	1463	Apparel
12	4 Edw. IV c. 1	1464–1465	Wages
13	8 Edw. IV c. 2	1468	Livery and retaining
14	17 Edw. IV c. 4	1477–1478	Tile manufacture
15	22 Edw. IV c. 1	1482–1483	Apparel
16	1 Hen. VII c. 7	1485	Unlawful hunting
17	11 Hen. VII c. 2	1495	Gaming
18	11 Hen. VII c. 4	1495	Weights and measures
19	11 Hen. VII c. 15	1495	Sheriffs
20	11 Hen. VII c. 17	1495	Game poaching
21	11 Hen. VII c. 22	1495	Wages
22	19 Hen. VII c. 12	1503–1504	Gaming
23	19 Hen. VII c. 14	1503–1504	Retaining
24	1 Hen. VIII c. 7	1509–1510	Coroners
25	3 Hen. VIII c. 3	1511–1512	Arms
26	32 Hen. VIII c. 13	1540	Horse breeding
27	33 Hen. VIII c. 1	1541–1542	Forgery
28	1 Edw. VI c. 1	1547	Nonconforming priests
29	1 Edw. VI c. 3	1547	Vagabonds
30	2 & 3 Edw. VI c. 9	1548	Leather trade
31	5 & 6 Edw. VI c. 14	1551–1552	Commodity speculation

subsequent reference. Others about whose meaning there might be some question have been excluded. The remainder of this section discusses the examination provisions of each statute. The translation from the French in pre-Tudor statutes here and throughout the chapter is that of the *Statutes of the Realm,* and virtually all of the material in square brackets is original to its editors. Editorial commentary and footnotes to conflicting texts have been omitted. Section 2 studies this class of evidence more analytically in its bearing on the Marian legislation.

The earliest instance which is unambiguous is a statute of 1383 against vagabonds (No. 1). It empowers the JPs and their counterparts in the towns (mayors, bailiffs, and constables) "to examine [the vagabonds] diligently, and to compel them to find Surety . . . ," failing which the vagabonds are to be gaoled pending gaol delivery. In language immediately preceding, the statute preserves as an alternative mode of investigation the traditional inquiry before the presenting jury at assizes or in sessions. The examination procedure differs from the Marian in that the examination before the magistrates does not merely supplement, rather it displaces, presentment or indictment. The examination is preliminary to final process at gaol delivery, hence an alternative to presentment or indictment. This is a feature common to much of the pre-Marian legislation; we discuss it in the next section.

A single statute (No. 2, 1414) under Henry V, regulating laborers, directs the JPs "to examine . . . all Manner of Labourers, Servants and their Masters . . . by their Oaths, . . . and upon that to punish them them upon their [Confession] . . . as though they were convict by Inquest . . . ." Examination takes the place of both presentment and jury trial. The statute exhibits a scheme of summary process conducted wholly by examination. The use of oath is interesting, because it all but disappears from later statutes.

Seven of the statutes (Nos. 3–9) date from the reign of Henry VI. An act of 1423 (No. 3) addressed to the judges of both benches, JPs, and mayors who sit as JPs, empowers them to hear complaints in certain matters regulating cordwainers. They "shall have Power to enquire, hear and determine . . . ," that is, to try accused persons by traditional process, "or to attaint them by Examination . . . ," that is, in a summary trial conducted by examination. Similarly, in a statute of 1427 (No. 4) regulating wages, JPs and mayors are authorized

to examine by their Discretion [and Knowledge], as well such Servants,

Artificers, and Workmen, as their Masters, how much such Servants, Aritficers, and Workmen do take by the Year, by the Day, and by the Week; and if they find . . . [violations, the violators] shall be punished . . . .

An act of 1429 against livery (No. 5) recites former legislation against livery still in effect and complains that it has not been successfully enforced. The new act therefore propounds an alternative procedure of summoning suspected offenders before the JPs in sessions. The JPs "shall have Power . . . to examine them . . .; and they whom they find [guilty] by Examination . . . shall incur [the same sanctions] as they ought if they were by Inquest duly . . . convict . . . ." Examination is a summary procedure obviating both presentment and jury trial. A pair of statutes (Nos. 6–7) of 1429 and 1433 empowers JPs and mayors to proceed against users of faulty weights and measures either "by Inquests, or by Examination . . . ." Another act of 1433 (No. 8) regulating the candle trade empowers the JPs and mayors, as an alternative to ordinary "enquire hear and determine" procedure, "to examine and search" (by weighing or otherwise) candles and other wax products "and to punish [violators] that by such Examination or Search shall be found guilty . . . ." Examination again obviates both presentment and jury trial. The final examination statute of the reign (No. 9, 1444–1445), one of several treating wages and labor, empowers "every Justice of Peace . . . to call . . . to Examination" persons refusing to labor as required, "and such as they find defective, to commit to the Gaol . . . ." Examination by a single justice out of sessions is the whole of the procedure.

Six examination statutes under Edward IV deal with similar subjects in similar procedural fashion. An act regulating the wool trade (No. 10, 1463) authorizes the JPs of county and city "to hear and determine [cases of violation] as well by due Examination as otherwise." Here appears something of a stock drafting phrase which, with slight variations, recurs often in later statutes. The same Parliament empowered JPs and mayors "to enquire, hear, and determine" offenses of apparel "as well by Enquiry as by due Examination . . ." (No. 11). The next Parliament enacted a complex statute (No. 12) of wage regulation for the cloth trade, providing for examination in varied litigational situations—private suit as well as criminal action. An act of 1468 (No. 13) against livery and retaining lays down a procedure for use in the royal courts and at assizes as well as at the sessions of the peace. Suit may be begun by information rather than indictment, and the trial court is empowered

> to examine all Persons Defendants, and every of them, upon every such Information, and to judge him or them convicted or attainted, as well by such Examination as by Trial as the Case requireth, after the Discretion [of] the Judges; . . . .

A statute regulating tile manufacture (No. 14, 1477–1478) authorizes JPs "to inquire, hear, and determine by their Discretions, as well by Examination or otherwise, the Defaults, Offences, and Trespasses which shall happen to be committed contrary to this Ordinance . . . ." Another section of the statute devises an alternative procedure of presentment by a special jury of tile experts, who are empowered to inform themselves by search of a suspect's premises. And an act of 1482–1483 (No. 15) again regulating apparel provides that the JPs, among others, may "inquire, hear and determine . . . as well by Enquiry as by due Examination . . . ."

The accession of the Tudors cannot be said to have materially affected the development of examination before the justices of the peace. Precisely as many of the pre-Marian statutes predate 1485 as postdate it, with one (No. 16) being enacted in that year. As it happens, this one statute of 1485 is among the most interesting of the series. It is directed against unlawful hunting in forests and elsewhere and provides for initiation of proceedings by information laid before any JP or any member of the Council. The sheriff or constable is to bring the accused before the councilor or JP, who is authorized to examine him.

> And if the same persone wilfully concele the said huntyngs or any persone with hym defective therin, that then the same concelement be, ayenst every suche persone so concelyng, Felonye, and the same felonye to be enquered of and determyned as othir felonyes within this Realme have used to be; And if he then confesse the trouthe & all that he shalbe examyned of and knoweth in that behalf, that then the same offences of huntyngs by hym done be as ayeinst [the Kynge our] Soverayn Lord but trespasse finable, by reason of the same confession, at the next generall Sessions of the Peax . . . .

Here, in convoluted fashion, is statutory preliminary inquiry for felony. It is the sole example before the Marian acts. The procedure of the statute has two branches. Summons and examination of the suspect precede either. If a confession results, conviction for misdemeanor on the basis of the confession follows at sessions. If confession is not forthcoming, subsequent trial will be for felony. The examination in that case is solely preliminary to later determinative proceedings. Nothing is said of the use of the unsuccessful examination at the felony trial. Were the JP to testify at the trial, this scheme would square exactly with the Marian procedure: preliminary inquiry for felony with the JP subsequently adducing the results of his investigation to the trial court. It does seem unlikely that a JP whose unsuccessful attempt to secure a confession had nonetheless turned up criminating evidence would abstain from the trial. The grant of examination powers in this statute indifferently to councilors and to JPs may also be significant. It is tempting to think that the strong medieval tradition of examination before the Council may have influenced the growing examination practice of the magistrates. The equation, if such it may be called, of the JPs' power and mode of investigation with that of the councilors suggests that, at least in this instance, it may have been the conciliar tradition of examination which was being extended to the justices.

Seven other examination statutes were enacted under Henry VII, five of them (Nos. 17–21) in the year 1495. An act against vagabondage (No. 17) recites the examination provisions of the statute of 1383 (No. 1 above) and adds new provisions against gaming by servants and artificers; examination is permitted as an alternative to presentment. Another statute (No. 18) returns to the regulation of weights and measures with a two-tier examination system. Initially, it directs the mayors and bailiffs of cities, boroughs, and market towns to inspect periodically all weights and measures, those revealed by the "seid examynacion" to be "broken and brent." Second, two justices, one of the quorum, "have auctorite aswell by examynacion as by enquerry to here and determyn" complaints both against the city officials for dereliction of their duty to investigate and against persons employing noncomplying weights and measures. The requirement that two justices examine, and that one be of the quorum, is not an innovation of the Marian bail statute. A third statute of 1495 (No. 19) empowers one or more JPs to examine sheriffs and undersheriffs accused of extortion in the conduct of county court proceedings, and to "convycte and atteynt . . . [the offender] without ferther enquerre or examynacion . . . ." Examination displaces both indictment and jury trial; the procedure is mandatory. The same Parliament passed another statute (No. 20) against game poaching, listing among the alternative modes of trial "examynacion before the Justices of the peas . . . ." Finally, the Parliament of 1495 enacted yet another statute (No. 21) regulating wages and directing violaters

> to be convicted for every suche defaute by presentment afore the Justices of Peas in the Sessions according to the comen Lawe, or by examynacion of the same Justices in the same Sessions, or by examynacion of [two] Justices of the Peas out of the Sessions . . . .

The requirement that two justices examine when out of sessions appears again. Curiously, the draftsman draws a contrast between presentment according to "the comen Lawe" and procedure by examination. If the implication is that examination was not "comen Lawe," it is singular in the stream of legislation we are considering. It comes in a Parliament which enacted more examination statutes than any other.

Two further examination statutes were enacted under Henry VII, both in the Parliament of 1503–1504. One (No. 22) reenacts the examination procedure of the 1495 statute against gaming (No. 17 above) and adds a power, to be exercised by no fewer than two JPs, to make "a dewe and a diligent & a secrete serche" for such "mysruled persons." The other (No. 23) is an important statute against retaining. It provides for normal indictment and trial at sessions, but in the alternative it authorizes one or more JPs, one of the quorum, to summon and examine suspected violators. The JPs must certify to King's Bench the names of the violators discovered in their investigation, and the certificate shall have "the lyke effect and strength ayenst all theym so examened and by that examinacion founde in defaute as though they were convycted thereof by due order of the Kynges Lawes[.]" There is much of the future in this procedure. Here again is the requirement that two JPs, one of the quorum, should examine. Here too is the idea of certification of the results of examination to the central officers. Further, the dissatisfaction with presentment as a means of law enforcement appears with particular clarity. Retaining was perhaps the prototypical case of the inadequacy of the presentment system. By definition the offense concerned offenders of some power, often of sufficient power to intimidate a presenting jury. When the crown sought an alternative procedure, it chose to have the justices examine and certify. It should be further noted that this statute continued on to erect yet another alternative procedure: examination in Council or Star Chamber. We note again, therefore, an association of examination before the JPs and examination in the prerogative process.

Only four of the pre-Marian examination statutes stem from the long reign of Henry VIII, despite the prolific output of other legisation. In the first Parliament of the reign a statute (No. 24, 1509–1510) imposed a fine of forty shillings on any coroner who extorted a fee for discharging his office. The assize justices and the JPs "have auctoritie and power to enquere thereof and determyn the same aswell by examinacion as by presentement." An act of 1511–1512 (No. 25) called for the arming of the populace with longbows and ordered the JPs (and others) to enforce the legislation by inquiry or by examination. A lapse of three decades preceded the next statute: an act of 1540 (No. 26) regulating horse breeding. The JPs in sessions are to procede upon presentment to hear and determine "as well by examination as otherwise . . . ." This is the unusual case where examination is strictly a mode of "trial" or final disposition, with presentment the exclusive mode of preliminary proceeding. The last examination statute of the reign (No. 27) is an act of 1541–1542 to punish obtaining by forged and counterfeit instruments. It provides for conviction upon the basis of "examinacion of Witnesses or confession" in Star Chamber, Council, assize, or sessions—exhibiting again the sharing of a Council–Star Chamber examination procedure with the justices of the peace.

The final four examination statutes (Nos. 28–31) stem from the reign of Edward VI. The first (No. 28, 1547) is the most novel. It is aimed at nonconforming preachers whose sermons have shown contempt for the Eucharist. When accusation is made to the JPs, they

> or three of them at the least . . . before whome any such presentment Information and accusacion shalbe made or taken as is aforesaide shall examyne the accusors what other witnes were by and present at the tyme of doing and committing of thoffence whereof the Informacion accusacion and presentment shalbe made and how manny others then the accusors have Knowledge thereof, and shall have [full] power and authoritie by their discretions to bynde by Recognisaunce to be taken afore them aswell the saide accusors as all suche other parsons whom the saide accusors shall declare to have Knowledge of the Offences by them presented and Informed, every of them in five pounds to the King to appere before the saide Justices of Peace afore whom the Offendor or Offendors shall be tryed at the daye of the Tryall and deliveraunce of such Offendors.

With one crucial difference, this procedure is highly reminiscent of the Marian. Like the Marian statutes, this act enables the JPs to seek out and to bind over further witnesses for the trial. The examination is out of sessions, this time before three JPs, one of the quorum. The sharp difference from the Marian, and from the previous examination statutes, is that it is not the accused who is to be examined, rather his accusers. Thus examination is being employed as a safeguard for the accused. This is reinforced by the requirement that there be two accusers and that they accuse under oath in writing. The statute seems to be an outgrowth of an act of 35 Hen. VIII c. 5 (1543–1544), limiting prosecution for heresy and related matters because "secret and untrue accusacions and presentments" had theretofore been made of "malice." The intensity of the infighting in religious questions had been spilling over into abuse of legal process. The Edwardian statute is setting its new safeguards in the pretrial process, using the long-familiar prosecutorial device of examination as a restraint on abusive prosecution. Herein it anticipates by three centuries the spirit of Sir John Jervis' Act (1848).[8] The phenomenon of prosecutorial devices becoming safeguards over the passage of time is one of the deepest themes in the history of English criminal procedure.[9] Indictment and jury trial are among the examples, as is the magistrate's preliminary examination. Here in 1547 is some faint stirring of this last transformation. Not its least important aspect is that it demonstrates how accustomed the pre-Marian criminal process was to the technique of examination by the magistrates. The transmutation of a prosecutorial device into a safeguard is latter-day business. It comes when the device itself has been long entrenched and has revealed its possibilities for cutting the other way.

The remaining three Edwardian statutes continue the tradition unexceptionally. Still another act against vagabonds (No. 29, 1547) provides that if any JP "doo espie any such vacaboundes or Idle parsone or yf anny suche be detected unto them, [he shall] examyn him or her of the tyme of their vagaboundrye . . . ." The single JP is empowered to convict. An act for the regulation of the leather trade (No. 30, 1548) empowers the JPs (and others) to "enquire . . . and heare and determyne [offenses], and also by their discretions examyn all persons supposed to offende this Acte or any parte thereof." Finally, three years before the first Marian statute, appears an act of 1551–1552 (No. 31) against commodity speculation, authorizing the JPs to proceed

> by Inquisicion presentment Bill or Informacion before them exhibited, and by examinacion of two laufull witnes or by any of the same wayes or meanes by the discretion of the saide Justices and to make process

8. 11 & 12 Vic. c. 42 (1848).
9. P. Devlin, *The Criminal Prosecution in England* (London, 1960) 3–11.

thereupon as though they were endyted before them by Inquisicion or by Verdicte of twelve Men or more; . . . .

2. *An Overview*

The argument to be made from this body of legislation is not that the Marian statutes represent no innovation. Rather, the Marian scheme shares so much with the earlier statutes that it must be understood to have been an evolution from them.

There are, of course, grounds of distinction. Most important, perhaps, is that the earlier legislation is generally concerned with summary accusation and trial procedure, not with exclusively pretrial procedure. Yet the mechanics for which the word examination is used differ little whether it be preliminary or determinative: the magistrate interrogates those who may know something of the offense, in particular the man suspected of it.

Another major difference, tightly connected with the first, is that the pre-Marian statutes are preoccupied with misdemeanor. We noted only one contorted instance (No. 16) in which the examination was designed to figure in felony proceedings. By contrast, the Marian scheme itself concerns exclusively felony and manslaughter. The line of continuity is nonetheless discernible. Examination was being employed in the pre-Marian statutes to displace indictment and jury trial, a development which could not have been extended to cases of serious crime. For felony the older procedure had become entrenched in the fourteenth century. A series of statutes, reacting to abuses of factionalism and favoritism in the conduct of conciliar criminal procedure, had denied capital jurisdiction to the prerogative courts, reinforcing the older procedure at common law.[10] Both indictment and jury trial had been constitutionalized for cases of felony. But the clumsiness of jury proceedings as a system of detection and denunciation was perpetually felt. Procedural innovation had remained possible for lesser offenses, whose sanction was comparatively mild, and the pre-Marian legislation is the record of its progress. Says Lambarde of some of these statutes:[11]

The obstinacie of evil dooers that woulde shewe no conscience in

10. Holdsworth I 486–488.
11. Lambarde 431 (italics in original).

acknowleging of their faultes, and the corruption of *Jurors* that would presente nothing, that lay onlie in their owne knowledges, hath begotten and brought into our Lawe thys triall by *Examination*, wherewith it was not before acquainted.

The Marian statutes themselves represent the perception that the magistrate's investigation could also be employed in cases of felony—not to displace, but to supplement the entrenched procedures of indictment and jury trial. For the technique was mechanically identical in Marian and pre-Marian usage: the JP examined suspect and witnesses.

It may still be objected that the earlier statutes were judicial, the Marian ministerial—that is, the earlier function of examination was typically in-court adjudication, whereas the latter was out-of-court investigation. One answer has already been indicated, that between the two situations the technique of examination did not vary. Another answer is that the generalization itself is unsound. Many of the pre-Marian statutes stipulate some out-of-sessions invesitgation (Nos. 1, 9, 16, 18, 19, 21, 22, 28, 29), and others must inevitably have presumed it.

That the pre-Marian statutes differ thus from the Marian scheme rather heightens the argument to be made from them. Precisely because the summary regulation of dicing, dress, wages, and game poaching differs so fundamentally from the sophisticated, elaborate Continental inquisitorial procedure for serious crime,[12] the steady reliance upon examination before the justices in these petty matters seems to illuminate the later employment of the same technique for felony. The very remoteness of the early context from the Continental mainstream buttresses the proposition that examination by the justices developed without reference to the Continental process.

Various other features of the pre-Marian statutes interest the student of Marian examination. There is a good deal of experimenting with a designated but fluctuating number of examining justices: four statutes empowered a single justice to examine (Nos. 9, 12, 19, 29), three required two JPs (Nos. 18, 21, 22), one called for three (No. 28). With but two exceptions (Nos. 2, 28) the pre-Marian statutes, like the Marian statutes, contain no provision for examination under oath. Finally, three of the pre-Marian statutes (Nos. 16, 23, 27) associate the justices' examination powers with parallel conciliar procedure.

12. In this respect England presents a contrast with Germany and France, where examination was first employed in cases of serious crime.

There is no need to belabor the force of this statutory prehistory as an argument against reception. In more than 30 statutes spread over two centuries before the reign of Philip and Mary, the central device of the Marian scheme was being applied in England: examination of the accused and of witnesses by the justices of the peace.

B. THE MAGISTRATES' EXAMINATION PRACTICE

To complete the argument of this chapter, the present section makes two points. First, examination by the magistrates *in cases of felony* had an informal existence before the Marian statutes. Second, the justices' examination practice made no distinction between Marian felony and pre-Marian misdemeanor procedure; that is, the JPs themselves understood the Marian statutes as a continuation and confirmation of the powers of examination they had long possessed.

1. The Sources

Because we want to change focus away from the formal commands of the statutes to observe the actual examination practice of the magistrates, we shall have to be prepared from the outset for quite imperfect results. For in the main our sources have vanished. Elton has written that "the difficulties of knowing about crime and law-enforcement are greater in the sixteenth century than the thirteenth . . . ." [13] Further, speaking of the entire span of years 1200–1640: "The problems of public peace are worst documented in the fifteenth and early sixteenth centuries." [14]

Two key factors underlie the dismal state of the sources for the common law[15] criminal process. First, the absence of defense counsel, and the practical absence of prosecution counsel at all but exceptional trials, stunted the development of criminal law reporting. Lawyers' literature does not emerge where lawyers have no role. Common law criminal trials in the sixteenth century were not the subject of contemporary

13. G. R. Elton, *The Sources of History: England 1200–1640* (London, 1969) 62.
14. Id. at 65.
15. As opposed to the prerogative criminal process (Council, Star Chamber, Admiralty, and the palatinate courts, among others), for which substantial fifteenth- and sixteenth-century archives survive in the Public Record Office.

law reports. The *State Trials* are reconstructions, seldom drawn from neutral sources.[16] For example, perhaps as reliable as any of the sixteenth-century *State Trials* is Sir Thomas More's; it was drawn principally from a manuscript composed by his son-in-law more than 20 years after the events.[17]

Second, the surviving archives reflect the distinctive decentralization of the common law criminal process, which retarded orderly record-keeping. The system of *nisi prius*—of pleading to issue in the central courts followed by disposition in the localities—was not duplicated in criminal procedure. In civil cases, the pretrial stage, aimed primarily at definition of the question to be directed to juries, was highly centralized. In the criminal law, indictment or presentment was completely localized. To the extent that law professionals were involved in this stage, their work was conditioned by the need to extract results from the lay panel and it was substantially merged in the work of the accusing jury. The illustrious record of the Westminster pleaders finds scant echo in the monotonous indictment files.[18] A principal reason why statutory and conciliar intervention became so frequent in criminal as compared with noncriminal procedure is that the criminal law lacked the possibilities for central direction and development which inhered in common law pleading on the civil side.[19]

The lack of central archives is not compensated by careful local record-keeping until the seventeenth century. Quarter sessions records are patchy and late for the sixteenth century in the few counties where they exist at all.[20] As indicated in Chapter 2, the lack of records is not only explicable in the light of the function of the Marian examination, it helps explain that function. No aspect of the Marian or the pre-Marian statutes called for or inspired systematic retention of examination documents. Because the Marian bail statute had a largely deterrent function,

16. See G. K. Clark, *The Critical Historian* (London, 1967) 92–115.

17. E. E. Reynolds, *The Trial of St. Thomas More* (London, 1964) 23–24. Compare the admirable reconstruction and analysis of the sources in J. D. M. Derrett, "The Trial of Sir Thomas More," *English Historical Review* 79:449 (1964).

18. Elton (supra, note 13) at 59–60.

19. See S. F. C. Milsom, *Historical Foundations of the Common Law* (London, 1969) 360–361; T. F. T. Plucknett, *Edward I and Criminal Law* (Cambridge, 1960) 75–76, 100–101.

20. A competent list of local archives and published local records appears in M. G. Davies, *The Enforcement of English Apprenticeship 1563–1642* (Cambridge, Mass., 1956) 283–286, 290–292. (I am indebted to Professor J. H. Gleason for this reference.)

not many examinations may have been transcribed.[21] Even the committal examinations, owing to their time-bound function, had short lives. Similar considerations apply *a fortiori* to the procedures under the pre-Marian statutes. Most of the statutes required no writing, since they were really devising a mode of summary accusation and, in some instances, of summary trial. Further, because the writ of error issued so seldom, even for felony, and turned on formal defects (usually in the framing of indictments), examination documents were not preserved for appellate record. Their whole function would have been fulfilled at trial, whether the trial produced conviction or acquittal.

The one substantial set of pre-Marian examinations which I have discovered, those preserved by the city of Norwich, seem to have survived because their function was felt not to have been wholly fulfilled, for reasons best discussed in the light of their contents.

2. *Pre-Marian Examination*

The pre-Marian legislation empowering the magistrates to examine into a variety of misdemeanors might in itself have suggested the Marian legislation. It would seem more probable, however, that the development was not so sharp. Preliminary examination of suspected felons may have arisen in advance of the Marian statutes as a customary practice among JPs who were already examining for the myriad of lesser offenses.

(*a*) *The JPs in the prerogative criminal process*

There are some traces of pre-Marian examination by magistrates apart from the Norwich records, but the evidence on the whole is too vulnerable to contrary interpretation to add much weight to our argument. For example, it is clear that the prerogative courts, especially the

21. Lambarde's "Ephemeris," discussed supra, pages 39–41, reports his having made some bailments pursuant to the Marian procedure. E.g.:

> 3 *April* [1581] My father-in-law [also a JP] and I took the examination of John Gladwell, charged with the felonious taking of wheat and peas, and the information of Reignold Hawkes and [blank] Innifer, concerning the same, and bailed the said Gladwell under his bond of 20 [pounds] and the bond of 10 [pounds] of John Burges. This examination, with the information and recognizances, I certified at Rochester, 3 July.

Lambarde, *Ephemeris & Charges* 20. Other bailments: id. at 24, 26, 31, 35 (two), 36, 37, 45, 46 (two), 47 (two).

Star Chamber,[22] employed JPs as special examining commissioners in cases of alleged crime. The Privy Council, too, frequently used the JPs as examiners, and with less formality.[23] In such cases, however, the justice was only incidentally justice: his authority derived from his commission to examine. In essence the examination was conciliar, not magistrative. Not uncommonly an opposite flow is detectable: examinations seemingly instigated by the justices of the peace by virtue of office and transmitted to the Council on their own initiative. For example,[24] an entry dated 1550 records:

> Sir Christopher Glenham and John Stone, Justices of Peace in Suffolk, sent the confession of one Seman tooching woordes and matter of rebellion that he accused one Stanton of, whereupon lettres were addressed to the same Justices to sende up both parties for further examinacion of the matter.

Again, it seems overly hazardous to generalize about the ordinary criminal procedure from this sort of evidence. The felt need to inform the Privy Council in cases of sedition may have induced some justices to employ a procedure they would not normally have used. On the other hand, the procedure they did select was examination and deposition. The argument is inviting that the idiosyncrasy was not examination but the report of examination. Because these political crimes touched the interests of the Council, they alone were communicated to the Council, whereas investigations not of interest to the Council obviously were not reported there. The question is, which was likely to have been extraordinary, the report to the Council or the underlying technique, or both? One's inclination is to think that while the report to the Council may have motivated special alertness and the use of writing, it did not inspire, but resulted from, the practice of investigation and examination by the

22. E.g., the illustration provided by G. R. Elton, *Star Chamber Stories* (London, 1958) 34–35.

23. E.g., an entry for May 29, 1545, in *Acts of the Privy Council (New Series): 1542–1547* (J. R. Dasent, ed.) (London, 1890) I 173–174:

> Uppon informacion that one John Farnold servant to Sir George Bayneham, was lately murdered in Wiltshire, letters were addressed to the Sherif and Justices of Peax to make diligent enquirye who were doers of it, and for further examinacion to sende hither the bodies of John Smith of Wroughton and Thomas Fluell, myller.

24. *Acts of the Privy Council (New Series): 1550–1552* (J. R. Dasent, ed.) (London, 1891) III 18.

JPs in cases of serious crime. However plausible, that view remains conjectural.

Another class of pre-Marian records, perhaps closer to those of the ordinary criminal procedure at common law, is the set of archives left by the High Court of Admiralty. It has been mentioned that in 1535–1536 Parliament enacted the Statute of Pirates,[25] converting Admiralty criminal jurisdiction from civilian to English common law procedure. Coincident with that legislation begin the Admiralty criminal records in the Public Record Office.[26] Prominent among these are examinations of suspects and witnesses, later stitched up into bound volumes.[27] Hence, in a jurisdiction which is self-consciously imitating common law procedure, complete with grand jury indictment and trial to a petty jury at an Admiralty gaol delivery, there appear examination documents from the 1530s.[28] Presumably the Admiralty's examination practice was in imitation of that at common law, as was the rest of the newly "received" procedure. On the other hand, this was an ancient civilian jurisdiction, the Statute of Pirates did not by terms address itself to preliminary procedure, and most important, the sixteenth-century examiners seem typically to have been Admiralty functionaries, hardly local JPs. It is therefore open to contention that Admiralty preliminary examination continued beyond 1535 in an inherited civilian pattern, the court functionaries gathering evidence as of old, save that jury process was substituted for civilian final process in order to make convictions easier to secure. Once again it seems unwise to try to extrapolate from prerogative court practice to that of the JPs at common law.

(*b*) *Examination before the magistrates in Norwich*

The Norwich records, on the other hand, seem free of involvement with the prerogative process. The collection which interests us has been calendared under the title *Depositions Taken before the Mayor and Aldermen of Norwich 1549–1567*.[29] The documents were individually

25. 27 Hen. VIII c. 4 (1535–36), 28 Hen. VIII c. 15 (1536).

26. Under class mark H.C.A. 1. See generally the introduction, "Criminal Records of the High Court of Admiralty (H.C.A. 1)," in the P.R.O.'s typescript calendar, *Oyer and Terminer Records (H.C.A. 1) Descriptive List: 1535–1834*, reproduced as List and Index Society Vol. 45 (London, 1969) 1–4.

27. H.C.A. 1/33 ff.

28. E.g., H.C.A. 1/33/5–7, 1/33/9, 1/33/12.

29. (W. Rye, ed.) (Norwich, 1905) [hereafter cited as Rye].

composed. At some later time the papers for the years 1549–1554 were stitched into a volume, not always in precise sequence but in a generally chronological order. The collection continues through the Elizabethan years. However, there is a high proportion of criminal matters only to the year 1561, after which the series becomes preponderantly civil. For the present, we shall speak solely of documents predating the passage of the Marian bail statute in January 1555. In addition to this collection of depositions, Norwich has preserved an earlier series of bound volumes, the Mayor's Court Books, which commence in 1510 and continue without interruption well into the seventeenth century. There are a few criminal investigation documents in this overwhelmingly civil collection.

One suspects that similar records must have survived elsewhere, but to my knowledge the Norwich collections are virtually unique for pre-Marian times.[30] Even they are scarcely known, although calendared in 1905. Presumably because it was published under the obscure auspices of the Norfolk and Norwich Archaeological Society, rather than by the Norfolk Record Society, the calendar has escaped conventional indexing.[31] It abstracts two documents from the Mayor's Court Books in an appendix,[32] but is otherwise devoted to the collection of depositions. This is rendered from its beginning in 1549 to 1567, by which time the collection had become essentially civil. The editing technique was not a modern one,[33] and it has been necessary to refer to various of the original

30. See infra, pages 87 and 93 n. 76, for reference to pre-Marian examination authority from the borough of Leicester and from Caernarvonshire.

31. *Texts and Calendars* (Royal Historical Society) (E. L. C. Mullins, ed.) (London, 1958).

32. Rye 91–95.

33. As his preface declares, Rye wanted to extract substance, and he was uninterested in judicial procedure. He purports to have compiled a "précis of [the] contents, giving all the facts and dates they contain but omitting all verbiage." Id. at 18. His disregard for procedure can be misleading. He renders the deposition of Agnes Mychell, id. at 59, as a straightforward criminal investigation of Agnes' part in the theft of merchandise from her master, one Crane, at the importuning of a neighborhood couple named Clerke. He neglects to note that the actual document is headed "Crane contra Clerke" and is a deposition taken before the mayor and two aldermen in response to interrogatories (which are missing). "Agnes Mychell of Norwich, of thage of [20] yeres sworn, and Examyned uppon certain Interrogatoryes a[d]mynistered unto her saith and deposeth by virtu of her othe in maner and forme following. To the first she saith . . . ." Norfolk and Norwich Record Office (N. & N.R.O.): Interrogatories and Depositions, Case 12, Shelf a, Bundle 1b (loose deposition dated August 20, 1554). Agnes was apparently deposed as a witness in a civil suit concerning the converted merchandise, not as a criminal defendant.

Unfortunately, the calendar is also unreliable for nonprocedural matters. Rye was an accomplished, although occasionally careless, paleographer. His transcrip-

documents now housed in the Norfolk and Norwich Record Office.

These records need to be prefaced with a word about the bearing of municipal practice on ordinary magistrate's practice outside the boroughs. Roughy speaking, the mayor's court, staffed by the mayor and aldermen, was the municipal counterpart to the sessions of the peace in the country. "The Mayor, Recorder, Steward, and all the Aldermen who had passed the Chair were Justices of the Peace throughout the City, holding Petty and Special Sessions, and a Court of Quarter Sessions having exclusive and complete criminal jurisdiction. . . . The City had been since 1404 a County of itself, with a jurisdiction extending over ten square miles of adjacent commons, cornfields, and villages outside the walls, from which the Sheriff and the Justices of the County of Norfolk were entirely excluded."[34] Norwich was not in this respect unusual. It will be recalled that much of the pre-Marian legislation discussed above pertained indifferently to mayors and JPs. Elizabethan borough charters contained a " 'usual clause . . . which makes the Mayor and some of the Aldermen Justices of the Peace, and gives the Borough the power of holding Sessions of the Peace.' "[35] Hence it is no telling point that the mayor and aldermen of Norwich were municipal officers rather than prototypical rural JPs. They were the JPs of their jurisdiction,[36] assimi-

---

tion of the crucial case of Fuir & Ely (1552), Rye 40–43, is masterly. ("This is written in a very vile hand, little better than shorthand." Id. at 41 n. 1.) See infra, pages 90–91. Yet the calendar elsewhere makes gross errors of transcription. For example, Rye at 20, line 6, renders as "it" what is in the original palpably the proper name "Kette" (Ket of Ket's rebellion), making nonsense of the document. Compare N. &. N.R.O.: Interrogatories and Depositions, Case 12, Shelf a, Bundle Ia, fol. 2ᵛ, at line 27. (Bundle Ia is the first bound volume, containing material dated 1549–1554; it will hereafter be cited as Norwich Depositions 1549–54. Spelling and punctuation will hereafter be modernized.) Another example of severely garbled substance is Rye's account, at 21, of William Leese's Case (1550), discussed infra, pages 89–90; cf. infra note 70.

34. S. & B. Webb, *English Local Government: The Manor and the Borough* (London, 1908) II 533–534 (footnotes omitted).

35. Id. at I 349, quoting H. A. Merewether, *A Sketch of the History of Boroughs . . .* (1822) 22.

36. The examination document in William Leese's Case (1550), discussed infra, pages 89–90, is captioned: "Examinations taken against William Leese . . . before Robert Rug[ge], Mayor of the city of Norwich, Thomas Gawdy, Recorder, Augustine Steward, alderman, and other justices." Norwich Depositions 1549–54 fol. 6. Rugge had been mayor in 1545 and was serving his second term in 1550. Steward was thrice mayor—in 1534, 1546, and 1556. Another caption showing the contemporary understanding that the city officials were examining as justices of the peace: the examination in Chapman's Case (1552), infra, page 88, recorded as having been taken before Thomas Cock (the then-mayor), Augustine Steward, Richard Davye (mayor in 1551 and 1563), "& other Justices." Id. fol. 77ᵛ. (On the dating of Norwich mayorships see the sources cited infra, note 69.)

lated to the role of the country justices through legislation and charter.

Of course, the urban setting did influence the character of some of the criminal business—there are cases involving merchants and foreigners, for example. Moreover, the need for official criminal investigation is greater in the hustle and impersonality of a major city than in the more static countryside. But these are qualifications of degree, not kind. The really significant difference which stems from the borough jurisdiction is that record-keeping was more competent. The Norwich documents may have survived while country records did not. However, this is an issue best deferred until the documents have been reviewed.

The depositions collection from 1549 to 1554 contains documents relating to about seventy-five different matters or cases. Of these a third (twenty-six by my count) are unmistakably civil. There is testimony about realty transfers and boundary problems;[37] about debts (usually disputed repayments);[38] occasionally there are formal interrogatories and deposed replies in property matters.[39] The remainder of the collection relates to criminal matters.[40]

The largest element among the criminal depositions are cases of seditious words. Twenty of the cases appear to deal with such matters. The characteristic scenario is that the accused casts aspersions upon the crown, the church, or the municipality, often while drinking in a public house.[41] A hearer thereafter bears witness to these words before the mayor and some aldermen (or before their clerk at least; the depositions sometimes do not disclose who the examiner is). The accused is then examined; he typically explains away his remarks as the hearer's misunderstanding. This is not an invariable sequence—sometimes there are several accusing deponents; sometimes there is accusing testimony only, without any statement from the accused.

Typical is *William Mordewe's Case* (1551?).[42] Elizabeth Brooke, the

37. Norwich Depositions 1549–54 fol. 24 (1551), 26–26ᵛ (1551), 48–50 (1555), 115–118 (1557) (note the interruption in chronological sequence), 132–134 (1554).

38. Id. fol. 60–61ᵛ (probably 1551), 79ᵛ (1553), 91–91ᵛ (1552), 92–92ᵛ (1552?), 94 (1552).

39. Id. fol. 95 (1552 or 1553) (interrupted at 96, resumed at 109–111) (demise of a vicarage); 96–105 (1552) (testamentary dispute).

40. Some of which are ambiguous; there are cases which may have raised either civil or criminal issues, and it is not clear from the documents which motivated the taking of the deposition. See infra, page 89.

41. Norwich Depositions 1549–54 fol. 87–88 (1553), 135–136ᵛ (1554) (cases of pub chat).

42. Id. fol. 37–37ᵛ. The reader may find it instructive to have a verbatim transcript of one of these depositions, hence Mordewe's Case follows in full. There is

servant of Robert Woode, gentleman, declares that she overheard Mordewe, a baker, in his bakeshop threaten "that if it pleased the king to make him hangman to a great many gentlemen, he could find in his heart [to] hang a great many of them . . . ." Margaret, wife of Ralph Sutton, to whom these remarks were addressed, had replied, according to Elizabeth Brooke, that her husband Ralph was in agreement. A second deposition appears on the same page, that of Elizabeth Balles, age 12, daughter of John Balles, gentleman. She heard Mordewe say he would hang a hundred or two, but she cannot say whether he meant gentlemen. She also heard Mrs. Sutton affirm that "they were very traitors," but again the girl had not heard who "they" were. Overleaf appears the examina-

---

no heading or other introduction, only the four paragraphs set out below. The date of 1551 is suggested because the depositions bound before and after in the volume are dated that year. Spelling and punctuation have been modernized.

> Elizabeth Brooke, servant with Robert Woode, Gentleman, sworn and examined, sayeth and deposeth by virtue of her oath that she, being this day at one Mordewe's house, Baker, in the bakehouse there, towards the setting in of bread, heard the said Mordewe amongst other words there said in communication [that is, conversation] say these words: that if it pleased the king to make him hangman to a great many gentlemen, he could find in his heart the [*sic;* "to"?] hang a great many of them; saying further upon her oath that one Sutton's wife being there present said these words: That her husband was in the same mind, also; and further she sayeth not.
>
> Elizabeth Balles, daughter of John Balles, Gentleman, of the age of 12 years, examined, sayeth that she heard Mordewe the Baker say that he would hang a hundred or two, whether he meant gentlemen or not she cannot say; and that Sutton's wife said to him that by the mass they were very traitors; whom she meant she knew not.
>
> Margaret Sutton, the wife of Ralph Sutton, sworn and examined, sayeth and deposeth that she was this day at Mordewe's house in the bakehouse there, and upon many words touching the hard world and the loss of money amongst them, then had Mordewe spake of extortioners and bribers of the "counwith" [country? commonwealth?], and said that if it pleased the king to make him, he would be hangman to a hundred of them; and sayeth further that she said and answered him that her husband was of the same mind that he was; and further she cannot say.
>
> William Mordewe, examined, confesseth and sayeth that divers folks being in his bakehouse this day, amongst them had communication upon the great prices of grains and victuals and the fall and loss of money; and he himself alleged amongst them that the fault thereof was in the men of the "conwith," for they would not obey the king's proclamations nor the king's proceedings, and confesseth that he said these words: that if it please the king to make him hangman he would hang a sort of them that will not obey the king's proclamations nor the king's proceedings, and confesseth that he said these words: that if it please the king to make him hangman he would hang a sort of them that will not obey; and further sayeth not.

Mordewe appears in an earlier deposition in the opposite role as accusing informant, claiming to have overheard seditious talk by another: Scotter's Case, id. fol. 31 (1551).

tion of the two suspects. Mrs. Sutton explains that she and the baker had been bemoaning the general hard times and drop in the value of money, to which Mordewe had said that extortioners and bribers were to blame. Such had Mordewe been willing to hang, and she had replied that her husband agreed. The examination of Mordewe follows. The conversation had been about the rising price of grain and victuals and the falling value of money. He had put the blame on people who refused to obey the king's proclamations, and he had said he would have served the king as hangman of those who refused to obey.

The examinations in cases of seditious words like *Mordewe's Case* do not appear to have been made in order to be sent to the Council. The cases were not serious enough. The closest to an active conspirator is a carpenter named Toppylow who had fallen in with Wyatt's forces in the rebellion of 1554, but hid out in Southwark during the battle and escaped disguised as one of the queen's men. (He blurted all this out in a pub in Norwich upon his arrival there, and several of his hearers reported it to the authorities.[43] We hear no more of it.) None of the cases of seditious words involves an unconditional confession. Either the accusing testimony constitutes the whole record (*Toppylow's Case*), or the accused denies or qualifies the remarks ascribed to him (*Mordewe's Case*).

Most of the sedition cases date from the years 1549–1551. One of the most serious insurrections in English history, Ket's rebellion, had occurred in and around Norwich in the summer of 1549. Mention of Ket figures in several of the cases of seditious words in the depositions collection.[44] The underlying grievance which provoked the rebellion was the enclosure movement, whose dislocations were being felt not only by dispossessed rural folk, but also by townspeople like Baker Mordewe "smarting under the famine prices which the change of culture had brought with it . . . ; while the gentlemen were doubling, trebling, quadrupling their incomes with their sheep-farms, and adorning their persons and their houses with splendour hitherto unknown." [45] Ket's rebellion started among an assembly gathered near Norwich for an annual festival. Ket, a tanner, led the rising, which soon collected some sixteen thousand men in a camp just north of Norwich. "Ket sat daily to admin-

43. Id. fol. 135–136^v (1554). On Wyatt's rebellion see J. A. Froude, *History of England from the Fall of Wolsey to the Death of Elizabeth* (London, 1870 ed.) IV 143–181.

44. Norwich Depositions 1549–54 fol. 1^v (1549), 2–2^v (1550), 2^v (1550), 31 (1551); cf. id. fol. 5–5^v (1550).

45. Froude (supra, note 43) at V 201–202.

ister justice; and there, day after day, the offending country gentlemen were brought up for trial, charged with robbing the poor." [46] The rebels seized Norwich, abandoned it to the royal forces, then seized it again. They were finally defeated after seven weeks by an army commanded by the Earl of Warwick and newly fortified with German and Italian mercenaries. Perhaps thirty-five hundred of the insurgents were killed in the battle. Ket and his brother were thereafter hanged.[47] The tenderness of the Norwich authorities about seditious words is, therefore, easy to understand. On the other hand, Norwich was not alone in pre-Marian times in taking written examinations in such cases. There survive among the borough records of Leicester three examinations, locally generated and retained, dated 1532, 1533, and 1534, all cases of seditious words.[48]

The documents in cases of seditious words may not have been prepared in contemplation of subsequent trial. Several other functions are imaginable. First, the investigation was itself a chastening experience for someone like Baker Mordewe or Housewife Sutton. It might achieve the desired inhibiting effect without more formal criminal sanction. Second, the examination might have been the basis for a binding over to keep the peace and to abstain from such chatter in the future. Third, the examination may have been transcribed and saved in the event that the accused's subsequent conduct imparted a more sinister meaning to it. Each case was ostensibly one of mere intemperate grumbling, yet potentially of the greatest seriousness should it later develop into active sedition.

Many of the examinations for ordinary crime seem to have been transcribed and preserved for a similar reason: the absence of the culprit made prosecution momentarily impossible. The evidence against him was recorded for the contingency that he might in the future reappear. A good illustration is *Harman's Case* (1551).[49] A single document exists, the sworn examination of Robert Crowe, glover. He explains that he and another local man, John Denman, were gambling with dice. On Denman's suggestion the two went to the market to a pub called The Angel

46. Id. at 202.

47. Id. at 204–215. Documents from the trial of Ket appear in the appendix to F. W. Russell, *Kett's Rebellion in Norfolk* (London, 1859) 215–240. Russell's text itself is premodern. Cf. S. T. Bindoff, *Ket's Rebellion 1549* (London, 1949).

48. *Records of the Borough of Leicester* (M. Bateson, ed.) (Cambridge, 1905) III 31–32, 34–35. Note also in this collection a series of memoranda from 1550 recording that the mayor and four JPs had, pursuant to the pre-Marian statutes, "calle[d] before them . . . al maner of mettes and measures" from particular sectors of the borough. Id. at 62–63.

49. Norwich Depositions 1549–54 fol. 46.

to play together against Harman, a barber who cannot be further identified. In a day of dicing, Crowe literally lost his shirt (which he valued, remarkably, at twelve shillings) together with quantities of his stock-in-trade (gloves, leather, and so on) and his money. Harman then induced him to borrow more money, which he promptly lost. Denman too was cleaned out. One supposes that Harman moved on, and that the mayor's court made record in the event he returned. Dicing, it will be recalled, was the subject of two of the pre-Marian examination statutes.[50]

Others of the dozen or so cases of petty offense involve absent defendants. Elizabeth Dawson of Pulham Mary, caught selling rancid butter in the Norwich market, deposes that it was not her husband's, but belonged to a Mrs. Pallante of Pulham.[51] James Wharton, minstrel, examined about the singing of irreverent songs ten days before by two of his apprentice boys, first replies that he never heard them singing such songs. But a search of a song book of his reveals a piece of paper containing a "very evil and lewd song," which he concedes he had sung with the boys. It was given him, he says, by a minstrel named Robert Gold, and undersigned by one William Mason.[52] Presumably the examination was recorded should either Gold or Mason reappear.

Not all the petty cases involve absent defendants, however. An examination taken in August 1554 records the admission of John Harrison that he had twice removed some pears from the yard of Giles Vanderbrook, followed by the examinations of three accomplices.[53] There is an examination of a vagabond, one Robert Stokay, noting his movements.[54] A quarrel in the market between the mayor's servant, Simon Chapman, and another is recorded,[55] as are instances of threatening or insulting words (doubtless the basis of bindings over to keep the peace).[56]

It is palpable that this handful of cases[57] cannot have been the total of petty crime in the second largest city in England in the years 1549–1554. The archive is very far from complete. From the Norwich court records of the time (quarter sessions, mayor's court, guildhall court) it

50. 11 Hen. VII c. 2 (1495); 19 Hen. VII c. 12 (1503–04).

51. Norwich Depositions 1549–54 fol. 51^{v} (probably 1553).

52. Id. fol. 130–131 (1554).

53. Id. (loose deposition, unpaginated).

54. Id. fol. 126 (1553). Post-Marian examinations for vagabondage are elsewhere relatively common; cf. infra, notes 78, 79, and 84.

55. Id. fol. 77^{v}–78 (1552) (the mayor's servant being the deponent-complainant).

56. Id. fol. 32–32^{v} (1551), 33 (1551).

57. Another half-dozen have not been described.

is known that many more cases were actually processed. Although some possible reasons have been given, there is no fully satisfactory explanation of why these few examinations were transcribed and saved.[58] Nonetheless, they give us glimpses of seemingly unexceptional examination practice for petty crime in the years 1549–1555. It seems to have been common enough to go to the town officials with complaints of wrongdoing, and for the officials to investigate by examination where appropriate. Their examinations do not seem referable to special statutory authority, even when we know it to have been applicable. Examination was simply a technique of office, used alike for dicing (where there was statutory authority for investigation by examination) and petty larceny (where there was not).

Examination did extend to felony. Municipal officers were not prepared to leave serious crime to the archaic presentment system, having once developed a pattern of official investigation for lesser offenses. Several Norwich depositions raise issues which might pertain to felony prosecutions, but which can be distinguished from Marian examination procedure. One of the depositions concerns grand larceny committed in the Netherlands by one Englishman against another;[59] the culprit turned fugitive and sailed for England, and there was some thought that he might appear in Norwich. Two sets of depositions[60] contain only defensive evidence, to the effect that each defendant had bought a horse in an arm's-length transaction; since accusations do not appear, it seems that the potential defendants themselves instigated the examinations to perpetuate the testimony. In *William Leese's Case* (1550)[61] chalices had been stolen from the church in Felthorpe, Norfolk, and the deponents had

58. In addition to the perpetuation of evidence in cases not ripe for prosecution (or not immediately susceptible to prosecution on account of the absence of the defendant), another theme is disproportionately prominent in the collection: a surprising number touch the municipal officers personally. Three witnesses depose to an incident of name-calling between Leonard Osborn, the defendant, and the wife of Alderman Marsham. Id. fol. 32–32^v (1551). Thomas Sharpe, mason, deposes to the menacing words of Thomas Woode, joiner, who hoped to "make the Aldermen to sweat." Id. fol. 76 (1552). Simon Chapman, the mayor's cook, deposes to a brawl in the market between himself and the servant of Sir William Woodhouse, originating in the competition of both servants to buy the same dozen eggs. Id. fol. 77^v–78 (1552). Two bystanders are examined about an altercation between the mayor and an alderman. Id. fol. 89–89^v (1553). (More of these cases appear among the Elizabethan documents.)

59. Id. fol. 119–120 (1552).

60. Id. fol. 28–28^v (1551), 42–44 (1551).

61. Id. fol. 6–7^v.

come from Felthorpe to notify the goldsmiths of Norwich "if any such Challices should hereafter come in to their hands . . . ." Leese, whom they met in a pub, purported to sell them information (probably in the nature of a conjuration) leading to the discovery of the chalices and the information turned out to be false. It seems likely that it was not the theft, committed outside Norwich, but the fraud or conjuration which the mayor's court was investigating. Leese himself appears not to have been examined, and it would seem that he had turned fugitive. Several other depositions record serious crimes whose perpetrators seem either unknown or fugitive. One sets out the pathetic story of Joan Hall, who was swindled of a total of at least 20 shillings to pay a "cunning man" (that is, a conjurer) to "get a rich marriage for her." [62] Others are less clear, but seem to allege robbery[63] and sheep-stealing.[64]

There is one felony case, however, whose documents contain not mere accusations, but the confessions of apprehended felons. The case of *Fuir & Ely* (1552)[65] is the prime example of examination for felony in the Norwich deposition collection. The examinations are precisely those which the Marian committal statute will prescribe for felony, but the case antedates the statute by three years. The examination document records the statements both of a witness and of the two felons in a case of church robbery. The witness, Roger Pyne, is the 16-year-old apprentice of John Ely, a smith, one of the defendants. He accompanied his master to the scene of the crime and witnessed the events, although he says he did not participate and went solely out of fear. He says that on the previous Friday night Thomas Fuir, the other defendant, broke the glass in a window of St. Giles' Church, Norwich, and entered the building. Fuir unlatched the door for Ely to enter. The two men removed organ pipes, cushions, and two surplices, as well as parts of the church bells. Ely, the smith, later melted down some of the pipes. Next follows the examination of Fuir. He confesses the breaking in, the taking of the pipes, bell clappers, two cushions, and two surplices, and the melting down of the pipes. The cushions and surplices he left at Ely's house. Finally follows Ely's statement. He too confesses all.

The examination document in *Fuir & Ely* is indistinguishable from those taken by JPs in post-Marian felony practice, except in one matter

62. Id. fol. 56 (1552).
63. Id. fol. 22b^{v}–22c^{v} (1550).
64. Id. fol. 9^{v}–10 (1550).
65. Id. fol. 82–85; see supra, note 33.

of form. It became customary for JPs to put an indented heading on examinations, disclosing the date and place of the examination and the names and titles of the examiners and examinees. The pre-Marian Norwich criminal documents sometimes lack such headings,[66] and there is none in *Fuir & Ely.*

In the earlier Norwich collection, the Mayor's Court Books, appear a handful of depositions touching criminal matters;[67] one is particularly striking, and it is reproduced in full as an appendix to this chapter. It has an indented heading similar to those of post-Marian practice: "Memorandum: Examination taken before William Hart, mayor of the said city, John Marsham, Thomas Aldrich, Robert Long, John Clerk, Robert Jannys, Thomas Bauburgh, the Saturday before Saint Andrew in the 11th year of the reign of King Henry the 8th, for the death of [blank] Ganton." [68] Six of the seven examiners must have been justices of the peace, since they had all passed the mayor's chair; the seventh was a former sheriff and future mayor who could well have been in the commission of the peace.[69] This substantial panel of authorities was constituted to examine into a case of felony, a homicide, in the year 1519. Five witnesses [70] were deposed—the four survivors of the fatal brawl and the innkeeper in whose pub the killing occurred. Their testimony runs for eleven pages in the court book. There are numerous cross-outs and interlineations. Thus the document appears to be the contemporaneous transcript of the testimony given the examining panel. The events:[71]

66. Cf. supra, note 42.

67. N. & N.R.O.: Mayor's Court Book 1510–1532, fol. 43–44 (seditious words against the Duke of Norfolk); 307–308 (larceny).

68. Id. fol. 79–90.

69. The mayor, Hart, had also held the office in 1512; Aldrich had been mayor in 1507 and 1516; Long in 1509; Marsham in 1518; Clerk in 1515 (and later again in 1520); and Jannys in 1517 (and later again in 1524). Bauburgh, sheriff in 1516, would become mayor in 1530. H. Le Strange, *Norfolk Official Lists* (Norwich, 1890) 105–106. Cf. B. Cozens-Hardy and E. A. Kent, *The Mayors of Norwich 1403–1835* (Norwich, 1938) 39–47. On the significance of having passed the mayor's chair, see supra, page 83.

70. Rye, at 91–93, noticed the case and abstracted the first two depositions, apparently overlooking (or at least omitting to mention) the other three; cf. id. at 10–11.

71. This account is a composite of the five depositions, necessarily ignoring some minor discrepancies in the several versions. Deponent Robert Abell reported that Ganton and Godfrey were gambling between themselves, rather than on the outcome of Godfrey's game with his companions. Godfrey alone deposed that just previous to insisting on his winnings, he let Ganton pick up his money and have a new round when it appeared that he, Ganton, was losing. Pethouse remembered Ganton's last words as "Alas, I am slain"; whereas the innkeeper, Cowper, heard "I am sticked." Further examples could be given.

Four local men, three weavers and a tailor, gathered at the Maid's Head Inn to eat and drink. Apparently on account of cresting flood waters, they decided to stay the night. They hired a room near the stables and began playing dice among themselves for a quart of wine. One John Ganton approached them and offered to gamble for forty-pence stakes. They all declined, and he departed to drink. He reappeared half-an-hour later, and again failed to persuade any of them to gamble with him. A third time he returned, seated himself among the players, and commenced to kibitz fractiously. To Richard Godfrey, one of the four, he volunteered that Godfrey had now lost the game in progress. "Nay, I shall win it," replied Godfrey. "Ye shall lose it," insisted Ganton, "and thereupon I lay two groats against one." Godfrey took the wager, and both men laid down their stakes. As the game drew to its close, a misunderstanding developed about who was winning. Godfrey, thinking himself ahead, saw Ganton start for the money. Godfrey was faster, grasped the money and put it in his purse. Cursing, Ganton began striking him. One of Godfrey's three companions, John Pethouse, came up and separated the two men. Ganton transferred his fury to Pethouse, saying, "By the mass, if thou wilt not let me strike him, I shall strike thee." Ganton drew his dagger and slashed at Pethouse, who avoided the blow by stumbling backwards into the fireplace. The dagger struck into the masonry of the chimney. A third of the companions, Robert Senior, then hastened forward and grappled for the dagger with Ganton. Ganton was stabbed in the scuffle, and died uttering his last words: "By the mass, I am slain." The proprietor of the inn detained the four companions and summoned the constable, who took them into custody tied and bound.

The investigation before the seven examiners took place three weeks after the slaying.[72] Numerous minor discrepancies in the testimony of the four companions[73] imply that each was deposed out of the others' hearing and that all had been held in custody separately from one another during the interval.

No explanation seems to suggest itself for the survival of this document among the largely civil matters recorded in the Mayor's Court Books. Yet it seems that the exceptional survival records an unexceptional procedure. There is no apology, no explanation for the investigation. The participants think it normal enough; each deposition begins with stylized phraseology ("Robert Senior of Norwich, worsted weaver, sayeth and deposeth that . . ."). It seems that the irregularity was not the investigation, but the survival of the transcript.[74]

72. The slaying occurred on Saturday, November 5, 1519 (Saint Leonard's Eve). The investigation was held three weeks later, on November 26 ("the Saturday before Saint Andrew"). See C. R. Cheney, *Handbook of Dates* (Royal Historical Society) (London, 1945) 44, 54, 150–151.

73. Supra, note 71.

74. Even that, however, was no simple filing error. The eleven pages of depositions in the case occupy pages 79–90 of a quire paginated 78–113 as bound. Page 78,

This case of 1519 displays Marian preliminary inquiry in operation more than 35 years before the Marian statute. Suspects and witnesses have been examined by the magistrates in a case of felony and the examination transcribed. The inquiry is consciously "for the death of [blank] Ganton." It was not, therefore, conducted pursuant to the authority granted in the statutes against gaming. From the outset the case was understood as homicide,[75] not gambling regulation.

Isolated cases[76] such as this one and *Fuir & Ely* do not provide the quantitative basis one would desire. Nonetheless, they do constitute hard evidence that pre-Marian magistrates did not confine their examination practice to petty crime. Examination for felony predated the Marian statutes. This bears decisively on the question of the origins of Marian preliminary inquiry. The Marian draftsman took his inspiration not from Continental codes, but from existing practice within the native magistracy.

3. *Post-Marian Examination*

The same point can be inferred from indirect evidence. For in post-Marian practice, examination was identical for felony and nonfelony.

---

on the back of which leaf these depositions commence, contains a series of routine entries in clerical hand recording appearances and fines in petty regulatory matters. And the rest of the quire, from 91 on, chronicles mundane city jurisdiction. Its position in the sequence of the quire does not explain why the Ganton homicide investigation was transcribed, but it does imply that the investigation was considered appropriate official business of the municipality.

75. Notwithstanding which, it seems clear that this was no coroner proceeding. There were seven examiners and no jury. "The Coroner is one chosen . . . of the meaner sort of gentlemen," wrote Sir Thomas Smith, *De Republica* bk. 2, ch. 21, at 72, scarcely a fitting description for seven once and future mayors of the second largest city in England. The depositions do not resemble coroner proceedings of the century as displayed, e.g., in the *Calendar of Nottinghamshire Coroners' Inquests 1485–1558* (R. F. Hunnisett, ed.) (Thoroton Society, 1969); and *Middlesex County Records: Indictments, Coroners Inquests-Post-Mortem and Recognizances from 3 Edward VI*, . . . (J. C. Jeaffreson, ed.) (London, 1886) I. Moreover, the gap of three weeks between the slaying of Ganton and the holding of the municipal investigation should not have occurred in a coroner proceeding. "When informed of [a sudden and unnatural] death, the coroner had to go immediately to the body. In Nottinghamshire in 1330 the interval between death and inquest rarely exceeded three days, and the same is true of most other counties in normal circumstances. In towns which had their own coroners there was naturally even less delay." R. F. Hunnisett, *The Medieval Coroner* (Cambridge, 1961) 13 (footnotes omitted).

76. Outside Norwich there is mention of what seems to have been pretrial examination before a magistrate for larceny in Caernarvonshire in 1550: "Memorandum of Commitment to Gaol" in the *Calendar of the Caernarvonshire Quarter Sessions Records 1541–1558* (W. O. Williams, ed.) (Caernarvon Historical Society, 1956) I 68.

Nothing altered when a justice put on his Marian cap; there was no sense in felony cases of a particular effort to comply with special Marian terms. Examination appears as a generalized technique. The justices themselves, in complying with the Marian statute, treated it as part of their older tradition of examination.

As luck would have it, the Essex County Quarter Sessions Rolls, which commence in 1556, contain two examination documents from that year—one for burglary, the other for vagabondage.[77] Examination documents are quite scarce for the first decades of the Essex rolls,[78] although from 1575 on they become more plentiful.[79] It is instructive, therefore, that the two 1556 documents are alike in form,[80] although one treats felony and the other a petty infraction. They are similarly headed and similarly phrased. Neither examination is said to have been sworn. In fact, it is doubtful that the burglary examination was conducted in conscious compliance with the Marian committal statute, because it records solely the statement of a witness and not those of the three defendants (who were almost certainly committed and hence available for examination).[81]

The indistinguishability of the form of examination for petty and serious crime was observable before the Marian statutes in the Norwich archives, and it continues to be true of post-Marian Norwich documents.[82] It remains true of the Essex records when they appear in quan-

77. Essex County Record Office: Quarter Sessions Rolls (Q/SR) 2/21; 2/42.

78. Q/SR 31/35 (counterfeiting, 1569); 41/4 (grand larceny, 1572); 47/17 (vagabondage, 1573); 47/59 (vagabondage, 1573).

79. Q/SR 53/51 (receiving stolen property, 1575); 54/5 (bastardy?, 1575); 55/4 (fornication, 1575); 56/21 (game poaching?, 1575); 58/55 (vagabondage, assault, 1576); 58/56–57 (vagabondage, 1576); 58/58 (vagabondage, 1576); 59/34 (vagabondage?, 1576); 62/45 (vagabondage, 1577); 62/46 ("upon suspicion of felony," 1577); 64/44–45 (heretical words, 1577); 65/61 (heretical words, 1577); 67/44–46 (sorcery, 1578); 68/42–43 (horse theft, 1578); 68/58 (mayhem, 1578); 69/50 (adultery, 1578).

80. Save that overleaf on the burglary examination are noted two recognizances, discussed infra, note 81, binding the deponent and another witness to appear and to prosecute at trial. Q/SR 2/42ᵛ. These are not part of the examination proper.

81. Because the defendants (who were vagabonds as well) were indicted and stood trial for grand larceny, Q/SR 3/18–19, it is to be inferred that they were committed pending trial. (They were acquitted.)

Another curiosity of the document in the burglary case suggests that the examiner was not following Marian procedure. One of the two recognizances binds the witness to appear and to prosecute only at quarter sessions, the other at both quarter sessions and gaol delivery. Q/SR 2/42ᵛ. The Marian statutes called for the certification of examination to gaol delivery, not quarter sessions. (This feature of the Marian statutes is discussed in Chapter 5.)

82. Compare the rape case of October 27, 1561, N. & N.R.O.: Interrogatories and Depositions, Case 12, Shelf a, Bundle 1b (loose deposition), with the prostitution case of July 25, 1563, N. & N.R.O.: Interrogatories and Depositions, Case 12, Shelf a, Bundle Ic, fol. 28–39ᵛ.

tity in the 1570s. The Leicester examinations of the 1580s and 1590s read like the Leicester examinations of the 1530s.[83] It is true of other collections of Elizabethan examinations that those for felony read like those for petty crime.[84] It might, of course, be contended that the Marian model was influencing examination for lesser crime. Were there distinctive traits to the Marian statutes which had not existed in the earlier legislation, that argument would be more tenable. But the force of the thirty-odd examination statutes which preceded the Marian statutes is that they had put in currency among the JPs the features of Marian examination. When we come to find that post-Marian examinations under Marian and pre-Marian authority are indistinguishable, the inference seems stronger that we are observing in practice the relationship we appear to see in design: extension of the older tradition to felony under Mary.[85]

83. The Leicester examinations of the 1530s, cited supra, note 48, appear in *Records of the Borough of Leicester* (M. Bateson, ed.) (Cambridge, 1905) III 31–32, 34–35. Compare the examinations, either for seditious words or for suspected felony, id. at 196–197, 229, 259–260, 341–344, 351–352 (continued at 370–372), 366, 383–384 (1584–1599). Other examinations are cited, inter alia, id. at 200, 268, 328, 384, 426. Cf. "The examination of William Hance, Priest," taken at Leicestershire in 1582, in *The Letters of Sir Frances Hastings 1574–1609* (C. Cross, ed.) (Somerset Record Society, 1969) 24–25.

84. With the published felony examinations cited supra, note 83, compare the examinations in *Quarter Sessions Records with other Records of the Justices of the Peace for the County Palatine of Chester 1559–1760* (J. Bennett and J. Dewhurst, eds.) (Lancaster and Cheshire Record Society, 1940) 42–43 (vagabondage, 1577); and *The Staffordshire Quarter Sessions Rolls 1581–89* (S. A. H. Burne, ed.) (Kendal, 1929) I 338 (bastardy, 1589). For substantial numbers of late Elizabethan examinations published or calendared, see *The Book of Examinations and Depositions 1570–1594* (G. H. Hamilton, ed.) (Southampton Record Society, 1914), and *The Book of Examinations 1601–1602* (R. C. Anderson, ed.) (Southampton Record Society, 1926); *The Staffordshire Quarter Sessions Rolls* (S. A. H. Burne, ed.) II and III (Kendal, 1930, 1932); *Worcestershire County Records: Calendar of the Quarter Sessions Papers 1591–1643* (Worcester, 1900); *Kentish Sources VI: Crime and Punishment* (E. Melling, ed.) (Maidstone, 1969).

85. Professor Barnes to the contrary notwithstanding:

> One innovation, seemingly without statutory basis or explicit conciliar sanction, was the justices' examination of offenders in misdemeanor as well as in felony. Neither the Marian statutes, Lambarde, nor Dalton gave any direction that in cases of misdemeanor the offender's examination should be taken. Yet, among the sessions rolls appear many such examinations certified to quarter sessions, which formed the basis of an indictment for misdemeanor. It was a wholly natural development, and it extended the useful inquisitorial procedure to the many lesser offences which were increasingly the concern of the justices.

T. G. Barnes, *Somerset 1625–1640: A County's Government During the "Personal Rule"* (Cambridge, Mass., 1961) 56–57 (footnote omitted). Manifestly, the pre-Marian examination legislation for cases of lesser crime, described in Section A of this chapter, has been overlooked, as well as subsequent legislation of the same

Finally, it ought to be noticed that Sir Thomas Smith's *De Republica Anglorum* (written 1565, published 1583) supplies important confirmation. Smith recounts the taking of examination in two passages. The first supposes a robber caught red-handed and describes his examination.[86] The second shows the JP actively instigating investigation (the context is the control exercised by the JP over the constables); it is there that Smith conflates examination for felony and for petty crime:[87]

> For the Justice of peace as soone as he understandeth by complaint that any man hath stolen, robbed, slaine, or any servant or labourer without license hath departed out of his maisters service, or any that liveth idle and suspectly, knowing once in what parish he is, he writeth to the Constable of the parish, commanding him in the Princes name to bring that man before him: the Constable dareth not disobey. The man is brought and examined by the Justice, and if the Justice doe find cause, hee committeth him to the same Constable to convey him further to the Princes gaole, where the partie must lie till the Justices of peace doe meete either at their quarter sessions, or at their goale deliverie, and that the lawe hath either condemned or acquited him.

Smith's account adds to the evidence of the primary sources that of the contemporary perception. Writing a decade after the Marian acts, Smith attributes no civilian influence to the procedure, and his civilian's eye[88] has not inspired him even to make analogy to the civilian process

---

sort. Nor have the JP manuals been given their due. See Lambarde 431–434; Dalton 123–127.

86. Smith, *De Republica* bk. 2, ch. 20, at 72:

> So soone as any is brought to the Justices of peace by this hue or crie, by the Constable or anie other who doth pursue the malefactor, he doeth examine the malefactor, and writeth the examination and his confession: then he doth binde the partie that is robbed or him that sueth, and the Constable, and so manie as can give evidence against the malefactor to be at the next sessions of gaole deliverie to give their evidence for the Queene. He bindeth them in recognisance of [ten, twenty, thirty, forty or a hundred pounds] according to his discretion, and the qualitie of the crime: which certified under his hande, is levied upon the recognizance if they faile of being there.

Strype's biography of Smith, first published in 1698, records Smith himself examining as a JP in a pair of witchcraft cases in Essex in 1570. J. Strype, *The Life of the Learned Sir Thomas Smith* (Oxford, 1820 ed.) 97–100.

87. Smith, *De Republica* bk. 2, ch. 22, at 74–75.

88. Sir Thomas Smith, born in 1513, was the first Regius Professor of Civil Law at Cambridge, although he began as a lecturer in Greek and was self-taught in Roman law. He wrote *De Republica Anglorum* in 1565 while on embassy from Elizabeth in France. See M. Dewar, *Sir Thomas Smith: A Tudor Intellectual in Office* (London, 1964) 13–22, 110–114.

Smith attributed English chancery process to civilian inspiration, and he found

(as he is elsewhere wont to do). He treats Marian and pre-Marian situations as indistinguishable. Had the Marian scheme, only a decade old, been a major innovation, we would expect him to have said so. Instead, he conflates it with the older examination powers and implies a like antiquity to the lot.

---

authority for civil jury trial in Cicero and Quintillian. Smith, *De Republica* bk. 2, ch. 11, at 54–55; id., bk. 2, ch. 15, at 62. Yet he regarded the whole of the criminal process, including examination before the JPs, as indigenous. Smith emphasized the several roles of the justices of the peace. We have commented on his discussion of their activity at trial in Chapter 2. Smith's ch. 19, bk. 2, describes the social standing of the JPs, their numbers, and something of their jurisdiction. The chapter concludes with a paean stressing not only the virtue of the JP system, but its singularity ("[T]he invention of this . . . is the most benefitte that can be devised for the common wealth of Englande . . . ."). Id., bk. 2, ch. 19, at 70–71. Cf. E. Coke, *The Fourth Part of the Institutes of the Laws of England* (London, 1644) 170: "[I]t is such a forme of subordinate government for the tranquillity and quiet of the Realm, as no part of the Christian world hath the like, if the same be duly executed."

Appendix to Chapter 4—The Slaying of John Ganton (1519)[89]

Memorandum: Examination taken before William Hart, mayor of the said city, John Marsham, Thomas Aldrich, Robert Long, John Clerk, Robert Jannys, Thomas Bauburgh, the Saturday before Saint Andrew in the 11th year of the reign of King Henry the 8th, for the death of [blank] Ganton.

Robert Abell of Norwich, worstead weaver, sayeth and deposeth that about eight of the clock in the night on Saint Leonard's Eve at the Maid's Head of a sudden met together the same Robert Abell, John Pethouse, tailor, Robert Senior, worstead weaver, and Richard Godfrey, and there supped in the hall within the said inn in the presence of Roger Cowper and others with him. The cause why that the said persons stayed so late was for that the great abundance of the water, etc. And after supper done, the said John Pethouse, Robert Senior, and Richard agreed to play at the tables and desired me the said Robert Abell to be one, and they would play at double hand. [Abell] answered and said he could not play at the tables. And thereunto said the said Robert Senior said [*sic*], "Do rest the dice and I shall play for you." And thereupon the said John Pethouse and Godfrey called for a chamber for them in the said inn. And thereupon one Joan, servant to the said Roger [Cowper, innkeeper], assigned to them one little chamber or parlor lying atwixt the two stables there. And thereupon the said Pethouse or Godfrey entered into the said chamber and one of them two brought the tables into the same chamber or parlor and the ostler made them one fire. And the said Pethouse and Godfrey on the one side and the said Senior and this deponent on the other side sat them[selves] to the tables and played for a quart of wine. And as they were playing there for the said quart of wine, one John Ganton came into the said chamber or parlor to the said players and said to them, "God speed, sirs, would any of you go fare at dice?", whereunto the said Pethouse and Godfrey said to Ganton they would not play at that game that night. And thereupon Ganton drank and departed. And after that about half an hour he came again and eftsoons [that is, soon after] he asked the the [*sic*] said Pethouse and

89. Transcribed from the Mayor's Court Book 1510–1532, at 79–90, now preserved in the Norfolk and Norwich Record Office. Spelling and capitalization have been modernized, punctuation (including quotation marks) has been supplied, and words abbreviated in the manuscript have been written out. Various of the sentences are grammatically deficient, and these have been left unaltered. Interpolated words are indicated by square brackets. Published by permission.

Godfrey if they would play at dice, and they eftsoons denied [that is, declined] then to play at that game. And [Ganton] eftsoons returned out of the said chamber, and yet in likewise within a little while the same Ganton came again into the said chamber to the said Pethouse, Godfrey, Senior, and this deponent, and required them to play at the farying, and they refused to play at that game that night. And thereupon the said Ganton did set him[self] down in the chair there then being at the tables and by John Pethouse on the one side and Robert Senior on the other side, whilst they were still playing for the said wine. And the same Ganton did say to Richard Godfrey, "That game is lost, and thereupon I will lay two groats to one and let me play it." And thereunto answered the same Godfrey, "I will hold that groat," and both parties did lay down their said hold. And thereupon John Pethouse and this deponent did arise and went to the fire and there tarried. And Senior sat still by the said Ganton, albeit they played none other at that game but only Ganton and Godfrey. And upon that and before the same game was played out between the said Ganton and Godfrey. And for that the same Godfrey supposed that he had won the same game and that perceiving [in other words, perceiving that] Ganton would suddenly have taken up the said 12^{d}, and that perceiving, the said Godfrey more swiftly caught the same 12^{d} in his hands and readily put it in his purse. Whereupon the same Ganton did swear great oaths that he should not have his money, whereupon the same Ganton rose suddenly and and [*sic*] took the said Godfrey by the head and smote him upon the breast with his fist. And thereupon the said Senior and Pethouse stepped to the same Ganton and Godfrey to depart [that is, separate] them, and Godfrey with their help departed from the said Ganton out of that parlor and called the said Roger Cowper, albeit the same Roger came not immediately. And then said the said Ganton to Pethouse, "By the mass, if you will not suffer me to have yonder boy by the head for my money, I will strike ye." And thereupon the same Ganton did follow Pethouse with his dagger in his hand into [the] chimney for to strike him, and as he went he put down the candle with the swing of his gown, and there was not other light but only the light of ye fire. And the said Pethouse, intending to flee the stroke, fell down in the same chimney side. And that perceiving Senior, he followeth the same Ganton, took hold of the said dagger with both his hands. And thereupon this deponent, fearing that the said Pethouse had a be [been] slain by the said Ganton, went out of the said parlor into the yard of the said inn and called and cried for the said Roger in these words: "Come away for the passion of God, for John Pethouse is slain." And thereupon the same Roger same to the said parlor door, commanded the same deponent to return into the same parlor before him, and so the deponent did. And the same Roger followed him, at the which entry of the said door and the same Roger together did hear the same Ganton say: "By the mass, I am slain," and therewith fell down afore them dead.

Roger Cowper, keeper of the Maid's Head in Norwich, sayeth that the said Senior, Godfrey, Pethouse, and Abell did sup together with Robert Brown and others in the hall within the said inn. And after that about the hour of 9 of the clock on Saint Leonard's Eve as he sat in the said hall by the fire with one John Bek and the wife of the said Roger and his maidens, he heard a sudden calling which sounded to be the voice of the said Godfrey saying in these words: "Here is one hath out his dagger." Whereupon the same Roger together with the said John Bek and one servant of the abbot of Saint Bennet's went to the door of the great parlor in the said inn. And there in the said door, the said Cowper, Bek, and the said servant did see Ganton with a dagger in his hand saying, "I am sticked," and suddenly groveling, fell down in the said door dead. And thereupon the same Cowper caused the great gate of his said inn to be shut, whereupon the said Senior, Pethouse, Godfrey, and Abell came to the said Roger into the said hall. And there the said Senior said to the same Roger, "Open the gate foresaid," whereunto the said Cowper answered, "Thou shalt abide a while." And thereupon the same Cowper required the said Bek and the said servant to keep the said Senior, Godfrey, Pethouse, and Abell while the same Roger went for one Mallerd, constable, etc., and so did, and brought with him four halters to pinion the said 4 persons. And thereupon the same Cowper and Mallerd took the said halters and pinioned the said 4 persons. And so the said Cowper and Cowper [*sic;* Mallerd?] with others brought them to the hall for the premises.

John Pethouse of Norwich, tailor, sayeth and deposeth that about 6 of the clock after noon on Saint Leonard Even[ing] Robert Senior of Norwich, worstead weaver, Robert Abell, and Richard Godfrey came to the house of the said deponent to have him to the Maid's Head. And the servant of the said deponent showed the same Senior, etc., that the said deponent was at William Claxton. Whereupon the same Senior, etc., came to the said William Claxton's and there found the said deponent. And then the said Senior asked the said deponent if he would go with them to the Maid's Head. And the said deponent answered and said, "Yea, I must go thither to drink with one Kerver [Carver] and Miller, servants to the abbot of Saint Bennet. Whereupon the said Senior and deponent went forth together to the Maid's Head. And they found Robert Brown, jailer, Thomas Leek, butcher, and other [*sic*] going toward supper, and they supped in the hall within the said inn with Brown and Leek aforesaid at the same table. And after supper the said Senior, Godfrey, and Abell said that they would be there that night, for that they could not go home for abundance of water, and so desired the wife there to have a bed. And thereupon the said Senior, Godfrey, and Abell desired the said deponent to lie with them all that night, whereupon the said deponent agreed, saying that he would go home to his mother, showed her thereof, and fetch him a clean shirt; and so did. Whereupon one Joan, servant of the said Roger, assigned to them one little chamber or parlor next onto the stable there. And thereupon they agreed to play at tables for a quart of malvesey at double hand. And thereupon one of the servants brought into them tables and the said said [*sic*] Senior and Abell played against the said deponent and Godfrey. [Interlineated: "And after that sat the said Senior and Godfrey played together only at the tables."] And as they were playing for the said malvesey, one John Ganton came into the said chamber to the said players and said, "God speed." And thereupon the said deponent offered the said Ganton the cup to drink. And immediately after he had drunken, the said Ganton asked the said players if any of them would go fare at dice for 40^{d}, whereunto the said deponent said that he would not fare and play for any money for his part. And on that the said deponent said that if any man could find him at dice for 1^{d}, he would give him all the money in his purse. And thereupon the Ganton [*sic*] departed. And after that about a quarter of an hour the said Ganton came again and found the said Senior and

Godfrey playing together at the tables, and he asked Senior if he would fare for 40[d], for he cared not whether he lost or won "for I have a fair pair of dice." And Senior said he would play for no money. And then the same Ganton asked the said Senior if he would go with him to the White Horse and see if any man would play there. And Senior said nay, he would [not] go. And then said Ganton departed from them and in like wise, within half an hour after, the said Ganton came again to the said chamber and found the said Senior and Godfrey still playing and Abell standing looking upon them and the said deponent sitting before the fire. And then the said Ganton said to the same Godfrey that he had lost the game. And Godfrey said, "Nay, I shall win it." "Ye shall lose it," said Ganton, "and thereupon I lay two groats against one." And thereupon the said Godfrey said that he would hold that groat. And thereupon both said parties laid down their said money. And so it chanced that Godfrey won the game and took it up—the money—and put it up. And then said Ganton called Godfrey "knave" and "boy," saying and swearing great oaths that he should not have his money. Whereupon the same Ganton rose suddenly and gave the same Godfrey 2 or 3 blows upon the ears with his hand. And the said deponent, perceiving that the said Ganton would have drawn his dagger and have stricken the same Godfrey, came to the said Ganton and laid his hand upon the same Ganton's hand that he should not draw out his dagger, and departed [that is, separated] them. And after that the said deponent turned himself toward the fire. And the said Ganton rose suddenly and with the swing of his gown sleeve put out the candle. And then the said Ganton drew out his dagger and struck at the said deponent. And the same deponent fell into the chimney, and so the same Ganton missed the said deponent and struck into the masonry of the same chimney. And this perceiving, Senior stepped to Ganton and laid hold upon Ganton's dagger. And the said deponent, fearing that he should have been slain, stayed still in the chimney and would have lighted the candle. And in the meantime the said Ganton said, "Alas, I am slain," and thereupon fell down.

Richard Godfrey of Norwich, worstead weaver, sayeth and deposeth that about 6 of the clock in the night on Saint Leonard's eve at William Claxton's of a sudden met the said deponent John Pethouse, tailor, Robert Senior, and Robert Abell, worstead weavers. And so they agreed there to go to the Maid's Head together, and so did. And after that they supped there together in the hall within the said Maid's Head with others then being there present. And after supper the said deponent Robert Senior, Robert Abell, and John Pethouse desired to have a chamber, whereupon they had assigned to them a chamber or parlor next unto the stable. And when they were in the said chamber the same deponent, Robert Senior, Robert Abell, and John Pethouse agreed to play at the table for a quart of wine and against each other. And whereupon the said deponent and John Pethouse played against Robert Senior and Abell. In the mean season while they were playing, John Ganton came in to the said players and asked John Pethouse if they would fare for 40[d]. And he answered [in] these words: "If ye might find or see me farying, take all the money in my purse." And thereupon the same Ganton drank and departed. And about a quarter of an hour after that the same Ganton returned again to the said players into the said chamber and asked them if they would play 40[d] a piece. And they answered and said nay. "What," said Ganton, "ye are young men.

It shall little skill you to play 40d a piece." And within a little while after, the same Ganton said to the said deponent that he should lose the game. And the said deponent answered and said, "Ganton, ye cannot tell." "Yea, by the mass," said Ganton, "and upon that I hold one a groat." And so the same deponent and Ganton laid down either of them a groat. And when Ganton perceived that the said deponent would win the game, the same Ganton took up his groat again and put it in his purse. And then the same deponent said to the same Ganton, "It was in fair play, for ye would not be so served yourself." And upon that the said Ganton said, "I hold two groats against one upon the game." And did set the men again as they were. And so when their money was down and the men set them[selves] again, Ganton, perceiving that he should lose his money if that game had been played, intended to have taken up his 8d again. And that perceiving, the said deponent was more ready and took up the said 12d. And thereupon the said Ganton said: "By the mass, knave, thou shalt not have my money," and thereupon struck the said deponent upon the head with his first 2 or 3 [times]. And thereupon the same deponent said to Ganton, "That is no good manner, for if ye will not be content, I will call my father Cowper [the innkeeper]." [Whereupon Ganton replied:] "Call whom thou wilt, I shall serve ye like a boy." And with that the same John Pethouse said, "Ganton, strike him no more." "By the mass," said Ganton, "if thou wilt not let me strike him, I shall strike thee like a boy and knave." And in the meantime the said deponent fled from them out of the same chamber and called once or twice and said these words: "Father Cowper, come away for the passion of Christ, for Ganton will strike me with his dagger." And with that Cowper came toward the said chamber. And the said deponent being without the same chamber heard the said Ganton say, "By the mass, I am slain." And after this deponent and other for the premises were brought into prison, the said Senior said openly to the deponent before divers persons then being in the said prison these words following: "Richard, I am sorry that thou should be troubled for the premises, for if any man were in defense thereof, it was I. For with wrestling of Ganton's dagger between me and the same Ganton, and with mine power and the power of the same Ganton, the same Ganton drew the dagger to himwards." And so the same Senior had the fleece or paxwax [?] crush Senior by the same violence that thereof came great wound but not deep.

Robert Senior of Norwich, worstead weaver, sayeth and deposeth that about 6 of the clock toward night upon Saint Leonard's eve at Maid's Head met of a sudden the said deponent, John Pethouse, Robert Abell, Richard Godfrey, and Ganton. And the said Ganton then asked the same deponent if he would go to the White Horse and fare 40d, whereunto the same deponent answered and sayeth he would not play. And thereupon the same Ganton departed. And the said deponent, Pethouse, Abell, and Godfrey tarried there and supped together in the hall within the said inn with Sir Thomas Watts and other. And after supper the same deponent and Abell departed from them and went to Fivrigge to look upon the water, and immediately after came together and drank at the George Inn. And the said deponent and Abell departed incontinently from thence and Claxton's. And they, the said deponent and Abell, met again with the said Pethouse and Godfrey. And after that, incontinent, the said deponent, Abell, Pethouse, and Godfrey came again to the Maid's Head. And they desired to have a chamber, whereupon the ostler there brought them to a parlor or chamber next unto the stables. And so they commanded to have a fire, and then they agreed to play at tables and again and for a quart of wine. And thereupon Senior and Abell played against Pethouse and Godfrey. In the meantime, while they were playing for the said wine, Sir Thomas Watts and Ganton came in to the said players in the same chamber or parlor and said, "God speed." And after that the same Ganton asked Pethouse if he would fare 40^d, and he answered that he would play for no money. And so Ganton drank and departed. And within a while after, the said Ganton returned again to the said players and set him[self] down at the table, and looking upon the said players, and said to Godfrey and Pethouse: "Play no more, ye have lost the game." And they answered and said nay, and then said Ganton, "It is lost, a groat to a penny." Whereunto Godfrey said, "Nay, I hold one groat to another," and thereupon they agreed and laid down each of them a groat. And for that Ganton supposed to have lost his groat, he took up his groat again. And that same game not ended, the said Ganton and Godfrey travased again upon the same game, each against other one groat. And also then Ganton said to Godfrey that he would play that game himself. And the said deponent answered to Ganton saying that he would lay half loss with him. And for that the same Ganton perceived to have lost the same game, he would have taken up his money. And Godfrey perceived that, laid first hand upon the same two groats, and kept it still. And thereupon Ganton said and swore great oaths that he would have his money again, whereunto Godfrey said that the money was lost and he should not have it. And thereupon Ganton struck Godfrey upon the head with his fist once or twice. And that perceived, Pethouse stepped to Ganton and bade him be in peace and strike no more. And thereunto Ganton swore, "By the mass," and said, "I defy you boys and knaves," saying to John Pethouse: "If thou wilt not let me strike him, I shall strike thee." And then said Godfrey to Ganton, "Be in peace or I shall call my father Cowper." Whereunto Ganton answered and bade them call whom they would, for he defied them, boys and knaves. And the same Godfrey by the help of the said Pethouse fled from them into the yard and called the said Roger Cowper. And while Godfrey was calling of the same Roger Cowper, Ganton and Pethouse were together by the hair and their hands. And then the said Robert Senior stepped to them to have departed them. And after that they were parted, the said Pethouse fled toward the fire. And the said Ganton followed him, and with his gown bore down the candle, and incontinently drew out his dagger and struck at Pethouse therewith. And Pethouse perceiving that, he fled from the stroke and it lighted upon the masonry. And then the said deponent, perceiving that the same Ganton would have stricken the said Pethouse again, he stepped to the same Ganton and laid hand upon his dagger for to have taken it from him. And so the said deponent, having his hand upon the blade of the same dagger and the said Ganton his hand upon the haste of the same dagger, the same Ganton with wrestling slew himself.

CHAPTER 5 The Institutions of Criminal Justice after the Marian Statutes

It has been customary to understand that the office of the justice of the peace underwent a wholesale expansion of powers under the Tudors. Lambarde, in a well-worn phrase, laments the "Stacks of Statutes" [1] with which his generation of JPs had been loaded. "By the end of Elizabeth's reign Lambarde could list 309 statutes which in one way or another referred to the duties of justices of the peace; of these only 133 (going back to the thirteenth century) preceded 1485, 60 were made between 1485 and 1547, 39 under Edward VI and Mary, and 77 under Elizabeth." [2] Obviously, the Marian legislation of 1554–1555 must be reckoned as an enhancement of one side of the justices' office. It extended and systematized their prosecutorial role for cases of serious crime.

It has been less appreciated that the justices were simultaneously losing ground—their office was being diminished. The expanded power of the JPs in the pretrial process came at the expense of their ancient role in the trial process. In that, too, the Marian statutes were a landmark. The Marian scheme imposed a specialization of function in cases of serious crime. Although its antecedents were very old, the systematic division of function between the JP as investigating prosecutor and the assize judge as trier was a sixteenth-century creation and, indeed, one mandated by the Marian statutes. That peculiar divided judiciary, together with the persistence of jury trial, kept the English procedure consistently remote from Continental Inquisitionsprozess as it underwent the rationalization of Tudor times.

The present chapter examines the new balance which was struck in the Marian scheme among the three institutions whose roles were adjusted: the JPs, the central royal judiciary, and the juries of accusation and of trial. Section A deals with the decline in the truly magisterial side

1. Lambarde 38. The phrase originates in the first edition, and insistence to the contrary is mistaken; compare T. G. Barnes, *Somerset 1625–1640: A County's Government During the "Personal Rule"* (Cambridge, Mass., 1961) 40–41.

2. G. R. Elton, *The Tudor Constitution* (Cambridge, 1965) 454.

of the magistrates' office, their power to hear and determine cases of serious crime. In Section B we note the consequences of the Marian statutes for the juries of accusation and of trial. We have occasion to suggest that the Marian statutes laid the basis for the most profound transformation that common law criminal process ever knew: the formation of the law of criminal evidence.

A. THE MARIAN TRIAL COURT

In the fourteenth century when the powers of the magistracy were being first settled, it was common for commissions of the peace to include authority for justices to hear and determine cases of felony. Parliament confirmed the practice in statutes of 1344, 1361, and 1394, subject to the requirement that "men of law" be among the panel.[3] Miss Putnam's study of the shire peace rolls of the fourteenth and fifteenth centuries discloses a significant jurisdiction in felony;[4] the JPs had indeed exercised their power to try cases of serious crime.

By Elizabethan times the justices' trial powers had mostly fallen into disuse, although perpetuated notionally in the commission and in legislation treating various felonies. Lambarde remarked in 1588 that felonies were generally "reserved till the comming of the grave *Justices* of gaole deliverie . . . ."[5] Barnes' study of the Somerset quarter sessions records for the years 1625–1640 confirms that cases of serious crime "are extremely rare," implying "that assizes had assumed in practice the trial of virtually all felonies save larceny."[6]

The point at which the justices began finally to lose their trial powers in cases of felony has not been established. The Marian statutes seem not to have initiated the development,[7] but to have brought it to culmina-

3. R. B. Pugh, *Imprisonment in Medieval England* (Cambridge, 1968) 304–305.

4. B. Putnam, Introduction, *Proceedings before the Justices of the Peace in the Fourteenth and Fifteenth Centuries* (Ames Foundation) (London, 1938) cxii–cxvii; see id. at xxviii–xxix on the "vicissitudes" of the justices' power to determine felonies from 1327 into the sixteenth century.

5. Lambarde (1588 ed.) 549 (italics in original). Corresponding sections of earlier editions, e.g., the 1581 edition at 446, do not contain the remark.

6. Barnes (supra, note 1) at 51. The larceny cases are explained infra, page 112.

7. Miss Putnam traces to the reign of Henry VI

> a change in the character of the work of the justices of the peace; for determining felonies, that is for delivering gaols of prisoners indicted for felonies in the sessions of the peace, it was the justices of assize who were the successful

tion in Elizabethan times. The Marian statutes direct the justices to certify the Marian documents (examinations, bailments, and recognizances of persons bound over to appear) to "the next general Gaol Delivery," not therefore to quarter sessions. And that, Lambarde wrote in his first edition of 1581, was felt to be a factor "restrayning the *Justices* of Peace in the *Trial* of felonies, wherein also they are not now adaies much occupied, the rather bicause they deferre it til the comming of the *Justices* of *Assize,* by reason that the Statuts (1. & 2. Phil. & Mar. ca.13: & 2. & 3. Phil. & Mar. ca.10) doe enjoyne them, to *Certifie* at the next generall *Gaole* deliverie, both the *examinations* and bonds that they shal take, concerning Felons and suspects brought before them."[8] The Marian scheme left the JPs in full theoretical possession of their former trial powers. But, by making the Marian documents certifiable in the (assize) court of gaol delivery, it effectively required that the prosecution take place there.

Under this arrangement it remained possible for the JPs to activate their felony jurisdiction in at least two ways. One was to capitalize upon the circuitousness of the certification requirement by racing the

---

> competitors. The proof of their victory lies in the increasing number of such indictments found on gaol delivery rolls under Henry VI; also in the greater number of examples of correlation between the counties on the circuit of the justices of assize and the counties in which they are appointed as justices of the peace.

Putnam (supra, note 4) at liii (footnote omitted). Cf. Pugh (supra, note 3) at 305. Speaking of the 1530s, Elton has said: "Though commissions of the peace included all major crimes except treason, and though many misdemeanours as well as some felonies were tried at Quarter Sessions, most criminal trials in the shires were held before commissioners of oyer and terminer or of gaol delivery." G. R. Elton, *Policy and Police: The Enforcement of the Reformation in the Age of Thomas Cromwell* (Cambridge, 1972) 295.

8. Lambarde 452 (italics in original). This insight had only lately come to Lambarde. In the manuscript forerunner of the *Eirenarcha,* dated August 1579 and composed when Lambarde was first entering the Kent commission of the peace, there is a brief chapter "Of Sessions, for the Gaole delyverie." British Museum Additional Manuscript 41137, fol. 57v–58. It begins: "The Justices of p. may make gaole deliverie, so that they have two learned men in the Lawe at it." Id. fol. 57v. The chapter enumerates various offenses. Lambarde deleted the chapter from the first published edition of the *Eirenarcha* in January 1582 (see supra, Chapter 1, note 16). One supposes that in the interval between August 1579 and January 1582 Lambarde's further experience in the commission of the peace taught him what he records in the *Eirenarcha* in the passage quoted above in text: that the JPs' theoretical powers of gaol delivery had in reality lapsed through the operation of the certification requirement of the Marian statutes. On the dating of the manuscript and of Lambarde's tenure of office as a JP, see B. Putnam, "The Earliest Form of Lambard's 'Eirenarcha' and a Kent Wage Assessment of 1563," *English Historical Review* 41:260, 262–264 (1926).

commissioners of gaol delivery. Lambarde first remarks the possibility in the 1599 edition of the *Eirenarcha*, where he adds to the passage just quoted the concluding aside: "Nevertheles their [the JPs'] power is no whit restrained, to proceede before the comming of those *Justices.*"[9] What would then be certified to the judges at assizes would be the documentation from a prosecution already concluded at quarter sessions, with the defendant in all likelihood now acquitted or hanged. It seems remote that the judges on their busy assize circuits[10] were intended to be, or in fact permitted themselves to be, saddled with the review of documents from routine cases already dispatched at quarter sessions. Lambarde does not claim currency for such a practice, nor does other authority appear to exemplify it. Hence it is best to regard Lambarde's remark as simply a recognition that, in this respect as in so many others, the Marian statutes were less than tightly drafted.

Another means by which quarter sessions could retain trial jurisdiction over felony was by delegation from gaol delivery. The royal judges were always pressed for time by the list of civil causes to be tried at *nisi prius*, and it was in their power to refer to the JPs a portion of the assize criminal calendar. This, we gather from Lambarde, was actual usage. The "*Justices* [of gaol delivery] (being withal *Justices* of Peace) do leave wyth the *Clarke* of ye Peace, Inditements, & such causes of the Peace, as be not determined [at the sessions of gaol delivery], but hang in processe, to the end offendors may be more speedily *Justiced.*"[11]

9. Lambarde (1599 ed.) 534 (italics in original).

10. "Doe what the judges can they cannot deliver all the gaole many tymes before the latter ende of there sittinge, for even the laste half-daye thereof divers be indyted and not before, and that not in defaulte of the judges but for wante of evidence, bringing in of the prisoners, and defaulte sometymes in some of the justices of peace." This anonymous lament is from a document dated July 2, 1586, now in the British Museum Landsdowne collection: "A declaracion of the course used and nedeful to be used by the judges in the Westerne circuite in the delivery of the gaole and triall of *nisi prius*," transcribed and discussed in *Somerset Assize Orders 1629–1640* (T. G. Barnes, ed.) (Somerset Record Society, 1959) 54.

11. Lambarde 299 (italics in original). The county archivist for Essex has reported that "some [Essex] Sessions Rolls are entirely or largely comprised of such cases." F. G. Emmison, "Calendars of Essex Assize Files, 1559–1714, and King's Bench Indictments (Ancient), 1538–1675," *Essex Journal* 1:126, 129 (1966) (footnote omitted). Elsewhere he has explained how the Essex quarter sessions proceeded upon such delegated indictments. F. G. Emmison, "The Elizabethan Assize Files with Particular Reference to the County of Essex," *Bulletin of the Society of Local Archivists* (No. 13) 2, 11–12 (April 1954).

The passage from Lambarde quoted in text is garbled in the copy of the 1581 edition in the Harvard Law School Treasure Room; the Cambridge University Library copy contains the corrected version. Putnam, *Early Treatises*, at 234–235, identifies only one 1581 edition of the *Eirenarcha*.

In special circumstances at least, it was also feasible for the assize judge to authorize the JPs to try felons at general or special sessions of their own convened in advance or in lieu of the assizes. In Essex in 1595 Baron Clarke, an Exchequer judge regularly in the commissions both of assize and of peace for Essex, directed his warrant to the sheriff " 'at the request of the Keeper of the [County] Gaol of Colchester because he is charged with many more prisoners than he is able to maintain and the offences of many are of no great moment, for the holding of a Gaol Delivery at the next Quarter Sessions.' "[12] Clarke himself sat at the gaol delivery. An earlier instance in which Baron Clarke and a fellow assize judge held a gaol delivery at Essex quarter sessions in 1591 is also known.[13] The assize judges for Derbyshire wrote the JPs in 1597 that the next scheduled assizes would have to be postponed; but "as we understand that there are many poor prisoners in gaol charged with small offences, we hereby require you, at the midsummer or some other sessions to be held shortly, to try and deliver some of the smaller offenders, which will be a great ease to the country."[14]

Cases such as these are not seriously inconsistent with the view that the post-Marian magistracy had lost its authority to try cases of serious felony, because the JPs were proceeding on more than ordinary magistrative authority. Other evidence has come to light in recent years which does, however, suggest that up to the Restoration the Marian jurisdictional division was not invariably followed. For example, it has been noticed that the JPs in Kent in late Elizabethan–early Jacobean times, in addition to holding regular quarter sessions for lesser crime,[15]

> also held at other times to the normal sessions' dates, gaol delivery sessions at which they tried felons in custody mainly accused of theft and at which death sentences were passed. These gaol delivery sessions were quite distinct from the gaol deliveries held by the Assize judges twice a year for the county of Kent.

12. F. G. Emmison, "The Elizabethan Assize Files with Particular Reference to the County of Essex," *Bulletin of the Society of Local Archivists* (No. 13) 2, 10 (April 1954). For Baron Clarke see *Dictionary of National Biography* X 439–440.

13. Emmison (supra, note 12) at 10–11.

14. "Sir Edmund Anderson and J. Clench, Justices of Assize, to the Justices of the Peace in Derbyshire," calendared in *The Manuscripts of His Grace the Duke of Rutland* (Historical Manuscripts Com'n., 12th rpt., ap., pt. IV) (H. C. Maxwell Lyte, ed.) (London, 1888) I 339. I owe this reference to Dr. J. S. Cockburn.

15. E. Melling, Introduction, *Kentish Sources VI: Crime and Punishment* (Maidstone, 1969) 2.

An extract has been published[16] from one of the rolls for these sessions of gaol delivery for 1597 at which Lambarde himself (among other Kent justices) sat. It is reported that similar "[e]ngrossed records in roll form survive for ten sessions held between 1596 and 1605 headed, 'Delivery of the Gaol.'"[17] There is no question, therefore, that these JPs were trying felons. The issue is whether they purported to do so as JPs, under their authority as commissioners of the peace; or whether, consistent with the certification requirement of the Marian statutes, they convened under special authority—either special commission of gaol delivery[18] or special warrant of the assize judges—to clear overcrowded gaols in intervals between assizes. The self-conscious segregation of these felony trials as gaol deliveries may imply that the JPs in Kent were specially constituted. Other seventeenth-century evidence is harder to explain. Barnes reports finding eight cases in the period 1625–1640 in which felons were convicted and hanged for grand larceny by Somerset quarter sessions.[19] There is further evidence from Kent of quarter sessions held up to the Restoration at which death sentences for felony were pronounced.[20] A similar practice during the same period in Devonshire has been noticed.[21] It is conceivable that in all these instances where the JPs continued to try serious crimes at their regular sessions, they were acting on cases delegated from assizes, or they had been authorized by the assize judges (or by special commission). Whatever the explanation of these exceptions in the seventeenth century, it is enough for present purposes to emphasize that the exceptions were indeed exceptional, that in normal circumstances the Marian division pertained. Cases of serious felony were tried at assizes by the assize judges.

The requirement of the Marian statutes that the JPs certify their examinations, bailments, and recognizances in cases of serious crime to "the next general Gaol Delivery" tended to determine the content of the bailments and recognizances in a way which emphasized the jurisdictional allocation. The examining magistrate had to declare in the instrument which court the bound persons were obliged to attend as the con-

16. Id. at 134–136.
17. Letter from Miss Melling, March 20, 1972.
18. A suggestion I owe to Professor T. G. Barnes.
19. Barnes (supra, note 1) at 52.
20. Melling (supra, note 15) at 3.
21. A. H. A. Hamilton, *Quarter Sessions from Queen Elizabeth to Queen Anne* (London, 1878) 30–34; J. S. Cockburn, *A History of English Assizes 1558–1714* (Cambridge, 1972) 94–96.

dition of satisfying the bailment or recognizance.[22] The examiner, writes Bacon, binds the accused, accusers, and witnesses "to appeare either at the next Assizes, if it be a matter of Treason or Felonie; or else at quarter Sessions, if it bee concerning Ryot or mis-behavior, or some other small offence."[23] It was at the very outset that the JP had to determine the forum to which the case would be tried, in order to bind appearances.[24] Because any subsequent change of forum would be awkward,[25] the post-Marian jurisdictional division was becoming inflexible.[26]

What purpose had the Marian draftsman in restricting the justices' trial powers while expanding their pretrial role? The most reasonable view,[27] it is submitted, is that the concern was to restrain the develop-

22. For the forms of recognizance and bailment see Lambarde 206–208, 264–265.

23. F. Bacon, *The Use of the Law* (London, 1630) 14–15. The Marian statutes did not by their terms prevent the examining justice from binding appearances to both quarter sessions and assizes, but the duplication of obligation would have burdened witnesses considerably in an era of rude transport, and without any real benefit to the state. The practice is, however, exemplified in at least one document: the recognizance binding Thomas Hornesbye to produce his son to "appere att the next quarter Sessions to be holden att Chelmsforde, and to give evydence agaynst Henrye Wodeforde & Johanne Dodde for the Felonye aforesayde by them commytted/ And also to appere and give lyke evydence agaynst them for the same att the next Gayle delyverie to be kept within the said shire . . . ." Essex County Record Office: Q/SR 2/42v (1556). See supra, page 94 & n. 81, for discussion of why the examination and recognizance in this case may not have been made in conscious compliance with Marian procedure.

24. "A J.P. wrote the Somerset clerk of the peace in January 1634/5 that he had bound three men to assizes accused of the theft of three pairs of stockings, even though they had asked to be tried at Q[uarter] S[essions], 'but because I believe it wilbe above the vallew [of one shilling, hence grand larceny (see infra, page 112)], I doe think it will not be tryed at the sessyons . . . .'" T. G. Barnes, Introduction, *Somerset Assize Orders 1629–1640* (Somerset Record Society, 1959) xviii n. 3 (citation omitted).

25. See Emmison (supra, note 12) at 10–11, recounting a letter to Baron Clarke from a man who seems to have been bound to prosecute at assizes, and who planned to be away in Wales when Clarke convened his special gaol delivery at Essex quarter sessions in 1591.

26. Although it is quite correct to view quarter sessions and assizes as "part of the same highly integrated governmental system, which bestowed complementary functions upon them," Emmison (supra, note 12) at 8, the scanty case law of the period shows a sharp sense of jurisdictional limitation upon both. Compare Smith's Case, Cro. Eliz. 87, 78 Eng. Rep. 345 (1588), and Wilson's Case, Cro. Eliz. 601, 78 Eng. Rep. 843 (1598) (quashing forgery indictments taken at sessions, which under 5 Eliz. I c. 14 [1563] ought to have been taken at assizes); with Pursell's Case, Cro. Eliz. 179, 78 Eng. Rep. 435 (1590) (quashing an indictment taken before justices of gaol delivery, not justices of the peace). This is not to suggest that all points of the relationship between the two courts was clear; see, e.g., Lambarde at 79, wondering whether the effect of the sitting of assizes is to put the county commission of peace into abeyance.

27. There have been others. Blackstone improbably explained the desuetude of the justices' trial powers by reference to the *casus difficultatis* clause of the revised

ment of over-mighty local officers. Trial competence was detached from the magistracy to prevent abuse by the justices. The bail statute explicitly declares that it is instituting examination and certification as a check upon the justices. The committal statute carried forward the certification requirement and its checking function—understandably, since the committal statute otherwise effected such a considerable expansion of the magistrates' authority in the criminal process. Paradoxically, therefore, the Marian statutes both expanded and contracted the magistrates' office. The prosecutorial role occasioned the decline of the adjudicative.[28] That the Marian statutes should have had this jurisdictional message as well as the expressly processual one is a further sign of the scope of the reconstruction they were effecting. We shall see in the final section of this chapter that the new order extended to the institution of jury trial itself.

In actual practice the jurisdictional disposition of the Marian statutes proved too strict. By the time of Dalton's first edition (1618), and seemingly after Lambarde's last revision of his *Eirenarcha* (1599), judicial practice generalized an exception to the Marian statutes for "small felonies"—the lesser offenses which were technically still categorized as felony. Dalton reports the practice and its rationale:[29]

---

commission of the peace, discussed infra, pages 116–118, which first appeared in 1590, well after the justices had regularly ceased to exercise their jurisdiction. W. Blackstone, *Commentaries on the Laws of England* (Oxford, 1769) IV 268. Barnes (supra, note 1) at 53, has offered another account:

> As the local magistrates did not possess in like measure as the awesome judges the dignity and power in their persons and places sufficient to coerce a grand jury into returning a true bill and a trial jury a conviction that meant the noose, so felons were not brought to justice as King, Council and judges required. Anyone aware of the relative lawlessness of the age is even more aware of the unending exertion of the Council to suppress it. The King and Council did not scruple to reduce the justices' powers in felonies for the better preservation of the King's peace.

28. The temptation to see in this development the draftsman's recognition of the incompatibility of prosecutorial and judicial roles probably ought to be resisted. Even though the JP was becoming a persistent protagonist in criminal litigation, organizing many a prosecution case and often testifying himself, contemporaries may not have found it alarming that to permit the JP to continue to try such cases might constitute him judge in his own cause. That issue would have remained well submerged in a legal procedural scheme which forbade defense counsel and only rarely employed prosecuting counsel. Concern with the unfairness of a prosecutorially inclined judge had little currency until the political trials of the later Stuarts. In Tudor times, when policing was wholly amateur, when prosecution was nonprofessional, and when the communal basis of jury trial seemed to assure the elementary fairness of the criminal process, the state felt itself too threatened by serious crime to trouble itself with devising procedural protections for accused felons. See Stephen I 354–357.

29. Dalton 39 (italics in original). This division between greater and lesser

> But if it be for pety Larceny, or other small felonyes, the Just. of peace may bind over the Informers, and may certifie the examinations, and informations, to the next quarter Sessions of the peace; And this was the advice and direction of Syr *David Williams* Knight (late one of the Justices of the Kings Bench) at the Assises at Cambridge: For said he, it was not meet to keep poore prisoners in the gaole for small matters or felonies, from one Assises till another: And therefore he gave order, that the Ju. of P. (at their generall Sessions of the peace) should try and deliver offendors for small felonies[.]

Thus is explained the jurisdiction in lesser felonies, mostly larceny, which Barnes reports for Somerset quarter sessions in 1625–1640. The effect of judicial practice was to override the Marian draftsman on his use of the felony/nonfelony distinction in favor of the functional distinction between serious (generally capital) and lesser crime. But that was a technical revision. The essential Marian jurisdictional division remained: in cases of serious crime the JPs prosecuted and the assize judges tried.

Another development in the relations between lay and professional judiciary seems to have been occasioned by the Marian jurisdictional adjustment—the debasing of the quorum of the peace. The bare fact of the debasement is well known. What has not been remarked is the precise timing and its apparent connection to the Marian scheme.

The quorum clause has not yet found its historian—lamentably, because he would be able to tell us much about the means by which the expertise of bench and bar informed the work of the lay magistrates in late medieval and early modern times. Nonetheless, the outline is tolerably clear. The quorum "probably originated" in an act of 1344.[30] It expresses a limitation upon the trial powers granted in the commission of the peace. The formula as it ran in 1547 states: "And the commissioners or at least two of them, of whom (*quorum*) one of [certain named commissioners] must always be one, are to hear and determine the felonies aforesaid [and certain designated lesser offenses]."[31] The justices of the peace specially named in the quorum clause were (in the original usage) "common law judges or practitioners."[32] Lambarde in

felony seems nascent in the assize judges' instruction to the Derbyshire JPs in 1597 (supra, page 108).

30. The term first appears in a commission for Cornwall dated July 20, 1344, designating William Shareshull, later chief justice of King's Bench, to the quorum. Putnam (supra, note 4) at xxv, xli.

31. *Calendar of the Patent Rolls: 1547–1548* (London, 1924) 80.

32. Dawson, *Lay Judges 138.*

his first edition (when, we shall see, the clause was already anachronistic) explained the historic purpose: "These of the *Quorum,* were wont not without just cause to be chosen, specially for their learning in the laws of the Realme . . . [since the] power to hear and determine [is that] in which part that kinde of learning is most requisite and serviceable." [33] Lambarde had occasion to amplify this point when a new standard-form commission of the peace was adopted in 1590, perpetuating the anachronistic quorum clause:[34]

> For, albeit that a discreet person (not conversant in the studie of the lawes) may sufficiently follow sundry particular directions concerning this service of the Peace: yet when the proceeding must be by way of *presentment* upon the evidence of witnesses and othes of Jurors, and by the order of *hearing* and *determining* according to the streight rule & course of the *Law,* it must be confessed, that learning in the lawes is so necessary a light, as without the which all the labour is but groping in the darke, the end whereof must needes be error, and dangerous falling.

Common law trial was sufficiently complex that the quorum clause had been "wont" to insist on the participation of professional lawyers.

It was in the generation following the Marian statutes that the quorum, already grown large, was bloated into meaninglessness. In 1547, fairly shortly before the Marian statutes, the figures for five representative counties were as follows:[35]

County	*Commission*	*Quorum*
Kent	53	17
Northamptonshire	36	17
Somerset	39	16
Worcestershire	49	25
Yorkshire, North Riding	51	17

33. Lambarde 55–56 (italics in original).

34. Lambarde (1591 ed.) 48 (italics in original). The quoted paragraph is preceded by the view that, "(to say the trueth) all *Statutes,* that desire the presence of the *Quorum,* doe secretly signifie such a *learned* man." Id. (italics in original).

35. These five counties have been chosen for convenience in order to correlate with Gleason's data for the same five for later years (infra, notes 36–37). The year 1547 is taken because a set of commissions of the peace dated in that year survives on the patent rolls. It is calendared in *Calendar of the Patent Rolls: 1547–1548* (London, 1924) 80–92. The calendar does not disclose the figures for the quorum clause; these have been gathered from the roll itself in the Public Record Office: Patent Roll 1 Edw. VI, pt. III, P.R.O. C. 66/801. The editors of the calendar say in an aside, at 80, that the quorum tends to number "about one quarter" of the members of the commissions, an estimate too low for the results set out in the text.

The immediate impact of the Marian legislation was not great. In 1562, these were the statistics:[36]

Kent	56	28
Northamptonshire	29	15
Somerset	40	24
Worcestershire	28	17
Yorkshire, North Riding	35	20

But by 1584, the proportion of the justices in the quorum had burgeoned:

Kent	76	55
Northamptonshire	43	34
Somerset	49	33
Worcestershire	52	45
Yorkshire, North Riding	63	53

We suggest that it was the Marian scheme's transfer of felony trial jurisdiction from the JPs which occasioned the debasing of the quorum. The function of the quorum clause had been to condition the JPs' trial jurisdiction in serious crime upon the presence (and inferentially, upon the guidance) of legal professionals and others of great experience. When the trial jurisdiction itself all but ceased to be a component of the magistrates' office, the quorum designation could degenerate into a petty embellishment of dignity.[37]

36. Figures for 1562 and 1584 have been computed from the tabulations in Gleason 4, 15, 123–124; 164, 167–168; 187, 190–191; 207–208, 210–211; and 224–225, 227–228.

37. Gleason's figures on legal education rule out the possibility that the growth of the quorum reflects a commensurate leap in legal training among the justices. The number of matriculates at inns of court who appear in the commission did grow rapidly under Elizabeth. But the quorum grew faster. Moreover, matriculation at a fashionable inn was a matter of enrollment, no guarantee of a man having studied or learned anything. See Gleason 83–95; cf. id. at 50–51, 58.

The early tendency to put important central dignitaries in the quorum as well as in the commission itself may explain why the quorum designation came, in later years, to be treated as a dignitary distinction and thus was retained, rather than straightforwardly abolished, when its function had ceased. A lapidary inscription dated 1631 on the north choir aisle of Salisbury cathedral boasts: "Neere lies the body of John Lowe esquier, one of his ma[jesty]'s justice of the peace & quorum for

The divergent history of the parallel institution of the quorum clause in the commissions of assize provides indirect confirmation that the debasing of the quorum of the peace may have stemmed from the JPs' loss of their trial duties. It had been customary for the commissions of assize to designate, in addition to the royal judges and serjeants who in fact conducted the judicial proceedings, various local dignitaries whose attendance at the assize was ceremonial.[38] To prevent the local worthies from exceeding their decorative role, a quorum clause was inserted in the commissions of assize (gaol delivery and oyer and terminer), conditioning the exercise of the commission upon the presence of the professionals. Both the form and the function paralleled the quorum clause in the commission of the peace. However, when the quorum of the peace was being debased, the quorum of assize continued to designate only the professionals from the royal central courts.[39] We infer that the Marian juris-

this county . . . ." Another example, also from Salisbury cathedral, is mentioned in T. G. Barnes and A. H. Smith, "Justices of the Peace from 1558 to 1688—a Revised List of Sources," *Bulletin of the Institute of Historical Research* 32:221, 223 n. 4 (1959). Although Lawrence Stone's well-known chapter, "The Inflation of Honours," does not discuss the growth of the quorum, it seems to set the phenomenon in context. "The insatiable demand for status and honour between 1558 and 1641 is proof of the truth of what has been called 'Tawney's Law': that the greater the wealth and more even its distribution in a given society, the emptier become titles of personal distinction, but the more they multiply and are striven for." L. Stone, *The Crisis of the Aristocracy 1558–1641* (Oxford, 1965) 128.

38. Characteristically, they were justices of the peace in their own right. Conversely, the commission of the peace contained the names of various crown dignitaries, including the royal judges whose circuit put them in that county's assize commission. There was consequently a considerable overlap of personnel between the commissions of peace and of assize.

One gathers from the haphazard survivals in the patent rolls and the assize files that of the assize commissions, it was oyer and terminer rather than gaol delivery in which there would be designated a large panel of laymen whom the quorum clause excluded. Francis Bacon's little text, *The Use of the Law* (London, 1630), at 18, contrasts the commission of oyer and terminer, issued to the assize judges "and many others of the best accompt, in their Circuits" with the commission of gaol delivery, which "is only to the Judges themselves, & the Clearke of the Assize associate . . . ." Exemplars of commissions of oyer and terminer are cited infra, note 39. For contemporary gaol delivery commissions see, e.g., those for 1559–1561 cited supra, Chapter 2, note 12; and others for 1564 and 1571 calendared in *Calendar of the Patent Rolls: 1563–1566* (London, 1960) 37, 104–105; *Calendar of the Patent Rolls: 1569–1572* (London, 1966) 214–215.

39. Holdsworth I 280–281. Holdsworth prints full texts of the commissions of oyer and terminer and of gaol delivery, id. at 669–670, taken from Coke. The quorum clause appears on lines 7–8 of the former and on lines 2–3 of the latter.

The tiny professional quorum in a very large commission is exemplified in some oyer and terminer commissions preserved in the patent rolls, e.g., a commission of 1554 for several counties and cities in the Midlands designating thirty-three commissioners "or three of them, of whom James Dyer or Ralph Rokebye [serjeants-at-

dictional settlement explains the divergence in post-Marian times. The substantial demise of the trial jurisdiction of the commissioners of the peace undermined the purpose of the quorum of the peace and allowed it to burgeon. The monopolization of that jurisdiction by the gaol deliverers at assizes reinforced the purpose of the quorum clause in the assize commissions, which continued to restrict the exercise of these commissions to the professionals.[40]

When the commission of the peace underwent the definitive revision of 1590, the quorum of the peace was already an anachronism. It was retained, presumably for honorific reasons, although in practice it had attained a size which rendered it useless to its original purpose. However, the 1590 revision did introduce a frail functional substitute for the former quorum clause, one apparently deemed adequate to the diminished trial jurisdiction of the JPs. This was the *casus difficultatis* clause, which stipulated:[41]

> Provided always, that if a case of difficulty should arise before you or any two or more of you concerning the determination of any of the matters aforesaid, then you should not proceed to render judgment yourself or any two or more of you, except in the presence of one of our judges of one or the other of the Benches or of one of our judges assigned to taking assizes in the county aforesaid.

The clause does not explain what sort of casus might be difficultatis; in particular, it does not limit itself to cases of felony. A case of misdemeanor, too, could be held over for the coming of the assize judges if it perplexed the JPs.[42]

The casus difficultatis clause was so obviously the successor in

---

law] is to be one . . . ." *Calendar of the Patent Rolls: 1553–1554* (London, 1937) 29 (two similar appear on the same page). Further examples for 1564 appear in *Calendar of the Patent Rolls: 1563–1566* (London, 1960) 41–43, 105.

40. Miss Putnam suspected the relationship but reversed cause and effect:

> This change in the character of the quorum led eventually to a change in the character of the work of the justices of the peace; for determining felonies, that is for delivering gaols of prisoners indicted for felonies in the sessions of the peace, it was the justices of assize who were the successful competitors.

Putnam (supra, note 4) at lii–liii.

41. Translated from the Latin appearing in Lambarde (1591 ed.) 41–42.

42. Barnes (supra, note 1) at 51, 53, ought not be read to equate felony and casus difficultatis. Several instances in which the Somerset sessions held over nonfelony matters for the guidance of the assize judges are noted in T. G. Barnes, Introduction, *Somerset Assize Orders 1629–1640* (Somerset Record Society, 1959) xxvii–xxviii.

function to the quorum clause that we ought to mark well the difference between the two. Unlike the quorum clause, which suspended an entire class of jurisdiction until the professionals were present, the casus difficultatis clause operated in individual cases and at the discretion of the JPs. It was necessary for the JPs both to recognize that a "case of difficulty" was indeed before them, and to agree to forbear further proceedings until the coming of a royal judge. The new commission therefore provided a channel of assistance for the JPs without imposing any effective constraint upon them should they neglect to use it. Wrote Lambarde soon after the casus difficultatis clause appeared in the commission:[43]

> And here, least these *Justices* [of the peace] should rather ground their judgements upon the number of *voices,* then upon the weight of *reasons,* this latter *clause* [the *assignanimus* of the commission, giving the JPs power to hear and determine] is shut up with a *provision,* and restraint, that in all cases of ambiguitie and doubt, they shall spare to proceed to judgement, and shall expect the advise either of some one of the *Judges* of the Kings *Bench,* or of the *Common* place, or (at the least) of the one of the *Justices* of *Assise* in that Countie, which be their more neare and readie *Oracle.* And yet . . . is not their judgement void, if they lust to proceed without such advice; but it standeth good & effectuall, untill it shall be reversed by a writ of *Error.*

This new arrangement, which left to the discretion of the JPs the critical decision of when to admit that a case raised issues beyond their capabilities, was feasible only as a consequence of the Marian jurisdictional revision. The effective withdrawal of cases of serious crime from the JPs' trial competence set a tolerable ceiling on the amount of mischief they could work should they proceed to judgment where they ought to have awaited professional guidance.

Both the quorum clause and the casus difficultatis clause will interest us further for the remarkable parallel they suggest to the system used in the German Carolina to provide lay magistrates with expert guidance. The Carolina, we shall see, commands that in cases "not provided [for] or made sufficiently plain or understandable" in the statute, the lay court "shall seek advice how such odd and incomprehensible cases shall be best judged and dealt with . . . ."[44]

43. Lambarde (1591 ed.) 49 (italics in original; citation omitted). Some of this language appears in the 1581 edition, at 55, in another context. The 1592 edition, at 51, substitutes "expect the presence," where the 1591 edition has used the phrase "expect the advise."

44. Carolina Article 105.

The mechanics of the casus difficultatis clause are particularly close to the Carolina's *Aktenversendung;* both schemes contemplated that the lay court would itself recognize when legal issues were beyond it and would seek out the expertise of designated professionals.[45] It is easy enough to understand why some such arrangement is all but compelled when a legal system assigns an important adjudicative role to laymen. It must be foreseen that they will ultimately reach their depth and that, if justice is to be done, a channel needs to be provided for associating the professional hand with the lay.

Yet the similarity between the English and German schemes goes only that far. Each looked to a distinctive source of professionalism. The Carolina, by authorizing resort to the university law faculties, took the ultimately decisive step in the reception of Roman law in Germany. The draftsman had scant alternative. The failure of German national political life had prevented the growth of central institutions comparable to the English bench and bar which could have organized and preserved the native criminal process. Having employed Roman-canon sources extensively in the design of his code, the draftsman found it necessary to direct his lay courts to the Roman-canon professionals in cases of doubt. The parallel English devices in the commission of the peace—first the quorum clause, then the casus difficultatis clause—both had the effect of integrating the procedure of the local magistrates into that of the central courts and their professional judiciary. The deference of the JPs to the professionals in the English scheme reinforced the indigenous procedure by constituting "the *Justices* of *Assise* . . . their more neare and readie *Oracle.*"[46]

B. THE MARIAN JURIES

The ultimate context in which the Marian statutes were set, as we have several times said, was the fundamental transformation which had overcome the jury system in the years preceding. The juries had largely ceased to be self-informing and had become dependent upon outside

45. Nonetheless, there can be no question but that the English development was indigenous—for the reasons already canvassed in dealing with the reception issue, and because the casus difficultatis clause is so manifestly the successor to the late medieval quorum clause.

46. Lambarde (1591 ed.) 49 (italics in original).

agencies to supply them the information they needed for indictment or verdict. Yet the Marian scheme was not simply a reaction. It had important consequences of its own for the two juries. By raising up the justices of the peace as prosecutors, it sealed the fate of the jury of accusation, transferring to the justices the investigatory and instigatory functions of the former presentment system.

In giving the JPs' role the peculiar shape of evidence-gathering for oral public jury trial, the Marian scheme had an immense significance—to some extent contemporaneously recognized—for the petty jury. By instituting a procedure to assure the regular flow of information to a trial jury which was no longer self-informing, the Marian statutes reinforced the jury's role as trier-of-fact. In the next centuries the Marian scheme became the very core of the law of criminal evidence. It was the separation of the investigative and determinative functions, previously merged in the work of the jury, which became the occasion for regulating by rule what information the investigators might transmit to the determiners. The law of examination was found to have secreted the law of evidence.

The underlying phenomenon, the tendency of both juries toward a passive role, remains as mysterious as when Thayer's leading work[47] first appeared. Although the course of the development is sketchy, its timing seems fairly well established. There are increasing signs through the fifteenth century, and by the first third of the sixteenth century it had become expectable that the jurors would be themselves ignorant of the matters of fact they denounced and determined.[48]

This transformation affected the jury of accusation more deeply than the jury of trial, because the crux of the accusing function had been the gathering of information and suspicion upon which to decide whether to make the suspect stand trial. The accusing function had been primarily an informing function, only secondarily a deliberative one.[49] The

47. J. B. Thayer, *A Preliminary Treatise on Evidence at the Common Law* (London, 1898) 90–136, esp. 122–136.

48. Thayer emphasizes the primitiveness of the role of witness testimony as late as Fortescue's account (1460s), id. at 130–132. On the other hand, he points out, id. at 135 n. 1, that the Statute of Pirates of 1535–1536, supra, page 55, incontestably exhibits the notion of a jury of ignorant triers. It provided for jury trial in England for offenses committed thousands of miles from the jurymen.

49. Whereas, of course, it was the deliberative function which came to predominate when the informing function was externalized. We find in post-Marian archives many bills of indictment for felony endorsed "ignoramus." The deliberative role could be taken very seriously; e.g., in Richard Bernard's *A Guide to Grand Jury*

active presenting jury did not become the passive indicting jury in one leap. The power to present persisted into the twentieth century. Yet by Lambarde's time, at the latest, the passivity of the jury of accusation in cases of serious crime appears established. Nineteen speeches which Lambarde delivered to quarter sessions grand juries in Kent in the period 1582–1601 survive in manuscript and have been published under the editorship of Conyers Read.[50] Each was "a prologue to the formal charge to the grand jury, a long affair which fills some seventy-five pages in the several editions of *Eirenarcha*." [51] The charge itself was a summary statement of the substantive law upon the various offenses for which the jury might present or indict. The speeches, which repeat one another constantly, exhort the jurors to perform their duty to present of their own knowledge. "[H]ow shall we [the JPs] that be the mouth speak unless you the eyes will first show and tell us whereof?" [52] Again:[53]

> It hath been the common opinion of men in your place that they ought to present nothing unto the bench save that only which is given in evidence by others unto them. But this is a bypath, and therefore be not led out of your way with it. Your oath and duty is not only to hear and receive what others shall bring but also to inquire and present what yourselves do know.

These passages are deceptive, however; their context denies them the meaning they would otherwise assume. In fact, they are exclusively concerned with petty crime. The theme, incessantly repeated, is that little offenders left unpunished become great offenders, and that the jurors are appropriate to detect and denounce these petty offenders. Felony goes unmentioned. It is "the disorders of alehouses," bastardy,

Men (London, 1627), at 24–25, a clergyman's tract which warns the grand jurors in witchcraft cases to be reluctant to return a true bill unless well persuaded, since the "simple men" of the petty jury could be easily led to a mistaken conviction.

The present study has had to eschew the large and tempting subject of juror selection in early modern times. There is need for a monograph to sort out such questions as how much discretion the sheriff in fact exercised in selecting the panels, how tightly the lines of social class were drawn between grand and petty jurors, how extensively the JPs themselves sat on grand juries, and how much overlap there was in membership among the various accusing juries at quarter sessions and the grand jury at assizes.

50. Lambarde, *Ephemeris & Charges* 67–149. Read's introduction appears id. at 55–63. "So far as I know, these are the only extant speeches of their kind for Elizabeth's reign." Id. at 57.

51. Id. at 56.

52. Id. at 69 (1582).

53. Id. at 88 (1587).

gaming, and offenses of apparel which the jurors ought to present, since these constitute "the first steps, as it were, of those stairs which do lead up to pickery, theft, and robbing."[54] You should "present the names of regraters, engrossers, forestallers and transporters of victual,"[55] and of those who deal falsely with weights and measures. Failing presentment, "small seeds at the first wax in time to be great weeds . . . ."[56] By implication, the great weeds are for the justices to root out; and we have seen that Lambarde's diary shows him doing just that—routinely investigating in cases of serious crime. There the JPs had displaced the jurors in the conduct of the informing function. For petty crime alone was it "a false persuasion" that the jurors "ought to present nothing but that only which is brought in bill ready to your hands." For serious crime the initiative had shifted to the magistrates, who organized detection, detention, and prosecution, and who controlled the framing of bills of indictment for submission at sessions to the jury of accusation.[57] In felony cases the jurors' role was indictment, not presentment.[58]

In the *Eirenarcha,* we have seen,[59] Lambarde asserts a causal relationship between the decline of presentment and the development of what we have called the pre-Marian tradition of examination incident to summary trial for lesser offenses. Furthermore, Marian examination is "to enforme the *Jurie* towardes an Enditement . . . ."[60] Yet Marian examina-

54. Id. at 70 (1582).
55. Id. at 70–71.
56. Id. at 71.
57. In the *Eirenarcha* Lambarde explains that the JPs, when holding sessions, customarily "commaund, that the *Enqueste* shall take no *Billes,* but suche as the *Justices* themselves have firste perused: Howbeit, if the *Enquest* do the contrarie, it is good ynoughe, so long as their bils doe carrie sufficient forme and matter with them." Lambarde 384. The assize judges exercised a like power of review over bills submitted to the grand jury at gaol delivery. The cryer proclaimed: "All manner of persons that have any Bills of Indictment to put unto the great Inquest, put them into the Court first, that my Lords the Kings [*sic*] Justices may peruse them, or else they shall not be received." T. W., *The Clerk of Assize, Judges-Marshall, and Cryer* (London, 1660) 6.
58. Arguably, the unconcern with felony in these speeches reflects no more than the decline in quarter sessions' trial jurisdiction over felony, discussed in Section A of this chapter. However, quarter sessions remained competent to receive presentments for felony which would be remitted for trial to gaol delivery. Nor is it reasonable to think that the JPs expected the jurors to leave cases of serious crime unreported pending the convening of another court. The explanation is not the decline of the justices' trial powers, but the enhancement of their pretrial powers. The community no longer informed collectively through presentment, but individually (as bringers) to the investigating magistrate.
59. Supra, pages 75–76.
60. Lambarde 434 (italics in original).

tion is "to enforme the *Jurie* towardes an Enditement onelie, in so muche as the parties are bounde to give the matter of them in evidence *Viva voce,* when the Triall shall bee." [61] That is to say, Marian examination has largely displaced the jury of accusation, but not the jury of trial. The instrumental role in accusation has passed from the jury of accusation to the JPs. To the parallel problem of the ignorance and inactivity of the trial jury the Marian scheme was responding more indirectly: witnesses were to be discovered and bound over to testify at trial. In this way the trial jury was buttressed just when the jury of accusation was being ceremonialized.

The Marian statutes helped perpetuate jury trial. They gave the petty jury a new lease on life by systematizing the gathering of evidence and its production at oral public jury trial—at a point in time when the petty jury was as vulnerable to displacement as the grand jury. The Continental history will remind us that the Marian solution was not inevitable. We will have occasion to study the fate of the *Schöffen* court in the final *Rechttag* procedure of the German Carolina, to see how and why it came to be relegated to a ceremonial station, confirming in ritual the results of an externalized investigation and judgment. That development will underline something of the rationale in England for perpetuating the jury as trier-of-fact: its inexpensiveness and its efficiency compared with a wholly professional judiciary which was constricted by rigorous standards of proof and, in the French version, by a hierarchy of appellate review.

What seems noteworthy is that contemporaries understood something of the evidentiary import of the Marian statutes. The earliest authority is Staunford's *Les Plees del Coron* (1557).[62] His brief chapter on "Evidens" begins with the proposition for which it was subsequently cited:[63] *"A Doner evidence: chescun serra admitte pur le Roy."* [64] (To give evidence, anyone will be admitted for the king.) That sentence is immediately followed by a compressed statement of the Marian bail statute's provision that *"chescun justice de Quorum, devant que il baila ascun prisoner, prendra son examination ou informacion del fact, et le certefiera al prochein general gaole delivere . . . .*[65] (Each justice of the

61. Id. (italics in original).

62. [W. Staunford,] *Les Plees del Coron: divisees in plusiours titles & common lieux* (London, 1557).

63. See Dalton 262.

64. Staunford (supra, note 62) fol. 163 (italics in original).

65. Id. (italics in original).

quorum, before he bails any prisoner, shall take his examination or information of the fact, and certify it to the next general gaol delivery.) Then follows, in English, the verbatim text of the Marian committal statute.[66] The chapter concludes with a recital of the statutes specially regulating the number of witnesses in cases of treason.[67]

Staunford's curt chapter interests us for two reasons. First, in its paucity of rule it confirms the almost total lack of a law of criminal evidence up to the Marian years.[68] Second, in the primacy it gives to the Marian committal statute, it shows that contemporaries perceived the essential purpose of the Marian scheme: organizing the giving of evidence for the king at jury trial.

When, however, some decades of practice under the Marian statutes had elapsed, this organized production of prosecution testimony began to give rise to a true law of evidence. The still fragmentary and elementary rules of evidence in Dalton's treatise (1618) are set forth in a revealing way, as a digression from the substantial account of the JPs' examination practice under the Marian statutes. Because "[t]he Justices of peace have authoritie (by the wordes of the [committal] statute) to bind by Recognizance all such as do declare any thing materiall to prove the felony, to give evidence against the offendor . . . ," [69] Dalton has thought to set out rule on the subject. Hence he begins, notwithstanding the JPs' Marian authority, "the wife is not to be bound to give evidence, nor to be examined against her husband . . . ," which is said to be a concession to "the lawes of God . . . ." [70] On the other hand, Dalton recounts, two children were examined against their mother in preparation for a witch trial at Lancaster Assizes in 1612; the depositions were read in evidence and one of the two testified against the mother at the trial.[71] Dalton collects other disqualifications: conflicting evidence of accused accomplices; the remainder of the testimony of one who has been proven to

66. Id. fol. 163–163ᵛ. The opening part of the Preamble (which recites the contents of the bail statute) Staunford omits, since he has just supplied his own compressed summary of the bail statute.

67. Id. fol. 163ᵛ–164ᵛ.

68. Although elsewhere in the book one finds matters we deem evidentiary (e.g., interspousal immunity, id. fol. 26ᵛ).

69. Dalton 261.

70. Id.

71. Id. The examination documents were published together with trial narratives in 1613. Dalton cites to that volume, of which there is a record society edition: T. Potts, *Discovery of Witches in the County of Lancaster* (J. Crossley, ed.) (Chetham Society, 1845).

have perjured himself in another portion; the testimony of a perjurer who has received a royal pardon; and the testimony of a convicted forger.[72]

Dalton conflates the law of evidence with the law of examination,[73] suggesting that the Marian development of systematic production of prosecution witnesses may have helped pressure the formation of rules of evidence. The Marian scheme became the occasion for considering which witnesses ought to be excluded, and which ought to suffer in credibility. It thus raised an issue which the medieval system of self-informing juries had largely submerged. The theory, boastfully reasserted by Fortescue as late as the 1460s,[74] was that the jurors were themselves the witnesses. That left little room for rules about witness testimony, apart from the rules of juror selection. The Marian statutes recognized the sixteenth-century reality that the jury had effectively become a panel of lay judges, while the justices of the peace had assumed the direction of the active informing role. That differentiation and specialization of function made possible the formation of the law of evidence, for it exposed the jury as but a panel of nonprofessional fact-finders, informed through the efforts of another group of laymen, the magistrates. This was a situation which invited the elaboration of increasingly detailed rules of jury control—rules of evidence—by the assize judges, to whose job the task of jury control had long been incident. These rules were at

72. Dalton 261. The text continues, at 262:

> But if one be brought before a Justice upon suspition of felony, although the information against the prisoner shalbe by such witnesses, yet it seemeth safest for the King, and to binde them over to give evidence, &c. and to commit the partie suspected. And upon the triall to informe the Justices of gaole delivery, concerning the credit of those witnesses.

This advice to the JPs to err in favor of evidence-gathering, and to leave the decision on (admissibility or) credit to the judge at gaol delivery, is in fact limited by the opening phrase. It is when a suspect has been "brought" to the JP on private accusation that it is "safest" for the JP to examine, commit, and bind over. This is therefore the evidence-gathering consequence of the insistent rule, noted supra, pages 7–8, which denied to the justices the power to discharge persons already accused of felony, however flimsy the case.

Where, however, the JP was investigating on his own initiative rather than examining persons "brought," the decision on whether to build a case inevitably lay within his discretion. In that situation Dalton's instructions on the nascent law of evidence could spare the JP from working up an untenable prosecution, by warning him what proofs the trial court would be unlikely to allow or encourage.

73. It is a notion which long persists. Even after the law of evidence had developed to the extent that it could inspire its first treatise, W. Nelson's *The Law of Evidence* (London, 1717), G. Jacob's *The Modern Justice* (3rd ed., London, 1720) at 175–179 was continuing its composite entry "Evidence and Examination."

74. See Thayer (supra, note 47) at 132 ff.

once understood to relate back to the JP's examination function, since they told him which witnesses to avoid, or at least to avoid emphasizing. In Dalton's treatise they were expressed as limits or caveats upon the examination power; and in this way the law of evidence in its rudimentary state is found secreted in the justices' examination practice.

We conclude with a final suggestion about the nexus between examination and evidence at jury trial. As long as the jury was self-informing, there was little need for a courtroom proceeding to enlighten the jury. The jury came to court more to speak than to listen. But the metamorphosis of the jury into a passive trier-of-fact required that oral public jury trial become an instructional proceeding for the purpose of informing the jury's verdict. The particular form taken by this proceeding resembles rather strongly the process of examination before the justices of the peace. We still use the term "examination" in the dual sense which it had acquired by the time of Sir Thomas Smith: to mean pretrial interrogation, and to describe "examination" and "cross-examination" of witnesses at trial. It may have been the case that our trial proceeding developed to some extent in imitation of the earlier practice of the justices. Examination of individual defendants and witnesses became a regular feature of ordinary criminal law in the fifteenth century in the series of pre-Marian statutes. The technique was particularly well-suited to its purpose in those statutes: it enabled the magistrates to inform themselves for the exercise of their own summary powers in cases of lesser crime. In the next century in cases where private prosecution faltered, public jury trial for felony began to resemble a magistrate's examination restaged for the benefit of an audience of jurors. A JP who had informed himself in advance by having conducted the Marian pretrial examination of the defendant and the witnesses now reenacted material parts of his pretrial investigation by interrogating substantially the same persons in the presence of the jury.

PART II Inquisitionsprozess

CHAPTER 6 Roman-Canon Inquisitionsprozess

By the middle of the sixteenth century the major Continental legal systems exhibit a set of common characteristics of criminal procedure. Important dissimilarities persist as well, but the resemblances are for present purposes in view. These features share a common association with the Roman-canon prototype, whose outline had matured in the church courts by the end of the thirteenth century. They take the name *Inquisitionsprozess* from the leading German scholarship. By the sixteenth century Roman-can Inquisitionsprozess is visible nearly everywhere one would think to look: Spain (prominently in Aragon[1]), Italy,[2] remotely even in Sweden.[3] In three countries there is legislation of special preeminence: the *Constitutio Criminalis Carolina* of 1532 in the German Empire, the *ordonnance royale* of 1539 in France, and the *ordonnance criminelle* of 1570 in the Spanish Netherlands.[4] Largely on account of its date, the Spanish-Dutch code falls outside the present study.[5] It followed the English Marian statutes by fifteen years, whereas

1. See especially the 1521 ordinance under Ferdinand in *Fueros de Aragon* (Saragossa, 1517 and later; unpaginated) (Göttingen University copy: Jus. Statut./XIII/3400).

2. E.g., in Piedmont-Savoy: *Libro quarto delle cause criminali, et il modo di proceder in esse* (Vercelli, 1566).

3. See G. Schmidt, *Die Richterregeln des Olavus Petri: Ihre Bedeutung im allgemeinen und für die Entwicklung des schwedischen Strafprozessrechts vom 14. bis 16. Jahrhundert* (Göttingen, 1966).

4. Coing, for example, identifies both the German and the Spanish-Dutch statutes among the prominent forerunners of European codification. H. Coing, "Die europäische Privatrechtsgeschichte der neueren Zeit als einheitliches Forschungsgebiet: Probleme und Aufbau," *Ius Commune* 1:1, 16–17 (1967). The French statute is well known, most notably through Esmein's account. A. Esmein, *Histoire de la procédure criminelle en France, et spécialement de la procédure inquisitoire depuis le XIIIe siècle jusqu'à nos jours* (Paris, 1882) [hereafter cited as Esmein], substantially reproduced as *A History of Continental Criminal Procedure with Special Reference to France* (Continental Legal History Series, vol. V; J. Simpson, trans.) (Boston, 1913).

5. See the account given in M. G. Nypels, *Les ordonnances criminelles de Philippe II* (Brussels, 1856). An extensive discussion appears in E. Poullet, *Histoire du droit pénal dans le duché de Brabant* (Brussels, 1870) 163–226. For the statutory texts in both French and Dutch see B. Voorda, *De Crimineele Ordonnantien van Koning Philips van Spanje* . . . (Leiden, 1792) 3–73.

the French and German legislation of the 1530s was already influential in the Marian years. The following chapters study these two statutes in detail; English translations are provided in Appendixes B and C.

The German and French statutes are worthy of comparative study in their own right. Each was conditioned by its own historical milieu, the matrix of legal and social institutions into which it was set. Awareness of these contexts will illumine much within the statute books. Yet it happens that still more is at stake in an examination of the antecedent history than these familiar concerns of the student of legislation. For the English reception argument hints at a view of the Continental history which it is important to question. When Holdsworth speaks of "those new and effective codes of procedure with which the modern European states were arming themselves,"[6] the implication is that the content of the statutes was new to the enacting states, hence that the absorption of inquisitorial institutions was a recent occurrence. What turns on this point, in part, is the plausibility of English reception. English reception theory posits a sudden and severe break with the indigenous past. The theory finds helpful the belief that a similar break was contemporaneously effected on the Continent. Were it not, then the advocate of reception must contend that there occurred in Tudor England a more radical break with the indigenous legal tradition than on the Continent, despite the more evident continuity in English legal institutions.

Inquisitorial procedure is customarily contrasted with accusatorial; that is, one of the principal characteristics of Inquisitionsprozess is the mode of initiation. The private complainant still in theory instigates and conducts the criminal prosecution in England. In the classical view "[t]he essential difference between pure accusatorial and inquisitorial procedure consists in this, that in the former the injured party pursues his rights . . . . In inquisitorial procedure, on the other hand, the state prosecutes crime . . . ."[7] Modern scholarship has deemphasized this distinction between private and public modes of initiation. What is called Inquisitionsprozess could and did flourish in legal systems which

6. Holdsworth V 169–170. Apart from the French statute (which he knew through Simpson's translation of Esmein), Holdsworth does not identify the "codes" he has in mind.

7. F. A. Biener, *Beiträge zu der Geschichte des Inquisitionsprocesses und der Geschworenengerichte* (Leipzig, 1827) 8–9.

continued to permit private as well as official prosecution.[8] Historians today attribute to Inquisitionsprozess two cardinal and interconnected features, both evident in the sixteenth-century codes. The one, called *Offizialmaxime*[9] or *Offizialprinzip*,[10] parallels the idea of official initiation upon which earlier scholars generally seized; what is meant, however, is officialization of all the important phases *except* initiation. Eberhard Schmidt formulates Offizialmaxime as "the duty of governmental organs to conduct the entire proceeding ex officio, by virtue of office."[11] Where the mode of initiation was reduced to a formalism, lacking functional importance to the conduct of the prosecution, it mattered not whether it too was officialized or left in private hands.

The other dominant element, *Instruktionsmaxime,* refers to the duty of these organs "themselves to investigate judicially *(instruieren)*[12] and to establish the substantive facts and the objective truth."[13] These two features alone delimit Inquisitionsprozess; "Where both these elements conjoin, Inquisitionsprozess stands before us."[14] Inquisitionsprozess involves, therefore, definite ideas not only about who should conduct the criminal process, but about how he should go about it. For instruktionsmaxime is primarily concerned with the nature of judicial proof. In contradistinction to the nonrational proofs of ancient Germanic law, it represents the view that the object of criminal procedure is to permit a judgment to be made about the authorship of criminal acts, based upon a rational inquiry into the facts and circumstances. The crux of Inquisitionsprozess is that an officer of the state, typically a judge, is made responsible for investigating and assembling evidence upon which to rest rational judgment. Schmidt's summary:[15]

8. It will be remarked (infra, pages 177–178) that the Carolina in Germany exemplified this duality.

9. E. Schmidt, *Einführung in die Geschichte der deutschen Strafrechtspflege* (3d ed., Göttingen, 1965) 86 [hereafter cited as Schmidt, *Einführung*].

10. R. W. Millar, "The Formative Principles of Civil Procedure" in A. Engelmann and R. W. Millar, *A History of Continental Civil Procedure* (Continental Legal History Series, vol. VII) (Boston, 1927) 16.

11. Schmidt, *Einführung* 86.

12. The German word corresponds to the French *instruire,* noun form *instruction.* "The use of the term 'judicial investigation,' rather than 'investigation,' as a rendering of the French 'instruction' in relation to criminal procedure and, thus, as characterizing the Continental principle of criminal prosecution, originated with Professor Wigmore." Millar (supra, note 10) at 13.

13. Schmidt, *Einführung* 86–87.

14. Id. at 87.

15. E. Schmidt, *Inquisitionsprozess und Rezeption* (Leipzig, 1940) 9 [hereafter cited as Schmidt, *Inquisitionsprozess*]. This work originally appeared, differently

The essence of this Inquisitionsprozess consists in this, that public initiative tries from the appearance of the first signs of suspicion in the "case" to clarify things in the sense of investigating the substantive truth. The judge appears here as the governmental organ principally concerned. His task is to take the whole proceeding in hand with full responsibility for justice and by his own initiative to assemble the grounds for decision *(Urteilsgrundlage)* in the form of a comprehensive factual investigation. This picture of Inquisitionsprozess is offered us in numerous legislative acts from the sixteenth to the nineteenth centuries.

This is a bare-bones description of Inquisitionsprozess, one we shall flesh out considerably in looking at the detail of the sixteenth-century statutes. In particular, it does not emphasize the role of torture and confession, features endemic to Inquisitionsprozess for most of its long history and not severed until the eighteenth century. But the tortured confession was known before and apart from Inquisitionsprozess; and conversely, Inquisitionsprozess as it is now understood survived the eighteenth- and nineteenth-century reforms to live on in the modern Continental criminal procedural systems.

In the context of the present study, we should note the remoteness of Inquisitionsprozess from the formal English procedure for serious crime, especially before the Marian statutes of 1554–1555. Prior to that time, Offizialprinzip, in the sense of the continuing responsibility of an officer of the state to investigate upon suspicion of crime and to build the case against the accused, has not been acknowledged. The characteristic mode of prosecution was nonofficial. Even later, the binding-over-to-prosecute which the Marian committal statute required, together with the persistence of jury trial, continued to emphasize nonofficialization. It was nearly the contrary of what Eberhard Schmidt defines as Offizialmaxime—"the duty of governmental organs to conduct the entire proceeding ex officio . . . ."[16] Nor had English process any developed analogue to Instruktionsmaxime. The firm basing of judgment upon rational proofs, to the extent it is today present in our criminal law, is mostly a product of the law of criminal evidence—the law of jury control—which was fragmentary into the eighteenth century. The trial jury had been

paginated, in *Festschrift der Leipziger Juristenfakultät für Heinrich Siber*. Citation to the work in the present study is to the separate print, not to the Siber Festschrift.

16. Supra, note 11.

the sudden successor to the ordeals. "Like the ordeals, the jury also was inscrutable."[17]

It has never been doubted that the mature Inquisitionsprozess which appears in the sixteenth-century statutes in Germany, France, and elsewhere on the Continent was derived from the system developed by the Roman church, principally in the thirteenth century, and brought to a very high level of sophistication in the late Middle Ages in the practice of the church and of the North Italian city-states. More debatable, particularly with regard to Germany, has been the timing and the significance of this reception—whether the Roman-canon doctrine which found its way into the Carolina was really novel, ousting the indigenous procedure, or whether it constituted merely a refinement of an already-developed, indigenous inquisitorial procedure.

That the church should have played so central a role in the development of criminal procedure strikes the modern eye as curious and merits a word of explanation. Ecclesiastical criminal jurisdiction was in fact vast. It was also dynamic, expanding with the temporal power of the church in the early and high Middle Ages, receding upon the rise of the late medieval monarchies. The controversy between Becket and Henry II concerning the jurisdiction of the church courts over criminous clerks had an equally serious and only slightly less dramatic counterpart on the Continent, most notably in France.

At its apogee, ecclesiastical jurisdiction seemed nearly limitless. The church courts rested their claims of competence upon two bases, *ratione personae* (by virtue of person) and *ratione materiae* (by virtue of subject matter), roughly status and transaction. Ratione personae meant for the most part the jurisdiction over clerics. The position as Gratian summarized it in the twelfth century was complete immunity from lay process, coupled with positive disability to instigate or participate in lay process, as much for the least cleric as for bishops and metropolitans. A few limits were admitted in the course of the thirteenth and fourteenth centuries. Clerics of minor orders who led lives incompatible with priestly status (who married, for example, or became merchants) could

17. T. F. T. Plucknett, *Edward I and Criminal Law* (Cambridge, 1960) 75. "Of the actual conduct of a trial we know almost nothing before the sixteenth century, not nearly enough until the eighteenth. How the jury informed itself or was informed, how rules of evidence emerged, when and in what detail directions were given by the justices, these are things we do not know." S. F. C. Milsom, *Historical Foundations of the Common Law* (London, 1969) 360.

be excluded from the protection. Otherwise, the immunity was not waivable. It was less a right in the cleric than in the church. Jurisdiction ratione personae also extended to a few classes of nonclerical persons (wards, orphans, widows).

The other basis of jurisdiction, ratione materiae, was the more potent—theoretically all but infinite. For ratione materiae meant largely *ratione peccati* (by virtue of sin). The claim was made, most importantly by Boniface VIII, to an ecclesiastical criminal jurisdiction coterminous with sin. And since all crime is sinful, in theory none lay beyond the purview of the church courts. The church did not attempt to implement that claim, to monopolize criminal jurisdiction to the exclusion of the secular authorities. Nevertheless, over special categories of sin-crime—the more egregious offenses against the faith (heresy and sorcery), offenses against marriage, offenses against church property, simony—there was for a time a serious claim to exclusive jurisdiction.[18] Such was the range and volume of criminal law business that needed proceduralization in the high Middle Ages.

The evolution of Roman-canon Inquisitionsprozess was roughly contemporaneous with that of the juries in England. Both were responses to the undermining of the older private procedure which had held more or less universal sway in the Germanic West. "Between 1100 and 1200 the modes of proof which had prevailed for centuries went through a crisis which would eventually lead to their disappearance."[19] The decisive prohibition of the Fourth Lateran Council in 1215, reinforced by decretal of Honorius III in 1222, eliminated the ordeals from church practice, and effectively from secular courts as well.[20]

18. P. Fournier, *Les officialités au moyen age* (Paris, 1880) 233–290; A. Dumas, "Juridiction ecclésiastique," in *Dictionnaire de droit canonique* (Paris, 1957) VI columns 236–283.

19. R. van Caenegem, "The Law of Evidence in the Twelfth Century: European Perspectives and Intellectual Background," in *Proceedings of the Second International Congress of Medieval Canon Law* (Vatican City, 1965) 297.

20. J. W. Baldwin, "The Intellectual Preparation for the Canon of 1215 against Ordeals," *Speculum* 36:613, 615 (1961). The prohibition affected secular courts whether it intended to or not. For one thing, church court practice had long been an influential model for secular jurisdictions. More important was that the priests were forbidden to continue their former role in the ceremonies of secular trial. Withdrawal of the priest from procuring the judgment of God precipitated the crisis in the secular legal systems. In England, for example, the dislocation was all but instant. See F. Pollock and F. W. Maitland, *The History of English Law* (2d ed., Cambridge, 1898) II 599 and n. 5; Milsom (supra, note 17) at 359 ("The whole mechanism turned upon the invocation of the priest . . . . It is today impossible to imagine the practical and intellectual disarray caused by this decision [of the Lateran Council].")

Criticism of the ordeals had been growing steadily through the twelfth century, particularly in the latter half.[21] In a recent essay the Belgian scholar van Caenegem has sketched the relations of this phenomenon to the intellectual and political movements of the time beyond the legal systems. His leitmotif is that "the history of evidence is connected with that of governmental institutions, with the political structure and the forms of government."[22] The abolition of the ordeals could have occurred only when alternatives were in sight. The Roman-canon alternative, nascent Inquisitionsprozess (officialized prosecution and rational judgment), mirrored the ongoing officialization and rationalization of government and public life. These "great changes . . . were essentially a process of rationalization . . . ,"[23] and as such were part of the "astounding and miraculous"[24] rationalization of government which characterized what has elsewhere been called the "twelfth century Renaissance."[25]

Although these developments were more visible in ecclesiastical than in secular government (since these years saw the acme of papal government), van Caenegem stresses "how alike [they] . . . were in Church and State . . . ."[26] Among them was increasing centralization, especially of judicial life. The "tremendous expansion [of] the judicial functions of the Roman curia"[27] and the rise of the ecclesiastical judicial corps, the ordinaries, had counterparts in several secular jurisdictions, of which "the most remarkable was perhaps the rise of the court of common pleas in England with its ever-widening national jurisdiction at the expense of local and regional, i.e. feudal and county courts."[28] With centralization came internal structural differentiation: the courts and the judicial corps and the chanceries crystallized.[29] The primitive bureaucracies accelerated a "process of 'Verschriftlichung', of increased use of writing, [which] was not confined to the sphere of administration. It

21. Admirably recounted in Baldwin's essay (supra, note 20).

22. Van Caenegem (supra, note 19) at 299. Compare the theme of a recent comparative study of modern European civil procedural systems: M. Cappelletti, *Processo e Ideologie* (Bologna, 1969).

23. Van Caenegem (supra, note 19) at 300.

24. Id.

25. C. H. Haskins, *The Renaissance of the Twelfth Century* (Cambridge, Mass., 1927).

26. Van Caenegem (supra, note 19) at 299.

27. Id. at 300.

28. Id. at 301.

29. Id. at 302–303.

affected the the practice of the law courts, and especially the rise of written evidence."[30]

Dissatisfaction with the ordeals had numerous grounds. The contemporary tracts objected that the old proofs were barbarous, arbitrary, inefficient, unjust, and susceptible to extortive or otherwise oppressive misemployment. The theologians came full circle when the *Gottesurteil* was denounced for its sinfulness in tempting God.[31] The defects were as old as the ordeals themselves. The complaints could come to expression in the twelfth century because new forces were highlighting the clumsiness of the ordeals. Stronger governments, papal and monarchical, than had been seen since the Franks were emerging. Restoration of order, suppression of crime, was fundamental to their mission. Not only could an age of intellectual revival perceive the weaknesses of the ordeals, it could begin to contemplate alternatives. Van Caenegem reports what appear to be steps toward a procedure of "rational inquiry into the truth of the matter"[32] in lieu of the ordeals in twelfth-century Flanders and Hainaut. "And we find the king of England introducing the jury of twelve knights or twelve lawful men as principal mode of proof in the realm, reducing the old irrational techniques to a very inferior status."[33]

Van Caenegem's views on the nexus between the demise of the ordeals and the governmental and intellectual movements of the age are worthy of summary here because Inquisitionsprozess did appear as successor to the older system of proofs. Although there were probably some earlier antecedents, and a vast later elaboration, the decisive innovations came in the papacy of Innocent III (1198–1216). The Fourth Lateran Council of 1215, which proscribed the ordeal, prescribed the *inquisitio* (as one mode of criminal procedure alongside surviving older ones). This general legislation had been preceded by a series of decretals—essentially papal adjudication—from 1198 on, exhibiting in hesitant form the fundamentals of ex officio and rational process for particular cases.[34]

30. Id. at 303.

31. Baldwin (supra, note 20) at 628–629, reciting the argument of Petrus Cantor's tract *Verbum Abbreviatum* (Paris, 1190).

32. Van Caenegem (supra, note 19) at 309; cf. R. van Caenegem, *Geschiedenis van het Strafprocesrecht in Vlaanderen van de XIe tot de XIVe eeuw (Avec résume français)* (Brussels, 1956) 326–327.

33. Van Caenegem (supra, note 19) at 309–310; cf. Pollock and Maitland (supra, note 20) at II 603–604.

34. R. Schmidt, "Der Herkunft des Inquisitionsprozesses," in *Festschrift der Albrecht-Ludwigs-Universität in Freiburg zum fünfzigjährigen Regierungs-Jubiläum*

Toward the middle of the thirteenth century inquisitorial procedure seems to have shed much of its character as an exceptional process. The most important step toward its normalization was a relaxation of the standard of *infamia*, the degree of suspicion necessary for the official to initiate proceedings in lieu of the former private complaint. Investigation under torture was confirmed.[35] The Inquisitionsprozess which enters Durantis' *Speculum Judiciale* (1271) is elaborate and unmistakable. Rather parallel development occurred in the practice of the statutists of the North Italian city-states—sometimes, indeed, in advance of the canonist practice.[36]

There is a special reason why the church played so predominant a role in the development of the new criminal process: "the enormous spread of heresy during the twelfth century."[37] It ought not to surprise us that the rationalism of an age which came to doubt divine judgment in the courts might undermine still more of what had been claimed for Providence. The great heretical movements[38] defied effective repression through the older procedures. "Of all the others the crime of heresy was the most difficult to discover and to prove . . . ."[39] There was no injured private victim to shoulder the load of prosecution. Moreover, the problem of detection was severe. "In the absence of overt acts it was difficult to reach the secret thoughts of the sectary. Trained experts were needed whose sole business it should be to unearth the offenders and extort a confession of their guilt."[40] The heresy inquisition tended, therefore, to exhibit in exaggerated manner the characteristics of Inquisitionsprozess —official instead of private process, and rational rather than ritual proofs and evidence-gathering. The heresy inquisition soon spun off from the main Roman-canon process it had helped to inspire (already in the thir-

seiner königlichen Hoheit des Grossherzogs Friedrich (Freiburg/Breisgau, 1902) 65, 84–88; P. Hinschius, *System des katholischen Kirchenrechts mit besonderer Rücksicht auf Deutschland* (Berlin, 1895) V 350 ff.; cf. Biener (supra, note 7) at 38 ff.

35. P. Fiorelli, *La tortura giudiziaria nel diritto comune* (Milan, 1953) I 79–80; R. von Hippel, *Deutsches Strafrecht* (Berlin, 1925) 88 n. 1 [hereafter cited as von Hippel]. See also Esmein 77; Fournier (supra, note 18) at 280–281.

36. R. Schmidt (supra, note 34) at 89–91. Comparable to Durantis was the statutist Gandinus. See H. Kantorowicz, *Albertus Gandinus und das Strafrecht der Scholastik*, I and II (Berlin and Leipzig, 1907, 1926).

37. H. C. Lea, *A History of the Inquisition of the Middle Ages* (New York, 1888) I 305.

38. See generally id. at 57–208; A. S. Turberville, *Medieval Heresy and the Inquisition* (London, 1920).

39. Lea (supra, note 37) at I 305.

40. Id. at I 318.

teenth century) and was separately institutionalized with the mendicant orders who supplemented the ordinary almost to the point of supplanting him.[41]

Roman-canon Inquisitionsprozess was considerably more canon than Roman in its sources. That is, the notoriously ill-developed[42] Justinianian sources could not and did not sustain the extensive medieval elaboration. There has been considerable controversy about whether certain institutions from the Germanic, particularly Frankish, past might have survived in curious ways to have inspired Innocent III and the Italians of the thirteenth century. Perhaps the best known of these theories is Richard Schmidt's conjecture that Carolingian *inquisitio* had been salvaged by the Normans and transmitted by them to Sicily, from whence it met the attention of Innocent III.[43] On the other side is the evidence of broad movement toward Inquisitionsprozess in the late twelfth century—for example, in Hainaut and Flanders as well as in Rome and North Italy—the point being that the ongoing rationalization of judicial and governmental procedures was highly likely to uncover independently the efficiency of officialized investigation and rational evaluation of the evidence.

More important than this sort of question about the parentage of the stimulus to Inquisitionsprozess is the fact that the subsequent development through the thirteenth century and beyond took place within the learned Roman-canon tradition. The principles of the new procedure were formulated in terms of the tendencies or biases of Roman law, above all the Justinianian predilection for documentary proof. By the time the ordeals were abolished, there was a formed alternative in civil as well as criminal procedure. "[T]he canonists by 1215 had generally adopted the Romanist emphasis on written instruments and witnesses as principal means of proof."[44]

The working out of rational procedure in the thirteenth century made possible an extensive learned development of substantive criminal

41. Id. at I 328 ff., 399 ff.; Fournier (supra, note 18) at 278–281.

42. See, e.g., F. Wieacker, *Privatrechtsgeschichte der Neuzeit* (2d ed., Göttingen, 1967) 136–137; W. Ullmann, "Some Medieval Principles of Criminal Procedure," *Juridical Review* 59:1, 2–3 (1947).

43. R. Schmidt (supra, note 34) at 107 ff. Many of the prominent *Germanisten* have had competing theories of this sort. See the list in Schmidt, *Inquisitionsprozess* 9 n. 18.

44. Baldwin (supra, note 20) at 617.

law—offense definition and aspects of "the general part"[45]—particularly in the fourteenth century. Hence, when the reception of Italian jurisprudence became significant in Germany at the end of the fifteenth and the beginning of the sixteenth centuries, the medieval tradition[46] had long since overcome the deficiencies of the Justinianian sources and had evolved a comprehensive and learned body of criminal law and procedure.

45. The term is known in English, e.g., G. Williams, *Criminal Law: The General Part* (2d ed., London, 1961), but the notion is basically Continental. What is meant is the set of issues about criminal liability which inhere regardless of the particular crime—mens rea, actus reus, causation, liability for inchoate crimes, defenses, mitigation, and so forth.

46. See generally W. Ullmann, "Some Medieval Principles of Criminal Procedure," (supra, note 42) at 1; W. Ullmann, "Reflections on Medieval Torture," *Juridical Review* 56:123 (1944); G. Dahm, *Das Strafrecht Italiens im ausgehenden Mittelalter* (Berlin and Leipzig, 1931). On later developments see F. Schaffstein, *Die europäische Strafrechtswissenschaft im Zeitalter des Humanismus* (Göttingen, 1954); L. Chevailler, "Droit roman et droit pénal dans la doctrine du XVIe siècle," in *Studi in memoria di Paolo Koschaker* (Milan, 1954) II 95.

CHAPTER 7 The German Empire before the Carolina

The *Constitutio Criminalis Carolina* of 1532 was the first in time of the major criminal procedural codes of the sixteenth century. It was also the most copious. The procedural sections of the Carolina number nearly 140 paragraphs, compared with about 30 in the French *ordonnance royale* of 1539 and 75 in the Spanish Netherlands *ordonnance* of 1570. But the Carolina was also the most influential, both in space and time. It spread to the limits of the German Empire and far beyond.[1] Alone of the three it was repeatedly translated—into French,[2] Latin,[3] Polish,[4] Niederdeutsch,[5] and Russian.[6] In the 1870s, long years after the French and Spanish Netherlands codes had been superseded, there were German courts basing decisions upon the Carolina.[7] Nor do the other statutes occupy in their own national legal traditions the centrality of the Carolina for the Germans. The very language of the Carolina has been offered up for celebration. Said Savigny: "I know no German statute of the 18th century which could be compared with the [Carolina] in

1. See, for example, A. Meier, *Die Geltung der Peinlichen Gerichtsordnung Kaiser Karls V. im Gebiete der heutigen Schweiz* (Bern, 1910); J. Nagler, "Die Geltung der Carolina in Basel," in *Festschrift zur Feier des 450jährigen Bestehens der Universität Basel* (Basel, 1910) 35–109; A. Baumgärtner, *Die Geltung der Peinlichen Gerichtsordnung Kaiser Karls V. in gemeinen III Bünden* (Bern, 1929); L. Dargun, "Die Reception der Peinlichen Halsgerichtsordnung Kaiser Karls V. in Polen," *Zeitschrift der Savigny-Stiftung für Rechtsgeschichte (germanistische Abteilung)* 10:168 (1889).

2. Editions discussed by E. von Künssberg, Introduction to K. Saueracker, *Wortschatz der Peinlichen Gerichtsordnung Karls V.* (Heidelberg, 1929) 8 n. 32.

3. Id. at 9 n. 36.

4. Id. at 9 n. 33; cf. Dargun (supra, note 1).

5. Von Künssberg (supra, note 2) at 10 nn. 41–42.

6. *Karolina: Ugolovno sudebnoe uloshenie* (Alma-Ata, 1967). In an introduction to this modern edition Professor S. J. Bulatov records that the Carolina was a work of high authority in the literature of pre-Bolshevik criminal procedure. Id. at 4. Peter the Great is said to have studied the Carolina in preparing a code of military law. Id. at 3–4. (I am indebted to Dr. Norbert Reich for this reference, and for translating the introduction.)

7. E. Schmidt, "Die Carolina," *Zeitschrift der Savigny-Stiftung für Rechtsgeschichte (germanistische Abteilung)* 53:1, 34 (1933) [hereafter cited as Schmidt, *Carolina*].

force and power of expression."[8] The importance of the Carolina has made it the subject of a vast body of scholarship[9] which has no counterpart, Continental or English, in historical writing about the criminal process.

For such reasons, reasons internal to the Continental sources themselves, the Carolina would deserve pride of place. Still, there are more compelling grounds for the primacy of the German sources to comparative study. Like England, Germany came almost to the end of the Middle Ages with a native, customary legal tradition substantially undisturbed by Roman law.[10] And like the English, the German legal tradition was one which had entrenched laymen into the administration of the criminal law. Yet Roman-canon criminal procedure was received, ultimately massively, in the sixteenth century, and the Carolina was the decisive event in that reception. For the student of the question of reception in sixteenth-century England, the German history serves—quite uniquely—as a model of actual reception over roughly the same period in a legal system certain of whose features bore pronounced resemblance to the English.

A. GERMAN CRIMINAL PROCEDURE BEFORE THE CAROLINA

1. *The Medieval Origins of German Inquisitionsprozess*

Historians have never doubted that the enactment of the Constitutio Criminalis Carolina constituted the major event in the reception of Roman law (that is, of medieval Italian jurisprudence) into the German criminal process. But a radical change of view in the past generation has overtaken an issue nearly as fundamental: whether the Romanized Carolina introduced Inquisitionsprozess into Germany, or whether it repre-

8. F. C. von Savigny, *Vom Beruf unserer Zeit für Gesetzgebung und Rechtswissenschaft* (Heidelberg, 1814) 52, quoted in G. Radbruch, "Zur Einführung in die Carolina," in *Die Peinliche Gerichtsordnung Karls V. von 1532 (Carolina)* (Reclam ed., Stuttgart, 1949) 13 [hereafter cited as Radbruch].

9. Competent bibliographic compilations appear in Schmidt, *Einführung* 464–465; Radbruch 153–155; and H. Conrad, *Deutsche Rechtsgeschichte* (Karlsruhe, 1962, 1966) I 450, II 416–418.

10. Dawson, *Lay Judges* 94. The nature and scope of Roman law influence in the Middle Ages in Germany is the subject of an exhaustive restatement in the Ius Romanum Medii Aevi project: H. Coing, *Römisches Recht in Deutschland* (I.R.M.A. pt. V:6) (Milan, 1964).

sented simply a *Verwissenschaftlichung*,[11] a scientific or learned recasting of an Inquisitionsprozess already present in the indigenous law. Reception granted, what was received? Inquisitionsprozess where there had been none, or an Italianate version of Inquisitionsprozess where there had been a German one? Into the 1930s there was no serious suggestion of the latter position; today it is entrenched. The revision was the achievement of Eberhard Schmidt; the present account, when it reaches that issue, will follow in the main the organization, the evidence, and (save in one respect) the conclusions of Schmidt's 1940 monograph, *Inquisitionsprozess und Rezeption*.[12] The medieval background is pursued here in some detail both for the light it throws on the Carolina and because it suggests so many parallels to the problems of the English history.

German criminal procedure entered the high Middle Ages a fairly rudimentary system. Its highest ambition was to channel and limit private vengeance. The substantive criminal law understood for its goal either private compensation or private retribution. Its proofs were divine judgment procured through battle, ordeal, oath, and oath-helping. It lacked the sense of serving public or social purposes broader than the conditioning of private struggle. Of course, there had been no time when the notion of a public interest was wholly lacking. Some few offenses (desertion upon the battlefield being the prototype) were perceived to victimize the entire community and were the subject of a communal process.[13] It is also apparent that the Frankish empire had, before its dissolution in the ninth century, been moving toward a public criminal process, initially incident to fiscal administration. The *Rügeverfahren*, perhaps the progenitor of the English jury of presentment, involved a mode of public accusation resting on public power and requiring the intervention of public officers.[14] Individual capitularies hint at the existence of an extraordinary process yet more officialized and explicitly

11. The term made current by F. Wieacker, *Privatrechtsgeschichte der Neuzeit* (2d ed., Göttingen, 1967) 132.

12. Schmidt, *Inquisitionsprozess*, cited supra, Chapter 6, note 15.

13. Tacitus, *Germania* (H. Mattingly, trans.) (Penguin ed., 1948) ch. 12: "One can launch an accusation before the Council or bring a capital charge. The punishment varies to suit the crime. The traitor and deserter are hanged on trees, the coward, the shirker and the unnaturally vicious are drowned in miry swamps under a cover of wattled hurdles." Cited by Schmidt, *Einführung* 25.

14. R. Schmidt (supra, Chapter 6, note 34) at 73–82; H. Brunner, *Die Entstehung der Schwurgerichte* (Berlin, 1872) 84–126.

rational in proofs.[15] In Germany, neither survived the Carolingians. The business of uprooting the Germanic private composition system in favor of a recognizably "criminal" law of public prosecution for public purposes on account of wrongs done to the public—this commences in Germany only in the twelfth century and is not completed in all detail until the *gemeines deutsches Strafrecht* of the seventeenth and eighteenth centuries.[16]

The initial stimulus toward a public process came from the church. The dangers of private warfare, only minimally restrained, magnified themselves appreciably when the reconstruction of society along feudal lines raised up a class of professional warriors. The church began to promulgate the several *Gottesfrieden* (literally, "peace of God"). The earliest stipulated that a "peace," precluding the conduct of feud, would apply to particular persons or to all persons within a particular place. In 1023 appeared the device of general pacification made applicable to all persons for particular days, initially Sundays and holy days. Within fifty years this type of prohibition consumed three-quarters of each calendar year. At the beginning the sanctions for breach, for feuding within these periods, were exclusively ecclesiastical, preeminently excommunication. Late in the eleventh century the participation of secular authorities was won, in order to enforce the Gottesfrieden with secular sanctions.

At roughly the time of the investiture crisis, this sort of ecclesiastical legislation disappeared and was succeeded by the first of the long series of *Landfrieden* (declarations of "territorial peace").[17] More was involved than the displacement of ecclesiastical by secular authority. The unit of pacification became once again territorial, the proscription attaching more to space than to time. The Landfrieden resembled less the modern statute than a nonaggression pact among putative belligerents. The form was not the command of the prince, but the renunciation of force among the participants (though at the instigation of the prince). The sanctions on life and property derived from the sworn compact, rather than from customary law. One feature of the Landfrieden particularly emphasizes their contractual character: individual compacts were valid only for designated periods, two to five years, following which renewal was necessary.[18]

15. Schmidt, *Einführung* 43–45.
16. On periodization see id. at 11–13, 17–18.
17. Id. at 48–50.
18. W. Ebel, *Geschichte der Gesetzgebung in Deutschland* (2d ed., Göttingen, 1958) 47.

The rudiments of recognizable criminal law began to be laid down in the centuries-long course of expansion of the Landfrieden. The compacts became more complex. No longer did they speak solely to the feud. They began to proscribe, with penal sanction, other particularly odious conduct—to begin a primitive offense definition. The first Reichslandfriede of 1103, for example, prescribed the loss of hand or eye for larger thefts, with lesser corporal punishment for lesser thefts.[19] A century later the accretion of offenses in the Reichslandfriede of 1224 had reached most of the basics of criminal law—murder and homicide, rape, wounding, robbery and highway robbery, heresy, and sorcery. Where the cities were involved, the offenses characteristic of an urban setting came to be proscribed—burglary, counterfeiting, adultery, pandering, and blasphemy.[20] By the time of the *Sachsenspiegel* (1221–1224) the notion of general public proscription of serious offenses had been absorbed into the customary law and was no longer dependent solely upon the compacts.[21]

Inescapably there was a procedural concomitant to this "revolution, which developed in the eleventh through thirteenth centuries with the transition from the composition system to the system of criminal sanctions . . . ."[22] For obviously, different processes are needed to vindicate public interests than to channel private interests. The ancient Germanic process had played itself out before a large court of passive laymen, who witnessed ceremonial proofs and were absolved of any investigative duty.[23] Abolition of the ordeals, even where fully implemented, left a panoply of nonrational proofs, above all oath and oath-helping. It was the defense by oath or oath-helper which was so difficult, yet so essential, to overcome. Most of the devices attempted had the effect of narrowing or eliminating the accused's right to defend by oath. For the defense by oath, though entrenched and time-honored, was fundamentally incompatible with an officialized criminal procedure, especially

19. Schmidt, *Einführung* 50–51, 58.

20. Id. at 58–59. Schmidt, *Inquisitionsprozess* 12 and n. 25, repeats His' description of the Reichslandfriede of 1224 and a Saxon Landfriede of 1223 as "*eigentliche Strafgesetzbücher*." R. His, *Das Strafrecht des deutschen Mittelalters* (Weimar, 1920) I 14.

21. E.g., the punishment of death for rape, bk. 3, art. 1, sec. 1. E. von Repgow, *Der Sachsenspiegel* (H. Hirsch, ed.) (Berlin and Leipzig, 1936) 228.

22. Schmidt, *Einführung* 76.

23. Id.

when the defense was claimed by "professional" criminals from without the community.[24]

A single discrete inquisitorial alternative and successor to the old procedures did not harden in Germany until the sixteenth century. In the later Middle Ages when Germany lacked central political direction capable of imposing a unified process, diversity was inevitable. The English presentment system had needed Henry II; the Roman-canon Inquisitionsprozess, Innocent III. There could be no German analogue in the very years of the collapse and dissolution of the monarchy. Instead, there appeared a bewildering variety of procedural techniques. Perhaps the simplest was the notion of substituting an official for a private complainant in an otherwise unaltered proceeding.[25] For many reasons the future could not lie there; in particular, the ancient proofs continued to pertain. However, the idea persisted and came in various places to be coupled with Inquisitionsprozess, so that ceremonial official complaint could serve to trigger the newer inquisitorial procedures.[26] Another device, particularly characteristic of Saxon law, analogized wider classes of defendants to the paradigm of the culprit caught in the act, to whom the old law had itself denied a defense based upon oath.[27] That analogy could not be the basis for a more general reformulation of procedure, which had of necessity to be able to reach unwitnessed crimes.

The notorious *Vemgerichte* in the North were another response.[28] They did not spread south, where there had already appeared the procedure which was to typify the later enforcement of the Landfrieden: the procedure against the *Landschädlichen* (*Verfahren gegen die landschädlichen Leute*).[29] The Landschädlichen were the serious criminals against whom the later Landfrieden were largely directed, exemplified by the robber knight and the peasant vagabond.[30] Landschädlichkeit

24. See id. at 89–90.

25. Id. at 84.

26. See the striking case from Frankfurt (1411), discussed in A. Vogt, "Die Anfänge des Inquisitionsprozesses in Frankfurt am Main," *Zeitschrift der Savigny-Stiftung für Rechtsgeschichte (germanistische Abteilung)* 68:234, 281 (1951).

27. Schmidt, *Einführung* 81, 82.

28. See generally Dawson, *Lay Judges* 99–101; Schmidt, *Einführung* 84–86; H. Finke, "Vemgericht und Inquisition?" in *Historisches Jahrbuch* 11:491 (1890); T. Lindner, *Veme und Inquisition* (Halle, 1893).

29. "[T]he Vemgerichte with their distinctive process served essentially the same mission and purpose as this procedure [against the Landschädlichen] in the South." O. von Zallinger, *Das Verfahren gegen die landschädlichen Leute in Süddeutschland* (Innsbruck, 1895) vi.

30. Schmidt, *Einführung* 82–83. Definitional quibbles persist; see Vogt (supra, note 26) at 262 ff.

was a status. Prove that one was landschädlich, and he lost his right to defend himself by oath; he was effectively assimilated to the culprit caught in the act.[31] Originally, the so-called *Übersiebnungsverfahren* required for conviction that there be several sworn complaints against the accused and that the complainants be possessed of personal knowledge of his deeds. Ad hoc enforcement officials (designated in the Landfrieden) and not private victims or relatives prosecuted. Over time this *Verfahren gegen die landschädlichen Leute* evolved into the *Verfahren auf Leumund*—the "proceeding upon repute." The officials were able to convict by swearing to the evil repute of the accused. The gravamen need not be conduct, but status, repute for dangerousness or harmfulness. Proceeding was summary; death could follow.[32]

The Landfrieden therefore generated not only the transition from private to penal law, but the appearance of corresponding public procedures, however crude. Implicit in both developments was yet another: the end of official passivity, the nascent officialization of crime repression. The Landfrieden imposed enforcement duties upon participating authorities.[33]

We have been speaking in a summary way of the developments in Germany into the late 1200s. It is from about that time that the evidence commences upon which Eberhard Schmidt rested his thesis of medieval Inquisitionsprozess. Schmidt's was a feat of reinterpretation; his sources were hardly novel. To some extent it was a feat of definition, of emphasizing the narrow, rather than the broad, notion of Inquisitionsprozess. He looked beyond the hallowed opposition between accusatorial and inquisitorial modes of initiation and focused on Offizialprinzip and Instrukstionsmaxime as the functional requisites of Inquisitionsprozess.[34] The formulation did not originate with Schmidt; but it was he who first understood its significance to the events of the later Middle Ages. The thesis Schmidt advanced, insofar as it relates to timing, is irrefutable: in the development leading out of the Landfrieden, particularly in the fourteenth and fifteenth centuries, Offizialprinzip and Instruktionsmaxime became commonplace in Germany; with them Inquisi-

31. Schmidt, *Einführung* 82–83.

32. Id. at 83.

33. Vogt (supra, note 26) at 249–254; e.g., the Landfriede concluded in the Wetterau (north of Frankfurt) in 1265, setting up an eight-man enforcement committee. Id. at 251.

34. Schmidt, *Inquisitionsprozess* 7–8.

tionsprozess had arrived. The legislation of the Renaissance confirmed, recast, and Italianized an Inquisitionsprozess which had been demonstrable at least since the middle of the fourteenth century.

There is a subsidiary line of argument—really of assumption—in Schmidt's monograph, which is unproven at best, and in fact probably wrong. It is the proposition that this late medieval Inquisitionsprozess in Germany developed wholly indigenously, "without the influence of foreign legal models."[35] I suggest below that the influence of the church may have been undervalued. This second issue must be kept distinct; it is a matter of sources, not of timing. And what we are initially concerned with is Schmidt's principal thesis of timing—that the German Inquisitionsprozess first formed in the late Middle Ages, not during the high tide of Renaissance reception; hence that Inquisitionsprozess had long preceded the Carolina in Germany.

Schmidt organized his evidence around the two functional concepts of Inquisitionsprozess. Offizialprinzip was the easier to demonstrate from medieval sources. The treaty-like documents of the later Landfrieden not infrequently required enforcement undertakings of the participating authorities.[36] More revealing glimpses of the later activities of municipal officials survive in city records of the fourteenth century. By 1350 a regular arrangement for official prosecution of the Landschädlichen is evidenced, for example in Basel and in Brünn.[37] Prosecution without private complainant, a sure sign of official activity, appears in the records with increasing frequency.[38] Late in the development, the evidence of official prosecution is voluminous and quite unambiguous in the grants of imperial privileges. The privileges, from the later fourteenth and early fifteenth centuries, were issued to the urban authorities and confirmed their practices.[39] They represent the height of central, monarchical participation in the transformation of the criminal process in Germany. Inquisitionsprozess formed in the absence of central direction and control. The imperial privileges came late and served a reinforcing, legitimating function.

Schmidt emphasized "the connection between the development of

35. Id. at 61.
36. Id. at 13–15; see supra, note 33.
37. Schmidt, *Inquisitionsprozess* 16.
38. Id. and n. 46.
39. Id. at 17 n. 52, collecting a half-dozen; cf. id. at 44–46; Schmidt, *Einführung* 88.

Offizialprinzip and the expansion of the concept of things schädliche . . . ."[40] It was a matter of importance, to which we shall return, that the characteristic concern of early official process was the outsider, the criminal from without, the Landschädlichen. The struggle against the criminal from abroad was the wedge, but the new prosecuting officials called into existence for that purpose could not long be held at that line. Their competence to deal with their own citizenry became apparent in the fourteenth, and especially in the early fifteenth, century.[41]

The increasing official responsibility for apprehension and prosecution accompanied a transition to rational modes of proof (Instruktionsmaxime). The ancient proofs were replaced by rational evaluation of the evidence of the circumstances of the crime. It would be pointless for the authorities to conduct rational investigation and thereafter to ignore the results in favor of trial by the ordeal of hot iron or the rote of oath-helpers. The archaic proofs were incompatible with the developing notion that crime offended the public and ought to be prosecuted on behalf of the public by officers of authority. The tension went deeper than the contrast between the rationalism of the new and the formalism of the old. The new public process inescapably undercut certain of the assumptions on which the old rested. The official who prosecuted in the absence of private complaint could not be made to do battle with the accused; his interest was not a personal or a family one, and he was not willing to undergo the highest personal hazard as an incident of (unpaid) community office. Similarly, the Landschädlichen as outsiders lacked the bonds to community presupposed by the whole of the oath and oath-helping system; it was no accident that the heart of the earlier judicial procedures devised against them—the Übersiebnungsverfahren and the Verfahren auf Leumund—was the denial to them of the right to defend by oath. What differentiates the German history of movement away from the archaic proofs from the English or the French or the canon is the lack of central direction. The splintered politics of the thirteenth through the fifteenth centuries prevented systematic reform. The development was groping, confused, occasionally relapsing, as the new and the old competed.[42]

Schmidt's sources depict a steady increase of torture-induced con-

40. Schmidt, *Inquisitionsprozess* 17.
41. Id. at 18–19.
42. Id. at 21.

fessions in Germany in each century from the thirteenth into the sixteenth. Predictably, the earliest sources are skimpy. In the thirteenth century there was a notable reference in the city law of Neustadt (Vienna), circa 1220–1230,[43] and the *Schwabenspiegel* (1275–1276) stipulated a month-long torture.[44] The list lengthens for the first half of the fourteenth century: the use of torture is recorded in Augsburg and Strasbourg in the 1320s, the Strasbourg source emphasizing official participation.[45] A wave of proceedings against Jews in 1348–1349 left particularly firm evidence of officially exacted confessions.[46] Much is special to these cases. The Jews were being blamed for the Black Death (which began in Germany in 1347).[47] The alleged crime was typically clandestine poisoning, for which the "evidence" required seeking out. The plague took so many lives that the sense of community-as-victim was strong. The Jews were an order apart, hence perhaps more easily analogized to the landschädlichen outsiders. These were factors which simplified the resort to Inquisitionsprozess. Says Schmidt of the sources: "One sees before oneself the whole of Inquisitionsprozess: examination conducted in the torture chamber by personnel of the municipal council; questioning of the accused about all the details; repetition of examination following the intervening arrest of accomplices; extraction of confessions with torture, in case the accused was not prepared without the application of force to admit the facts which it was desired to hear from him."[48]

These Jewish cases foreshadowed the next half-century's growth. The period from 1350 to 1400 effectively normalized the tortured confession in the German criminal process, and with it Inquisitionsprozess. A pair of sources[49] from these years are known which counseled against it, but they are quantitatively insignificant and speak as well to the presence of the danger they opposed. Characteristic of these years was

43. Id. at 24–28. Authorities interpret the Neustadt passage variously; see R. Lieberwirth, "Die Aufnahme der Folter in das mittelalterlich-deutsche Strafverfahren: Einleitung," prefacing C. Thomasius, *Ueber die Folter* (R. Lieberwirth, trans.) (Weimar, 1960) 71.

44. Schmidt, *Inquisitionsprozess* 29–30.

45. Id. at 30.

46. Id. at 31–33.

47. "In the middle of the fourteenth century, . . . when the plague of the 'Black Death' broke over Europe, decimating the population and raising the fury against the Jews to its peak, most of the flourishing Jewish settlements were destroyed. There was hardly a German city that did not witness persecution either by expulsion or by burning of its Jews." G. Kisch, *The Jews in Medieval Germany: A Study of Their Legal and Social Status* (Chicago, 1949) 4 (footnote omitted).

48. Schmidt, *Inquisitionsprozess* 32.

49. Id. at 34–36.

the widespread appearance of the investigating commission, a small group of city councilors or Schöffen who attended the actual questioning and torturing and who bore witness to the confession if it were recanted at the final proceedings before the full court.[50] This represented a crucial change not only in court structure, but in criminal procedure as well. The former practice had treated as binding only a confession made in full court—logically enough, since there had been no preliminary stage. The development of questioning before the investigating commission presented an opportunity to validate in full court a confession previously made to the commission. The last apparent instances of refusal to do so are contained in the so-called Magdeburg Questions dating from the end of the fourteenth century, in which confessions made to the commissioners under torture were declared not to preclude the accused from his right to defend by oath before the full court.[51] These were also the last authoritative pronouncements opposing torture. Thereafter the practice became settled in Germany that the accused's oath in full court was no defense to the sworn testimony of the commissioners, themselves members of the court, to the fact of the confession. It was that step which finally made of Inquisitionsprozess a procedure usable against citizens as well as outsiders. The regularization of official witness testimony in this indirect, two-step way was the device which proved capable of cutting off the claims to ancient proofs.[52]

For the fifteenth century the evidence of routinized Inquisitionsprozess is massive.[53] Several features of this evolution merit emphasis:

(1) The connection between officialization and rationalization, between Offizialprinzip and Instruktionsmaxime, was intimate. Official process had to be rational, both because the archaic proofs were not designed for parties who lacked personal interest in the litigation, and because the archaic process was woefully inadequate to protect the social interest in crime control which motivated the official intervention. Correspondingly, rational public process presupposed official administration. Power was needed to apprehend and detain, investigate, punish.

50. Id. at 37–38. For the view that the North German courts, under the influence of Saxon law, were more resistant to torture than those in the South, see H. Dreisbach, *Der Einfluss der Carolina auf die Rechtsprechung norddeutscher Oberhöfe* (Marburg/Lahn, 1969) 53, 56.

51. Schmidt, *Einführung* 96–97.

52. Id. at 100–101; Schmidt, *Inquisitionsprozess* 38, 39–43.

53. Schmidt, *Inquisitionsprozess* 43–53; Vogt (supra, note 26) at 301–304, esp. n. 164, reciting over forty instances of officially conducted torture identifiable from the surviving Frankfurt municipal records of the fifteenth century.

(2) The form of the official intervention is related to the nature and power of the officialdom. Although Schmidt's evidence may in degree be distorted by virtue of the preponderance of municipal as opposed to principality or "territorial" sources which have survived, it is clear that the German procedure developed without central direction and authority in relatively small and weak governments. There could be no counterpart to the Angevin monarchy's decisive imposition of the presentment system. Hence the contest with older procedures lasted for centuries and conditioned the choice of new process. The attractiveness of confession, albeit under torture, was that it avoided the old process. Political power to overcome the archaic process by means less dangerous had simply not developed.

(3) The new procedures worked back upon the officials who instituted them. The development of small two-, three-, or four-man investigating and examining panels within the larger body of Schöffen was, in retrospect, the first step toward the ouster of the Schöffen in favor of a professionalized magistracy. Later stages will be seen in the Carolina. This change in court structure fulfilled a vital precondition for the full reception of learned Italian law in the Renaissance. The differentiation of a smaller, functionally specialized—but still collegial and lay—investigating panel out of the larger Schöffen court was a key transitional phase.[54]

(4) Repeatedly instrumental in the progress of Inquisitionsprozess was the distinction made between outsiders and citizens. The problem of dislodging the archaic process without the help of central authority was awesome. Defense by oath was birthright. Consequently, the new process developed first "for export," for use against the Landschädlichen. The Jewish cases seem to illustrate the same phenomenon. Resistance to procedural innovation is diminished when its objects are conceived as standing apart from the community; such lines blur, once new institutions have been allowed to arise. Dahm described a parallel phenomenon in the North Italian city-states.[55]

54. Schmidt, *Inquisitionsprozess*, does not emphasize these changes, but see Schmidt, *Einführung* 134–135; Vogt (supra, note 26) at 243, 267–269.

55. G. Dahm, *Untersuchungen zur Verfassungs- und Strafrechtsgeschichte der italienischen Stadt im Mittelalter* (Hamburg, 1941), esp. ch. 2, "Das Strafrecht als Kampfmittel gegen die Aussenseiter," at 30–56. Dahm's point is somewhat different—the use of Inquisitionsprozess in the political struggles, first of the cities against the territorial nobility, then of the urban aristocracy against its own widening "proletariat."

(5) Inquisitionsprozess developed slowly. Too many changes were involved in areas of fundamental structural importance for there to be sudden transformation in a legal system of customary law operated by laymen.

2. *The Relation of Roman-Canon Inquisitionsprozess to the Medieval German Procedure*

Schmidt's monograph was principally concerned with describing and dating the appearance of Inquisitionsprozess in Germany. Above all, Schmidt was correcting earlier views about the timing of German Inquisitionsprozess. But there is a second line of argument about the sources: "Inquisitionsprozess developed on German soil in the thirteenth through the fifteenth centuries, both in its fundamental principles and also as regards its methods of carrying out prosecution for crime, without the influence of foreign legal models."[56] In support of that view Schmidt made two points. First, he found it incongruous that "the reception" should be operating to bring in Roman-canon law some two and a half centuries before the turn of the sixteenth century, the customary date of the commencement of full reception.[57] Second, he felt, surely correctly, that the sources were consistent with the view that the use of torture developed indigenously in Germany, perhaps out of affinity to the physically discomforting ordeals.[58]

Schmidt's conclusion about the lack of canon influence is unproven, and the evidence which has so far been adduced implies that the doubt ought to run the other way. Although the point is far from settled, the better view would seem to be that canon process did influence the medieval German. To begin with, Schmidt's argument is overstated. The decisive normalization of Inquisitionsprozess in Schmidt's own opinion came in the period after 1350.[59] Hence the disparity between full Inquisitionsprozess and the customary dating of full reception (in the late 1400s or early 1500s) is of the order of one and a half centuries or less.[60]

56. Schmidt, *Inquisitionsprozess* 61.

57. Id. at 56.

58. Id. at 56–61. Compare P. Fiorelli, *La tortura giudiziaria nel diritto comune* (Milan, 1953) I 3: "Dreadful or not, compelling a person through violence to admit or disclose something against his will is a method of procedure so humanly obvious that it proves difficult to imagine an age in which it could not have been known."

59. Schmidt, *Inquisitionsprozess* 37–38.

60. Schmidt himself later refers to the period of development in Germany as

More important, this notion of "the reception" as a datable event of the years around 1500 lacks the support it had in the 1930s when Schmidt wrote. The dating of reception has changed with the treatment of the event itself—with the increasing understanding that the major event was less the acceptance of the doctrinal substance of Italian law than the appearance in Germany of Italian-trained jurists disposed to refer to Roman-canon practice and sources.[61]

The movements which culminated in the full reception of the Renaissance were medieval in inception. Of these, Coing emphasizes "the importance of the reorganization of ecclesiastical jurisdiction in Germany in the thirteenth century, which for the first time caused to be created [in Germany] learned courts with broad jurisdiction . . . ."[62] Following the collapse of the Staufen dynasty, the church had been left as the principal institutional influence on German legal life; from the church courts and "from the form of ecclesiastical procedure, above all, emanated the decisive impulse for the spread of the learned law in practice; these the German territories and cities followed."[63] Further, no aspect of ecclesiastical jurisdiction was more likely to attract the attention of secular authorities, for the church depended upon their active assistance in inflicting penal sanctions of a nonecclesiastical nature. The canon criminal process insistently employed secular authority. This was especially true of those great and special exercises of the canon jurisdiction in the Middle Ages, the heresy inquisitions. Heresy inquisitions per-

---

having been one and a half centuries: "*diesen Inquisitionsprozess . . . , wie er sich seit anderthalb Jahrhunderten in Deutschland entwickelt hatte, ...*" Id. at 68.

61. The changed historiography is well characterized in Coing's recent restatement of the history of Roman law in medieval Germany:

> The understanding of the history of Roman law in the German Middle Ages has suffered deeply under certain fundamental assumptions of the Historical School concerning the nature of law and of legal history, corresponding to which the reigning viewpoint regarded [reception as] the penetration of a "foreign" law and its "struggle" with the national law. What thereby resulted was not only the danger of formulating the question in a historically unsound fashion, but also, in particular, disproportionate attention was given to the results of the process, while questions about the men who had brought about that process—their knowledge and consciousness—stood in the background. Contrariwise, current research has been concerned to understand the event in the context of the age and in the conceptions of the participating figures. The fundamental realization is that the revival of Roman law was above all a cultural and intellectual event. There must have been people who had acquired understanding of Roman law before it could have been applied.

Coing (supra, note 10) at 11–12.

62. Id. at 12.

63. Id. at 13.

sisted in Germany from the 1200s into the Renaissance.[64] The literature is not such that one can even begin to speculate about the scope and influence of the regular canon criminal jurisdiction; it is said that there was ecclesiastical criminal jurisdiction of some vigor in Frankfurt in the 1370s, particularly efficacious in lesser matters.[65]

Against this general background, the glimpses of Roman-canon process which one sees in Schmidt's own evidence acquire their significance. (1) The foundations for German Inquisitionsprozess were laid in the Gottesfrieden movement of the eleventh century. (2) The *Schwabenspiegel,* among the earliest of Schmidt's sources which is absolutely unambiguous about the use of torture, originated in Franciscan circles in Augsburg.[66] The volume was an unsophisticated, Romanized reworking of parts of the *Sachsenspiegel.*[67] (3) Schmidt reports a case, circa 1345, from the Mecklenburg Record Book in which ecclesiastics, through counsel, instituted what was essentially canon inquisition against a woman for working magic.[68] (4) There is a striking instance of explicit tracking of Justinianian language in the *Brünner Schöffenbuch,* circa 1350, relating to torture.[69] Schmidt dismisses it as bearing on the mode of resort to torture, not "its procedural permissibility as such."[70] Of course, what impresses is the fact of the usage itself.

It is appropriate in these pages only to raise, not to resolve, doubts which relate to an important, unresearched aspect of German legal history—the scope of ecclesiastical criminal jurisdiction and its influence upon the developing secular procedure. The present argument is not that the medieval German Inquisitionsprozess represented an extensive infusion of Roman-canon learning. It is clear that Schmidt is right, that the Verwissenschaftlichung of German Inquisitionsprozess was the work of the sixteenth-century reception. The present point is more modest: extensive ecclesiastical criminal jurisdiction employing a mature and efficient canon Inquisitionsprozess in often intimate association with

64. Cases of political significance are discussed in H. C. Lea, *A History of the Inquisition of the Middle Ages* (New York, 1888) II 316–426. There is also a monograph, not the archive study which is needed, but sufficient to hint at the quantitative significance of the heresy inquisitions: P. Flade, *Das römische Inquisitionsverfahren in Deutschland bis zu den Hexenprozessen* (Leipzig, 1902).

65. Vogt (supra, note 26) at 270.

66. Coing (supra, note 10) at 111.

67. Id. at 113.

68. Schmidt, *Inquisitionsprozess* 33–34.

69. Id. at 40, 56.

70. Id. at 56.

secular authority[71] probably served as a model influencing the evolution of a parallel secular process and legitimating it against resistance. Not the detail of the canon Inquisitionsprozess, but its broad outline, seems likely to have derived from the church. The detail was to come later.

B. THE ORIGINS OF THE CAROLINA

1. *The Problem of Torture*

The achievement of the medieval German Inquisitionsprozess had been to solve one set of problems at the expense of creating another. While a rationalized, officialized public process had come into being to deal with crime, for its efficacy it depended upon torture. About three centuries had been required to institute Inquisitionsprozess. Another three centuries would pass before Germans (and Europeans generally) abandoned the effort to regulate torture and banished it entirely from the criminal process. In its most significant aspect the Carolina was among the earliest attempts of secular authority in Germany to confine the use of torture.

The legislative history of the Carolina spans four decades, from the first expressions of concern to the Reichstag until final passage of the statute in 1532. It was the Reichstag of Lindau in 1496–1497 to which the Reichskammergericht reported abuses, and the Reichstag of Freiburg in 1497–1498 which resolved: "Because complaints are brought to court daily against princes, imperial cities and other authorities, that they have allowed innocent people to be condemned to death and executed unlawfully *(on Recht)* and without sufficient cause . . . it is therefore necessary to undertake a general reformation and ordering in the empire of the mode of proceeding in criminal matters." [72] Although it is customary to

71. Secular authorities were not restricted to an executioner's role in canon process. A recent critical edition of the dossier of a heresy inquisition held at Worms in 1422 shows the ecclesiastical inquisitors using local secular officials as witnesses in much the way that they were used as witnesses to examination in contemporary secular procedure. Those participating include one of the two Bürgermeister of the city of Worms and at least four of the city council members (*Ratsherren*). H. Heimpel, *Zwei Wormser Inquisitionen aus den Jahren 1421 und 1422* (*Abhandlung der Akademie der Wissenschaften in Göttingen*) (Göttingen, 1969) 17, 44.

72. *Reichsabschiede* (1498) sec. 34, NS II (Frankfurt, 1747) 46. The portion of the quoted passage before the ellipses, although recorded in the Reichsabschied of 1498, dates back to 1496. It is the Lindau complaint. C. Güterbock, *Die Entstehungsgeschichte der Carolina* (Würzburg, 1876) 18 n. 3 [hereafter cited as Güterbock].

trace the history of the Carolina to these first stirrings, it needs also to be said that nothing came of them. The brief revival of imperial institutions of these years[73] subsided in political difficulty,[74] and after 1500 the project lay dormant for two decades, there being no significant progress until the draft of 1521.[75]

The historical importance of this agitation at the imperial level is that it left a record of dissatisfaction with criminal procedure among politically vocal elements within the empire. To account for this phenomenon is to explain the milieu of the Carolina and its predecessor legislation. This protest against brusque and summary criminal procedure was the reaction of ordinary, respectable elements within the estates who had found their liberties undercut by the growth of Inquisitionsprozess. What had been acceptable enough as a rough-and-ready remedy against outsiders was now being applied to ordinary citizens. The regularization of Inquisitionsprozess denied the right to defend by oath to all, no longer just to the Landschädlichen. The ordinary citizen was becoming a victim of the summary procedures operated by the increasingly confident authorities. His safeguard in archaic process—in defense by oath—having dissolved, his demand had to be, and was, that Inquisitionsprozess itself be domesticated, that the officials be bound to procedures which recognized the interests of the individual as well as of the government.[76]

Although the reception statutes dealt with other matters, the essential concern, especially in the Carolina, was the regulation of torture. Torture had rendered Inquisitionsprozess effective against crime, but the efficacy of torture was in fact too great. Under sufficient coercion an

73. Including the reconstruction of the Reichskammergericht in 1495 and the promulgation of the perpetual Landfriede in the same year. See J. P. Dawson, *The Oracles of the Law* (Ann Arbor, 1968) 185–191 [hereafter cited as Dawson, *Oracles*]. Also including the first legislation in what became the series of Reichspolizeiordnungen, again in 1495 (J. Segall, *Geschichte und Strafrecht der Reichspolizeiordnungen* [Kirchhain, 1914] 35–43); the creation of the Reichsregiment in 1500 (Conrad, supra, note 9, at II 74–76); and the commissioning of the Reichsregiment and the Reichskammergericht in 1500 to draft a criminal procedure ordinance—a charge not fulfilled (id. at II 406; Güterbock 20–22). See generally H. Holborn, *A History of Modern Germany: The Reformation* (New York, 1959) 39–50; and Gebhardt, *Handbuch der deutschen Geschichte* (9th ed., H. Grundmann, ed.) (Stuttgart, 1970) II 54–56, 369–370.

74. Güterbock 22.

75. Id. at 23–31.

76. See Schmidt, *Inquisitionsprozess* 73–76, in connection with the Wormser Reformation.

innocent man will confess as readily as a guilty one. On the other hand, although torture could be used crudely to extract confession in a way resembling a coerced plea of guilty, it could also with far greater reliability elicit evidence which would corroborate confession. Given the high standard of proof demanded for conviction, there was no feasible alternative to torture as the mode of evidence-gathering. At first there had been the need for confession to obviate the archaic proofs; later the Roman-canon system of proofs provided that confession would substitute for its requirement that there be two eyewitnesses to the gravamen of the crime.[77] The territorial competence of the evidence-gathering authorities, their jurisdiction, was often severely confined, and nearly all the modern investigative techniques which facilitate the collection of evidence from sources other than the accused were nonexistent.

Even more important, perhaps, than the paucity of alternative means of gathering evidence was the inability to deal with the evidence, to evaluate it, to decide whether it justified condemning the accused. The Carolina is all but myopic in its preference for confession, albeit corroborated and verified confession.[78] Because confession operated as a waiver on the fundamental question, it spared the court the task of weighing the evidence. And that was a function the lay courts of the time were ill equipped to perform. "Had it been desired no longer to torture confessions, it would have been necessary to resolve for the cases where there had previously been torture (that is, where considerable suspicious circumstances were known) to pass judgment without confession—that is, to replace the Carolina's theory of legal proof with free judicial evaluation of the evidence. That, however, presumed a mature and trustworthy judicial corps. The Carolina, to the contrary, was obliged to count on [unlearned] court personnel . . . ."[79] Given high standards of proof on the one hand and low standards of judicial professionalism on the other, it was inevitable that the maxim would continue: *confessio est regina probationum.* The movement for a "reformation," which came to early expression in the Reichstag of 1496–1497, left no record of having inspired doubts among contemporaries about whether to continue to employ torture. The response throughout the sixteenth century

77. These issues are canvassed in the work of Fiorelli (supra, note 58). In English see W. Ullmann, "Reflections on Medieval Torture" (supra, note 46).

78. See Article 69, directing that the judge attempt to secure confession even when witness testimony sufficient to convict has been established.

79. Radbruch 19.

(and long before and long beyond) was to compromise, to devise rules which might rescue only the innocent from the torture chamber. We shall have occasion below to examine the detail of the Carolina's solution.[80]

2. *The Predecessor Legislation*

Given the fractionated state of German political and legal life, it is not surprising that the first fruits of the reaction against unfettered Inquisitionsprozess should have come at the same level as the abuses to be remedied: in the cities and the territories. Three of the pre-Carolina statutes have attracted particular emphasis in the German literature; the present account follows Eberhard Schmidt.[81]

a. The Maximilianischen Halsgerichtsordnungen[82]

The medieval tradition of German Inquisitionsprozess reached its laconic culmination in the Tyrolean territorial criminal procedure ordinance of 1499. A lightly revised version of the ordinance was promulgated elsewhere in the Hapsburg lands in Radolfzell in 1506. The two statutes are known as the *Maximilianischen Halsgerichtsordnungen* (the criminal court ordinances of Emperor Maximilian I). The statutes record a procedure which is unquestionably Inquisitionsprozess, yet which in essence proved capable of redaction in a single paragraph. The Tyrolean version:[83]

Where it is decided to question someone, male or female, under torture. The judge shall take with him three persons from the council

80. Infra, pages 179–183.
81. Schmidt, *Inquisitionsprozess* 61–85.
82. Schmidt's critical edition of the texts supersedes earlier prints. *Die Maximilianischen Halsgerichtsordnungen für Tirol (1499) und Radolfzell (1506) als Zeugnisse mittelalterlicher Strafrechtspflege* (E. Schmidt, ed.) (Bleckede/Elbe, 1949).
83. Id. at 99. This is Article VII in Schmidt's assigned numbering; note his commentary, id. at 152–155. The italics in the text are supplied, expressing my sense that the grammatically deficient sentences had the effect of titles, marking in each instance a progression in time and process. The word rendered as *Schöffen* is in the original *Gsworn* (modern: *Geschworenen*); the difference appears to be one of regional idiom. See A. Zycha, *Deutsche Rechtsgeschichte der Neuzeit* (2d. ed., Marburg/Lahn, 1949) 144.

or from the Schöffen. In the presence of them and of the court scribe, the said person is to be interrogated as previously decided upon and ordered. *And what the wrongdoer admits and confirms.* The court scribe shall transcribe the confession uncorrupted. The judge and the persons he has had with him shall read it over. *And when it is desired to proceed to judgment thereon,* [the confession] shall be read out to the councilors or Schöffen. Then the three who were present shall testify to the confession unanimously by their oaths before the judge and the other Schöffen. Thereupon the said confession will suffice. And accordingly [at the sitting of the Schöffen] one of the three should be the first to be asked his judgment.

What is striking about this scheme is not its contrast with the past, but with the future. It is a summation of the "practical" Inquisitionsprozess[84] of the Middle Ages. There is torture before the lay investigating commission, whose later testimony will support the confession if the accused attempts to recant. Archaic or ritual process has disappeared. Yet the elaborate limitations on torture—on when and whom to torture and what to torture for—these matters which preoccupy the Carolina and its forerunners are lacking. The procedure is untouched by Roman-canon learning.[85] All is remitted, as in the medieval sources, to the discretion of the officials. The movement of reaction traceable in the Reichstags of 1496–1497 and 1497–1498 seems not to have reached Tyrol in 1499. The imperial free city of Worms, however, was showing itself a more fertile ground.

b. The Wormser Reformation[86]

A markedly different spirit animates the Inquisitionsprozess promulgated for Worms in 1498. A summary of its "titles" of criminal

84. The term comes from Schmidt, *Inquisitionsprozess* 68.

85. This was misunderstood among earlier historians, who equated the inquisitorial format, especially the absence of private complainant, with reception. See Schmidt's refutation, id. at 64–69, esp. 67; cf. Schmidt's introduction to the texts (supra, note 82) at 74–79, esp. 79.

86. The Wormser Reformation was a general "code" of law for the city of Worms, composed by the year 1498. The last of its six books deals with criminal law and procedure. There is no modern edition of the whole; the most recent was apparently printed in 1561. Books 3–5 (private law) have been printed in *Quellen zur neueren Privatrechtsgeschichte Deutschlands* (Weimar, 1936) (W. Kunkel and H. Thieme, eds.) I (erster Halbband) 95–220. Books 1–2 (civil procedure, instance and appellate) appear in the widely circulated collection of A. Saur, *Fasciculus Judiciarri Ordinis Singularis* (Frankfurt, 1588) I. A reprint of that work, edited by Dr.

procedure will show why the *Wormser Reformation* has been described as "the first comprehensive law which takes a demonstrably new path in the handling of Inquisitionsprozess . . . ."[87]

(1) An introductory statement of Inquisitionsprozess. Because it happens that crimes are committed whose authorship is not clear, save that "general repute or strong suspicion or credible indication" may suggest the guilt of someone, the Bürgermeister and Council are directed to investigate diligently and to take report from witnesses or those with knowledge or understanding of the matter. They may gaol a suspect and question him. Should he fail to confess, there shall be inquiry of the accusers looking to whether there is sufficient indication to justify questioning the accused by torture.

(2) Upon what grounds there may be examination under torture. Before there may be examination under torture, there needs be sufficient indication. Now this determination defies precise formulation. There can be "no certainty or rule established, rather it depends upon the judgment of each judge." This so, it is ordered that no one be finally adjudged guilty or condemned to punishment upon mere suspicion or doubted indication, but examined under torture upon that basis. Although a general rule for what is sufficient to justify torture is impossible, illustrations can be given, a dozen of which follow: for example, when someone of wanton character is found with the stolen goods; when the accused is found with the bloody dagger and the victim has been stabbed.

(3) How to conduct examination under torture. The law officers are instructed not to torture if there is an easier way to get at the truth; to use reason and restraint lest the investigation be worse than the crime; to try to elicit the factual details, not mere confession of guilt.

(4) When witnesses, as opposed to suspects, may be examined under torture.

(5) Which persons shall not be examined under torture. Save for the case of high treason, doctors of law, physicians, academicians, and public officials are immune.

(6) The order of proceeding in examining under torture when several persons may be examined. The rule: torture first the person most likely to talk, for example, the young and the weak before the older, the son before the father (in the presence of the father), the wife before the husband.

(7) Although there be sufficient justification for examination under torture, it is nonetheless not to be employed until any defenses or grounds of exculpation raised by the accused are investigated, including the hearing of his witnesses. Again a dozen illustrative cases are set forth.

(8 & 9) The private complaint procedure.[88]

Gerhard Immel, is currently in progress. The sixth book (criminal law and procedure) has not been reprinted since the sixteenth century. I have used a copy of the first printing of 1499 located in the Stadt-und-Universitätsbibliothek, Frankfurt. For citation to sixteenth-century editions see Schmidt, *Inquisitionsprozess* 69 n. 243. Citation below is to title numbers. All titles are subsections of bk. 6, pt. 2, fol. cliii–clix.

87. Schmidt, *Inquisitionsprozess* 69.

88. The private complaint procedure of the Wormser Reformation is sharply

(10) The criteria for final judgment, that is, the grounds upon which the accused may be condemned to final criminal sanction as opposed to the indicia justifying torture. Preeminent is voluntary confession, failing which, confession extracted by torture; otherwise, "sufficient" witness proofs.

A striking concern with limiting Inquisitionsprozess has overcome this ordinance. Every section expresses humanity and attempts to translate it into safeguards. One giant advance has been made. The statute imposes a so-called *Indizienlehre*—a system of evaluating the indicia, the circumstantial evidence, against the accused to determine whether there is justification for examination under torture. Without "sufficient indication," something close to the Anglo-American law's idea of probable cause, torture is impermissible. The Carolina will exhibit a much expanded Indizienlehre. But already the Wormser Reformation contrasts strongly with the Maximilianischen Halsgerichtsordnungen and with the whole of the medieval past. At last, limits upon the power and the procedures of the officials were being included in the procedure to protect the accused. Further, the Wormser Reformation, like the Carolina to come, makes a distinction between the evidence needed to torture and that needed finally to condemn.[89] The ordinance made another important advance in its substantive criminal law (not summarized above). It displays a fairly sophisticated scheme of defining offenses, categorizing the most important crimes, especially homicide in its several degrees. These provisions too will be surpassed in the Carolina. They are important because they implement the same paramount value as the procedural

---

differentiated from the officially operated procedure, in which respect it follows the Roman-canon mainstream. E. Brunnenmeister, *Die Quellen der Bambergensis* (Leipzig, 1879) 104 [hereafter cited as Brunnenmeister]. The intermixture of the two, characteristic of the late medieval procedure, still finds an echo in the Carolina, but had already disappeared in the Worms ordinance. There the two procedures are segregated. The complainant who opts for private process cannot employ the tools of the official process, hence cannot put the accused to examination under torture irrespective of how strong the criminating "indications." The complainant is limited to investigation by written interrogatory. His burden of proof is coupled with the sanction that, should he fail to procure evidence sufficient to condemn the accused, he is liable to the accused in damages.

Final process (Title 10) is the same for private and official process, that is, the same standards govern the evaluation of the evidence to determine guilt or innocence.

No particular advantage pertained to private suit, apart from the joinder of a private compensatory action. The burden and the hazard to the complainant were severe, the gain over official process nugatory. Hence the observation that the draftsman's intent could only have been to discourage the private complainant. Schmidt, *Inquisitionsprozess* 69–71.

89. See Brunnenmeister 105.

reforms—binding the officials to the law by spelling out the substantive component of their jurisdiction. Serious crime was to be less what the officials said it was and more what statute defined.

Because, therefore, the Wormser Reformation strove both in substance and procedure to confine official discretion, to elaborate protections for the accused within its Inquisitionsprozess, it deserves the accolade it bears in the literature as the first clear break with medieval tradition. It inaugurated the themes of the later and greater statutes of German criminal procedure in the Renaissance. Instructively, it was also the first criminal procedural ordinance in Germany to borrow heavily and systematically from Roman-canon law.[90] "There is no legal source of the fifteenth or sixteenth centuries which to such a degree as the Wormser Reformation, put aside the law contemporaneously in practice, and presented in essence only the common [Roman] law—not indeed from the Roman [Justinianian] sources themselves, but from the writings of the [medieval] jurists."[91] The whole of the procedural structure of the Worms Inquisitionsprozess imitated Roman-canon process and can occasionally be traced in various details to specific sections of the thirteenth-century treatise of Gandinus.[92] The Indizienlehre, the standards of proof for final process, the offense definitions—all features which distinguish Worms and anticipate the Carolina—these are the German reception.[93]

90. Id. at 102–136; cf. Schmidt, *Einführung* 109.

91. O. Stobbe, *Geschichte der deutschen Rechtsquellen* (Leipzig, 1860) I 334, quoted in Brunnenmeister 103. Although Worms was unique in the extent of its Romanism, many of the South German cities were instituting reformed "codes" of Roman impress in these decades. See Wieacker (supra, note 11) at 193. Nonetheless, Worms was remarkably doctrinaire. I owe to Dr. Gerhard Immel the suggestion that the Wormser Reformation may in fact have begun as a textbook. Medieval European legal history provides many examples of the phenomenon of a privately produced textbook being transmuted into something close to a statutebook (among them Beaumanoir and the *Sachsenspiegel*). The city of Worms was at the time competing to be designated the seat of the Reichskammergericht and might in that connection have had occasion to commission a jurist to produce a German-language "treatise" of Roman law, especially civil and criminal procedure (which received disproportionate attention in the Wormser Reformation).

92. E.g., Brunnenmeister 104 and n. 1. See supra, Chapter 6, note 36.

93. I pass over, as I must in a specialized study, the vast questions of the nature and causes of the whole German reception. There now exists in English a concise and sophisticated account of the principal events and issues: Dawson, *Oracles* 176–232.

c. *The Bambergensis*[94]

The most important of the Carolina's predecessors must receive short shrift in these pages. Because the Carolina was so completely dependent upon the *Bambergensis,* because the Carolina is generally but a glossed version of the Bambergensis,[95] it would be unduly repetitive in the present study to speak to the contents of both. We pass over the Bambergensis to reach the Carolina, in which cast the Bambergensis achieved its greatest influence.[96] What remains, therefore, is to speak

94. The modern critical edition, complete with reproductions of the original woodcuts, is *Die Bambergische Halsgerichtsordnung* (J. Kohler and W. Scheel, eds.) (Halle, 1902).

95. Students of the English Marian legislation will note the coincidence (of no particular significance) that the Carolina, like the English committal statute of 1555, was a derivative piece of drafting, couching itself in the language of an earlier act. Much has already been said about the difficulty which that technique caused for the later English statute (supra, Chapter 3, note 20, and references there supplied). With regard to the Carolina, it should be illustrated that even more embarrassing, though less important, confusion resulted from slavish copying. The final paragraph of Article 198 of the Carolina, dealing with the written forms-of-words of certain criminal judgments having property consequences, cross-refers to several of the substantive law sections of the statute purportedly imposing such property sanctions. Two of these references are senseless—the substantive sections do not in fact impose property sanctions. But if one goes behind these Carolina provisions to the corresponding articles of the Bambergensis, one does find the appropriate provision. In each case the Carolina had altered the substantive provision it took from the Bambergensis and failed to adjust Article 198 accordingly.

The two Carolina provisions are Articles 120 and 121. Article 198 identifies Article 120 as treating immoral sexual relations between a married man and a single girl. Article 120 is in fact a brief and general proscription of adultery. The corresponding section in the Bambergensis, Article 145, does deal more extensively with adultery; does specially treat the case of the married man and the single girl; and does impose a property sanction. The omission of this feature of the Bambergensis occurs in the first Carolina draft. Yet it and each subsequent draft of the Carolina carry forward in Article 198 the now-mistaken reference. See the texts in *Die Peinliche Gerichtsordnung Kaiser Karl's V. nebst der Bamberger und der Brandenburger Halsgerichtsordnung* (H. Zoepfl, ed.) (2d ed., Leipzig and Heidelberg, 1876) 100–102, 164–165.

The other mistaken reference in Article 198, to Article 121, again continues to ascribe a property sanction which the Bambergensis counterpart had contained but which the Carolina dropped. Id. at 102–104, 164–165.

Oddly enough, the French ordonnance royale of 1539 was also a work of derivative draftsmanship. Chancellor Poyet, its author, had done an earlier version for the province of Brittany. See infra, Chapter 9, page 236 and n. 125; Esmein 139.

96. Zoepfl's synoptic edition of the Carolina (supra, note 95) displays the Bambergensis alongside the Carolina in parallel columns, facilitating comparison. A conversion table, id. at xiii–xvi, shows which Bambergensis article became which Carolina article. The Carolina is no base reprinting or rearrangement of the Bambergensis. Roughly a fifth of the Bambergensis articles did not find their way into the Carolina; and a handful of Carolina articles have no Bambergensis counterparts. The Carolina not infrequently revises a Bambergensis provision. However, in the

about the draftsman of the Bambergensis, but not directly of his work.

The *Bambergische Halsgerichtsordnung* was promulgated in 1507 for the Bistum of Bamberg—the easternmost of the major cities of the Main, an episcopal principality possessed of territorial dominions once as distant as modern Austria. The draftsman, Baron Johann von Schwarzenberg, has been lionized as the greatest figure of German law in the Renaissance. Schwarzenberg was born in 1465 to an established line of Franconian nobility. He received the low-grade provincial education of the time, emphasizing physical and military prowess. He never learned Latin. After an early career as a soldier and in imperial service, he held in the 1490s a series of diplomatic-administrative-judicial posts under various princes, secular and episcopal. Returning to Bamberg, Schwarzenberg rose to preeminence among the secular servants of the prince-bishop. Like his father before him, Schwarzenberg was long a lay judge, a member of his local criminal court. What became the Bambergensis was originally devised for that court's practice, although as early as 1503 an intermediate draft was prepared to apply throughout the Bistum.[97]

Like the Wormser Reformation, the Bambergensis was a reform statute, responding to the kinds of complaint expressed a decade before in the Reichstag. Like the Wormser Reformation, but much more extensively, the Bambergensis limits torture and sets forth a catalog of substantive offenses. Schwarzenberg's sources were not, however, exclusively Roman-canon. Although there was major borrowing from the Italians, much of the indigenous practice also survived. Brunnenmeister's important study, *Die Quellen der Bambergensis,* is centrally concerned with separating the Italianate and Germanic components, and we shall

perspective of the whole work the revisions are minor. The Carolina is effectively a version of the Bambergensis.

97. E. Wolf, *Grosse Rechtsdenker der deutschen Geistesgeschichte* (4th ed., Tübingen, 1963) 106–116. Schwarzenberg was a larger figure than present purposes permit recounting. He was a minor poet. It is said that his contribution to the settling of *Frühneuhochdeutsch* was exceeded only by Luther's. He became in his later years a supporter of Luther and had previously been a tractician in behalf of the prerogatives of the aristocracy. He sat in the Reichstag more than once, and more significantly, in the Reichsregiment. His adherence to the Reformation party cost him his office under the Bamberg episcopacy, although without the enmity which would have seemed likely under the circumstances. He finished his career in the service of the Brandenburg electorate. Schwarzenberg died in Nuremberg in 1528, four years before the Carolina elevated his Bamberg criminal procedure ordinance to Reichsgesetz. Id. at 129–134. Bibliography on Schwarzenberg and his works appears id. at 136–137.

allude to this issue often in looking at the detail of the Carolina. Schwarzenberg's own hand is somewhat harder to detect, because his knowledge of the Italian sources had to be derivative. It is believed that he had translations of the Latin works of the medieval jurists rendered into German for him.[98] Whether his advisers were more than translators is not known. Regardless, Schwarzenberg had control of the whole and gave it a consistency of theme and execution which is emphasized time and again in the voluminous German literature which celebrates Schwarzenberg and the Bambergensis-Carolina.

3. *Legislative History of the Carolina*

It is believed, but cannot be proven, that Schwarzenberg sat on the committee formed by the Reichstag of Worms in 1521 to draft an imperial criminal procedure ordinance. Schwarzenberg did sit in that Reichstag and his prestige at the time was great enough to win him office in the re-revived Reichsregiment, which later became involved with the drafting. Irrespective of the personal participation of Schwarzenberg, the important event was that his Bambergensis was taken as the 1521 committee's basic text. The Bambergensis even then had a wide renown. Five editions had been published between 1507 and 1510.[99] The Brandenburg rulers in 1516 had adopted the ordinance without alteration for their territories of Ansbach and Bayreuth (near Bamberg).[100]

Several proposed drafts of the Carolina were produced in the years 1521–1529, each fundamentally a mild revision of the Bambergensis. This process, which has been carefully reconstructed,[101] is an exemplary display of the painful difficulties which then beset any attempt at imperial legislation of significance. The draft of 1529 brought the issue to a head. The city fathers of Esslingen had denounced the 1521 draft as an interference with municipal privileges, and indeed as a scheme which

98. Kohler and Scheel (supra, note 94) at lxvi–lxvii. It is conceivable that the Bambergensis was first designed as a handbook rather than a statutebook, as has been suggested with respect to the Wormser Reformation (supra, note 91).

99. Id. at viii–ix.

100. Of course, there were technical adjustments such as substituting Brandenburg princes for Bamberg bishops as promulgators. See Zoepfl (supra, note 95) at 10 nn. III-1, V-1; 12 nn. V-2–4, VII-1; 14 nn. IX-1–3.

101. Güterbock, at 32–215, recounts the several drafts. Zoepfl's synoptic edition (supra, note 95) displays the 1521 and 1529 drafts as well as the Bambergensis and the final Carolina draft in parallel columns.

encouraged and protected criminals.[102] The latter objection, to substance, seems not to have been widely shared. The constitutional issue, however, alarmed interests far more powerful than the city of Esslingen. For the 1529 draft, which by its terms intended mandatory effect in every jurisdiction in the German Empire, would have set a threatening precedent against territorial autonomy. Although its motives were laudable and its substance generally unobjectionable, the 1529 draft was cast as imperial legislation authoritatively intervening in the operation of the courts of the cities and territories. Major electorates—Saxony, the Palatinate, Brandenburg proper—moved into opposition,[103] compelling the crucial compromise of the 1530 draft which salvaged but weakened the reform: the so-called saving clause of the Preamble, stipulating that the Carolina would pertain only when not in conflict with the "old, well-established, lawful, and equitable usages" of the territories. In consequence, the Carolina could claim only subsidiary validity if local usage were effectively marshaled against it. Thus hobbled, it was finally enacted in 1532. The Carolina would achieve its great influence indirectly, not as command but as model.

102. Schmidt, *Einführung* 131.
103. Id. at 132, Güterbock 128–140.

CHAPTER 8 The Carolina

Although the Carolina[1] is overwhelmingly a work of criminal procedure, it does contain important substantive provisions. "In its fundamentals the Carolina is not really a code of criminal law *(Strafgesetzbuch)*, but a code of criminal procedure (*Strafprozessordnung*) into the middle of which a code of criminal law has been intromitted."[2] These substantive law provisions of the Carolina have received the preponderant scholarly attention. The reason is easy to imagine. The jurisprudence of torture which the Carolina sought to modify finally had to be abandoned in the eighteenth century. The liberal scholars of the later nineteenth and early twentieth centuries could not develop much admiration for the procedural system whose destruction had been among the dearest objects of liberal politics. Still, where the procedure of the Carolina seemed to be a dead end, the substantive law had about itself much of the look of the future. One could see, usually quite rightly, important lines of continuity from the Carolina down to the modern codes. It is thus the case today that a good Carolina bibliography[3] will disclose in fair number titles such as "Robbery in the Carolina,"[4] "The Conception of Guilt of the Carolina,"[5] or "Concerning the Concept and the Penalty for Child Murder in the Carolina with Regard to the Roman and Ancient Germanic Law."[6] Von Hippel's important history of German criminal law found room to discuss virtually every substantive article in the

1. Citation is to the article numbers of the statute, which are uniform in the various editions. The two modern scholarly editions are discussed in the preface to the translation in Appendix B, where my preference for the Zoepfl edition (supra, Chapter 7, note 95) is explained.

2. Radbruch 14. Schmidt, *Carolina* 10: "[T]he Carolina is in the main a criminal procedure ordinance . . . ."

3. Supra, Chapter 7, note 9.

4. G. Radbruch, "Der Raub in der Carolina," in *Elegantiae Juris Criminalis* (2d ed., Basel, 1950) 49.

5. H. Kollmann, "Die Schuldauffassung der Carolina," *Zeitschrift für die gesamte Strafrechtswissenschaft* 34:605 (1913).

6. L. Jordan, *Ueber den Begriff und die Strafe des Kindsmordes nach der Peinlichen Gerichtsordnung Karls V. mit Rücksicht auf das römische und altgermanische Recht: Ein Beitrag zur Interpretation der Artikel 35, 36 und 131 der Carolina* (Heidelberg, 1844).

statute.[7] The procedural sections, by contrast, have rather seldom been the subject of such close study.

A. SUBSTANTIVE CRIMINAL LAW

The Carolina treats substantive criminal law in a continuous series of 77 articles, Numbers 104 to 180. The translation in Appendix B contains the individual titles of these articles,[8] from which the range of subject matter is apparent. Save for sexual offenses and others of particularly ecclesiastical concern, the Carolina deals only with serious crime—most extensively with homicide and theft, also arson, robbery, riot, counterfeiting, and forgery. The preoccupation with major crime[9] is related to the broader procedural purposes of the statute. These offenses bring Inquisitionsprozess into operation. Careful definition of the substantive liabilities involved is part of the enterprise of binding the officials to the law. More generally, the dominant purposes and techniques of the procedural portions of the statute underlie the substantive part as well. The draftsman intermixed them in a common plan; hence we pause over the Carolina's substantive law to notice themes which will preoccupy us in the study of the procedure.

Virtually every offense definition in the Carolina marks an advance in conceptualization. Relatively few of the major crimes go undefined, and these are quaintly worded: Article 125 speaks not of arson but of the arsonist, Article 126 of the robber; and in these instances punishment is ordained without any description of the elements of the of-

7. Von Hippel 159–213.

8. Articles 104 and 105 are fully translated.

9. It should be remarked that lesser crime was being simultaneously regulated in other compendious imperial legislation. The Reichspolizeiordnung of 1530 traces back to the same Reichstags of the 1490s and the 1520s as the Carolina. Although some provisions dealt with such ancient evils as blasphemy, the preponderant concern was economic regulation. The body of petty economic offenses which had been created by the end of the sixteenth century in England had substantial counterpart in the Reichspolizeiordnungen of 1530, 1548, and 1577, which regulated, e.g., usury, weights and measures, monopolies, begging, liquor and drunkenness. See J. Segall, *Geschichte und Strafrecht der Reichspolizeiordnungen* (Kirchhain, 1914) 4–7, 35 ff., 144 ff. Generally, however, lesser crime was an inappropriate subject for imperial as opposed to territorial or local law. Further, much of what is today handled in the criminal process was still in the sixteenth century remitted to the civil process. See von Hippel 195 n. 6.

fenses.[10] "The malevolent proven arsonist shall be put to death by fire," runs Article 125 in its totality. Article 126 prescribes death by the sword for the robber, unless the locality has its own "good custom" for such cases. These curt and simple provisions, distinctive for their rarity in the Carolina, were the norm of prior Germanic compilations. They are the staples of the Maximilianischen Halsgerichtsordnungen: "Every murderer shall be executed upon the wheel. A traitor dragged and drawn and quartered. Robber with the sword."[11] In the main, the Carolina cuts loose from this tradition. To illustrate: among the most important of the Carolina's definitions from the standpoint of the future refinement of offense classification is the treatment of homicide in Article 137. It follows a series of special provisions for poisoning, child murder, and others, and precedes a lengthy series of articles (to be discussed below) which explain the grounds of exculpation for homicide.

> Every murderer or killer, when he can establish no lawful exculpation, has forfeited his life. Although according to the custom of some areas the premeditated murderer and the killer are executed alike upon the wheel, a distinction should be taken between them, viz: following the custom, a wanton premeditated murderer shall be punished upon the wheel, and someone else who has committed a homicide out of sudden anger or wrath, yet otherwise has no acceptable exculpation, shall be put to death with the sword . . . .

The conceptual advance over the Tyrolean ordinance of 1498 ("Every murderer shall be executed upon the wheel") is patent. Brunnenmeister has shown the Italian origins of the distinction between *homicidium deliberatum* and *non deliberatum*,[12] which continued into the modern German law of graded homicide.[13] The Italianate ideas were not woodenly transposed, but adapted—in this instance to the harsher realities of German penal law. For whereas the Romanist practice had generally distinguished *homicidium non deliberatum* in order to rescue its

10. An oft-remarked point. See Wolf (supra, Chapter 7, note 97) at 126; Schmidt, *Einführung* 116, notes the particularly archaic language: "bosshafftigen überwunden brenner" (Article 125), "bosshafftiger überwundner rauber" (Article 126). Carolina, Zoepfl ed. (supra, Chapter 7, note 95) at 107.

11. *Maximilianischen Halsgerichtsordnungen* (supra, Chapter 7, note 82) at 100 (Tyrol, Articles IX–XI) (1499).

12. Brunnenmeister 249 (treating Article 162 of the Bambergensis, the analogue to Carolina Article 137. Hereafter in citation to Brunnenmeister the conversion from Bambergensis to Carolina will not be specified; the book has a conversion table).

13. Id. at 249–251 n. 4.

perpetrator from capital punishment,[14] Schwarzenberg employed the distinction simply to justify a less gruesome death for the less deliberate killer.

This sort of mining of the conceptual richness of Italian law is most evident and most successful in the Carolina's handling of aspects of what is called the "general part" of the criminal law: those problems of intent, causation, exculpation, and the like which are common to the variety of specific offenses. The concerns which promoted clarity in offense definition encouraged it in the general part as well. Medieval Germanic law had focused on character as much as conduct. Directed against outsiders, the Verfahren auf Leumund had inquired whether the accused was the evil sort, landschädlich. The extension of official process to ordinary citizens made it more pressing to sort out what conduct was criminal. The individual had a claim to protection from needless or, worse, oppressive interference. That interest had long since achieved a more philosophic formulation to implement the canon law's pervasive concern with individual guilt in criminal law. Because crime had been equated with sin, and because sin was a matter of the individual's exercise of his free will, it had been essential to devise rules which reflected individual volition. The distinction between premeditated and impassioned homicide instances this concern of the Roman-canon law, and the Carolina took it over.[15] The interest in causation is related: the crime must be genuinely the product of the accused's will. Hence the Carolina limits criminal liability for sorcery to the case where the accused thereby "inflicts injury or disadvantage . . . ."[16] The law of attempts poses the converse problem, willed but uncompleted harm. Roman-canon law had developed the doctrine of liability for attempts in the Middle Ages, Germanic law had not, and the strikingly modern treatment in Article 178 of the Carolina represents unmistakable reception.[17] The Carolina also identified as a problem the question of the capacity of youthful offenders, although the paucity of solution in both

14. Id. at 249.

15. Concisely discussed in von Hippel 204–206. Cf. Schmidt, *Carolina* 17–22; Kollmann, supra, note 5.

16. Article 109. See the particular implementing procedural provisions, Articles 21, 44, and 52, translated in Appendix B. Other causation rules are supplied in several homicide situations. See von Hippel 190–191. Especially interesting is Article 147 concerning the remoteness problem: "When someone is struck and dies, and it is mooted whether he died of the wounds."

17. Brunnenmeister 173–177. Cf. Wolf (supra, Chapter 7, note 97) at 126–127; Radbruch 13; Schmidt, *Einführung* 119–120.

the indigenous and the Roman-canon sources left the draftsman no alternative but to direct that such cases be abandoned to legal experts,[18] a phenomenon to be discussed below.

Justification, above all self-defense, is the most extensively developed of the "general part" notions in the Carolina. The preoccupation with self-defense may reflect the draftsman's experience that the plea was frequently made in the homicides which are the ordinance's predominant group of offenses. The scheme, whose Italianate origins have been established,[19] may be briefly summarized. Article 139 establishes the general proposition that there can be justified homicide. Article 140 ("What genuine self-defense is") ranks among the most precocious of the Carolina's generalizing, conceptualizing dispositions:

> When someone challenges, attacks or strikes another with a deadly weapon or arm, and the imperiled person cannot reasonably escape without danger or injury to his body, life, honor and good repute, he may save his body and life through appropriate counterforce without any criminal penalty. Should he thereby kill his attacker, he is not liable for that, nor is he liable if he has failed to hold his counterforce until he is struck; notwithstanding whether written law and custom have been to the contrary.

The requirement that self-help be avoided where reasonable is a measure of the distance traveled from the ancient Germanic law of institutionalized self-help, and was even in the sixteenth century a clarifying advance.[20] But by authorizing the jeopardized person to strike the first blow, the provision recognized the countervailing concern, and with it, the perpetual tension between the extremes of excessive and inadequate force.

To operate under a rule so abstract, without more guidance, in the lay courts of the time was not feasible. Hence, coupled to the rule is a stern allocation of the burden of proof (Article 141) which required that

18. Carolina Article 179 ("Concerning criminals who, owing to youth or other reasons, lack understanding"): "Should a crime be committed by someone who, on account of youth or other infirmity, has not his understanding, that [case] shall be sent with all the circumstances to the place and location indicated at the conclusion of this our ordinance, and dealt with or punished according to the advice of those and of other knowledgeable persons."

19. Brunnenmeister 177–185, esp. 183–185.

20. Schmidt, *Einführung* 121; Wolf (supra, Chapter 7, note 97) at 126–127.

the party relying upon self-defense prove it "sufficiently."[21] Article 142 continues with the problem of proof. It is among the lengthiest articles in the statute, and it displays various of the draftsman's characteristic devices. It retreats from generality to proceed by example. This technique will be seen repeatedly in the Carolina's procedural law. A series of hypothetical cases illustrate situations in which the person claiming self-defense has in fact exceeded the permissible counterforce.[22] Following the examples comes stern language about the difficulty of deciding such cases when they turn on "highly subtle distinctions . . . which . . . cannot be explained to the comprehension of the common man." This being so, cases of difficulty are to be referred to outside experts.

These are deep themes in the Carolina—the limits of the lay judges and the consequent need for resort to expert advice where difficulty appears. We shall have occasion to return to these matters, and to their bearing upon the nature of the German reception. We note here that they illustrate the interrelation of substance and procedure in the scheme of the Carolina. The commonest feature of the substantive sections of the statute is that they tend to conclude with the advice that in case of doubt about the applicability of a definition or a rule, reference should be made to the legally knowledgeable *(rechtverstendigen)*.[23] By my count, 42 of the Carolina's 77 substantive law articles contain or refer to this instruction.[24] Not only the complicated business of exculpation, but many of the relatively straightforward offense definitions are concluded with similar caution. The draftsman was possessed of an astounding distrust of the competence of the courts for which he was legislating. Hence the recurrent use of the devices associated in Articles 140 and 142: concise Italianate definition; popularization of the definition by example; warning about the hazards of adjudication of the more difficult cases by untrained lay judges; and reference of such cases to the legally knowledgeable.[25] Indeed, the Carolina generalizes much of this in a provision (Article 105) prefacing the substantive law articles:

[I]n those criminal cases or complaints as to which punishment is

21. Roman-canon origins are doubtful. See von Hippel 203; Radbruch 16.

22. Schmidt, *Einführung* 121.

23. On the translation of *rechtverstendigen* see infra, note 143.

24. Articles 105–106, 109, 111–114, 117–119, 123–124, 127–129, 131–134, 136, 142–144, 146–148, 150–153, 160, 164–166, 168–169, 172–173, 176, 178–180.

25. The Carolina treats further particularities of self-defense in Articles 143–145; Articles 146–147 deal with other problems of exculpation.

not provided or made sufficiently plain or understandable in the following articles, judge and judgment-givers (when guilt is apparent) shall seek advice how such odd and incomprehensible cases shall be best judged and dealt with according to this our Imperial law and to this our ordinance, and they shall give judgment accordingly. For not every conceivable sentence and punishment can be sufficiently set forth in this our ordinance.

This referral system explains what would otherwise have been an impossible contradiction within the substantive law of the Carolina. It has been said that the goal and effect of the conceptualization in offense definition and "general part" dispositions had been to narrow the arbitrariness of the medieval law, to bind the officials to the law; and it has been promised that the Carolina's procedural system will be shown to have exemplified this policy even more dramatically. Yet Article 105 in fact authorizes judicial offense definitions beyond the statute, contrary to the modern principle of strict construction *(nulla poena sine lege),*[26] seemingly perpetuating the very evil against which the rest of the statute strains. Moreover, Article 105 has echoes elsewhere in the Carolina, where careful offense definitions conclude with expansive grants of discretion in punishment. Article 113 ("Punishment of someone who falsifies weights, measures, and goods") for example,[27] provides that one found guilty of the offense

shall be put to penal sanction, banished from the territory or flogged with rods upon his body or the like, according to the nature and character of the conviction; and it may be that when such falsification has been frequently substantial and wilful, the criminal should be punished with death, all according to the advice which is discussed at the end of this our ordinance [a reference to Article 219, containing the Carolina's general scheme establishing where a perplexed local court should look for legal advice].

What reconciles such discretion with the commitment to a criminal law of rule is the effort to have the discretion be rule-guided and professionally administered. Discretion to fit the punishment to the seriousness of the crime, as in the article just quoted, or discretion in Article 105 to analogize in unforeseen cases—neither is discretion to proceed

26. Radbruch 14; Schmidt, *Carolina* 22; von Hippel 177.
27. Articles 114, 115, and 119 instance similar latitude.

by fiat. Flexibility in sentencing offends no modern scruples, and Article 105 would offend no Anglo-American jurisdiction which retained a common law of crimes. The Carolina itself, in a lengthy introduction to its substantive part (Article 104),[28] stresses that discretion in setting punishment pertains only in the absence of authoritative disposition in the statute, or failing that, in Roman law. Even then, it is a discretion granted to "a good, legally knowledgeable judge who can rule upon [the] circumstances and seriousness of the crime." Still, discretion thus conditioned had to confront the fundamental complaint of the Carolina, that "most criminal courts are staffed with persons who have not studied, had experience with, or exercised our Imperial law."[29] The solution was to trust the lay court in clear cases, to instruct it where possible,[30] and to direct it to seek learned advice in cases of complexity. This scheme, already apparent in the Carolina's substantive law, comes to full vigor and will be better understood in the realm of adjective law. It will unravel the great strands of the German reception in the criminal process.

B. THE CRIMINAL PROCEDURE OF THE CAROLINA

After so much prologue we reach our principal object of comparative study, the Carolina's explicitly procedural sections. They are extensive: the Preamble and Articles 1–103, 181–206, and 218–219. (A translation appears in Appendix B.) The size of the statute poses a less serious problem of organization for present purposes than might be supposed, because its provisions are fairly systematically grouped around the phases of the process and arranged in what is essentially sequence-in-time. That the statute should be so conveniently arranged was no accident to the draftsman, concerned as he was to simplify his product for unlearned users. Although other divisions—either more or less detailed—are possible, it will be convenient for the present study to discuss the procedural scheme of the Carolina in seven sections:

28. Translated in Appendix B.
29. Preamble.
30. The final sentence of Article 104 explains:
And in order that judges and judgment-givers who are not learned in such law may, in deciding upon such punishment, act that much less against the said law or against good and permissible custom, there is below set out regarding some punishments when and how the said law shall operate in accord with good custom and reason.

(1) Court structure and staffing (Preamble, Articles 1–5)

(2) Initiation of proceedings, both ex officio and by formal private complaint (Articles 6–17)

(3) The inquiry procedure, including the Indizienlehre regulating the use of torture and the rules controlling confessions and witness testimony (Articles 18–77)

(4) The ceremonial final process of condemnation and execution (Articles 78–103)

(5) The system of recordation during the inquiry procedure and the formulary practice for final judgment (Articles 181–203)

(6) Regulation of court costs and rectification of certain improprieties (Articles 204–206, 218)

(7) Provision for the taking of outside legal advice (Article 219).

1. Court Structure and Staffing[31]

The Carolina often voices its dissatisfaction with the traditional lay courts which the political disarray of the Middle Ages had bequeathed. The Preamble announces the predicate of the statute to be that "most criminal courts are staffed with [laymen]," in consequence of which "in many places proceedings are often contrary to law and reason, and either the innocent are punished and killed or the guilty reprieved, dismissed and set free through irregular, deceitful, and protracted proceeding . . . ." Among the most fundamental events of what is called the reception of Roman law in Germany was the functional displacement of these lay courts in matters civil and criminal, and to the Carolina has been attributed a vital part in the transition to a professional judiciary.

The Carolina did not operate directly in the matter of court structure. Imperial legislation abolishing the customary courts and substituting professional ones by fiat would have been unthinkable. Elsewhere in Europe more potent central authorities would be unable to effect drastic legislative change in court structure for several centuries.[32] The Carolina's Preamble concedes the impossibility of imperial reconstruction of the lay courts whose incompetence it protests, for "according to long-established usage in German territory in these matters, the criminal courts in many places cannot be staffed with legally knowledgeable, ex-

31. Preamble, Articles 1–5.

32. Systematic legislative rationalization of court structure and administration in France awaited the Revolution, prior to which there was "a complexity bordering on utter confusion." F. Ford, *Robe and Sword* (Harper Torchbook ed., New York, 1953) 35. In England the debris from the medieval profusion of courts was cleared away only with the Judicature Acts of the 1870s and successor legislation.

perienced and practiced persons." The Preamble in fact contains the great trophy of German legal particularism, the saving clause which remitted the statute to subsidiary validity as against contrary local practice.

The Carolina's contribution to the professionalization of the courts needed to be circuitous. The ordinance promulgated as a model a vast and complex criminal law, both substance and procedure, drawn heavily from learned Italian jurisprudence and capable of adequate administration only by professionals; it exhorted the laymen to apply that law when they could and to defer to professional administration when they could not. In the main this is a story more appropriately told in connection with the concluding provisions of the Carolina, and we shall return to it there.

The Carolina does at its outset make a few dispositions bearing directly on court structure and staffing (Articles 1–5). They are interesting for their skimpiness, their failure to attempt to remedy the deficiencies the Preamble bemoans. Article 1 addresses the problem of lay staffing only to say that the personnel of the courts should be "the best and most upright" available. Anything more serious falls to the local authorities, whose responsibility it is to "exert all appropriate diligence to see that the criminal courts are ordered to the best, and that injustice be done to no one . . . ." The rest of these opening articles is detail, mostly taken over from the Bambergensis: provision for deputation in the patrimonial (proprietary) courts and for the seating of aristocrats in the customary courts.[33] Articles 3, 4, and 5 prescribe the forms of oath of office for judge, Schöffen, and court scribe. While one commentator has found in the oaths a further expression of the concern that the officials be bound to the law,[34] these rituals may simply reflect the Carolina's general propensity to codify the ceremonious.[35]

In sum, the opening paragraphs of the ordinance raise a problem they do not solve. It will be shown that the ordinance is elsewhere more responsive to the chords struck in its Preamble. Political reality prevented frontal assault on the lay courts. Against the route which the

33. Articles 1 and 2. These provisions are said to confirm then-current practice. H. von Weber, "Die Peinliche Halsgerichtsordnung Kaiser Karls V.," *Zeitschrift der Savigny-Stiftung für Rechtsgeschichte* (*germanistische Abteilung*) 77:288, 300 (1960) [hereafter cited as von Weber].

34. Schmidt, *Inquisitionsprozess* 79.

35. Typified by the final *Rechttag* procedure of Articles 78–103, discussed infra, pages 187–192.

Carolina in fact took, there was considerably less defense: the introduction of procedures which obsoleted the customary courts in function but not in form.

2. *Initiation of Proceedings*[36]

As had the Wormser Reformation before it, the Carolina both retained and discouraged the medieval private complaint procedure. The Carolina, however, integrated its private complaint procedure into its Inquisitionsprozess.

Official or public process is the norm of the Carolina. Article 6 empowers the local authorities to arrest upon suspicion and directs them thereafter to investigate *without* torture. It cautions them at the very outset that examination of the suspect under torture is subject to the further constraints of the statute. Article 6 contrasts a lower standard of suspicion to arrest someone than to examine him under torture; the latter requires the "legally sufficient . . . indication" of the Indizienlehre, the former nothing more than "common repute" or notoriety.[37] The necessity for somewhat hasty arrest arose not only from the substantial absence of the modern detective force, but also from the fragmentation of jurisdiction which made flight from a city or territory an effective way to avoid its criminal process.[38]

The private process of the Carolina is in a sense illusory. The Wormser Reformation had resolved the problem of the relation between private process and Inquisitionsprozess by placing the two in irreconcilable opposition. The private party who chose to pursue the ancient private form of initiation was denied access to official help and was bound at his peril to prosecute successfully.[39] The private action was conditioned upon terms so onerous that the inducement to leave prosecution

36. Articles 6–17.

37. In a Frankfurt case, for example, a pair of nonresidents were detained on the ground that the source of their money was not evident. K. E. Meinhardt, *Das peinliche Strafrecht der freien Reichsstadt Frankfurt am Main im Spiegel der Strafpraxis des 16. und 17. Jahrhunderts* (Frankfurt, 1957) 63 and n. 10. Hasty arrest had its obvious drawbacks, which the Carolina disowns in Article 218.

38. Apart from setting the standard for arrest, however, Articles 6–10 do little more than summarize and preface the Inquisitionsprozess which the statute is about to detail. It has been suggested that the purpose of the summary was to show the self-sufficiency of the official process, its independence of the private complaint procedure treated in Articles 11–15 following. Schmidt, *Carolina* 27.

39. Supra, Chapter 7, note 88.

to the officials would be irresistible in any case short of palpable guilt. The Carolina's tactic is nearly the reverse: it hampers the private action not by isolation but by assimilation. The Carolina permits private initiation, but subjects it to the subsequent stages of the ex officio process.[40] The private complainant may remain active to assist the official investigation,[41] but control over the later phases of the process passes to the officials: "It is above all to be noticed that the accusatorial process of the Bambergensis and the Carolina is really nothing more than a pure Inquisitionsprozess in which the complaint of a private party . . . has been retained simply as a still-possible mode of initiation of proceedings [which] meant absolutely nothing."[42] Understandably, the ancient private form died hard, since it had about it the sense of individual entitlement. The force of conservatism, therefore, induced the Carolina to retain something of the traditional private form. Nonetheless, the draftsman wanted to discourage such interference with Offizialprinzip. In pure Inquisitionsprozess the proceeding would be instituted only when the official wished it. Between private denunciation (not complaint) and official prosecution was interposed official discretion to decide whether or not the proceeding was warranted. The Carolina favors that Roman-canon safeguard for the accused, and it adopts the Roman-canon sanction designed to prevent its avoidance: Article 12 stipulates that when the private complainant insists upon his ancient right to institute prosecution, he must provide surety of an amount set by the court. The fund will compensate the accused should the complaint be found malevolent, dilatory, or mistaken.[43] Moreover, should the complainant be unable to make surety, yet insist upon prosecution in his own right, the statute requires that he be gaoled along with the accused.[44] These drastic deterrents assured "that the victim would find himself ever less prepared to institute private complaint, and were crimes not to go unpunished, Inquisitionsprozess would remain the only way."[45]

40. See the closing words of Articles 8 and 9.

41. E.g., Article 45; cf. Articles 70–77. It should nonetheless be emphasized that the Carolina's norm was passivity on the part of the complainant. Revealing in that regard is Article 17, reminding the complainant to leave his address with the court after he has had the accused gaoled: "don't-call-us,-we'll-call-you."

42. Schmidt, *Einführung* 126.

43. Articles 12 and 13 detail these arrangements.

44. Article 14.

45. Radbruch 16.

3. The Inquiry Procedure[46]

The crux of the Carolina's procedural scheme is the series of provisions regulating the means by which judicial proof is gathered and evaluated: the preconditions for torture, the verification of confessions extracted under torture, and the use of witness testimony.

The Carolina's achievement, remarkable for its time, was to strike a balance between the perpetually competing concerns of the criminal law. The statute sought simultaneously to advance the social interest in crime repression and to protect the individual against its excesses—"from esteem of justice and for the sake of the common weal."[47] Of the two policies, the concern to safeguard the individual seems more dominant in the Carolina, not necessarily because the draftsman valued it more in absolute terms, but because it had been the neglected aspect while the structure of official process was being elaborated in the later Middle Ages.

a. The Indizienlehre[48]

The most striking manifestation of the Carolina's concern with safeguard is the Indizienlehre, the set of rules generally taken over from Roman-canon procedure establishing preconditions for examination under torture. The student of the constitutionalized safeguards of modern American criminal procedure will find the system of the Carolina not unfamiliar: it amounts to a requirement of probable cause enforced by an exclusionary rule. The Carolina's term for probable cause is "sufficient indication," rendered throughout this book as "legally sufficient indication" *(redliche anzeygung)*, for examination under torture.[49] Article 20 imposes the exclusionary rule:

When legally sufficient indication of the crime which it is desired to

46. This section treats Articles 18–69. Mention should be made of Article 16, which rather falls between this and the preceding section. It seems to carry over the medieval summary procedure for persons caught red-handed or felt to be *friedbrecher*. This distinctive term implies that the landschädlichen Leute are meant; see Radbruch 13. The statute's own justification: to dispose of "such obvious and undoubted crimes . . . at the least possible cost."

47. The famous phrase of Article 104 (*"auss lieb der gerechtigkeyt, und umb gemeynes nutz willen"*).

48. Articles 18–44.

49. Article 18 imposes the standard, Article 19 defines it after a fashion, Article 20 insists upon its exclusivity.

> investigate has not been produced and proven beforehand, then no one shall be examined; and should, however, the crime be confessed under torture, it shall not be believed nor shall anyone be condemned upon that basis.

Moreover, the Carolina grants to the person who was illegally examined under torture a money recovery against the offending officials.[50]

The Carolina expostulates its Indizienlehre in the style we noticed in connection with the statute's substantive law sections. The general principle, once enunciated, is developed by example. Article 18 announces the standard of legally sufficient indication, and in the same sentence abandons the attempt to work out its meaning in a body of ordered doctrine ("it is not possible to set forth all of these matters . . . .").

> Nonetheless, however, in order that the officials, judges, and judgment-givers, who are otherwise uninstructed in these matters, may be the better informed as to what establishes a legally sufficient indication or suspicion, the following examples of legally sufficient indication or suspicion are hereafter set forth in a manner that everyone, to the extent of his German, can identify or distinguish.

Where possible, "an analogy shall be drawn in cases not named in these articles."[51] Failing that, the statute has its panacea: referral of the problem to outside experts.[52]

The catalog of exemplary situations is preceded by a few other qualifications. Suspicion arrived at through soothsaying is declared incredible.[53] Article 22 warns against confusing the standards for investigation with those for final judgment. Following classic Roman-canon evidence law, the Carolina will indicate in later articles that the require-

50. Article 20. Note too the final paragraph, which eliminates any waiver defense to the compensation claim. See also the final sentence of Article 21. Article 61 repeats the sanction.

51. Article 24. See W. Ullmann, "Reflections on Medieval Torture," *Juridical Review* 56:123, 128–129 (1944).

52. Article 7:

> When the aforementioned judgment-givers are in doubt about the decision whether, in a particular case, the adduced suspicion is or is not sufficient for examination by torture, they shall in consequence seek advice from the authorities—from the local authorities directly in charge of the penal jurisdiction, or from those places cited at the end of this our ordinance; and moreover, they shall accurately report in writing to the said authorities in such advice-seeking all the details and circumstances of suspicion known to them.

53. Article 21.

ment for conviction is either confession or the testimony of two eyewitnesses. This standard is higher than the standard of proof necessary to justify examination under torture. The relationship between the standards for preliminary process and for dispositive adjudication is further explained in Articles 22 and 30, which regulate the use of witness testimony in the preliminary process to establish "sufficient indication" for torture. There the two-witness requirement of the final process is employed in the preliminary process as well, when the testimony pertains to lesser matters of circumstantial import. When the gravamen of the crime is attested to by a single witness, that "half proof," although insufficient for conviction, will justify examination under torture.

The distinction between the sufficiency of one witness and of two is part of a larger division in the Indizienlehre based roughly upon the importance of the proposition or circumstance being proven. In general it can be said that the more remote the proposition from the probandum, the more insistent the statute that (1) it be corroborated by a second witness, and that (2) it be reinforced by evidence of some additional suspicious matter. The former is the gist of Articles 23 and 30, and the latter is the express standard of Article 27. Article 27 governs eight categories of more remote evidence itemized in Articles 25 and 26. (Later articles speak to the more cogent evidence of which a single item, well proven, suffices.) The eight categories, two of which—well proven—justify torture, are general to all crime, whereas the single-item categories of Articles 29–44 pertain to specific crimes or groups of crimes. Typical of the general categories are the following:[54]

> Second: When the suspected person has been caught or found at a place suspicious in the context of the deed. . . .
>
> Fifth: In cases of damage to property or person, attention shall be paid to whether the suspected person could have been motivated to the present crime out of envy, enmity, former threat, or in the expectation of some advantage.

The requirement that two such items be proven to justify torture is Italianate.[55]

One of the most sophisticated passages in the whole of the Carolina appears as a sort of proviso to these rules of remoter circumstantial evi-

54. Article 25.
55. Brunnenmeister 229–230.

dence. It is a plea that such seemingly simple rules not be applied mechanically. It is necessary, says Article 28, to consider fairly whatever favors the accused as well as what inculpates:

And when in consequence it is decided that the weight of suspicion is greater than the weight of exculpation, then torture may be employed. When, however, the grounds of exculpation have higher regard and attention than some lesser suspicions which have been made out, then examination under torture shall not be employed.

The Carolina approaches the balancing methodology of modern interest analysis in these sentences. Characteristically, the article concludes that "when something is doubtful in these matters, those responsible for ordering and conducting examination under torture shall seek advice from the legally knowledgeable . . . ."

The larger part of the Indizienlehre concerns the more cogent circumstances which, when properly established, singly suffice for examination under torture. Articles 29–32 regulate the situation collectively, Articles 33–44 govern individual offenses. The latter provisions exemplify the draftsman's technique of describing unambiguous hypothetical cases in lieu of generalizing a standard.[56] A convenient illustration is Article 41 ("Concerning sufficient indication of clandestine arson"):

When someone is suspected or accused of a covertly committed act of arson, and when this person is otherwise a fellow to be suspicious of, and it can be discovered that shortly before the fire he was in a stealthy and suspicious manner concerned with unusual and suspicious incendiary materials of the sort typically used to set fires clandestinely, that provides legally sufficient indication of the crime unless he can show with good, credible basis that he used or wanted to use them to noncriminal ends.

What is strange to the modern eye is that the draftsman thought it necessary to belabor anything so obvious. The same point arises when Article 43 draws out the nexus between burglary and burglary tools, or when Article 37 soberly links the purchase of poison to the crime of poisoning. These paragraphs do suggest the degree of naïveté the Carolina must have ascribed to its users.

A final point of interest in the Indizienlehre is Article 31, which

56. With the consequence foreseen in Articles 18 and 24.

cautions against the dangers of accomplice testimony. In the context of the more cogent sort of matter, the testimony of a single witness[57] to the gravamen could justify torture. Hence comes a caveat to look for improper motivation in the denunciation of an accomplice. Certain of the practices instituted in the next section of the statute are anticipated: emphasis on criminating circumstances rather than on mere conclusory denunciation, and avoidance of "suggestive questioning" by which the examiner supplies the declarant with the factual detail for false witness.

b. Torture and Confession Practice[58]

Much of the spirit which animates the Indizienlehre carries over to the Carolina's rules for handling those examinations under torture which the Indizienlehre does permit. The concern with the unreliability of coerced testimony which underlies the Indizienlehre's threshold limits on resort to coercion is manifest in the rules which regulate the subsequent application of coercion. The purpose of these rules is to increase the likelihood that coerced confessions will still be truthful.

Initially, however, one more threshold determination is interposed before torture is permitted. It is the rule that matters in exculpation which might exonerate the accused of the crime be first investigated:[59]

> When . . . the accused denies the crime under consideration, then it shall be assiduously inquired of him whether he can show that he is innocent of the alleged crime, and the prisoner shall in particular be asked to remember whether he can prove and establish that at the time the crime under consideration was committed he was with people or at a place or location whereby it can be recognized that he cannot have done the crime of which he is suspected. *And such exhortation is thus needed because many a person out of simpleness or fright, even when he is quite innocent, does not know how he should proceed to exculpate himself of the thing.* And when the prisoner in this manner or in like-serving way indicates his innocence, then the judge shall as quickly as possible investigate the exculpation proffered . . . .

The italicized language, whose compassion has been justly praised,[60] shows itself the product of an experienced judge.

57. Articles 23, 30.
58. Articles 45–61.
59. Article 47 (italics added).
60. E.g., Radbruch 18.

Failing exculpation, the Carolina directs as a last alternative to torture that the accused be examined under the mere threat of torture.[61]

The Carolina does not regulate the modes of torture. Article 58 remits the problem, which it conceptualizes as quantum ("much, often or seldom, hard or lenient"), to the discretion of the supervising judge. The statute's sole disposition is the optimistic prescription of Article 59 that "[w]hen the accused has serious wounds or other injury to his body, examination under torture against him shall be conducted so that he is as little as possible hurt in these wounds or injury." What the Carolina does regulate is the testimonial product of examination under torture. The statute imposes safeguards at several levels, by placing limits upon (1) what may be asked, (2) who shall ask it, (3) when it may be transcribed and attested, and (4) how it shall be verified.

The limitation upon what may be asked is Article 56's prohibition of the suggestive question, some anticipation of which has been noticed above in the Indizienlehre's provision governing accomplice denunciation. Questions administered under torture should elicit detail, not supply it. Confession should be more than conclusory self-crimination; it should disclose enough detail to be independently verifiable. It is particularly desirable for the accused to divulge matters "which no innocent person can know."[62] Because that design would "probably be frustrated when the said circumstances of the crime were previously told to the prisoner," Article 56 instructs that "nothing . . . be put to the accused before or during examination . . . ."

The Carolina directs in Article 46 that it is the judge who should interrogate the accused in the presence of two Schöffen and the court scribe. The statute speaks constantly of the judge himself examining. This active role[63] of the judge represents one of the great departures from ancient Germanic practice and exemplifies the Carolina's ancillary effect upon court structure. We shall have further occasion to discuss it.[64] In the present context it is to be noted that the Carolina authorized a system of judicial torture, not some broader creature we might call police torture. The safeguards of the statute had more chance of being

61. Article 46.
62. Article 54.
63. Noticed in R. Blankenhorn, *Die Gerichtsverfassung der Carolina* (Tübingen, 1939) 29.
64. Infra, pages 187, 191–192, 194, 200–201.

adhered to in practice when the judge himself was operating the most sensitive phase of the process.

The Carolina distrusted its tortured confession. The statute propounded a pair of rules designed to capture whatever enhanced reliability might result from the passage of time between physical agony and testimonial utterance. First, Article 58 directs that "what the tortured person says shall not be taken down or transcribed while he is being tortured, rather he shall make his statement when he is released from torture." Of course this is a pallid safeguard, since the fellow can be promptly strung up for more. Nonetheless, it points up again the draftsman's awareness that torture might coerce falsehood as well as truth, and it reveals him searching for remedy. Similarly motivated and similarly defective to the purpose is the procedure of confirmation in Article 56:

> [T]he prisoner shall also, at minimum two or more days after the torture and his confession . . . , be brought before the competent judge and two Schöffen in the guard room or in another room and his confession read to him by the court scribe, after which he shall be asked a second time whether his confession is true, and what he says to that shall also be transcribed.

A more effective device to enhance the reliability of confession testimony is the scheme of subsequent investigation and verification. Once the accused has confessed, the statute directs that he should "be questioned subsequently without torture for further information."[65] The purpose is to elicit the maximum amount of factual detail bearing upon the crime, to maximize the opportunity for successful verification of the confession. Again the draftsman prefers to illustrate rather than generalize: Articles 48–52 suggest the focus of questioning for particular cases (murder, arson, and so forth). As with other instances of this technique, the statute joins to its hard cases the command to analogize in cases it does not specifically regulate (because "it is all too long to be described"[66]).

Indicative of the handling of particular cases is Article 48, dis-

65. The quoted language is from the group title for Articles 48 ff., preceding the title for Article 48.

66. Article 53. Further: "Any knowledgeable person can surely deduce from the above exposition how he should handle such additional questioning in other cases . . . ."

cussing the further questioning of a confessed murderer which should be undertaken for "the discovery of the truth . . . ." As striking here as in earlier instances is the simpleness of the points toward which the draftsman feels it necessary to instruct his magistrate:

[W]hen [the accused] has confessed to a murder, he shall be asked the reason he did the crime, on which day, at what hour, and at what place, whether anyone helped him to it and who; also where he buried or put the dead man, with what weapons the said murder was committed, how and what sort of blows or wounds he gave or inflicted upon the dead man, or how otherwise he killed him, what the murdered person had upon him by way of money or other things, and what he took from him, where he put this, or sold, dispersed, parted with, or hid it; and such questions as in many respects apply just as well to a robber or thief.

Having elicited such details, the Carolina requires that the judge have them checked to the extent feasible. He should "send to the places and . . . have it inquired whether the confession . . . is or is not true . . . ."[67] Ideally, we have said, this process will induce the confessed criminal to divulge "such circumstances as occurred in the event and which no innocent person can know."[68]

c. *Witness Testimony*[69]

The preoccupation of the Carolina with instituting limitations upon torture and confession as protections for the accused reflects rather faithfully an internal counterweight: the extent of the underlying commitment to the jurisprudence of the tortured confession. The Carolina does contemplate conviction upon the basis of witness testimony in the absence of confession;[70] but the bias for confession is overpowering. Remarkably, the statute commands that even when adequate witness testimony has been marshaled, a last try should be made to get the confession. "When the accused still will not confess after sufficient proof, it shall be declared to him that the crime is proven of him, in order that his confession can be secured . . . ."[71]

67. Article 54.
68. Id.
69. Articles 62–77.
70. Articles 22, 62 ff., esp. 67.
71. Article 69. In Frankfurt it is said that torture was employed even where there were two sufficient witnesses. Condemnation only rarely rested upon witness testimony alone. Meinhardt (supra, note 37) at 74.

The transparently Roman-canon basis of the Carolina's witness proof system has been long remarked.[72] The requirement of "full proof" by at least two [73] eyewitnesses [74] is taken over, elaborated with the expected disqualifications for bribed [75] or false [76] testimony. The indigenous peculiarities of the scheme concern court structure. Article 72 says in essence that a court not professionally staffed is not fit to conduct witness proof proceedings, and it provides for the calling in of surrogates—a substitute professional court. Article 71 discloses that among the virtues it ascribes to a learned judge is his capacity to observe and record demeanor and to discern factual inconsistency. It seems that the formal witness proof proceeding was an exceptional one, derived from Roman-canon practice and invoked principally at the insistence of a private complainant.[77]

d. Evaluating the Evidence

It will be seen that the Carolina purported to preserve the ancient Germanic analogue to English public trial, the final *Rechttag*. It will also be observed that there was left to that proceeding a wholly ceremonial role; it promulgated a judgment previously concluded. The key provision is Article 81 ("The conference of the judgment-givers before the Rechttag"):[78]

> Before the Rechttag all that has been gone into shall be read out before the judge and judgment-givers; [all the prior proceedings which the court scribe has transcribed shall be] brought before the judge and judgment-givers. On that basis judge and judgment-givers can discuss among themselves and decide what judgment they wish to speak.

One gathers that even this session was in the nature of a dress rehearsal for the Rechttag spectacle. The judge who had conducted the inquiry was not likely to call this meeting of the full court until he had elicited the requisite confession or full witness proof. The proof,

72. See Brunnenmeister 222.
73. Article 67.
74. Article 65.
75. Article 64.
76. Article 68.
77. See Articles 62, 70, 186; cf. Article 151 ff.
78. Article 81 continues to require that in event of doubt about the disposition, advice of the legally knowledgeable be sought.

typically confession, was simply read out by the court scribe, together with the record of its verification. Such deliberation as occurred in this ex parte proceeding was probably directed to the various options in sentencing, Article 81 suggests.

There is in fact no formal stage of the Carolina's main procedure at which the question of the sufficiency of the evidence is in question. This follows logically enough from the predominance of confession in the Carolina's system of proof. Confession concludes the issue from the mouth of the accused. Hence the confident prescription of Article 60: when the confession has been obtained in accord with the rules set forth, it is "undoubtedly credible; and upon it, according to the nature of the case, penal sanction is to be pronounced . . . . " As long as confession has not been secured, the tendency is to keep trying to obtain it; once confession is secured, the problem of evidentiary sufficiency is concluded. The gap between these two possibilities is the confession once uttered and then recanted, a problem which Article 57 deals with, principally by further torture looking to reutterance of the confession.[79]

4. *Final Process: The Rechttag*[80]

One would be hard pressed to describe the Carolina's final phase of public condemnation and execution without resort to the language of the theater. For the Rechttag is theater. It is in fact the ceremonial spectacle at which a decision already concluded among the members of the court is publicly promulgated. The elaborate formalism of stage directions and set speeches harkens back to the days of the ritual proofs, where the words of "pleading" were themselves operative. Only now there is no waiting for the judgment of God. "[T]he judgment lay already completed on the court table . . . "[81] for insertion into the ancient drama.

The Carolina scripts the performance meticulously. The curtain

79. There is occasion for the evaluation of the proofs when proceeding is by formal witness testimony and not confession. This is why the draftsman in Articles 71 and 72 provides for a panel of learned examiners.

80. Articles 78–103. The term *Rechttag* has not been rendered into English here or in the translation of the Carolina in Appendix B. The literal "law day" is hopelessly wooden, whereas the word "trial" could be taken to import the idiosyncrasies of English common law procedure into the Germanic folk court.

81. Radbruch 21.

rises, as it were, to "the customary bell-ringing,"[82] at whose peal judge and Schöffen parade to the local court seat (generally the marketplace). There they seat themselves, the judge remembering to display an attention-riveting prop: a staff or a bared sword.[83] Dialogue ensues among the court, the statute supplying each performer his lines:[84]

> When the court has thus seated itself, then the judge shall ask each of the Schöffen individually: "N., I ask you whether the final court is properly staffed for criminal proceedings." When the said court is staffed with not less than seven or eight Schöffen, then each Schöffe shall answer: "Lord judge, the final criminal court is properly staffed according to Emperor Charles V's and the holy Empire's ordinance."

Jurisdiction thereby resolved, the accused is escorted on by, among others, the executioner.[85] If this strikes him as not a propitious augury, it confirms the trend of some earlier signals to him—priestly visitations and public pillorying.[86]

With the dramatis personae in place, "pleading" commences. Subject to local desuetude, the Carolina preserves a ceremonial denunciation to be performed at the behest of an aggrieved complainant.[87] This done, the statute provides for orators for and against the accused.[88] Each is given a set speech, with fill-in blanks for the various proper names and for the offense.[89] The draftsman anticipated incompetence even here, hence the concluding provision of Article 89:

> [W]hen the orator cannot make the said complaint and motion orally he may submit it to the court in writing and say the following: "Lord judge: I ask that you might let your scribe publicly read out the complainant's complaint and plea from the sheet of paper submitted."

The prosecutorial speech itself is utter rote, reciting the presence of the accused and praying judgment on the complaint "with regard to all the proceedings and to the writings produced . . . ."[90] As for the response,

82. Article 82.
83. Id.
84. Article 84.
85. Article 86.
86. Articles 79, 85.
87. Article 87.
88. Customarily chosen from among the Schöffen: Article 88.
89. For the prosecution, Articles 89–90; for the accused, Articles 90–91.
90. Article 89.

when the accused has no defense, "he may do nothing other than plead for mercy or let it be pleaded for him . . . ."[91] When he has adduced a defense in the course of the prior inquiry proceedings and now persists in it, the set speech in his behalf recites the fact of defense and prays judgment. The actual merits of the attempted exculpation are not reopened in the Rechttag. The function of the defendant's submission is mere *litis contestatio,* joinder. The closest that the Rechttag comes to true deliberation is the procedure for sustaining a confession recanted at the Rechttag itself. One can understand the danger that such would occur as the accused, still accompanied by the executioner, saw the hopelessness of his situation. The Carolina's solution is the one already noted in the Maximilianischen Halsgerichtsordnungen: "the judge shall inquire on oath of the two commissioned Schöffen who with him heard the said confession read out whether they heard the confession read out."[92]

Submissions to the court being concluded, an open-air "deliberative" phase follows in which the judge and Schöffen among themselves formulate "in writing the most appropriate and even-handed judgment . . . ."[93] This is pantomime, since they have just met privately in advance of the public sitting and have "decide[d] what judgment they wish to speak" and have had "the concluded judgment written down for the [Rechttag] proceeding . . . ."[94] Each then replies in an identical set speech that the written judgment just formulated is his.[95] The judge then orders the court scribe to read out the judgment.[96] The finale calls for the judge to break his staff,[97] then surrender the prisoner to the executioner, whom he commands to his duty. (The mode of execution will have been contained in the judgment.) Execution follows at once.[98]

There is provision for holding a Rechttag at which the accused is declared innocent,[99] but it would rarely have taken place. The Carolina intends that determinations of innocence take place in the

91. Article 90.
92. Article 91.
93. Article 92.
94. Article 81.
95. Article 93.
96. Article 94.
97. Article 96 (subject to contrary local custom).
98. Articles 97–98, 102.
99. Article 99.

investigative stage at the latest, and that they not be the subject of ceremony.[100] The Carolina's procedure for public display of innocence may have been a survival of the medieval *Inzichtverfahren*, a procedure in which a person laboring under community suspicion was himself able to institute public legal proceedings.[101]

Schwarzenberg did state something of the rationale for the Rechttag procedure in Article 123 of the Bambergensis, a counterpart of which was dropped from the final Carolina draft where it had followed the present Article 101.[102] He discussed the function of the final Rechttag in the course of explaining why he rigidified it—why he propounded a public procedure all of whose elements were "prescribed and appointed" rather than one in which "complaint, answer, motions, questioning, finding and so forth should vary with the character and the justice of each case":[103]

Following the custom and usage of this territory, our local criminal courts may be staffed with none other than common people, who necessarily have not learned or exercised the law; therefore throughout this our ordinance is found in all clarity, with the diligence appropriate to the need, the way all such judicial matters shall be conducted, heard and recorded at the final Rechttag; also where necessary how the judgment shall be made according to the advice of the legally knowledgeable; in order that at the final Rechttag no one be disadvantaged . . . .

Should submissions other than the ritual ones of the statute be allowed,[104]

such judges and court members would easily be confused in this regard, so that the judgment could not be resolved at the same final Rechttag. That would be a pernicious hindrance to the punishing of wrongdoing and against the common weal; the parties would also in this way come to great disadvantage and expense.

In other words, the ancient public process has been ceremonialized

100. See Article 61.

101. See the last sentence of Article 78, which allows the accused to petition for the holding of a final Rechttag; cf. Article 87. On the Inzichtverfahren see generally R. Müller, *Studien zum Inzichtverfahren nach bayerischen Quellen* (Leipzig, 1939).

102. See E. Schmidt, "Der Inquisitionsprozess in ober- und niederbayerischen Rechtsquellen des 15. und 16. Jahrhunderts," in *Festschrift für Hellmuth von Weber* (Bonn, 1963) 32, 35.

103. Article 123, *Die Bambergische Halsgerichtsordnung* (supra, Chapter 7, note 94) at 48.

104. Id. at 49.

out of fear that the incompetence of the lay courts might interfere with the essentially judge-operated Inquisitionsprozess of the rest of the statute. Nonetheless, says the draftsman, the show must go on, the ancient formalities must be complied with, since judge, Schöffen, and scribe are all "bound and obligated to see to it that no one is abridged in his rights . . . ." And those rights included the final Rechttag —"on account of [the expectations of] the common people and ancient custom . . . ." The ceremony supplied reassuring continuity to tradition-bound communities. Criminal justice was still being settled in the folk court of Germanic antiquity.

Schwarzenberg's candor has supplied us with evidence of the changing relationship between Inquisitionsprozess and the ancient forms. The newer preliminary process (the *Vorverfahren)* had become the exclusive deliberative process. The customary process of final public condemnation (the *Hauptverfahren)* had been reduced to rote and rite. The lay court was being ousted in function but retained in form. Article 93 of the Carolina still puts in the mouth of each Schöffe the words, "Lord judge: it is my judgment which has been formulated in writing . . . . " But it is his by adoption, not conception. The whole of the Vorverfahren has been conducted by the judge. He has administered the Indizienlehre's "probable cause" determination, he has supervised the examination under torture (in the presence of two passive Schöffen-witnesses), he has arranged the verification of the confession, he has handled the taking of witness proofs. Only then, when he has secured confession or full proof, does the judge summon the Schöffen for the pre-Rechttag session of Article 81 at which judge and Schöffen take up the case on the basis of the written record which has been compiled under the direction of the judge. This is already the dress rehearsal, where the judgment is being settled for the Rechttag. When Article 123 of the Bambergensis lays its petrification of the final Rechttag to the danger that the untrained laymen "would easily be confused," it puts the capstone on all that we have seen. The Vorverfahren has become the functional Hauptverfahren. And the layman is being displaced by the professional—a substitution which the Carolina did not simply confirm and refine, rather one which the Carolina itself facilitated enormously in the later sixteenth century. As we shall see, that is the story of Article 219 at the Carolina's close.

5. The Formulary Practice[105]

A lengthy section of the Carolina's procedural regulation consists in instructions and literal forms to be employed by the clerk, called throughout the statute the court scribe. These provisions, translated in Appendix B, belong to two groups. Articles 181–189 instruct the scribe on recording the stages of the Vorverfahren, Articles 190–203 contain instructions and forms-of-words for the framing of final sentence.

The instructions of Articles 181–189 specify that the significant events and utterances of the preliminary process be recorded in a continuous dossier: complaint (whether private[106] or ex-officio[107]), response,[108] "probable cause" for torture,[109] the accused's response under threat of torture,[110] confession under torture and any corroborating evidence secured to verify it,[111] witness proofs in default of confession,[112] and proceedings in exculpation.[113] Article 189 summarizes these directions in the light of their purposes. The record shall be carefully transcribed

> sequentially and in the form of a file; and there shall always be reported for every proceeding the year, day, and hour it transpired; in addition the scribe shall affirm . . . that he heard and transcribed everything, in order that upon the basis of a thorough transcript done in this way judgment may be firmly and surely given, or where it is necessary, that advice may be sought thereupon as to proposed judgment as need be; . . . .

The shaping of the record as a continuous file, the notion of the French *dossier*, the German *Akte*,[114] is canon-derived, as is the practice of careful dating of entries.[115] The *Aktenversendung* system we are

105. Articles 181–203. With the Carolina's forms of judgment compare those for the English assize court in the 1681–1682 edition of the *Clerk of Assize* manual cited supra, Chapter 2, note 15, at 63–68.
106. Article 181.
107. Article 188.
108. Articles 181–182.
109. Article 183.
110. Article 184.
111. Article 185.
112. Article 186.
113. Article 187.
114. See von Hippel 209 and n. 4.
115. Cf. Article 182. The Roman-canon continuous dossier complete with dating to the half-day is exhibited in the Worms heresy inquisition cited supra, Chapter 7, note 71.

shortly to discuss was absolutely dependent upon the creation of proper Akten. Article 189 itself speaks to the connection between its instructions for transcription and the contingency "that advice may be sought thereupon . . . . " Otherwise, the dossier is commanded "in order that upon the basis of a thorough transcript done in this way judgment may be firmly and surely given . . . . " Judgment is settled at the meeting of the Schöffen and the judge just in advance of the Rechttag sitting.[116] Because it is required (both in Article 189 and in Article 81) that the judgment be based upon the dossier, control of the dossier is effectively control of the result. And the dossier chronicles what the judge has done.

The formulary practice of Articles 190–203 has a like effect. In guise, these rules and forms bind the scribe. In effect, they limit the Schöffen. These are the rules for formulating the final judgment promulgated at the Rechttag sitting, although decided upon at the advance meeting of the court. Ostensibly this section of the statute is no more than a catalog of ceremonious proclamations. But the catalog is exclusive, hence it precludes improvisation from within the court. The forms correspond to the sanctions authorized in the Carolina's substantive law. They stylize the full range of alternatives, reinforcing the insistence of Article 104 that what discretion it allows in adapting punishments be that of "a good, legally knowledgeable judge who can rule upon [the] circumstances and seriousness of the crime."

6. Miscellaneous Reforms[117]

The thoughtful, genuinely systematic organization of the Carolina ceases with the judgment forms. The remainder of the statute dribbles off into the typical late medieval catchall of barely related dispositions. Some rules are set forth concerning property rights in stolen goods recovered, for example, and concerning the customary liability of carpenters and such to construct gallows.[118] Certain of these "reformations" have closer connection, however, to the Carolina's procedural structure and to the dominating concern of the draftsman to provide procedural protection for the individual.

116. Article 81. See supra, page 187.
117. Articles 204–206, 218.
118. Articles 207–214. Other property matters are dealt with in Article 206 and at the outset of Article 218.

One expression of that impulse is the effort to regulate costs—to set ceilings on some charges, prohibit others, and get the whole business under rule. The Carolina itself propounds no general tariff, but mandates that the authorities of each local court issue a schedule of charges "in order that thereby no one be excessively burdened . . . ."[119] The Carolina also shows a precocious disdain for the endemic fee system of the age, which obliged the litigant to pay various court functionaries for their services.[120] When the officials have a financial stake in criminal justice, the conflict of interest risks extortion or worse. Hence the statute's strident denunciation of the "abuse . . . by which the judges request and receive special payment from the complainant [for] every criminal who is punished, which practice is wholly contrary to the office and dignity of a judge . . . ."[121]

Closer still to the Carolina's procedure is the complaint voiced in Article 218, "that the gaols are contrived more to torture than to keep custody of the prisoners and persons confined." It must be remembered that the Carolina dates from half a century before the advent in Europe of the sentence of imprisonment as a regular mode of punishment.[122] Detention in the Carolina serves an exclusively custodial function, pending judicial investigation and disposition. It is not itself intended as a punishment.[123] In theory, even the scheme of incarcerating the private complainant intended not a penal deterrent to private complaint procedure but a custodial guarantee that someone wrongfully accused by a private complainant would not have his civil damage remedy defeated by the physical escape of the complainant.[124] The Carolina's exhortation "that the gaols should be erected and established for the custody of the prisoner and not intentionally to intensify his suffering"[125] is part of the broader program of protecting the individual in Inquisitionsprozess.

119. Article 204. Cf. Article 75.

120. See the concluding portion of Article 204; see also Article 205.

121. Article 205. Cf. Article 206, forbidding judge and authorities to confiscate any property of a fugitive for their own benefit. A similar provision is among the reforms of Article 218 with regard to the property of convicts.

122. Von Hippel 242–249.

123. Save possibly for an obscure preventive detention scheme in Article 176.

124. Article 14 authorizes detention of the complainant only when he has proved unable to post the money surety specified in Article 12.

125. Article 11, anticipating Article 218. It should be remarked that the Wormser Reformation had expressed a like concern:

Those who are put in gaol or lockup should not be held there for more than

This policy manifests itself elsewhere in Article 218's catalog of grievances. In language resembling the Preamble's anguish at the injustice inflicted upon the innocent by ignorant courts, Article 218 decries

> that occasionally through the authorities carelessness, honorable persons are seized, without previous denunciation, ill repute and other sufficient indication, and brought into gaol, and that in the said seizure there is occasionally hasty and thoughtless conduct by the authorities, through which the person suffers detriment to his honor.

In the scholarly literature discussing the Carolina these self-conscious "reformations" figure in the debate about the Carolina's validity as obligatory law. The Carolina confronts local law at three levels. There are some instances where the Carolina encourages local custom; there are opposite cases where the Carolina seems to override local practice regardless of the saving clause; and there is the norm dictated by the saving clause in which the Carolina stands presumptively but subsidiarily valid, subject to contrary local practice.

The statute encourages local variation, for example, in several provisions in the final Rechttag scheme which validate the substitution of local customary ceremonial forms of proclamation, assembly, denunciation, and so forth;[126] or in the cost provisions already mentioned. There is controversy among historians regarding the opposite phenomenon in the Carolina, the overriding of local usage. It seems clear that at least a few of the Carolina's provisions were meant to survive the saving clause. The clause concedes to local practice its "old, well-established, lawful, and equitable usages."[127] When, therefore, the Carolina denounces some practices as unjust, hence unlawful and inequitable, this has been read as avoiding the clause. The more specific

---

> a few months, since gaol or lockup is instituted and authorized by law not to punish, but only to keep custody of those liable to punishment. Therefore our Bürgermeister or those set in his place shall be diligent in investigating to get at the truth, in order that the prisoner be discharged or punished according to law.

Wormser Reformation (supra, Chapter 7, note 86) bk. 6, pt. 2, tit. 11.

126. Articles 80, 82, 87, 96. By contrast note Article 100, aimed essentially at any attempt to open up the Rechttag phase and restore it a deliberative function. Local custom is abrogated: "And where the authorities learn that something to the contrary is practiced, they shall vigorously abolish it and punish for it, as often as it wrongfully appears."

127. Preamble.

of the reforms in Article 218 are the obvious examples: the "abuse" in some places "that the sentence is pronounced and proclaimed by the executioner rather than the judge or judgment-givers" or that local authorities are imposing forfeitures upon criminals' estates. The concluding disposition of Article 218 states:

> Concerning these and similar customs we desire that each of the authorities abolish them and pay attention that they be not practiced, used, or maintained in the future; hence we now by Imperial authority hereby abolish, nullify, and do away with them; and they shall in the future not be introduced.

This language would seem to apply as well to the more diffuse grievances of Article 218, concerning arrest and gaol conditions, although it is difficult to see how the statute could have been expected to have more than hortatory effect. The issue is murkier elsewhere in the statute, where less emphatic language is used which might suggest overriding force.[128]

Carolina enthusiasts have tried to analogize from the clearer instances of provisions falling outside the saving clause to a more general theory of obligatory force of the Carolina notwithstanding the saving clause. According to Robert von Hippel, the Carolina was a *Reichsgesetz* whose promulgation as a model would have been pointless, because the Bambergensis was already widely circulated. The saving clause could be dismissed as pertaining only to areas of "old" law, not to the "new" reception law of the Carolina.[129]

Von Hippel's arguments are not very attractive today. He overlooked the enormous enhancement of authority, albeit indirect authority, which the Bambergensis acquired when the Carolina translated it into an imperial model. His view of the Carolina as "new" law reflects the older view of reception which held sway until Eberhard Schmidt's work. Moreover, the later history of the Carolina unmistakably contradicts the notion that it was generally obligatory.[130] Long after its promulgation, the Carolina was being ignored or being

128. For example, Articles 1 and 100.

129. Von Hippel 211–212.

130. I take this point from G. Schmidt, "Sinn und Bedeutung der Constitutio Criminalis Carolina als Ordnung des materiellen und prozessualen Rechts," *Zeitschrift der Savigny-Stiftung für Rechtsgeschichte (germanistische Abteilung)* 83:239, 248 ff. (1966).

only partially applied in various places. Hennenberg in 1539 enacted a Landesordnung whose criminal procedure took over not the Carolina, but one of the Maximilianischen Halsgerichtsordnungen (the Radolfzell statute of 1506).[131] Bavaria's Landesordnung of 1553 discloses a criminal procedure untouched by the Carolina.[132] The city of Zwickau issued a Stadtrechtsreformation in 1569 (revising a 1539 draft) which followed the Carolina in various matters but garbled the Indizienlehre.[133] On the other hand, many of the territories, Hesse and the Electorate of Cologne included, confirmed the Carolina by adoption virtually from its issuance.[134] Nor ought the practical influence of subsidiary validity be minimized.

7. *Advice-Seeking and Aktenversendung*[135]

The concluding paragraph of the Carolina became the essential historical text for one of the more remarkable phenomena in Western legal history: the system of Aktenversendung, by which German courts effectively referred lawsuits for binding decision to professionals outside the court, in particular to university law faculties. Evidenced in its mature form after 1600,[136] the court of first instance would "simply . . . ship a full written record of the case to its expert advisers, who would thus have before them all the materials needed for a final decree . . . . [T]hat astonishing practice . . . one wise scholar long ago termed 'the decisive turning point' in the reception . . . . "[137]

131. Id. at 249 n. 36. See *Hennenberg Landesordnung . . . nach dem wahren Original de an. 1539* (Meiningen, 1720) 211–245.

132. G. Schmidt (supra, note 130) at 249 and n. 35. Cf. E. Schmidt (supra, note 102) at 38 ff., esp. 46–48.

133. *Die Zwickauer Stadtrechtsreformation 1539–69* (H. Berthold, K. Hahn, and A. Schultze, eds.) (Leipzig, 1935) 180–192. Cf. J. Vogel, *Der strafprozessuale Teil der Zwickauer Stadtrechtsreformation von 1539/1569 als Ausfluss des Rezeptionsgeistes* (Heidelberg, 1960) 32–57.

134. Schmidt, *Einführung* 142–143.

135. Article 219.

136. Dawson, *Oracles* 200 and n. 11.

137. Id. at 200, citing A. Stölzel, *Die Entwicklung des gelehrten Richterthums in deutschen Territorien* (Stuttgart, 1872) I 189, concluding the following discussion (Dawson, *Oracles* 199) of the development of Aktenversendung as "collective" and "binding" dispatch:

> [The] conviction that when law professors spoke collectively their conclusions were more than highly persuasive, indeed were formally binding . . . took time to grow. It was not a direct inheritance from the older *Oberhöfe*, whose influence, great as it was, was diffused too indirectly, through too many types of questioners and by procedures too unorganized for their responses to

The Carolina

The Carolina of 1532 did not compel this practice. It contemplated what it described—the advice, and not the decision, of the outside experts. "[B]efore 1550 [Aktenversendung] had not yet been organized in anything like its ultimate form . . . ."[138] Many later factors influenced the result, including the persistence of a "multitude" of local courts of first instance not made subject to an effective appellate structure or other control;[139] the demise of the *Oberhöfe*, the traditional sources of guidance for perplexed lay courts;[140] and the advance of Roman private law doctrine and procedure through the submissions of the parties, who would increasingly employ learned counsel.[141] Although the Carolina was not the immediate progenitor of the formed practice of Aktenversendung which substituted collective and binding decision of the law faculties for that of the court, it had "given a special impetus and also official sanction" to the court's practice of "consultation of learned experts."[142]

Article 219, the Carolina's provision for systematizing the seeking of advice, deals with the question of where to refer, not when or what (matters treated "in many places previously in this our . . . ordinance"). The perplexed local court should refer initially to that Oberhof (superior court) which the local court had traditionally used, and failing the availability of such, to the appropriate (political) authorities of the jurisdiction. However, the authorities are disqualified when they have themselves prosecuted the case ex officio. Then, and otherwise when doubt persists among the court or the authorities, advice

---

be invested with binding force. Nor could the result be ascribed to the Carolina, whose numerous references to aid from experts described it merely as seeking "advice" (*Rat*). But there were practical reasons that go far to explain the transition. Some collective responses by the faculties were written in German, but it was more natural for them to write in Latin, the normal medium for their own disputations. Whether written in German or Latin, the responses would usually be cast in technical language. If reasons were given or authorities cited, they would be, in any event, barely intelligible to their questioners. Under these circumstances the convenience of the inquiring court was actually served if the response was drawn up as a draft decree. As the sixteenth century progressed this was rendered more feasible by the rapid progress of Roman-canonist procedure, with its heavy emphasis on documentation. It became more common for the inquiring court to escape the task of formulating the legal questions that troubled them and merely to forward the documents.

138. Id. at 202.

139. Id. at 205.

140. Id. at 204.

141. See H. Coing, *Die Rezeption des römischen Rechts in Frankfurt am Main* (Frankfurt, 1939) 86–118, esp. 115–116.

142. Dawson, *Oracles* 197.

should be sought of the legally knowledgeable (*rechtverstendigen*)[143] at the nearest universities, cities, or elsewhere. "Roman-trained experts were not intended as the exclusive source,"[144] because the Oberhöfe of this time were still un-Romanized and the local authorities were only beginning to have professional jurists in their employ; on the other hand, the universities knew only civilians.[145]

The Carolina's insistent instruction that in case of doubt the court seek advice outside its members was the device which made the statute viable as a code of criminal law and procedure. Without advice-seeking, the Carolina would have been unworkable. The referral system explains how it was possible for a reception of learned law to take place in unlearned courts. The Carolina had three complementary solutions for that problem. First, it sought to instruct the laymen in the rudiments of principle. Second, it sought simultaneously to oust the laymen—to restrict the genuinely deliberative role of the unwieldly court of numerous laymen while enhancing the authority of the judge in their midst (who could increasingly be expected in the mid-sixteenth century in the more important local courts to have had some Roman-canon training). These two measures were not enough: there would inevitably be local jurisdictions so tiny or remote or for other reason resistant that the appearance of trained jurists as judges could not realistically be anticipated. And the Carolina's own 200-plus para-

143. The translation has been suggested by Dawson's, id. at 198: "those who know the law." The difficulty is to convey in English the idea that the rechtverstendigen were those thought to be informed in the law without necessarily being trained or professional.

144. Id.

145. Id. (footnote omitted):

> This clause was a complex compromise between the conflicting interests of the imperial government, the territorial princes who were struggling to extend their own power and the cities and subordinate court-keeping lords that had so far succeeded in eluding control. Earlier drafts of the Carolina had required merely that advice be sought from "higher authority," omitting even the *Oberhöfe*. This suited the interests of the territorial princes, whose efforts to cut off access to foreign *Oberhöfe* would soon cause most of them to dwindle away. But neither the imperial government nor court-keepers of subordinate rank wished to augment the powers of the great princes in an area so crucial as the criminal law. Many court-keepers of subordinate rank, though still claiming some degree of *Obrigkeit*, had no trained legal advisers in their entourages. And so the reference to the nearest "high school" (i.e., a university faculty of law) provided an alternative more acceptable to many. The consultation of the law faculties as authorized by the statute thus reflected the balance of forces that had so far been reached in Germany in the unremitting contest for political power.

graphs could not, as the draftsman so often acknowledged, predispose every case. Hence there had to be the third solution, the escape hatch. When neither code nor court could resolve a case within the sense of the code, an outlet had to be provided outside the court or the court would inescapably act outside the code.

The tightness of the interrelation of these three devices deserves some emphasis. Each presumed the other two. The Carolina had a seriously educative function. Its quality as a "law primer" *(Rechtsfibel)*[146] is striking. The concern was partially to educate the Schöffen to a level of some comprehension about why the judge had shaped the record as he had, why he had proposed the particular judgment, and why they should confirm it. But the critical concern was to educate the layman who served as judge, as inquisitor. Given the fractionation and dispersion of jurisdiction which permitted two thousand courts of first instance to operate in Saxony alone,[147] only partial professionalization of the judicial office could even be hoped for, mainly in the cities. The ordinance had to undertake to make laymen competent to perform the magistrate's role over the bulk of criminal administration—the easier cases. It had also to caution them about which problems were particularly difficult (for example, exculpation) and which particularly important (for example, the prerequisites for torture). In practice that was often education in when to abandon the job to the experts. The constant instruction to seek advice in difficulties procedural and substantive made viable the whole of the rest of the scheme. It deepened the infusion of learned law by providing for learned men. Article 219 does approve advice-seeking of the Oberhöfe, the ancient centers of non-Roman wisdom, as well as of the jurists, but that had no future. The Oberhöfe were atrophying or being Romanized, while the influence and numbers of the Roman-law-trained jurists in the courts, in practice, and in executive service was burgeoning. The Italianate basis of so much of the Carolina made it senseless to contemplate administration by persons ignorant of its principles when individual jurists and, above all, the law faculties were available. Having Romanized the law, the Carolina had in some measure to provide for Roman lawyers.

Another of the Carolina's most characteristic features, its emphasis

146. Von Weber 290. See supra, Chapter 7, note 98.

147. Dawson, *Oracles* 203–204, citing Boehm, "Der Schöppenstuhl zu Leipzig," *Zeitschrift für die gesamte Strafrechtswissenschaft* 59:371, 384–388 (1940).

on a comprehensive, consecutive dossier compiled from first suspicion through final sentence, was designed to facilitate the seeking of advice from distant experts. We shall see that the French procedure was as alert to have its dossier as the German its Akten. A major concern of the French process, like its canon model, was to facilitate review within a jurisdictional hierarchy. The German political-constitutional chaos had greatly retarded the development of ordered lines of appellate review. Nonetheless, we have seen that just that lack of larger system and control underlay the rise of Aktenversendung. The documentary tradition of canon process took a special twist in Germany and adapted itself to a special need—"that advice may be sought thereupon . . . ."[148]

C. THE GERMAN HISTORY IN COMPARATIVE PERSPECTIVE

While the Carolina is of itself an important object of historical study, in its comparative aspect it can add to the study of the English Marian legislation a dimension otherwise unobtainable. A proper understanding of the development of Inquisitionsprozes and the reception of Roman law in the German criminal process can bear upon several parallel issues in the English history.

First, a thesis of sudden reception as applied to Germany is unsupportable. Inquisitionsprozess developed there well in advance of the "full reception" of the Renaissance. The legislators of sixteenth-century Germany were not free agents transporting a fresh criminal process from foreign schoolbooks. All of the fundamental features of inquisitorial procedure were preexistent. The borrowings from Roman-canon process in the Wormser Reformation and the Bambergensis-Carolina were overwhelmingly conditioned by the needs of the extant system and by its parallels to the Roman-canon. Investigating magistrate and tortured confession had achieved general currency in crude form before the important reception statutes were enacted. The statutes brought refinement and safeguard, not structural innovation. Italian criminal science came to influence in Germany only after Inquisitionsprozess had already been largely established. What is called "the reception" was in fact a second-stage affair.

The importance of this matter of timing is that it undercuts the

148. Article 189.

powerful argument that formerly was made from another view of the facts. When the Renaissance reception was thought to have produced fundamental dislocation in the German criminal process, to have authored the transition to inquisitorial procedure; and when that had been the achievement of small bands of jurists in the employ and at the behest of the princes—then how much more likely a similar English pattern, given the greater power of the monarchy and the more centralized legal system. Thus Maitland extrapolated from Brunner's account of sixteenth-century German reception the "danger that [in England] *die fremdrechtlich geschulten Juristen,* [the jurists trained in foreign law] of whom there are a good many in the king's service, will gain the upper hand in the new courts that have emerged from the council, and will proceed [like Brunner's Germans] from *Verwaltung* to *Rechtsprechung* [from administration to adjudication]."[149] And Holdsworth, we have noted, spoke of "those new and effective codes of procedure with which the modern European states were arming themselves"[150] in terms implying that the appearance of Inquisitionsprozess in the Continental legal systems was an event of recency. On that rested something of the plausibility of the reception interpretation of the English developments. The reception thesis necessarily asserted a sudden rupture in the native tradition, and this thesis was sustained by an unsupported assumption that similar disruption had marked the Continental reception. However, Chapter 7 has shown that even in Germany, which experienced such an extraordinary reception in the Renaissance, the principal institutions of Inquisitionsprozess were already in place. That point established, we ought to reassert the significance ascribed to it in anticipation: the proponent of the English reception thesis must contend that there occurred in Tudor England a more radical break with the indigenous legal tradition than on the Continent, in this case in Germany, despite the more evident continuity in English legal institutions.

In fact, it is the evolutionary parallel between the late medieval developments in both systems which seems the more inviting. Both the German Inquisitionsprozess and the various late medieval English procedures involving the JPs as examiners (which Chapter 4 contends

149. F. W. Maitland, *English Law and the Renaissance* (Cambridge, 1901) 70 n. 43.

150. Holdsworth V 169–170.

were the true precursors of the Marian procedure) grew up as exceptions to the older criminal procedures and were then grafted on in ways which tended to empty the older competing procedures of substance while preserving their external forms. The balance struck in the Carolina between the newer inquisitorial process and the ancient final Rechttag has an analogue in the English development which was making the justices of the peace instrumental and the grand jury ceremonial.

The Carolina itself defies many of the preconceptions which a reader of Holdsworth might be expected to bring to it. It strikes one as a matter of crushing weight that the reception in German criminal procedure meant not a movement of enhanced crime repression, but of safeguard for individual rights against the existing machinery of repression. The Carolina was "*Reformwerk.*"[151] In England, on the other hand, agitation for reform of common law criminal procedure did not begin to stir until the Interregnum, nor to have effect until the end of the seventeenth century. There was a fundamental contrast of purpose between the changes in German criminal procedure through the reception and the innovations introduced in England under the Tudors. Whereas the English under a far more centralized government encountered the need for more organized means to repress crime, the Germans of that time, with governmental authority dispersed, had nevertheless already acquired repressive powers that needed to be contained. The Germans had Inquisitionsprozess and were principally concerned with limiting its excesses. If the English royal advisers of the day had turned to the German Empire's celebrated new ordinance, they would have laid it aside at once. For its essential purpose, manifested in virtually every paragraph, was running directly contrary to the contemporary English movement toward enhanced prosecutorial authority. It was not a model appropriate to the interests of Tudor crime control.

Even concentrating on those characteristic elements of Roman-canon process which bolstered the position of the state in Inquisitionsprozess, the Carolina had little to say to the problems of sixteenth-century English criminal procedure. In the main, it has been shown, the English needed to bridge a fissure which had opened in the jury system by the end of the Middle Ages. The grand jury was growing incapable of informing itself and thereby of initiating prosecution; and

151. H. Conrad, *Deutsche Rechtsgeschichte* (Karlsruhe, 1966) II 407.

this prosecutorial function had to be continued before the trial jury. The problem was to organize the gathering and presenting of evidence to the juries. Roman-canon process as exemplified in the Carolina was either unresponsive to the problem or else an overreaction. For it was predicated on the absence of jury trial. English procedure had permitted the trial jury, as successor to the ritual modes of trial, to convict without reference to objective standards for rational evaluation of evidence such as the Roman-canon system of arithmetic proofs. The jury system of ad hoc neighborhood triers had not called forth the limitations upon adjudicative discretion which the Roman-canon hierarchy had imposed upon its professionalized judicial corps. Roman-canon Inquisitionsprozess entered the Renaissance codes afflicted by the legacy of its own precocity: standards of proof high enough to contain judicial arbitrariness. Unwilling to let the judge convict much short of certainty (full proof = two eyewitnesses), the alternative was to rely upon inducing the accused to convict himself by confession.

The Roman-canon system of proofs which dominates the Carolina was perceived by the English of the day to be disadvantageous. As has been mentioned, the Statute of Pirates in 1535, three years after the Carolina and four years before the French ordonnance royale, makes a conscious substitution in Admiralty of common law jury trial for Roman-canon criminal process, explaining that efficient pirates seldom leave two witnesses.[152] The overwhelming preoccupation with judicial extraction of confession in the Carolina was all but pointless to the English law of proof. Not dependent upon confession for the efficacy of their criminal process, the English would have found themselves unattracted to a set of procedures which made confession the fundamental object. Of course there was no aversion to confession in English practice, then or since. Sir Thomas Smith portrayed his hypothetical JP securing a confession.[153] Confession evidence has always been highly persuasive to a jury; but the essential distinction from Continental practice was that conviction could easily be got without it. Time and again if one looks at the Indizienlehre of the Carolina, one is struck by the fact that an English jury could in the sixteenth century (and ever since) convict on the quantum of circumstantial evidence which the Carolina stipulates as a mere prerequisite for investigation

152. Supra, pages 55, 81.
153. Supra, Chapter 4, note 86.

under torture. And when reaction in the Enlightenment against the use of torture in the criminal process finally succeeded in Germany and generally in Europe in the eighteenth century, the Roman-canon standard of proof had to be abrogated.[154]

The Roman-canon system of torture and confession exacerbated rather than ameliorated the greatest problem of English criminal procedure, while disregarding its greatest strength. What it ignored, of course, was the efficiency of the jury standard of proof. It had the officers of the state do more; it required that they establish certainty. The problem it worsened was the underdevelopment of the investigative and prosecutorial function in English procedure, the task that had been stunted on account of the former efficacy of the presentment system. Roman-canon process required a vastly greater investigative-prosecutorial organization, because it effectively resolved all issues in the preliminary process. It imposed upon the preliminary process responsibilities so serious and time-consuming that it effectively compelled bureaucratization and professionalization. It has been suggested in Part I that the really critical problem which English procedure was facing in the sixteenth century was the need to organize the rudiments of a pretrial process. The Carolina would have been salt in the wound, calling as it did for a pretrial process so intricate that it all but presumed a professional magistracy.

It is difficult to think, therefore, that the Carolina would have appealed to an English draftsman of the time as a very instructive model. Preoccupied with confessions that the English did not need, based upon torture practices that the English had found unnecessary to employ,[155] operated by an increasingly professional and learned magistracy that the English did not possess, the Carolina's Roman-canon process was simply too foreign to the needs, the tradition, and the resources of common law process.

154. See Radbruch 19.

155. Jardine's admirable early work enumerates fifty-five cases from the years 1551–1640 in which the Privy Council ordered or referred to the use or threat of torture. Some of Jardine's cases are double-counted, but there are others in the Privy Council registers (then unpublished) which Jardine did not include. D. Jardine, *A Reading on the Use of Torture in the Criminal Law of England Previously to the Commonwealth* (London, 1837) 73–109. Holdsworth, at V 185, contends that Jardine's evidence "conclusively proved" that "torture was used all through this period . . . ." Elton has pointed out that Holdsworth, in "a very bad error," adduced no evidence for his contention that the court of Star Chamber employed torture. G. R. Elton, *The Tudor Constitution* (Cambridge, 1965) 170 n. 1. It is nevertheless an error which continues to be widely disseminated, e.g., R. van Caenegem, "La

The Carolina

The particular virtue of the Carolina as a model of actual reception in a legal system heavily staffed by laymen is that it suggests what would have had to be done in England to introduce Roman-canon procedure, had there been a wish to do so. The critical problem was the enormity and complexity of the learned procedure. We have seen that the Carolina's solution represented a diverse compromise. It sought to educate the lay magistrate to handle the basics, while encouraging him to defer to learned experts in cases of difficulty. This program was compelled, the Preamble said forthrightly, because "most criminal courts are staffed with persons who have not studied, had experience with or exercised [the learned] law." Since they cannot be got rid of, it has proven necessary to have "several learned, thoroughly experienced persons . . . make a summary . . . of how and in what manner judicial proceedings in criminal cases ought best to be conducted . . . ."

In von Weber's apt term, the Carolina was a *Rechtsfibel,* a law primer. It was not a work of learning, but of instruction. Novices cannot be expected to operate complicated machinery without a training manual. The Carolina contains 219 articles, about 140 of them procedural, exceeding 100 pages in most modern printed editions. The extensiveness of the ordinance should be contrasted with the Marian committal statute of 1555, whose operative provisions do not reach 200 words in length. The massive, comprehensive instructional manual which the engineers of the German reception provided for their lay judges finds no counterpart in the English statute. Equally lacking was any attempt to connect the English lay judges with that other modality of reception in the Carolina, the Roman-trained jurists. Neither the Marian statute nor other sources suggest any linkage between Doctors' Commons and the JPs.

---

preuve dans le droit du moyen âge occidental," *Recueils de la société Jean Bodin pour l'histoire comparative des institutions* 17:691, 737–738 (1965); J. Gilissen, "La preuve en Europe du XVIe au debut du XIXe siècle," *Recueils de la société Jean Bodin pour l'histoire comparative des institutions* 17:755, 790 (1965).

Although Jardine's cases typically are investigations of treason and affairs of state, others concerning "[m]urder, embezzlement, horse-stealing and various felonies" lack evident political overtones. Jardine, op. cit., at 66. Still, torture was used in such cases only because the highest political authority was lending its power—often at the behest of a well-placed complainant. "No magistrate or judge, and no individual Councillor or Secretary of State, was at liberty to use the rack or any lesser species of torture without a written warrant from the King himself, or from the Privy Council when assembled at the Board." Id. at 67. Constrained in this way, torture never threatened to invade the ordinary criminal process, and its "illegality" is celebrated in well-known passages "by some of the earliest panegyrists of English institutions, and in particular Fortescue, Smith and Coke." Stephen I 222.

The notion of broad-gauge English reception unmistakably suffers from comparison with the Carolina. It remains to consider whether the English draftsman might have been a more selective Romanist. Aware of the basic incompatibilities, he may have foresworn the grand design of Roman-canon criminal process while nonetheless extracting and transplanting from the Roman sources two useful techniques: the dossier and the underlying principle of investigation by the magistrate.

The Carolina's dossier provisions (Articles 181–189) do recall the command of the Marian statute that the statements of the accused and his "bringers" bearing on "the fact and circumstance [of the crime], . . . or as much thereof as shall be material to prove the Felony shall be put in writing, within two days after the said examination . . . . " Both statutes, therefore, direct the magistrate to prepare a narrative of the statements made by the accused and by the complainants in the course of the magistrate's investigation. But resemblance ceases there. The type of documentation differed markedly, corresponding to essential differences in purpose.

The Carolina demanded a record which outstripped the Marian in several respects. First, the Carolina required that every stage in the preliminary process be the subject of record, including the magistrate's attempts to get evidence beyond the original statements of complainant and accused. The Carolina covers the equivalent of the Marian statute's requirement in Articles 181 and 182, and continues in Articles 183–188 to specify writing in the further investigative phases. Second, the Carolina demanded that the record be comprehensive, and that it be attested as inclusive (Article 189). The Marian statute, by contrast, invited a partial document ("or as much thereof as shall be material to prove the Felony"). Moreover, the Carolina reinforced its requirement of comprehensiveness by one of contemporaneousness—to the day and hour in Article 182—whereas the English statute approved a delay of two days.

The differences in form reflect differences in function. The Carolina's dossier was supposed to provide, as Article 189 declares, the exclusive basis for final adjudication. It was functionally equivalent to the modern stenographic trial record compiled by and for a common law court sitting without a jury. The Marian statute, on the other hand, was looking to the creation of another sort of record—what we would today call the prosecutor's file. The purpose, as discussed in Chapter 2, was to bolster the prosecution's case at public oral trial, probably by aiding the magistrate's recall, rarely as a species of deposition evidence. The peculiarities of the writing requirement of the Marian statute seem explainable only by the more peripheral role which documentation served in the English procedure. The Marian requirement falls short of Roman-canon standards in crucial respects. Against the reception argument of bare similarity on the existence of a magistrative recordation requirement, these differences of form and function are too persuasive.

Much the same line of reasoning undermines the contention that magistrative investigation itself was Roman-canon derived in the Marian scheme. The similarities are superficial and the divergences profound. Both the Carolina and the Marian statute remit to a magistrate, typically lay, the investigation of serious crime. However, the Carolina provides its magistrate vastly larger duties and powers; and it looks forward to the professionalization of the magistracy, while providing even at the time for extensive professional guidance. The magistrate's responsibility is not simply to shape the prosecution's case, but the entire case. His obligation is, in the language of Article 56, "to get at the truth thoroughly . . . ." And as the Carolina defines it, his office is inextricably bound up with judicial torture. His most important job is to decide when torture is justified, then to supervise its application and to follow up its results. The likelihood that this could be a model for a nontorture system seems remote. The common lawyer errs if he analogizes the Roman-canon Vorverfahren to common law pretrial investigation. The Carolina's preliminary process was indeed succeeded by a sort of public oral trial. But that, we have seen, was a sham. The "pretrial" phase was the functional correspondent of common law trial in the sense that it was determinative; it produced confession, full proof, or release.

The Marian statute, by contrast, was concerned with organizing a less central function—not judicial investigation, but prosecutorial investigation. The trial jury could convict without confession; it would not convict without persuasion. The Marian scheme intended to institutionalize and officialize with the JPs the responsibility for organizing the job of persuasion. The idea that anything so peculiar to common law procedure could benefit from the diverse Roman-canon model is inherently suspect. When it is shown, as it has been in Chapter 4, that the JPs had been performing related functions for more than a century, and that they probably developed their role in the Marian scheme well in advance of the statute, the indigenous explanation looks the more appealing.

CHAPTER 9 Criminal Procedure in France

Seven years after the Reichstag of Regensburg finally approved the Carolina, the French King Francis I promulgated the ordonnance royale of August 1539—commonly called, after the place where it was issued, Villers-Cotterets.[1] Holdsworth, who knew of it through Esmein's account,[2] regarded it as the paradigm of those "new and effective codes"[3] of the sixteenth century which introduced into "many continental countries . . . an entirely new form of criminal procedure"[4] as a consequence of "the reception of Roman law . . . "[5] and whose "continental ideas"[6] influenced the draftsman of the Marian statutes. We shall see that the ordinance of Villers-Cotterets was rather less than the "revolution"[7] which older scholarship has sometimes made of it.

Because the point of perspective for comparative study in this book is the Marian legislation in England, the French history is less illuminating than the German. The characteristic of the German procedure which made it such an instructive object of comparative study was the persistence into the sixteenth century of a strong lay component in the criminal process. The Carolina provided an actual model of reception of Roman-canon process in a legal system which, like the English, had

1. The text appears in Isambert, Decrusy, and Jourdan, *Recueil général des anciennes lois françaises depuis l'an 420 jusqu'à la révolution de 1789* (Paris, 1823–1833) XII (pt. 2) 600–640 [hereafter cited as Isambert]. A translation of the criminal procedure articles appears in Appendix C.

2. Holdsworth, at V 170 n. 2 ff., refers to A. Esmein, *A History of Continental Criminal Procedure with Special Reference to France* (J. Simpson, trans.) (Boston, 1913). Citation in this chapter is to the original, A. Esmein, *Histoire de la procédure criminelle en France et spécialement de la procédure inquisitoire depuis le XIIIe siècle jusqu'à nos jours* (Paris, 1882) [hereafter cited as Esmein]. The translation is not so good as others in the Continental Legal History Series and, although not unhelpful, ought not to be relied upon.

3. Holdsworth V 169.

4. Id. at IV 528.

5. Id.

6. Id.

7. A. Allard, *Histoire de la justice criminelle au XVIe siècle* (Ghent, Paris, and Leipzig, 1868) 149.

preserved a significant adjudicative role for laymen. In France, for reasons about to be canvassed, the lay role had disappeared in the Middle Ages. Another factor which restricts the scope of compartive study is the relatively moribund state of French scholarship on the subject. There is no counterpart to the wealth of twentieth-century German monographs. Because the French have left their enormous resources of archive material[8] largely unworked, the foreign comparativist finds less at hand than may perhaps be there.

A. THE MEDIEVAL ORIGINS OF FRENCH INQUISITIONSPROZESS

The history of criminal procedure in France in the late Middle Ages is essentially the history of the criminal procedure of the royal courts. In this regard the French history resembles the English and diverges sharply from the German. Yet there were key differences in the resources available to the French and English monarchies which came to be reflected in the organization and in the procedures of the respective royal legal systems. These differences would prove so important that by the age of the Renaissance, French procedure, especially criminal procedure, would in its fundamental principles and techniques resemble the contemporary German vastly more than the contemporary English. The main element of the story, the adoption of Roman-canon procedure for civil and criminal adjudication, has been recently studied in Dawson's *A History of Lay Judges*,[9] and the present account follows that work. This section, by way of background, summarizes enough of the medieval history to set the criminal procedure of the sixteenth century into intelligible context.

The most decisive factor for the future shape of French legal history was the timing of the monarchical reconstruction. It came a century later than in England, in the thirteenth[10] rather than in the twelfth cen-

8. See generally Ministère de l'éducation nationale: Direction des archives de France, *Guide des recherches dans les fonds judiciares de l'ancien régime* (Paris, 1958).

9. Dawson, *Lay Judges* 35–94.

10. Id. at 46–48. Cf. R. van Caenegem, "L'histoire du droit et la chronologie: Reflexions sur la formation du 'Common Law' et la procédure romano-canonique," in *Etudes d'histoire du droit canonique dédiées à Gabriel Le Bras* (Paris, 1965) II 1459.

tury. The formative decisions made under Henry II in England in 1166 and shortly thereafter have their counterpart in France under Louis IX in 1258 and afterward. By 1258, however, the first phase of the Bolognese revival had run its course. The Accursian gloss, the culminating work of the glossatorial school, was produced within a decade or so of the French legislation of that year. Durantis' *Speculum Judiciale*[11] of canon civil and criminal procedure dates from 1271. Roman-canon process constituted a formed alternative which had not been plausible a century earlier when the procedure of the English courts was being worked out.[12]

Another significant consequence of the French monarchy's tardiness in elaborating royal central institutions of administration and governance was that feudal decentralization had had an extra century of unimpeded force. Older public communal courts had tended to merge with the courts of the feudal lords who held sway in the localities.[13] "[I]n most of France court-keeping functions had been distributed into innumerable private hands."[14] The monarchy was compelled to build afresh. "When the French crown belatedly, in the thirteenth century, commenced to reconstruct a system of royal justice, it found at hand no analogue to the English county and hundred courts which the Norman kings in England had already proceeded to reinforce and make agents of royal will."[15] Because the communal courts had been lost to the monarchy, the royal replacements would almost of necessity be professional. On the other hand, feudalization had strengthened some of the procedural characteristics of the communal courts in their privatized setting. The onerous duty of attendance and participation in Germanic folk-adjudication "became more and more a form of feudal service. The functions of the law-finders, over most of the land, became fused with the functions of vassals in courts held by their lords."[16] The assimilation was facilitated by the consultative aspect inherent in the feudal relationship, and by the collective nature of enforcement.[17]

11. Supra, page 137.
12. T. F. T. Plucknett, "The Relations between Roman Law and English Common Law," *University of Toronto Law Journal* 3:24, 50 (1939).
13. Dawson, *Lay Judges* 40–43.
14. Id. at 42.
15. Id.
16. Id. at 41 (footnote omitted).
17. Id.: "It was by no means always that a feudal lord, however great his estates, could be sure of his ability to put judgments in execution without help from

It was thus the case that when the French monarchy came to settle the procedures for its thirteenth-century courts, Germanic folk-judgment procedure had been widely perpetuated in France. The royal variant was the "group inquest" by which "a selected group of local inhabitants was compelled to answer under oath the questions put before them by royal inquisitors."[18] The procedure goes back to Carolingian roots and was the kernel of the English jury system.[19] The Capetians had employed a version of it in the twelfth and early thirteenth centuries "to ascertain and enforce crown rights."[20]

The Roman-canon alternative—characterized by Dawson as the "system of proof by individual witnesses"[21]—was not therefore preordained for the French courts. The formative legislation of 1258 nonetheless adopted it[22] because, by contrast with the folk-courts' "archaic modes of proof, the procedure . . . offered immense advantages."[23] The

---

his vassals. In rendering any judgment it was wise to engage with responsibility those persons, already bound by duties of service, who might be needed to enforce it."

18. Id. at 44.

19. Id. and sources there cited.

20. Id.

21. Id. at 44. Cf. id. at 45:

> [It was] a largely written procedure, involving an exchange between the parties of written statements of claim and defense, written interrogatories prepared by the parties to be administered to the witnesses, and written records that the judge was required to keep of his rulings, findings, and judgment. For present purposes it is even more important that the basic mode of proof was the testimony of individual witnesses under oath, under interrogation by the judge who then proceeded to make his own findings of fact.

22. In the early thirteenth century the choice between the group-inquest (jury) and the canonist modes of proof had not yet been decisively made. . . . The decisive step in choosing between the two available modes of proof was taken by Louis IX in 1258 by his ordinance abolishing the judicial duel in royal courts. The problem confronting the framers of this ordinance was evident: if duels were to be abolished, something must take their place. The same problem had appeared in England some forty years before when the crown had deferred to the church's newly declared hostility to the duel and had abolished it, thereby giving a sudden impetus to the growth of the common law jury. The abolition of the duel in France had still another implication, in that it removed the threat to witnesses that they might be required to defend themselves by battle against charges of perjury. In some parts of France this threat was so serious that witnesses were not compelled to testify unless they were exempt from the risk of challenge to a duel. So it was that elimination of the duel in royal courts operated both directly and indirectly to promote the use of witness-proof, with which many Frenchmen were becoming familiar. Louis IX ordered that instead of the duel his judges should use secret examination of individual witnesses under oath, through questions administered by the judges themselves.

Id. at 46–47 (footnotes omitted); cf. A. Tardif, *La procédure civile et criminelle aux XIIIe et XIVe siècles ou procédure de transition* (Paris, 1885) 145.

23. Dawson, *Lay Judges* 45.

church courts, with their enormous jurisdiction in France in the high Middle Ages, had long acclimated Frenchmen to canon process.[24] The century of delay had been a "century of experience" during which "many people in France must have become persuaded that interrogation of individual witnesses under oath was a far more rational mode of ascertaining truth."[25] Another fortuity of timing helped conceal the disadvantages of the Roman-canon process: the procedure had not reached the acme of its development "and had not yet been elaborated into bewildering complication."[26] Moreover, as a matter of administrative and political power, it appeared "easier, as well as far more rational," to examine individuals who had some familiarity with the particular case rather than to collect a group of community representatives, cart them to some seat of justice, and attempt to extract a verdict from them.[27]

The choice of adjudicative process in the ordinance of 1258 settled the "modes of fact determination," or more broadly "the modes of proof,"[28] not only for courts of first instance but for appellate courts as well. It was inevitable that the royal appellate courts supervising the royal courts of first instance would share with them a common procedural system. The Roman-canon procedure with its examining commissions and written evidence facilitated review *de novo*. The earliest evidence implies that the Parlement of Paris,[29] the principal royal appellate court, had from the outset "adopted a procedure which involved in most cases a full retrial of issues of fact through full-scale canonist inquest."[30] This was a matter of evident utility in the long struggle to subject the vast structure of seignorial courts to royal appellate review.[31]

24. See P. Fournier, *Les officialités au moyen age* (Paris, 1880) 64–127. Dawson notes the possibility that private arbitration of laymen's disputes by ecclesiastics and others conversant with the law and process of the church may have facilitated the spread of canon law procedure beyond the church. Dawson, *Lay Judges* 46 and n. 25.

25. Dawson, *Lay Judges* 47–48.

26. Id. at 46.

27. Id. at 48; cf. id. at 44 and n. 20; Esmein 81. Dawson remarks, *Lay Judges* 48 (footnote omitted): "The canonist methods of proof were soon to require a vast increase in the royal bureaucracy and the criminal inquisition came later to symbolize the overriding power of unlimited monarchy, but the initial choice of this procedure by the central government may well have been due much more to weakness than to strength."

28. Id. at 43.

29. See generally J. H. Shennan, *The Parlement of Paris* (London, 1968) 3–85; Dawson, *Oracles* 273–290.

30. Dawson, *Lay Judges* 57.

31. Id.

The fact that the royal process was appellate as well as instance helps to explain why Roman-canon process tended so rapidly to permeate the seignorial courts as well. Because "reversal meant money fines on the erring court . . . [t]he pressure [was] to conformity. . . ."[32] Other inducements were also operating,[33] in particular the "prestige not only of [Parlement] itself but of the highly trained professionals who built it. In this sense it was a model for other courts to follow."[34] "For all French courts, from the Parlement of Paris to the courts of the smallest lordships, the crucial decision had really been made in the thirteenth century when the group inquest had been allowed to disappear as a mode of establishing facts."[35]

The adoption of Roman-canon process was common to both civil and criminal procedure.[36] In England, too, the monarchy had chosen a common procedure for civil and criminal business in the royal courts when the jury system had been worked out and then extended to replace the ordeals. It will be recalled that in Germany the development was otherwise. A crude but rational criminal investigative procedure became common in the fourteenth century, a full hundred years before parallel notions began to overtake civil procedure in the "full reception." France, like England and unlike Germany, had central institutional direction. The choice of Roman-canon process was made and implemented in the course of the monarchy's determined establishment of its court system. Nonetheless, the choice was easier, hence more emphatic, for civil cases because less official exertion was needed:[37]

In civil cases the new modes of proof [required a lesser] assertion of judicial authority. Responsibility for selection of witnesses and for per-

32. Id. at 60.

33. Id. at 55 n. 60 (citations omitted): "It is worth noting that the canonist form of appeal had been early adopted within their own domains by some of the great feudal lords, even before the subjection of their courts to appellate review by the Parlement had put pressure on them to do so. In contests with their own local nobility the canonist appeal evidently offered advantages to the great feudataries when administered by trained judges that they themselves had appointed."

34. Id. at 60.

35. Id. at 59. Quaere whether the group inquest "was surely too much for the lesser nobility to organize if the crown did not lead the way" (id. at 49) if the explanation for the persistence of folk-judging in the feudal courts into the thirteenth century was the reinforcement given it in the immediate lord-vassal relation (id. at 40–42).

36. Tardif (supra, note 22) at 139; P. Guilhiermoz, *Enquêtes et procès: Etude sur la procédure et le fonctionnement du Parlement au XIVe siècle* (Paris, 1892) 95–98.

37. Dawson, *Lay Judges* 51–52 (footnote omitted).

suading them to testify was thrown on the interested parties. While the judge supervised the preparation of the questions and examined the witnesses himself or through his delegate, his role in civil cases was mainly to assemble and evaluate the evidence that the parties presented. The term *enquête* was soon applied to this kind of investigation, but it was not an inquisition of the kind that the canonists were developing for criminal or disciplinary proceedings, conducted by the judge ex officio. The *enquête* in civil cases was a court-conducted examination of individual witnesses, made available to private litigants to settle disputed issues of fact.

Conceptualized in the terms we have seen employed in the German scholarship, we might say that in France Instruktionsmaxime ran somewhat ahead of Offizialprinzip. Rational modes of proof, shared with civil process, came into use in criminal matters somewhat in advance of regularized official prosecution. In the later thirteenth and early fourteenth centuries private prosecution continued to prevail,[38] save increasingly with the proofs of the enquête, that is, individual witness testimony judicially extracted and evaluated.

The highly officialized criminal procedure which evolved in France does, however, derive from these thirteenth-century origins.[39] As in Germany, the problem case was that of covert crime in which no private prosecutor appeared. When victim or kin would make private accusation, the case would go forward substantially as a civil case; and even when no private complainant was present, the case of overt crime—that is, of flagrant delict—had not lacked an official, if summary, remedy. Moreover, the concept of flagrant delict could be expanded to reach the notorious criminal—the man of flagrantly bad repute.[40] We have seen a similar German pattern. For covert crime not privately prosecuted, the only effective possibility in a legal system whose final process depends heavily on official investigation and decision is official instigation. If dangerous suspected criminals were not to be released for want of prosecution, prosecution would have to be undertaken from within the court. There is some evidence to suggest that the canon model facilitated that development;[41] and some which hints at a procedure originally de-

38. Id. at 48; Esmein 100 ff.; cf. Tardif (supra, note 22) at 141–143.

39. See Esmein 78 ff.; Tardif (supra, note 22) at 138 ff.; Dawson, *Lay Judges* 49–51.

40. Esmein 78–79 and 79 n. 1 (citing Beaumanoir); cf. Dawson, *Lay Judges* 50.

41. Esmein 80–81, 103.

signed to reach especially dangerous *vilains*.[42] Judicial torture—that key indicator of the officialized prosecution—was already being regulated in an ordinance of 1254, and in the next century it became common enough.[43]

In France, unlike Germany, the prosecutorial function became separately institutionalized in the late Middle Ages in a prosecutorial office, that of the *procureur du roi.* Esmein suggests that the office antedates its first appearance in royal legislation (in 1302)[44] and that parallels in canon procedure provided the inspiration.[45] A lengthy series of fourteenth-century statutes isolated the public interest in criminal prosecution and assigned its superintendence to the procureur.[46] He was authorized to invoke the criminal process when there was no private complainant; his motions instigated judicial action and propelled the procedure through subsequent stages. By the sixteenth century, we shall see, he was exclusively competent to seek serious criminal sanction even when a formal private complainant had joined the case. The formation of the prosecutorial office already in the fourteenth century may also owe something to the early association of medieval French criminal procedure with the modes of civil adjudication. The role of judge tended to be defined in terms of duties in civil litigation, and that helped to provoke the crystallization of a separate prosecutorial office.[47]

The association of the civil with the criminal left another mark upon the scope of French Inquisitionsprozess. Well beyond the sixteenth century the notion persisted that civil procedure was an appropriate form for some criminal litigation, called the "ordinary" as opposed to the "extraordinary" (inquisitorial) procedure. This idea had originally taken hold in the late thirteenth and early fourteenth centuries, when the procedure for judicial examination of witnesses and adjudication had developed in advance of systematic official prosecution, that is, public instigation of charges and discovery and production of witnesses.

42. Tardif (supra, note 22) at 147–148. The parallel to the German *Verfahren gegen die Landschädlichen* is evident.

43. Esmein 98; cf. L. Tanon, *Histoire des justices des anciennes églises et communautés monastiques de Paris* (Paris, 1883) 58 ff.

44. Esmein 101.

45. Id. at 103.

46. These are noted by Guilhiermoz (supra, note 36) at 98 and n. 3; and by Allard (supra, note 7) at 69 and n. 2.

47. The medieval procureur had duties in civil litigation (as does the modern procureur). See Guilhiermoz (supra, note 36) at 98; Esmein 101. He was, as his title proclaimed, the king's lawyer.

It had then proved convenient to try to assimilate the criminal proceeding to something resembling a civil case by a "sort of procedural contract"[48] called "accepting the *enquête* (inquest)." The suspected person consented to judicial examination and to binding adjudication on a roughly civil standard of proof. In return he was allowed liberal defense, again of a civil standard, including the aid of counsel and immunity from torture.[49]

As long as the political power and judicial resources to conduct thorough official prosecution were lacking, this bargain- or waiver-based procedure was preferable to simply releasing suspects. Consequently, the requisite consent seems to have been not infrequently coerced[50] (much like the simultaneous English practice of extracting consent to jury trial by means of peine forte et dure). When the judicial and procuratorial offices became better developed, the procedural bargain was no longer advantageous to the state; proper official prosecution had become feasible. The procureur won effective control of the decision on whether to allow the accused to defend through the more liberal "ordinary process," and by the fifteenth century it was acknowledged that the grant of the milder procedure was proper only for relatively unimportant, noncapital offenses.[51] Otherwise, the "extraordinary" procedure was in fact ordinary enough. France, like Germany, saw Inquisitionsprozess established and regularized in the late Middle Ages. "By the [fourteenth century] all the important characteristics of inquisitorial procedure were already fixed . . . ."[52]

An inescapable result of this officialization and professionalization of the French courts and their procedure, civil and criminal, was its effect upon the former patterns of lay participation in judgment or at least in fact-finding. This important point is Dawson's, and we have had occasion in discussing the English Marian statutes to anticipate it:[53] "the active agent in driving out lay judges in France was the Roman-canonist system of procedure, especially its modes of investiga-

48. Dawson, *Lay Judges* 51.
49. Id. at 50–51.
50. Esmein 78.
51. See id. at 115 on the connection between "accepting the enquête" and "ordinary process." Article 117 of the ordinance of Blois (1498) explains that the procureur should allow "ordinary process" if it is established that the case does not merit corporal punishment. Isambert XI 367.
52. Esmein 107.
53. Supra, pages 22–23.

tion and proof."[54] The inherent complexity of the developed procedure assured that only men of some learning would be able to operate it.[55]

The royal courts in which the new procedures grew up merit some notice. The main court of first instance—that of the *bailli*—was attached to an officer who appeared in the royal service in the twelfth century, perhaps in conscious imitation of the Norman sheriff.[56] The baillis by 1190 were holding monthly assizes, exacting and recording fines to the king, and accounting at regular intervals to Paris.[57] The bailli in the thirteenth and fourteenth centuries became the principal royal local officer "who, like the English sheriff, combined in his office financial, military, administrative, and judicial functions."[58]

Inevitably, that agglomeration of duties required specialization over the course of time; the growth of royal power spurred the expansion of royal business in the localities. The bailli himself became a predominantly military officer, often away from the seat of his bailiwick in the service of the king in time of war. By the end of the Hundred Years

54. Dawson, *Lay Judges* 68.

55. By following the lead of the canonists in more refined methods of investigation, French courts committed themselves to a system that was likely to develop according to its own internal logic. When it was decided that witnesses were to be examined individually and in secret, a reliable examiner was needed and some record must be kept. If the examiner was to ask all the necessary questions, he would have to be prompted by a list of questions beforehand. In a case of any complexity it would be imperative that the questions be put into writing; it was natural to cast on the parties involved the burden of preparing the questions. To be sure that the draft interrogatories prepared by the parties were relevant and proper, it was convenient to have the initial statements of claim and defense put into writing. When this stage of documentation was reached, objections of each party to the other's claims or proposals would often need to be put into writing and the prolongation of the proceedings would make it imperative that the judge keep a written record of his actions at each stage. . . . By [the fourteenth century] it was already essential that the judge have not only an ability to read—a skill that was rare enough in itself—but an ability to dissect and scrutinize the contents of several layers of manuscript. As specialized personnel were assigned to these tasks and the paper work grew more complex, there was increasing distrust of informal, oral procedures not evidenced by writing. Each element of the system reinforced the rest.

Id. at 59–60 (footnote omitted). Dawson observes that lay judging obligations had always been onerous and unpopular, requiring time and exposing court members to risk of sanction for false judgment. Hence, the laymen who originally owed duties of attendance in the seignorial courts "saw nothing worth fighting for" (id. at 65) and "quietly deserted" (id. at 66) "as the successive steps in lawsuits were extended and the mounds of paper grew . . ." (id. at 67).

56. R. Fawtier, *The Capetian Kings of France* (L. Butler and R. J. Adam, trans.) (London, 1960) 174–176; Dawson, *Lay Judges* 54.

57. Fawtier (supra, note 56) at 178.

58. Dawson, *Lay Judges* 54.

War, his duties of adjudication had lapsed and his role was basically that of enforcer.[59] The judicial duties had passed to delegates, at first appropriately enough called *lieutenants.* The office of lieutenant traces back to the thirteenth century, when it was a truly provisional position, created ad hoc for the occasions when the bailli would be away.[60] The wars of the late Middle Ages lengthened those occasions. Simultaneously, the advance of Roman-canon procedure and the extension of the bailli's appellate jurisdiction over lesser seignorial courts brought about an increase in the judicial duties of the office. The complexities of the procedure tended to require that the judicial functions be exercised by persons of special training.[61] Around the year 1500, the splitting up of the former office of the bailli was complete. The lieutenant had become a permanent royal officer, no longer the surrogate of the bailli. Royal legislation fixed his salary and settled that he alone controlled the judicial process—which, however, he continued to conduct in the name of the bailli.[62] Further specialization spun off, in the early sixteenth century, a special lieutenant for criminal business.[63] This *lieutenant-criminel* was the judge who typically operated the French Inquisitionsprozess we are about to examine.

Some word must be said of the greatest of the courts of the ancien régime, the Parlement of Paris. It formed out of the curia regis in the early thirteenth century, and by the latter part of that century its procedure was unmistakably Roman-canon. Its jurisdiction was both instance and appellate, but principally appellate. It sat in appeal over both seignorial and lesser royal courts. It was professionally staffed already in the thirteenth century, and partially as a consequence of its procedures it became enormous, with tens of judges and cameral sectioning already in that century.[64] Criminal business became heavy enough to require a separate division of the court, the *Tournelle,* to be created in the fifteenth century.[65]

Three observations from the medieval history will help frame the criminal procedure.

59. Allard (supra, note 7) at 30–31.

60. A. Esmein, *Cours élémentaire d'histoire du droit français* (15th ed., Paris, 1925) 352.

61. Allard (supra, note 7) at 31.

62. Esmein (supra, note 60) at 352–353.

63. Id. at 353–354.

64. Dawson, *Lay Judges* 56–57; cf. id. at 57–58 on the phases of civil appellate litigation. See supra, note 29.

65. Shennan (supra, note 29) at 40–41.

First, French Inquisitionsprozess, like German, was a medieval development, not an innovation of the sixteenth century. The principle of judicial investigation, hence of individual witness proofs, became characteristic of French procedure in the thirteenth century, and the concept of official responsibility to initiate and carry forward the prosecution became entrenched in the course of the fourteenth century. French Inquisitionsprozess was from the outset deeply influenced by the Roman-canon model. The French history followed in this respect a course different from the German. The French procedure originated under Roman-canon influence but grew steadily away, the refinements of later centuries increasingly reflecting the experience, the needs, and the learning of the royal national legal system. We shall see that trend continue in the sixteenth-century legislation. Germany, by contrast, began with a crude and largely indigenous Inquisitionsprozess, which came to be recast in the late fifteenth and sixteenth centuries in greater conformity with Roman-canon learning. The divergence is no mystery, of course. The French had important resources of Roman-canon learning well in advance of the Germans,[66] which made possible an absorption of the essential elements of the learned procedure substantially within the century of its origin. Furthermore, the French monarchy supplied power and direction for a rational ordering of procedure within the royal courts, a force lacking a true counterpart in Germany.

Second, the "internal logic"[67] of Roman-canon process had produced a written procedure—civil and criminal—of great complexity. A rough but instructive comparison: a criminal proceeding for treason against the Maréchal de Gie from the years 1504–1506 has been published,[68] running to more than six hundred pages of documentation (articles, interrogations, *procès-verbaux*, and so forth). The closest contemporaneous English prosecution of which there is record, also for treason, is *Empson and Dudley's Case* (1509), the report of which covers two sides of a printed page in the *State Trials.*[69] The complexity of French procedure had required a large and professional magistracy—large because there were so many procedural stages, professional because the process was written and increasingly technical. The bureau-

66. See C. Lefebvre, "Juges et savants en Europe du 13ᵉ au 16ᵉ siècle," in *Ephemerides Iuris Canonici* 22:76, 148–157 (1966); Dawson, *Oracles* 273–290.
67. Dawson, *Lay Judges* 59.
68. De Maulde, *Procédures politiques du règne de Louis XII* (Paris, 1885) II.
69. 1 St. Tr. columns 283–287 (1509).

cratization of the French criminal process is quite striking. As the procedure grew, so did the officer corps needed to operate it. One significant functional differentiation had taken place in the fourteenth century: the splitting off from the judicial office of some consciously prosecutorial duties, which were lodged with the procureur. Even then the judicial role was unmanageable. Hence the practice developed of using surrogates (examiners) to conduct the initial phases of the procedure, the preliminary inquiry (*information préparatoire*). Into the fifteenth century, criminal and civil business had been handled by the same lieutenant; the sixteenth century had to specialize further. Moreover, we have been speaking only of royal instance jurisdiction. An appeal would multiply the number of professionals involved. Nor have we said anything of the lesser functionaries—clerks, scriveners, and others. We shall return to this phenomenon of burgeoning judicial bureaucratization in the light of the sixteenth-century practice. The point is raised here to emphasize that the basic structure of judicial bureaucracy which French criminal procedure presupposed had been created in the late Middle Ages along with the procedure itself. Further, the corollary to professionalization—the atrophy of lay participation in the criminal process—was likewise a medieval development.

Finally, the intimate association of final and preliminary process, which we have noticed in speaking of canon and of German procedure, we again observe in the French history. Instruktionsmaxime tended to call forth Offizialprinzip. The decision to replace the most persistent of the irrational modes of proof (judicial duel) with the most rational of alternatives (judicial evaluation of individual witness proof) was consciously made for civil litigation. Criminal business was carried along. And rational final process having been implemented, the preliminary process had to be created to sustain it—to dig out the evidence for decision even when there were no private prosecutors. The rationalization and professionalization of final process begun in the thirteenth century brought about the officialization of preliminary procedure in the fourteenth century. The sixteenth-century procedure whose detail we are about to examine was long matured in France.

B. FRENCH CRIMINAL PROCEDURE IN THE SIXTEENTH CENTURY

Although France, like Germany, entered the sixteenth century with a lengthy medieval tradition of Inquisitionsprozess, the procedure was a learned one, administered by professionals, principally within the courts of royal central authority. It should not surprise us, therefore, that the definitive French legislation of the 1530s bore little resemblance to the German. We have seen that the German Carolina was predominantly concerned with instructing lay magistrates in the principles of proof and the techniques of investigation. Moreover, it had to work its influence by example and instruction in jurisdictions not obliged to obey it. It was consequently both comprehensive and elementary. It set forth an entire procedural system, from first complaint to final judgment and execution. Because it was pitched to the understanding of the layman, it had to institute the remarkable arrangements for securing expert advice for cases beyond the layman's capacity.

The ordinance of Villers-Cotterets,[70] propounded for the quite different legal system of France of 1539, has a quite different look to it. It is much shorter—about 30 smallish paragraphs correspond to the Carolina's 140 criminal procedural sections. There is no earnest attempt to be comprehensive, to elaborate an entire procedural system. That would await the legislation of 1670.[71] The ordinance of Villers-Cotterets is in fact not even predominantly concerned with criminal procedure. The 29 paragraphs which treat that subject are embedded among 160-odd others.[72] There was no need to set forth the whole of the criminal procedure in a code for the professionals who already knew it well. The draftsman of the 1539 ordinance, we shall see, concentrated largely on the details he wanted to alter.

The peculiar thoroughness and simplicity of the Carolina helped us to study it. Its framers had taken special pains to organize it well, to make it intelligible and self-sufficient. The ordinance of Villers-Cotterets, however, being remedial and interstitial, and addressed to professionals, is scarcely understandable standing alone. The present sec-

70. See supra, note 1.

71. Isambert XVIII 371–423. See E. Detourbet, *La procédure criminelle au XVIIe siècle: Histoire de l'ordonnance du 28 août 1670* (Paris, 1881); Esmein 177–283, 329–396.

72. Infra, pages 243–244.

tion, therefore, locates its basic text elsewhere: in the account of the criminal procedure provided for the magistrates themselves in the contemporary practice manual written by a provincial lieutenant-criminel, Jean Imbert.[73] Imbert first wrote shortly before the ordinance of Villers-Cotterets, then revised later editions to give prominence to its dispositions. His manual permits us to depict the ordinance within its proper procedural context. Thereafter we can isolate the ordinance, in order to inquire (in Section C of this chapter) about its particular intention and effect. A translation of the criminal procedure portion of the ordinance is provided in Appendix C.

Although numerous alternatives would be feasible, I have found it convenient to group the procedural events into six stages, following the sequence of the process itself: preliminary inquiry, examination of the accused, confrontation procedure, examination of defense witnesses, torture, and final process.

1. *Preliminary Inquiry*

The initial stage of the criminal process, the preliminary inquiry (information préparatoire), occurs before the appearance of the accused. He has no role in it save as object. It includes both the formal instigation of the criminal action and the first investigation into the circumstances. In the paradigm the suspect remains at liberty during this inquiry; it could be conducted in secrecy in order to give him no cause for flight. This stage of the procedure functions to sift the idle and the palpably mistaken suspicion from the weighty. For serious crime the ap-

73. J. Imbert, *La pratique judiciaire, tant civile que criminelle, . . . enrichie . . . Par M. Pierre Guénois . . . et B. Automne* (Cologny, 1615) [hereafter cited as Imbert]. The first edition appeared in Latin in 1538, was several times reprinted, and was translated by Imbert himself into French in 1548. Subsequent editions of the French text dated 1563, 1579, 1585, 1593, 1609, 1616, 1624, and 1627 are recorded in the *Catalogue général des livres imprimés de la Bibliothèque Nationale* (Paris, 1922) LXXV 764–765. I have used a 1615 edition in the library of the Max-Planck-Institut für Europäische Rechtsgeschichte, Frankfurt, and have checked that edition against a 1571 edition in the library of Trinity College, Cambridge: *Les institutions forenses, ou pratique judiciare de M. Jean Imbert, Lieutenant criminel au siege Royal de Fontenay Lecomte: Traduittes de Latin en François, reveuz, corrigez, & augmentez par le mesme Autheur* (Paris, 1571). The work of later editors as evidenced in the 1615 edition was confined to an extensive gloss in the margin, citing to practical and scholarly literature and to legislation. Imbert's text was not rewritten.

Much the largest part of Imbert's manual is devoted to civil procedure. Book 3, at 564–727, treats criminal procedure, and all citations in the following notes are to that book. Book 4, devoted to criminal appeal, is slight.

propriate jurisdiction was typically, but by no means inevitably, that of the royal lieutenant-criminel.[74]

The division of responsibility between public prosecutor and private complainant which characterizes modern French criminal procedure was already highly developed. "We have two sorts of complainants (*accusateurs*)," Imbert writes,[75]

> one sort who prosecute in the interest of the King and of the public, whom we call the *gens du Roi*, comprising the *Avocat* and the *Procureur du Roi*. These seek corporal punishment and fines against the culprit. Parties of the other sort claim reparations for their civil interest, in which they have suffered on account of an offense committed upon their persons, or upon their goods, and never seek corporal punishment in our procedure, although according to common law (*droit commun*) [that is, Roman law] they can seek corporal punishment and reparation for their interest.

French procedure by the sixteenth century had separated the public and private interests in the law of wrongs and institutionalized them appropriately. The criminal sanction pertained to a wrong conceived to be against the king and the public; only the procureur might demand it. The aggrieved victim or kin was limited to civil damages in his own right. In one sense, therefore, the tendency to officialize the criminal process which we noticed in the Wormser Reformation and the Carolina is carried to completion in French practice. The private complainant of Roman-canon process, however restricted and discouraged, has here in France been wholly subordinated. On the other hand, having cleared the private party from the public action, the French welcome him alongside as a simultaneous civil plaintiff—as a tort plaintiff in our formulation. "Most often the *Procureur du Roi* and the *partie civile* are joint complainants," says Imbert.[76] The partie civile is not simply permitted, he is encouraged. The investigative stages of the procedure give him

74. Some seignorial courts retained rights of "high" (that is, capital) justice, and many more could deal with lesser crime. One author reckons that there were in the city of Angers in the sixteenth century nineteen separate courts with criminal jurisdiction of one sort or another; see V. Jeanvrot, "De l'évolution de la procédure criminelle en France," prefacing an edition of P. Ayrault, *Ordre et instruction judiciaire* [1588] (Paris, 1881) xlix–li. Imbert maintains that he is describing the procedure followed in all courts of high justice, not merely the royal courts, although the picture he in fact paints is that of royal court practice. Imbert, ch. 1, §2, at 567.

75. Id., ch. 1, §3, at 568.

76. Id., ch. 1, §6, at 569.

constant attention, to assure that his civil case is investigated as well as the procureur's criminal case. Doubtless the underlying rationale for the joinder of claims was the modern one—the inherent efficiency of litigating simultaneously both sets of legal issues arising from one congeries of events. But the sixteenth century had another inspiration: to shift to the partie civile the expenses of the combined action. Officialized prosecution might still be privately financed. The ordinance of Villers-Cotterets provides that costs other than those incurred in examining affirmative defenses raised by the accused "shall be charged to the parties civiles, if there be any, who might recover at the end of the case, and if there be none, or if they manifestly cannot bear the expense, then to the funds of our ordinary receipts . . . ."[77] The problem of the costs of official prosecution was part of the larger problem of financing the activities of the Renaissance state. What made the problem especially acute in France was the degree of procedural complexity, hence the number of people involved and the length of the procedings they administered—factors which inevitably increased costs.

The solicitude for the interests of the partie civile in his sphere ought not to obscure the decisive officialization which had occurred in the French procedure by the sixteenth century. The procureur had become indispensable, but not the partie civile. The partie civile might motion the procureur to initiate the preliminary inquiry, but the procureur could act alone in the absence of any partie civile.[78] Only the faintest traces of the earlier sort of private complainant survive.[79]

The preliminary inquiry is set in motion by the petition of the procureur and (generally) the partie civile.[80] The examiner who conducts this proceeding can in theory be the judge himself,[81] but in point of

77. Article 161.

78. Imbert, ch. 1, §6, at 569.

79. The device of imprisoning complainant and accused which the Carolina used was not, says Imbert, in general use in France. (The reason is that the preliminary inquiry went forward in secret while the accused was at liberty, and he was arrested only when that judicial inquiry established "probable cause.") Nevertheless, a Frenchman could constitute himself private complainant and be gaoled along with the accused if he insisted on having the accused arrested in advance of the preliminary inquiry. Imbert, ch. 1, §12, at 572. "Yet it is said that in Paris and Lyon, which places typically abound with foreigners, such [private complainants] are still received, and that until the accusing party has had the *informations* made which the case requires, and has verified the various witnesses, who support his accusation, the accusing party is held prisoner like the accused . . . ." Id., ch. 1, §14, at 573.

80. Imbert, ch. 2, §1, at 574.

81. Id.

fact is virtually always a surrogate. The delegation was routine even in the fifteenth century.[82] The reason seems obvious: the job became too big for the judge alone. The system stipulated a judicial investigation of every suspicion which the procureur took seriously. The result could only be a fractionation of the judicial office in function or in territorial competence. Either many persons would have to help with the work of the judge, or his bailiwick would have to be shrunk. The former was the principal solution, as it had been in the civil process where subordinate examiners had long been used. Because the examiner would not be the man to decide the case, he had to prepare a careful written record of his investigation for the use of the man who would decide the case.

The examiner interrogates each accusing witness, compiling his dossier of deposition testimony. "The witnesses are heard in a preliminary inquiry as in a hearing in a civil case, except that they may be heard in the presence of the partie [civile] . . . : because it is his libel and demand. And the witnesses are sworn as in a [civil] hearing and the deposition of each witness must be written out entirely (*tout au long*) . . . ."[83] The dossier should also contain the *plainte* of the partie civile; it should be headed up with the names of the parties; and it should show the year, day, and place of the examiner's sitting.[84]

The completed dossier then goes to the procureur, who recommends process against the accused appropriate to the case: bodily arrest where necessary, summons of personal appearance where not.[85] In this state the dossier reaches the judge for the first time for his decision on whether or not to follow the procureur's advice. The dossier comprises a written summary of the complaint and of the deposition testimony of accusing witnesses, together with the procureur's demand for process. It is, therefore, a prima facie case against the accused. (Its constituent elements would resemble the transcript of a modern American grand jury hearing—the prosecution charges and the testimony of accusing witnesses, produced at a session from which the accused is regularly

82. F. Hélie, *Traité de l'instruction criminelle* (Paris, 1845–1860) V 27. The practice of delegating the information préparatoire to examiners was recognized and its mechanics somewhat regulated in the ordinance of Blois (1498), the last major royal statute on criminal procedure before that of Villers-Cotterets. See Articles 95 ff. in Isambert XI 361 ff.

83. Imbert, ch. 2, §2, at 574–575.

84. Id., ch. 2, §3, at 575.

85. Id.

excluded and of whose convening he may be wholly ignorant. If the grand jury indicts, and it customarily does, the presiding judge issues his warrant for the accused.)

Inevitably, provision was made in case of flagrant delict and the like for reversing this somewhat leisurely course, the judge being empowered to authorize arrest in advance of the preliminary inquiry.[86]

It should be noticed that this inaugural stage of the procedure as Imbert depicts it derives mostly from judicial practice, suggested by the Roman-canon model. Legislation had nothing to do with the basic structure, and little with the detail. The sources which Imbert's glossators have cited in their marginalia comprise mainly the scholastic works of the late medieval Italian jurists (especially Baldus and Bartolus) and the practical writing of French lawyers. The ordinance of Villers-Cotterets in 1539 devotes a single paragraph[87] to the preliminary inquiry, enough to prevent any negative inference which might otherwise have been drawn had the subject been absolutely neglected, but far too summary to have had any shaping influence. Like the previous general regulation of criminal procedure, the ordinance of Blois (1498),[88] the ordinance of Villers-Cotterets is content to confirm rather than to direct this phase of the practice of the royal courts.

2. *Examination of the Accused*

The participants in the preliminary inquiry were typically the procureur, the partie civile, the examiner, and the accusing witnesses. In the second phase of the proceeding we exchange that supporting cast for the leading players: here appear the judge (accompanied by his clerk) and the accused.

The personal appearance of the accused, whether in response to

86. Id., ch. 2, §5, at 576; cf. id., ch. 2, §§6–7, at 577. The arrest stage is the subject of copious learning about contumacious and litigous defendants. The fugitive posed a serious problem in any European legal system of the day, exacerbated in France by claims founded upon the rights of competing ecclesiastical and feudal jurisdictions. Imbert, chs. 3–5, at 578–591. More quaint learning treats the mode of executing arrests, e.g., id., ch. 5, §2, at 592: according to *droit commun* it was forbidden to arrest anyone in his house. But French practice allows such arrest, during daylight hours, provided "nothing in the house shall be broken, nor shall anything be taken there. However, if the doors are shut, be they of the house or of the room where the fugitive is, they may be broken."

87. Article 145.

88. See supra, note 82.

summons or arrest, has required some formalized demands by the partie civile and the procureur—that the accused be "heard" (that is, examined) upon the charges and the evidence of the investigation contained in the dossier, and that he be gaoled pending the outcome of the case.[89] Immediately upon his first appearance, the accused must raise any challenge to the jurisdiction of the court (based typically upon feudal or ecclesiastical privilege). If he allows the judge to proceed further, he has waived the immunity he might have had.[90] Next, the interrogation of the accused is undertaken. "And in the first place, the [accused] is sworn to speak the truth, and afterwards questioned about what his occupation is, his age, his residence where he has lived and does live, and what occupation he has followed since reaching the age of fourteen until the day of examination."[91] Imbert continues in this rather detailed vein to describe the judge's examining duties; it is the sole occasion on which his treatise deals with matters so elementary and in a tone so belabored that it would put one in mind of the Carolina. The judge[92]

> must strain as hard as he can to extract whatever leads to the verification of the offense in question, and if there is variation, wavering or inconsistency, the judge shall record that and the fear and dread which the accused has, the gestures and mannerisms—if some argument could be deduced therefrom—and indication for the proof of the crime . . . .

This account further resembles the Carolina in the caveat it interposes against the danger that the judge will carry himself to excess and induce the accused to bear false witness against himself:[93]

> [N]onetheless the judge should not display too stern a manner *(visage)*, lest he intimidate the accused *(le confessant)* and lest through the said intimidation he be constrained to confess things which he did not do . . . .
>
> And it seems to me that the cunning which some employ is not a good thing, viz., to promise impunity and acquittal to the accused if he

89. Imbert, ch. 5, §6, at 594.

90. Id., ch. 6, §1, at 595. Imbert devotes four chapters to these jurisdictional objections, chs. 6–9, at 594–625. They encapsulate the results of a good bit of French constitutional history.

91. Id., ch. 10, §2, at 627–628.

92. Id., ch. 10, §2, at 628.

93. Id., ch. 10, §§2–3, at 628–629.

confesses in order to get it affirmed under oath: because there are many people so simple and frightened so much of prison, or of the legal system, that under the color of that promise they will confess to having done what they have not done. And the clerk must ascribe to the judge everything which the judge has said and stated.

Imbert seems to regard the clerk's transcription of the judge's words as something of a restraint or safeguard. We shall see that this dossier often leaves the hands of the judge for circulation within the bureaucracy.

It is a matter of importance, to which we shall refer in a later stage of the process, that the accused is expected to raise defenses at this point. "If the accused has pleas in bar (*fins de non recevoir*) against the complainant, or affirmative defenses (*faits justificatifs*), he should allege them now . . . ."[94] Indeed, the bulk of Imbert's chapter on judicial examination of the accused is devoted to these defensive pleas, "which are employed strenuously."[95] It is in no sense surprising that the examining magistrate should consider matters in exculpation as well as in crimination. The Carolina emphasized that duty.[96] This is a logical point for the accused to reply to allegations against him. He does not yet have a precise knowledge of the evidence against him. That comes later. But the interrogation would acquaint him with the contents of the dossier in a general way, since the judge uses it as a basis of examination, seeking to verify it. Of course the dominant purpose of this examination is to gather criminating evidence from the mouth of the accused. He has not yet had occasion to confront his accusers, to hear the detail of their testimony, and to call witnesses of his own. That is to follow. Here in the examination he does have the opportunity to raise defenses and by his own testimony to support them. This needs to be borne in mind in looking at the rigors that come next.

Bridging over to the subsequent stages is a review of the dossier by the procureur. These coming phases will not be needed if the accused has confessed the crime in the course of the interrogation—without torture, be it noticed. The procureur and the partie civile would then propound their *conclusions*, that is, their motions for final penal

94. Id., ch. 10, §5, at 629.

95. Id., ch. 10, §8, at 631. See id., ch. 10, §§8–14, at 631–636. Among the pleas (mostly against the partie civile): prescription, harassment, prior composition, and assignment of the claim.

96. Carolina Article 47.

and civil judgments. These would be shown to the accused, who might in reply raise matters in mitigation, but whose voluntary confession would have estopped any defenses.[97]

Otherwise the procureur moves for one of two sorts of interlocutory decree. The one is that the case be remitted to "ordinary procedure,"[98] meaning that the criminal case is not worth prosecuting and any remaining dispute is effectively left to the parties in civil litigation. The other is the motion for interlocutory decree ordering the confrontation phase, the next step in the procedure for serious crime. One gathers from Imbert that the procureur's motion was decisive, the judicial order routinely obliging.

Before continuing on to the confrontation procedure, which was the central concern of the ordinance of Villers-Cotterets, we should notice the dispositions of that statute regarding this second phase of the process, the judicial examination of the accused. Once again, the statute is content to summarize the procedure in terms which could not have been instrumental. Persons accused "shall immediately be properly and diligently examined and their examinations reiterated and repeated according to the legal form from our old ordinance . . . . "[99] The previous general ordinance, Blois, had been equally curt.[100] The marginalia in later editions of Imbert's manual again show that in the contemporary understanding, the procedure rested not on royal ordinance but on royal court practice.

3. *Confrontation Procedure*

The procedure for "the reexamination and confrontation of witnesses"[101] was the prime concern of the ordinance of Villers-Cotterets. Here the ordinance provided detail and affected structure. This phase of the procedure was entirely defensive in function, in that it supplied a set of checks on the accusing evidence in the dossier. It also laid the basis for the next phase, in which the accused might have his own witnesses called.

97. Imbert, ch. 10, §7, at 631.
98. Id., ch. 11, §§1–3, at 636–637.
99. Article 146.
100. Article 106, Isambert XI 364.
101. The quoted language is from the titles of Imbert's chapters 12 and 13, at 638, 639.

The confrontation proceeding followed an interlude during which the procureur's recommendations were formulated and submitted; then the judge arranged for the session. The period for procuratorial consideration was apparently susceptible to considerable delay. It was a natural point for neglect to occur if a heavy volume of court business was overtaxing the available personnel, because (for the state) it was the end of the investigative portion of the procedure in cases which did not require examination under torture. The ordinance of Villers-Cotterets—which is preeminently concerned with remedying delay in judicial procedure—attempts to prevent neglect of the case in this interval. It requires the procureur to review the dossier, to decide whether he wishes to continue the case, and to move for the scheduling of the confrontation phase and the summoning of its participants.[102] It further restricts to one, or at most two, the number of permissible postponements,[103] a restriction already disregarded in Imbert's day. He reports three or four postponements being granted "as before, owing to which the poor prisoners are sorely vexed . . . ."[104] The persistence of this practice in the teeth of recent and contrary legislation is a revealing indication of the pressures of volume upon the available personnel. Judicial practice could not, however, ameliorate the consequent hardship to the accused, whom the ordinance of Villers-Cotterets ordered confined until the confrontation.[105]

The ordinance spells out the actual procedure of reexamination and confrontation in some detail, and Imbert's manual indicates that practice did conform. The basic outline of the confrontation phase of the process was by no means novel to the statute. The ordinance of Blois had carried it forward from medieval practice in general language.[106] Beyond the generality there had been local variation, and in

102. Article 149.
103. Article 151.
104. Imbert, ch. 12, §4, at 638–639.
105. Article 152.
106. Hélie maintains, without authority, that Article 111 of the ordinance of Blois "is the first which . . . set up for the *regulation of the extraordinary* [procedure] the form of reexamination of witnesses and confrontation with the accused . . . ." Hélie (supra, note 82) at V 29 (italics in original). It seems unlikely that this complex proceeding was being innovated by anything as laconic as Article 111, which says in its entirety: "All necessary diligence shall be used for more ample *informations*, reexamination or confrontation of witnesses, or for the reexamination of the alibi, or other matter if there be such, admissible for or against the prisoner, as diligently and secretly as possible, so that none may know of it." Isambert XI 365.

some cases protraction of the proceedings. The ordinance of 1539 imposes a uniform (and restrictive) procedure. Principal among the variations which it expressly forbids is the grant of counsel to the accused for this stage of the process.[107]

What the ordinance calls reexamination is conducted by the judge. It will be recalled that until now the judge has not himself examined anyone but the accused. His knowledge of the witness testimony against the accused has been taken from the dossier of the preliminary inquiry, compiled by a subordinate examiner. These same witnesses are now made to come before the judge. They appear singly; each is sworn. The judge does not read back to the witness the deposition attributed to him, but asks him to summarize it. If the judge sees that the witness is saying what the deposition lays to him, he orders the clerk to read out the deposition and asks the witness to reaffirm it.[108]

The confrontation proper then commences. The accusing witness is brought into the presence of the accused; both are sworn; and the witness is asked whether the accused is the person of whom he spoke in his deposition.[109] The purpose is to negate the possibility of mistaken identity.

If the witness does identify the accused, the judge invites the accused to bring forward "any objections to the witness there present, and [he shall be] . . . enjoined to utter them promptly . . . , otherwise they shall not afterwards be received, of which [rule] he shall be well and expressly warned by the judge."[110] The object was to force personal objections—that is, those pertaining to the capacity or motivation of the witness—before the witness's testimony itself was disclosed to the accused and made subject to his reply. This was certainly a tactical disadvantage to the accused, but it was not positively unfair. It forced a separation of the accused's objections to the person of the witness and to the substance of his testimony, and presumably reflected the view that procrastinating defendants otherwise masked their inability to attack the merits of unfavorable testimony by making unjustified ad hominem challenges.

Objection to the witness aside, the deposition itself is read out. The judge then asks the witness whether he affirms it, which he does

107. Article 162.
108. Article 153; Imbert, ch. 13, §9, at 643.
109. Articles 153–154; Imbert, ch. 13, §9, at 643.
110. Article 154.

because he has just done so in private. The judge then asks the accused whether it is true. Here now is the opportunity to explain away the evidence, to put forward defenses to it, and, apparently, to conduct some cross-examination of the witness.[111] This procedure of physical confrontation followed by disclosure of the deposition is repeated for each witness.

Imbert suggests that the manifest safeguard function of the proceeding may also have effected a check on the lesser judicial bureaucracy. In a case in which a goodly number of the witnesses whose depositions have been taken at the preliminary inquiry retract and claim that the depositions do not contain their actual statements, the judge should call in the subordinate examiners responsible, examine them, and if they are culpable, punish them soundly. "For today this crime pullulates so that there is no man of substance who is not vexed and endangered by these [examiners]."[112]

The dossier with the results of this session is dispatched to the procureur. The ordinance of Villers-Cotterets again labors to breathe some urgency into the procuratorial review:[113]

> When the confrontations are done and finished, the dossier shall immediately be put in the hands of our procureur, who shall examine it well and diligently to see what *conclusions* he should make, be they definitive or peremptory, and he shall submit them promptly in writing.

Definitive *conclusions* would constitute a motion for final judgment and would be accompanied by a proposed form of judgment.[114]

Peremptory or provisional *conclusions* would be motions for further interlocutory process, of either of two sorts: the examination of defense witnesses or the use of judicial torture.

4. *Examination of Defense Witnesses*

When the accused's remarks in exculpation, either in the course of his examination before the judge or in reply to the accusing witnesses at the confrontation, raise a notionally tenable defense, such as alibi

111. Esmein 146.
112. Imbert, ch. 13, §13, at 646.
113. Article 156.
114. Imbert, ch. 13, §15, at 647.

(Imbert's example),[115] the procureur and the judge are expected to note it.[116] The procureur will move and the judge will order[117] "that the accused promptly name the witnesses by whom he intends to prove" the defense.[118] There follows an examination patterned on the examination of accusing witnesses in the preliminary inquiry: "the witnesses who shall thus be named by the said accused shall be heard and examined, *ex officio*, by the judges or their appointees or deputies...."[119]

These arrangements for the defense of the accused were regarded as excessively restrictive even in the sixteenth century. Imbert, in an exceptional interruption of his narrative, comments that the defensive procedures prescribed in the ordinance of Villers-Cotterets seem "*merveilleusement rigoureuses*":[120]

> [I]t is a very severe and harsh thing that a poor prisoner, who has languished in prison for a year or half-a-year, should have to designate his said witnesses at once, whereas in civil cases, which are much less dangerous, the parties have time to have their witnesses heard. Moreover, the prisoner has no one else for him [that is, no counsel], no one who can speak to the witnesses who might come to be heard for him; and the procureur, who is the adverse party, must require their appearance; and perchance they will be given to the charge of an [examiner] whose inclination and experience is to the party adverse to the prisoner.

Imbert's conclusion: perhaps it would be a good thing to ameliorate the ordinance by allowing the accused in some instances to organize his own defense. To prevent the suborning of witnesses by the accused, the court could rely on a statute of 1532 which prescribes the death penalty for those who utter perjured testimony.[121] Another contemporary lieutenant-criminel, Pierre Ayrault, published a more caustic critique of these matters.[122]

In addition to the insoluble problem of latent prosecutorial bias

115. Id.
116. Article 158.
117. Id.
118. Article 157.
119. Article 159. The paragraph continues on to deal with the costs of the proceeding.
120. Imbert, ch. 13, §16, at 648.
121. Id., ch. 13, §16, at 648–649.
122. Ayrault's tract (supra, note 74) was published in 1588, and was highly praised by nineteenth-century writers. See Allard (supra, note 7) at 457–461; Esmein 162–168; Jeanvrot (supra, note 74), at xcv–cxiii.

among an examiner corps accustomed to deposing accusing witnesses, two further aspects of the procedure as formulated in the ordinance of 1539 drew criticism from Imbert and Ayrault. One was the disparity in the amount of preparation time available to the procureur and to the accused, an imbalance they attributed to the malice of the draftsman of the ordinance of Villers-Cotterets. Another view is, however, open. We have seen that the ordinance in very clear language made efforts to cut down the procuratorial delay. The crush of business may have doomed that reform, but in design at least, the ordinance was attempting some evenhandedness. Motivated by the desire to expedite proceedings, it devised reforms which in the end proved more effective against the defense than the procureur.

The other aspect of the ordinance which offended Imbert and Ayrault was that the procureur became responsible for making the motion to commence the examination of defense witnesses and for issuing process to occasion their appearance. The procureur organized the defense of the accused. The conflict of interest being obvious, it ought to be asked how this arrangement could have commended itself to the draftsman. There is an answer other than Ayrault's (the malevolence of the draftsman, the politically unpopular Chancellor Poyet):[123] the draftsman felt himself without alternative, consistent with his goal of expediting the process. The grant of counsel to the accused would have been calamitous to expedition of the proceedings, and consequently the ordinance expressly forbids it.[124] Imbert suggests that the better solution would be that of prior royal legislation for Brittany, which allowed an accused who was not thought likely to "fabricate testimony . . . such as an ordinary woman or a poor peasant . . . to be received to allege and prove up the said matters."[125] That is, they might be allowed to organize and conduct the defensive proceedings in their own behalf.

Apart from liberality for hapless peasants, Imbert can think of no

123. Ayrault (supra, note 74) bk. 3, §65, at 236. Esmein, at 162, records Dumoulin's damning assessment of Poyet. Writers never tire of recalling that "[o]ne of the first victims of this Draconian system was the very author of the ordinance, Chancellor Poyet; prosecuted in 1543 in the Parlement [of Paris] for corruption, he sought the aid of counsel and met the reply: *'Patere legem quam fecisti'*: he was condemned to pay a fine of 100,000 livres." E. Chénon, *Histoire générale du droit français public et privé des origines à 1815* (Paris, 1926, 1929) II 356. One of Imbert's glossators has been moved to conclude his version of the tale with the pronouncement: *"L'histoire est fort vulgaire."* Imbert, ch. 13, §13, n.x., at 648.

124. Article 162.

125. Imbert, ch. 13, §16, at 648.

alternative. If a wily suspect were allowed to concoct defenses with outside collaborators, the laborious examination of those issues could be drawn out almost endlessly. The way to prevent such protraction was to officialize the defensive proofs—that is, to have public officials assume conduct of the defensive proofs as they had long ago the accusatory proofs. The defensive proceeding was analogized to the preliminary inquiry. The procureur invoked the proceeding and summoned the witnesses to it. The actual examination was conducted by the same class of examiner who had originated the dossier in the case. The inherent complexity of the procedural system almost compelled this step, as it had so many others. The vulnerability of the system to abusive protraction of proceedings having been revealed, the remedy, short of radical redesign, was a further officialization.

We need to remember that this was not the sole defensive opportunity open to the accused. When he was originally examined by the magistrate on the basis of the dossier of the preliminary inquiry, many an easy case must have resolved itself. It has been mentioned that this was the occasion for a number of formal defensive pleas and, inevitably, for informal exculpatory allegation and investigation. This may help explain one other feature of the formal defensive stage which we are now considering—that the theory of proof was oddly contorted. This is not a matter which the ordinance of Villers-Cotterets regulates, nor does Imbert speak to it with any care. Esmein's account:[126]

> A most astonishing and sadly ingenious theory was developed. It was not generally conceded that the accused could produce witnesses to prove that he was not guilty. Indeed, from the point of view of pure logic, a negative fact such as nonculpability cannot be proven, and according to the theory of legal proofs it was not a question of convincing the judge, but of establishing specific facts. If the fact was insufficiently proven by the accusing witnesses, all proof on the part of the accused was, so to speak, useless; if, on the contrary, the proceeding established by the requisite proofs that the crime had in fact been committed and that the accused was the perpetrator of it, he could only defeat the testimony through the objections he had raised [to the persons of the witnesses at the confrontation], or prove that these witnesses were suborned, or—finally—offer certain affirmative facts, which constituted his justification. These facts, called *justificatifs,* were of two sorts; one

126. Esmein 146–147. See also the discussion in Hélie (supra, note 82) at I 647–664.

sort showed, indirectly but undeniably, the accused's innocence, e.g., alibi, the appearance of the person thought dead, or the production of a prior judgment condemning the true perpetrator of the crime; the other sort, without contradicting the facts established in the proceeding, relieved the act of all criminality; for example, legitimate self-defense or the insanity of the actor at the moment of the deed.

Apart from personal challenges to the witnesses, therefore, only affirmative defenses—*faits justificatifs*—were properly the subject of formal defensive proceedings. Esmein remarks that it was the Roman-canon theory of proof which preeminently invited such a doctrine. It did not conceive of proof as the balance of persuasion. Rather, it intended to devise a set of mechanical rules for weighing evidence regardless of the opinion or convictions of the trier-of-fact. His job was to apply the rules, to assign arithmetic values to evidence according to the tariff of cogency which the later jurists had worked out.[127] Guilt or innocence was arithmetically determined; the judge cumulated the values assigned to the evidence. Conviction required "full proof," whose paradigm was the testimony of two eyewitnesses to the gravamen of the crime (each witness's testimony constituted a "half proof"). The gradations for circumstantial evidence were legion. But once the numbers added up properly to "full proof," contradiction had no place, because it could not alter the conclusiveness of the arithmetic. Evidence which inclined the other way simply fell outside the equation. Hence, the formal defenses open to the accused were the affirmative defenses, the proof of which goes to "a fact distinct from that proven by the prosecution."[128]

However, for that very reason, the exculpatory possibilities open to the accused in the prior phase of the procedure, in the judge's examination of the accused, need to be remembered. Matters within the knowledge of the accused bearing directly upon the prosecution evidence and exculpatory in import would be explained to the judge informally, and would affect the prosecution case informally, by influencing the decision on whether to go forward. Persuasion operated outside the calculus of the numerical proofs. By way of contrast, it should be recalled that the German Carolina, which so concerned itself with prob-

127. Esmein 261–262.
128. Id. at 147.

lems of exculpation, had relied almost entirely upon the informal raising of such pleas to the judge in the course of examination.

5. Torture

If formal defenses were either lacking or ultimately unsubstantiated, it was then in order for the procureur to move for final judgment, by submitting "definitive *conclusions.*" If the case remained short of full proof, yet was weighty, he could ask for a last interlocutory stage by submitting "peremptory *conclusions*" asking for examination of the accused under torture.[129] As in the opening stages of the procedure, the ordinance of Villers-Cotterets does not supply the basic text for the torture stage. Article 163 of the ordinance is the sole paragraph dealing with torture; its concern is to expedite an existing system:

> If upon the examination of the dossier the case is found to be subject to torture, or *question extraordinaire,* we will that the sentence to such torture be pronounced to the prisoner immediately, in order to be promptly executed if he does not appeal. And if there is an appeal [we will that] it be taken at once into our local supreme court *(cour souveraine du lieu)* where we wish all appeals in criminal cases to be brought immediately and without intermediary stage, on whatever [grounds] the said criminal matters be appealed.

The draftsman expresses two commands. One is that the decision to use torture be promptly communicated and carried out. The other is that any appeal against the decision be expedited by being sent up to the highest court at once.

Appeals presume standards, however, and these are not dealt with in the statute of 1539. The predecessor ordinance of Blois contains such statutory authority on that subject as Imbert can cite. Three consecutive articles[130] regulate judicial torture. Article 112 provides that the judge's decision on whether or not to use torture shall be taken after deliberation with the procureur and the council of local lawyers, minus any who have represented the accused or the partie civile. (The phenomenon of the court taking counsel with the bar in a formal session was common "in French lower courts, where the advisory councils,

129. Supra, page 234.
130. Isambert XI 365–366.

largely composed of local lawyers, had the closest connection with current litigation and were directly consulted in doubtful cases."[131]) Article 112 also exhorts the court to use dispatch in carrying out an interlocutory sentence to torture once decided upon. Article 113 prescribes the use of torture. The clerk shall be present to transcribe the names of those present, the details of the physical coercion applied including its frequency, "and the questions and answers, with the prisoner's persistence, his consistency or variation; and on the day after the said inquisition, the prisoner shall once more be examined away from the place where he had the said torture to check his persistence, and all shall be written down by the said clerk." Finally, Article 114 forbids further examinations under torture unless upon newly discovered evidence.

This Spartan scheme of statutory regulation in the two ordinances is preoccupied with the judicial mechanics: deliberation among the professionals, contents of the dossier, appeals, and so forth. The contrast with the Carolina is particularly striking. It too had directed the presence of the clerk and the preparation of a comprehensive dossier. But the great bulk of the Carolina is taken up with its Indizienlehre (the rules of evidence which justified the resort to torture) and with the detail of questioning the accused and verifying the confession. The French legislation, addressed to a professional magistracy, could presume an understanding of the jurisprudence of torture. Even Imbert's treatise deals only cursorily with the prerequisites of torture. He speaks of convening the meeting of the advisory council when the case against the accused "is enormous."[132] A single paragraph recalls the general proposition that "according to the opinion of some Doctors of civil Law, the deposition of one witness deposing to something which is a matter of some bodily sense like sight is sufficient, but if there are only *indices* [indications, that is, circumstantial evidence], these must be proven each by two witnesses."[133] A further slight section records that the rule of civil and canon law which exempted some persons from liability to examina-

131. Dawson, *Oracles* 283–284.

132. Imbert, ch. 14, §1, at 651.

133. Id., ch. 14, §2, at 652. Imbert discusses, as further authority for the rule, an ordinance of 1253 and a passage from the writer Le Coq. A few subrules are mentioned and attributed to the judgments of the Parlement of Bordeaux. Id. at 652–653.

tion under torture on account of their dignity is not followed in French royal court practice.[134]

Imbert's chapter on torture glosses the three articles from the ordinance of Blois. Imbert remarks that it is often impractical to proceed with the dispatch the statute calls for, and that when some delay in carrying out a sentence to torture is necessary, communication of the sentence should be withheld from the accused to prevent his taking any precaution to fortify himself against the pain.[135] Imbert describes the actual administration of torture. Together with the judge and the clerk come the procureur, two local lawyers, and two court functionaries. The normal mode of torture is called *brodequins,* meaning "laced boot," and involves driving wedges along the tightly bound ankle. The clerk records all of this, down to the number of wedges and the number of blows given each, as well as the questions, answers, and variations.[136] Confirmation of the confession is sought the next day, without torture.[137] To recant avails the accused not: he is condemned upon the confession "if it seems truthful and accords with or approaches the contents of the preliminary inquiry and the proofs taken in the criminal proceeding."[138]

It is difficult to sense how important torture was to the French system, how prevalent the tortured confession really was. It was obvious from the Carolina that torture was almost the first and only resort of the German investigating magistrate. The French system appears to treat examination under torture more exceptionally. It spells out a series of investigative stages short of torture. It has a professional prosecutor in charge of gathering evidence, who may have felt some pressure to do his job well enough to obviate the need for torture. The decision to torture is taken so seriously that the judge is obliged to put it to his legal advisory council. And even the expediting ordinance of Villers-Cotterets was unwilling to preclude the right of interlocutory appeal against such a sentence. These are grounds for believing that French practice may in fact have been somewhat less torture-prone than German, despite the greater concern of the German legislation with safeguarding the rights of the accused.

134. Id., ch. 14, §3 at 653–654; compare §5 of book 6 (pt. 1) of the Wormser Reformation, supra, page 160.

135. Imbert, ch. 14, §4, at 654.

136. Id., ch. 14, §5, at 654–655.

137. Id., ch. 14, §6, at 655.

138. Id., ch. 14, §7, at 655–656.

6. Final Process

It could happen that the proceeding would terminate in the accused's favor, notwithstanding its having come so far. After deliberation with the procureur and the advisory council, the judge would remit the parties to "ordinary process";[139] that is, he would release the accused, allow him counsel, and leave him to litigate the civil liabilities, including any action for wrongful prosecution, against the partie civile. A case would also be remitted to "ordinary process" if the investigation had disclosed that the accused's criminal liability was at most for petty crime.[140]

In the normal course, however, the judge finds the case against the accused to be established, either by confession or by sufficient witness proofs: he then notifies the procureur to submit his *conclusions.*[141] These "definitive *conclusions,*" demanding the condemnation of the accused, the judge discusses with the advisory council.[142] The judge alone passes sentence; the form of sentence indicates the specific offense in punishment of which the judgment is pronounced, although the practice of the Parlement of Paris is to pronounce a general condemnation disclosing nothing.[143] The sentence is ceremonially communicated to the prisoner by the judge in the council session or alone in the court room.[144] Unless the accused appeals, sentence is executed the same day.[145]

From the statutory texts and from Imbert one derives no fair picture of the appellate process. Imbert largely avoids the subject, perhaps because his readership was the instance magistrate corps.[146] It is particularly difficult to see how a system of notionally liberal appeal functioned in the absence of defense counsel to identify and raise appellate issues. It seems that there was some allowance of counsel in appellate

139. Id., ch. 15, §1, at 658.

140. Regulated in the ordinance of Blois (1498), Articles 117 ff.; Isambert XI 367 ff.

141. Imbert, ch. 20, §1, at 684–685.

142. Id., ch. 20, §4, at 685.

143. Id., ch. 20, §6, at 686. The Parlement's form-of-words: "*Pour la punition & reparation des cas dont il est trouvé attaint & convaincu par les procez.*"

144. Id., ch. 20, §5, at 686. This is said to pertain in lieu of a former usage in which the judge had the clerk convey the sentence to the prisoner in the guard room. Compare the disposition of Article 218 of the Carolina.

145. Imbert, ch. 20, §5, at 686.

146. See the brief treatment, id., bk. 4, at 728 ff.

matters, but one does not sense the dimensions of the practice.[147] In outline, in any event, the possibility of appeal was a feature pressing in upon the magistrate's practice. The expediting ordinance of Villers-Cotterets did not attempt to compromise it.[148] The ordinance of 1670 further facilitated appellate review of the final judgment in more serious cases.[149]

C. THE ORDINANCE OF VILLERS-COTTERETS

We have met provisions of the ordinance of Villers-Cotterets at various points in the sixteenth-century procedure. The present section takes up the ordinance by itself to ask what its intention was, and what its importance. We ought first to comment on what the ordinance contained.

The proper title of the statute is the *Ordonnance sur le fait de la justice,* roughly, "ordinance on the subject of the legal system." And its dispositions are correspondingly broad. It contains 192 separately numbered articles, without further subdivision. The first 8 articles treat the relations between lay and ecclesiastical courts, including appeals from the latter to the former—an ancient and perpetual subject of royal legislation.[150] Thereafter the statute regulates civil procedure in the royal courts, although a few of the provisions (such as those on contumacy)[151] are made applicable to criminal cases as well. The principal concern of these civil procedural dispositions is to remedy various practices which had been protracting proceedings. The language of Article 18 may suggest the flavor: "and we forbid all other delays wont to be taken, be they for advice, because of absence, waiting for counsel or any others . . . . "[152] Provisions abound which either fix the due date of a procedural step[153] or restrict the number of stays.[154] Default and

147. See Esmein 245–247. Further authority is collected in Allard (supra, note 7) at 370 n. 1.

148. See Article 163, contenting itself with avoiding intermediate review of interlocutory appeal against sentence to torture.

149. See Esmein 245–246.

150. Isambert XII (pt. 2) 601–602.

151. Articles 24–25, id. at 605.

152. Id. at 604.

153. E.g., Articles 19, 23, id. at 604, 605.

154. E.g., Articles 13, 18 (quoted in text above), 33–34, 46–47, id. at 603, 604, 607, 609–610.

contumacy[155] are regulated extensively, and various delaying practices are abolished.[156] The national system of parish registries in France was begun by this ordinance, which gives those records conclusive effect,[157] ostensibly to save litigation in property cases about times of birth and death.[158] A one-year statute of limitations in property matters is propounded.[159] Creditors' rights and modes of execution of judgment take up 17 articles.[160] Estimation of civil damages and related problems[161] are dealt with, followed by aspects of appellate practice,[162] including a measure to force greater particularity in the appellant's allegations of error.[163] There is the odd provision of more or less substantive law—nullifying gratuitous transfers to fiduciaries[164] and upholding certain contracts made by minors.[165] There is a good deal of instruction about the duties and compensation of various court functionaries, particularly the notaries, but also scriveners, clerks, guardians of seals, and examiners.[166] The ordinance concludes with 8 articles of guild regulation conducted through the law courts.[167] A terse Preamble prefaces the act, promulgating it "in order to provide in some measure for the good of our legal system, for the shortening of proceedings, and for the relief of our subjects . . . . "[168]

The 29 articles of criminal procedure are intromitted toward the close of the ordinance. We shall find it convenient to summarize them.

(139–140) Criminal proceedings have priority over civil. Criminal liabilities shall be decided before civil in a joint action.

(141–143) Judges have been making errors which have delayed proceedings and caused appeals. They shall be liable to sanctions for such errors, and for costs.

(144) Judges shall not delegate their own duties to other functionaries, such as the procureur or the clerk.

---

155. Articles 21–31, id. at 605–607.
156. E.g., Article 36 (id. at 607): "There shall be no more replies by *credit vel non credit*, nor rejoinders against the statements and depositions of witnesses . . . ."
157. Articles 51–56, id. at 610–611.
158. Article 57, id. at 611–612.
159. Article 61, id. at 612.
160. Articles 65–81, id. at 613–616.
161. Articles 88–108, id. at 617–622.
162. Articles 114–119, id. at 623–624.
163. Article 114, id. at 623.
164. Article 131, id. at 627.
165. Article 134, id. at 628.
166. Articles 120–125, 170–184, id. at 624–625, 635–638.
167. Articles 185–192, id. at 638–640.
168. Preamble, id. at 600–601.

(145) On complaint of wrongdoing, the judge shall investigate or have investigation made. He shall communicate it to the procureur, who will promptly enter his *conclusions* on the bottom of the document, without taking payment therefor. The judge shall order appropriate process against the accused.

(146) The judge shall examine the accused immediately.

(147) The examination shall be immediately sent to the procureur for his *conclusions*.

(148) If the accused has confessed, the confession is shown to the partie civile. His submissions and the procureur's are shown to the accused, who [having confessed guilt] may reply only by way of extenuation.

(149–150) If it is not considered that the accused's statement is sufficient to convict him, an order shall be made scheduling the next phase of the proceeding, the date depending on the distances and the people involved; unless the case is remitted to "ordinary process" at this point, on account of its triviality.

(151) A cutoff point on prosecution proofs is established.

(152) The accused shall not be released on bail pending the confrontation proceeding.

(153–155) The confrontation proceeding: witnesses are sworn and reexamined in the absence of the accused. Those who persist in accusation shall be immediately confronted with the accused, separately, one after another. The confrontation of each shall begin with the swearing of witness and accused. Before the reading of the deposition of the witness, the accused is asked whether he has objections to the witness, and enjoined to utter them promptly, after which they are waived. Then is read the deposition.

(156) The confrontation proceeding completed, the dossier is given to the procureur, whose *conclusions*, peremptory or definitive, he shall submit promptly.

(157) If the procureur finds that facts raising a tenable defense have been stated, he shall have the accused name the witnesses by whom he wishes to prove the matters alleged.

(158) The judge shall review these *conclusions*, decide which defenses are tenable, and order the accused to name his witnesses.

(159) The judge or an appointed examiner examines these witnesses, at the expense of the accused, or if he is indigent, of the partie civile, or if he is indigent, the crown.

(160–161) Payments for defensive proceedings out of crown funds are authorized. All other expenses may be paid from crown funds only when there is no partie civile who can afford them.

(162) There is no right to counsel in criminal cases; contrary usage is forbidden.

(163) If torture is ordered, it should be carried out at once. If there is an appeal, it should go to the highest competent court, without intermediate review.

(164) If neither the torture nor the examination produces the requisite evidence against the accused, he is to be declared innocent and remitted to "ordinary process" against the partie civile.

(165) Accusing testimony in the deposition of a witness who died before confrontation with the accused shall be credited anyhow if the confrontation

were delayed through the contumacy of the accused.

(166) Criminal proceedings do not stay civil ones.

(167) All prior royal legislation on criminal procedure is perpetuated, save where inconsistent.

The dominant theme of the ordinance of Villers-Cotterets, in its civil as well as its criminal procedural dispositions, is the need to remedy protraction of proceedings. Its Preamble proclaims the act "for the shortening of proceedings."[169] The reasons why protraction of proceedings had become such a serious problem should by now be fairly plain. The system of written evidence had developed complex multiple layers of evidence-taking and evaluation. Criminal procedure was less affected than civil because constraints on defensive opportunities, especially upon defense counsel, had retarded it somewhat. Yet unlike civil litigation, the criminal process tended to take place at the expense of the crown rather than the parties.[170] Hence the ordinance of Villers-Cotterets gives priority to criminal business and to correcting what it regards as points of blockage or protraction in the criminal procedure.

Alongside the complexity and procedural elaborateness which the system of written evidence had evoked appeared a related and indelible characteristic: the enormous judicial bureaucracy needed to administer it. It is a fair description of the criminal procedure portion of the ordinance of Villers-Cotterets that no subject is so extensively regulated as the relations of the judicial functionaries inter se. Which officer should take which step when, and having done it which other officer he should notify—this is the typical subject of these paragraphs. The constant exhortation that each of these steps be taken "immediately" or "promptly" is a further indication of the problems of coordination and delay inherent in a system where so many actions were to be performed by so many officers. We recall from Imbert the occasions where judicial practice had come flatly to contradict some statutory restriction upon delay. The rigidities of the process were so endemic that they could not always be responsive to legislative correction, even within such a hierarchic legal system with its appellate checks and its threatened personal sanctions upon the lower judiciary.

Nonetheless, the draftsman tried. He attempted to make the se-

169. Id. at 600.

170. Notwithstanding the wistful attempts to unload the expenses on the parties civiles, Articles 159–161.

quence of official duties as precise as possible. And he dealt at some length with that phase of the procedure which had become productive of the most delay—the procedure for raising formal defenses and the confrontation proceeding which set it up. Undeniably, the innovations of the ordinance worked to the detriment of the accused. The judge was strenuously forbidden any discretion to allow the accused the aid of counsel.[171] The accused was required to raise personal objections to a witness in advance of hearing his testimony; he was not allowed to discover how damaging the testimony was before deciding whether to press (or invent) objections to the capacity of the witness.[172] The accused had no leisure in raising defensive facts. He was obliged to bring forward all such matters at the confrontation hearing.[173] And the accused was limited merely to designating defense witnesses. Denied counsel and denied release on bail,[174] he could conduct no investigation to discover further witnesses. This was left to the initiative of the officials—the procureur and the judge or examiner—whose job it had previously been to convict him.[175]

Despite all the disadvantages which these measures involved for the accused, we should be reluctant to follow the view that such was the dominant intent of the ordinance. For the point remains that these were clumsy and indirect ways of compromising the position of the accused. Far more efficient alternatives were available. Torture could have been used sooner. Indeed, the entire process of defensive allegation and proof might have been combined with the prior phase of the procedure (examination of the accused) without formality. The German Carolina had done essentially that. Instead of taking any drastic moves to undermine the defense, the draftsman elaborated a series of lesser adjustments tightening up the existing procedure, with a time-saving motive always in evidence. It is difficult to believe that the position of the accused was grievously worsened by the statutory changes. On the whole, the statute did too little harm to have really intended it.

I suggest, therefore, that it has been error to attribute to the draftsman a malevolent design to harass the accused and render him defenseless. The ordinance of Villers-Cotterets is better taken at the face value

171. Article 162.
172. Articles 153–155.
173. Article 155.
174. Article 152.
175. Articles 157–159.

of its Preamble as an act "for the shortening of proceedings." In its civil procedural dispositions as well, but especially for present purposes in its criminal procedure section, the ordinance is composed of a series of interstitial adjustments designed to expedite proceedings, both by readjusting or refining the bureaucratic routine, and by eliminating or restricting individual steps in the long ladder which had proven awkward and time-consuming. A "revolution"[176] it was not.

D. THE FRENCH PROCEDURE IN COMPARATIVE PERSPECTIVE

The ordinance of Villers-Cotterets was neither a code nor a reception. It invites comparison, therefore, with the German Carolina, which was both, and with the English Marian statutes, which were surely no code and, in the argument of the present study, no reception either.

The ordinance of Villers-Cotterets dealt with many of the procedural stages in terms so general that it could only have been meant to confirm ongoing judicial practice rather than to formulate the procedure authoritatively. No magistrate could have found guidance in the articles treating preliminary inquiry, examination of the accused, or torture.[177] Nothing at all was said about promulgating final judgment or executing it. On the other hand, there was more detail about the confrontation and defensive proceedings, which the statute altered. The ordinance therefore presumed the existing system, which it expressly saved where not inconsistent.[178]

The contrast with the Carolina is particularly striking in this regard. The Carolina, being self-consciously a model procedural system, was a thoroughly comprehensive code in the sense that it covered every step from suspicion to sentence and execution. Moreover, because the Carolina was addressed to lay magistrates, it had an instructional quality to its organization, content, and language. It was a self-explanatory procedural system, indeed, an often oversimplified one. A nineteenth-century writer, commenting upon the Carolina from the perspective of the French system, marveled that it would "stoop to such truly ridiculous details, unworthy of a legislator who addresses intelligent men."[179]

176. Allard (supra, note 7) 149.
177. Articles 145, 146, 163.
178. Article 167.
179. Allard (supra, note 7) 423.

If the Carolina was excessively pedantic, however, it does not follow that the ordinance of Villers-Cotterets was a work of scholarly achievement. We have seen that it was nothing of the sort. Such fundamental matters of principle as the prerequisites for torture or the theory of proof, which the Carolina stated crudely, the French legislation of 1498 (Blois) and 1539 (Villers-Cotterets) did not discuss at all. Nor does Imbert's treatise pay serious attention to these elementary matters. The explanation, of course, lies in the expertise of the French magistracy. Being professionals, they had no need of schoolbooks done up as statutebooks. The French legislation thus is largely unintelligible standing alone. For the present study it has been necessary to rely on Imbert in order to construct a description of sixteenth-century French criminal procedure. A contemporary would not have had much better fortune trying to understand the system from the statute. The ordinance of Villers-Cotterets presumed familiarity with the whole of the bureaucratic routine of the procuratorial and magistrative corps. Had an English draftsman of the day come upon the ordinance, he would have turned away from it more rapidly even than from the Carolina. In all likelihood it would have been incomprehensible to him, precisely because of its interstitial character. But were he the exceptional scholar or traveler with an understanding of the system which the statute was repairing he would all the more surely have retreated before it. He would have known that the system presumed a vast and expensive corps of professional magistrates, examiners, prosecutors, and functionaries. He would have shuddered at the problems of financing, organizing, controlling, and training an English counterpart. And in the ordinance of Villers-Cotterets itself, he would have had a most alarming warning about the desirability of a system grown so complex, so heavily staffed, and so time-consuming that serious compromises with fairness had to be devised in the name of dispatch.

One of the key differences between the Inquisitionsprozess of the ordinance of Villers-Cotterets and that of the Carolina is that the prosecutorial function had crystallized into the prosecutorial office only in the former. The Carolina relied upon a single officer, the judge. The proliferation of officers in French procedure had made possible a functional differentiation between procureur and judge. It will be recalled that the procuratorial office appeared in the fourteenth century; that it may have been suggested in imitation of canon practice; and that the civil procedural model may have encouraged a tendency to analogize the royal and public interest in criminal business to that of a party plaintiff in civil litigation.

Because I have argued that the Marian statutes represent the decisive step in the formation and institutionalization of the prosecutorial office in England, it is worth stressing two points about the parallel phenomenon on the Continent. First, Inquisitionsprozess did not necessarily require that there be a discrete prosecutorial office; the Carolina had none. Second, the prototypical Continental prosecutor, the French procureur, had appeared in the Middle Ages. That office was created when it had become convenient to organize the judicial office in a fashion modeled on civil practice. The trier-of-fact became somewhat passive, examiner but not instigator or demandant, requiring that another officer take up the neglected duties. It goes without saying that these events were too remote in time and too particular to the idiosyncrasies of the French judicial bureaucracy to have served as a model for the Renaissance English. Still, the parallel is instructive, because the English of the sixteenth century were creating a prosecutorial office for the same reason the French had done it in the fourteenth century. The increasing passivity of the trier-of-fact—the petty jury—was requiring that another agency come forward to take up the active role in criminal prosecution.

It requires little demonstration that the ordinance of Villers-Cotterets constituted no reception of Roman-canon law. The underlying system was indeed a received one, dating back to the thirteenth and fourteenth centuries. This medieval reception had entrenched in France the Roman-canon theory of proofs, and above all, the principle of official examination and transcription of the testimony of individual witnesses—the building blocks of the system of numerical proofs. But the French procedural system had long since come to lead an institutional life of its own. We have seen that Imbert remarks upon the divergence of various French practices from the Roman-canon fundamentals underlying the system. The ordinance of Villers-Cotterets, coordinating the officialdom of the criminal process on the one hand, smoothing out what it deemed logjams in a long-evolved procedure on the other, was dealing with problems particular to French practice.

It remains to mention the role of the dossier in this classic system of written evidence. The Carolina, we have remarked, was primarily concerned with having its proceedings transcribed in order to facilitate referral of the case to outside experts if it became complicated. The dossier was the instrument of externalization. It was the device by which the court could rid itself of the case. Aktenversendung required Akten. Within the court the written documents were less significant, because a single officer—the judge—conducted the whole of the instrumental part of the proceeding. The French dossier, however, was the critical device of internal coordination within a bureaucratized instance court and within an appellate hierarchy of courts. The dossier commenced with the examiner's preliminary inquiry, picked up the repeated submissions of the procureur and the partie civile, then became the record of the judge's examinations and his deliberations with his advisory council. It is a revealing feature of the ordinance of Villers-Cotterets that it nearly always tells which officer has the dossier and to whom he ought next to send it. The dossier was the thread of physical continuity in a procedure ever more complex, with its multiple stages conducted over stretches of time by a variety of officials. The care with which legislation directs its progress[180] and retention[181] is therefore understandable.

Here too the lesson of comparison is that the written record served radically different purposes in France and in England. English criminal procedure had severely restricted possibilities of appeal, in contrast to the notional liberality of appeal, interlocutory and final, in the French procedure. The English system also lacked any serious counterpart to the French judicial bureaucracy which the dossier knit together, although in one respect the documents called for by the Marian committal statute had a remotely similar coordinating role in apprising the trial judge of the state of the case against the accused. But the greatest variation arose from the differences in the theories of proof. Final judgment would be passed in France upon the contents of the dossier, as in the Germany of the Carolina and everywhere in the Roman-canon procedural world. In England the trial court would pass judgment upon the verdict of the jury, "although it will seeme straunge to all nations that doe use the civill Lawe of the Romane Emperours, that for life and death there is nothing put in writing but the enditement onely."[182]

180. E.g., Article 145 of the ordinance of Villers-Cotterets, telling the procureur where on the page to enter his observations.

181. E.g., Article 95 ff. of the ordinance of Blois (1498), Isambert XI 361 ff., prescribing the use of special sacks for completed informations. Cf. Carolina Articles 189, 202.

182. Smith, *De Republica* bk. 2, ch. 23, at 81.

Appendixes Index

APPENDIX A. THE MARIAN STATUTES

Preface to the Texts

The following texts are based upon those in the *Statutes of the Realm* IV 259, 286. Spelling has been modernized, but capitalization, punctuation, and paragraphing are original. Footnotes in the *Statutes of the Realm* and variations noted therein have been omitted, save that in one instance (denoted by square brackets) a footnoted variation has been preferred. For more on the statutory texts see Chapter 3, note 18.

Marian Bail Statute

1 & 2 Philip & Mary c. 13 (1554–1555)

An Act appointing an Order to Justices of Peace for the Bailment of Prisoners.

Where in the Parliament holden at Westminster in the third year of the reign of the noble Prince King Henry the Seventh, It was among other things ordained and enacted, That no Prisoner arrested for Felony should be let to Bail or Mainprise by any one Justice of Peace, but by the whole Justices or at least by two of them whereof One to be of the Quorum: Since the making of which Statute one Justice of Peace, in the name of himself and one other of the Justices his companion, not making the said Justice party nor privy unto the case wherefore the Prisoner should be bailed, hath often times by sinister labor and means set at large the greatest and notablest Offenders, such as be not replevisable by the Laws of this Realm, and yet the rather to hide their affections in that behalf, have signified the cause of their apprehension to be but only for suspicion of Felony, whereby the said Offenders hath escaped unpunished, and do daily, to the high displeasure of Almighty God, the great peril of the King and Queen's true Subjects, and encouragement of all Thieves and evil doers: For Reformation whereof be it enacted and ordained by the King and Queen's Majesties the Lords Spiritual and Temporal and the Commons in this present Parliament assembled and by authority of the same, That from and after the first day of April next coming, no Justice or Justices of Peace shall let to bail or mainprise any such person or persons, which for any Offense or Offenses by them or any of them committed be declared not to be replevisable or bailed, or be forbidden to be replevied or bailed by the Statute of Westminster Primer, made in the Parliament holden in the third year of the reign of King Edward the first: And furthermore that any person or persons, arrested for manslaughter or felony or suspicion of manslaughter or felony, being bailable by the Law, shall not after the said first day of April be let to Bail or Mainprise by any Justices of Peace, if it be not in open Sessions, Except it be by two Justices of Peace at the least whereof One to be of the Quorum, and the same Justices to be present together at the time of the said Bailment or Mainprise; which Bailment or Mainprise they shall certify, in writing signed or subscribed with their own hands, at the next general Gaol Delivery to be holden within the County where the said person or persons shall be arrested or suspected: And that the said Justices or one of them being of the Quroum, when any such Prisoner is brought before them for any Manslaughter or Felony, before any Bailment or Mainprise, shall take the examination of the said Prisoner and information of them that bring him, of the fact and circumstances thereof, and the same, or as much thereof as shall be material to prove the felony, shall put in writing before they make the same Bailment, which said examination together with the said Bailment, the said Justices shall certify at the next general Gaol Delivery to be holden within the limits of their Commission: And that every Coroner, upon any Inquisition before him found, whereby any person or persons shall be indicted for murder or manslaughter, or as accessory or accessories to the same before the murder or manslaughter committed, shall put in writing the effect of the evidence given to the Jury before him being material; and as well the said Justices as the said Coroner shall have authority by this Act to bind all such by Recognizance or Obligation, as do declare any thing material to prove the said Murder or Manslaughter Offenses or Felonies or to be Accessory or Accessories to the same as is aforesaid, to appear at the next general Gaol Delivery to be holden within the County City or Town Corporate where the trial thereof shall be, then and there to give Evidence against the party so indicted at the time of his trial; and shall certify as well the same evidence as such bond and bonds in writing as he shall take, together with the inquisition or indictment before him taken and found, at or before the time of his said trial thereof to be had or made: And likewise the said Justices shall certify all and every such bond taken before them in like manner as before is said of Bailments and Examination: And in case any Justice of Peace or Quorum or Coroner, shall after the said first day of April offend in any thing contrary to the true intent and meaning of this present Act, that then the Justices of Gaol Delivery of the Shire City Town or Place where such Offense shall happen to be committed, upon due proof thereof by examination before them, shall for every such Offense set such fine, on every of the same Justices of Peace and Coroner, as the same Justices of Gaol Delivery shall think meet, and shall estreat the same as other Fines and Amercements assessed before Justices of Gaol Delivery ought to be.

Provided always and Be it further enacted by the authority aforesaid, That Justices of Peace and Coroners within the City of London and the County of Middlesex, and in other Cities Boroughs and Towns Corporate within this Realm and Wales, shall within their several jurisdictions have authority to let to bail Felons and Prisoners, in such manner and form as they have been heretofore accustomed, This Act or any thing therein contained to the contrary notwithstanding; And also shall take examinations and bonds as is aforesaid, upon every Bailment by them or any of them to be made, and shall Certify every such Bailments Bonds and Examinations [*sic*] by them or any of them taken or made, at the next Gaol Delivery to be holden within the Shire City Borough or Town where their several Jurisdictions extendeth; upon like pain and forfeiture as is before limited in this present Act.

And be it also Enacted by the authority aforesaid, That no Writs of Habeas [Corpus] or Certiorari shall be hereafter granted to remove any Prisoner out of any Gaol, or to remove any Recognizance, except the same Writs be signed with the proper hands of the Chief Justice, or in his absence One of the Justices of the Court out of which the same Writs shall be awarded or made; upon pain that he that writeth any such writs not being signed as is aforesaid to forfeit to our said Sovereign Lord the King and the Queen, for every such Writ and Writs, Five Pounds.

Marian Committal Statute

2 & 3 Philip & Mary c. 10 (1555)

An Act to take the examination of Prisoners suspected of Manslaughter or Felony.

Where in the last Parliament holden at Westminster, amongst other things it was enacted, That such Justices of the Peace as have authority to bail any Prisoners brought before them, for any Manslaughter or Felony, before any Bailment or Mainprise should take the examination of the said Prisoner, and information of them that bring him, of the fact and circumstances thereof, and the same or as much thereof as shall be material to prove the Felony, shall put in writing before they make the same Bailment, which said examination together with the said Bailment, the said Justices should certify at the next general Gaol Delivery to be holden within the limits of their Commission; as by the same Act more plainly is contained and may appear: And Forasmuch as the said Act doth not extend to such Prisoners as shall be brought before any Justices of Peace for Manslaughter or Felony, and by such Justice shall be committed to Ward for the suspicion of such Manslaughter or Felony, and not bailed, in which case examination of such Prisoner, and of such as shall bring him, is as necessary or rather more, than where such Prisoner shall be let to Bail or Mainprise: Be it therefore enacted by the authority of this present Parliament, That from henceforth such Justices or Justice before whom any person shall be brought for Manslaughter or Felony, or for suspicion thereof, before he or they shall commit or send such Prisoner to Ward, shall take the examination of such Prisoner, and information of those that bring him, of the fact and circumstance thereof, and the same or as much thereof as shall be material to prove the Felony shall put in writing, within two days after the said examination, and the same shall certify in such manner and form and at such time as they should and ought to do if such Prisoner so committed or sent to Ward had been bailed or let to Mainprise, upon such pain as in the said former Act is limited and appointed for not taking or not certifying such examinations as in the said former Act is expressed.

And Be it further enacted, That the said Justices shall have authority by this Act to bind all such by Recognizance or Obligation, as do declare anything material to prove the said Manslaughter or Felony, against such Prisoner as shall be so committed to ward, to appear at the next general Gaol Delivery to be holden within the County City or Town Corporate, where the trial of the said Manslaughter or Felony shall be, then and there to give evidence against the party; And that the said Justices shall certify the said Bonds taken before them, in like manner as they should and ought to certify the Bonds mentioned in the said former Act, upon the pain as in the said former Act is mentioned for not certifying such Bonds, as by the said former Act is limited and appointed to be certified.

APPENDIX B. *CONSTITUTIO CRIMINALIS CAROLINA*

Preface to the Translation

This translation renders into English the criminal procedural sections of the *Constitutio Criminalis Carolina.* The Carolina, although predominantly a procedural ordinance, was not exclusively that: Articles 104–180 deal with offense definition (the penalties for various specified offenses) and with matters of general substantive import, such as exculpation and mitigation. This middle portion of the Carolina, save for the first two articles (104 and 105, dealing with generalities of punishment), is omitted from the present translation. Also omitted are articles 207–214, which regulate matters we would regard as civil and administrative (the property rights in stolen goods recovered, the responsibility of local craftsmen to labor on the construction of gallows). The titles for the omitted sections are retained in the translation, however. Finally, the printer's privilege which prefaces the Carolina has been struck as an anachronism. These deletions intend to reduce the document to more manageable dimensions, while still preserving in its entirety its explicitly procedural portions.

The Carolina was composed (roughly contemporaneously with the Luther Bible) in what is today called *Frühneuhochdeutsch.* That tongue poses special problems for translation of a legal document into modern English. The difficulties of recondite vocabulary are usually surmountable, but the principal problem—archaic sentence structure—is probably not. The Carolina exemplifies the formless disorder of Frühneuhochdeutsch. Not uncommonly a single sentence runs on for a paragraph or a page, insufficiently and arbitrarily punctuated. The modern mind cannot cope with this, and comprehension has compelled, in my judgment, that a sentence structure of sorts be imposed upon the text. This is not, therefore, a close, quasi-literal translation. I suspect that such a job is impossible; in any event, it was impractical for present purposes. In the account of the statute given in this book, nothing of importance depends on the precise detail of linguistic formulation or syntax. Rather, the concern is to illustrate the issues to which the ordinance speaks, and to show the scope and character of the solutions. Accordingly, liberties have been taken in translation which might have been unjustifiable had the purpose been otherwise, and users must stand cautioned searching it for subtleties it will not support.

The serious intermeddling with the text has occurred in supplying punctuation marks, in particular the semicolon and the dash. Neither appears in the original, hence neither is bracketed in the translation. No terminal punctuation has been altered without disclosure in square brackets, apart from the occasional adjustment of supplying a period for a comma where the former was functionally meant but where the custom of the time was to print a comma. An interpolated full colon replaces a comma in the original in like circumstances; otherwise the full colon is original or is bracketed. I have not found it feasible to indicate when parentheses and commas are original and when interpolated. Paragraphing is generally original. So is almost all capitalization.

The translation is based upon Zoepfl's 1876 edition of the Carolina: *Die Peinliche Gerichtsordnung Kaiser Karl's V. nebst der Bamberger und der*

Brandenburger Halsgerichtsordnung, H. Zoepfl, ed. (2d ed., Leipzig and Heidelberg, 1876). The later critical edition by Kohler and Scheel has been intentionally avoided: *Die Carolina und ihre Vorgängerinnen: Die Peinliche Gerichtsordnung Kaiser Karls V.*, J. Kohler and W. Scheel, eds. (Halle, 1900). Despite its wealth of helpful footnoting, it is fatally defective at the root, because it fails to base itself upon the editio princeps. See R. von Hippel, *Deutsches Strafrecht* (Berlin, 1925) 174 and n. 4.

The Zoepfl text is based upon the 1532 official print, complete with contemporaneous flaws (mostly printer's errors); coherence requires that they be corrected in the translation. These problem passages are the subject of a chapter, "Die Text- und Redaktionsfehler in der Carolina," in C. Güterbock, *Die Entstehungsgeschichte der Carolina auf Grund archivalischer Forschungen und neu aufgefundener Entwürfe* (Würzburg, 1876) 216–253. The translation takes account of a number of the Güterbock corrections; deletions of this sort are typically not disclosed, whereas serious interpolations typically are (by square brackets). A few other, somewhat brazen interpolations in the translation are similarly indicated; routine tampering with relative pronouns and auxiliary verbs is not. The table of contents simply collects the titles of the text, next to the article numbers to which they pertain. It is not, however, a part of the official text.

The untranslated term *Rechttag* is discussed in Chapter 8 of the text, note 80. The translation of *rechtverstendigen* is discussed in the same chapter, note 143.

I am pleased to record my gratitude to Herr Hartmut Kokott of the Deutsches Seminar, Frankfurt University, who helped me convert many of the obscurities of Frühneuhochdeutsch into modern German; and to Frau Gertrud Ziemen of Munich, who reviewed the English translation and suggested many corrections and improvements.

The Carolina

The Criminal Courts Ordinance
of
His Highness the Mighty Invincible Emperor Charles V,
and of the Holy Roman Empire
Issued and Resolved at
the Reichstags of Augsburg and Regensburg,
Held in the Thirtieth and Thirty-Second Years

Concerning indications relative to particular crimes; and each article is enough for legally sufficient indication of that crime and therefore for examination under torture

(33) Concerning sufficient indication of a murder committed clandestinely

(34) Concerning sufficient indication of publicly committed homicides happening in brawls or riots among many people, and which no one admits to having done

(35–36) Concerning sufficient indication of the clandestine having of children and their killing by their mothers

(37) Concerning sufficient indication of secret poisoning

(38–39) Concerning sufficient indication of the suspicion of being a robber

(40) Concerning sufficient suspicion of those who aid robbers or thieves

(41) Concerning sufficient indication of clandestine arson

(42) Concerning sufficient indication of treason

(43) Concerning sufficient suspicion of theft

(44) Concerning sufficient indication of sorcery

(45–46) Concerning examination under torture

(47) Regarding demonstration of innocence before threatened torture, and further proceeding thereupon

How those who confess a crime when examined under torture shall be questioned subsequently without torture for further information

(48) First, concerning murder

(49) When the examined person confesses treason

(50) Upon confession of poisoning

(51) When the person examined confesses arson

(52) When the person examined confesses sorcery

(53) Concerning general, unparticularized questions regarding a confession secured under torture

(54) Concerning the checking out and investigating of the incriminating circumstances confessed

(55) When investigation reveals the circumstances confessed to be untrue

(56) That the circumstances of the crime not be told to any prisoner beforehand, rather that they be told entirely by him alone

(57) When the prisoner retracts the confession

(58) Concerning the extent of torture

(59) When the miserable fellow to be examined has serious wounds

(60) Establishing when the confession arising from examination under torture is ultimately to be believed

(61) When the prisoner has been put to examination under torture upon legally sufficient suspicion and not found guilty or the guilt not proven

(62) Concerning proving the crime

(63) Concerning unknown witnesses

(64) Concerning paid witnesses

(65) How witnesses shall testify

(66) Concerning adequate witnesses

(67) Concerning acceptable evidence

(68) Concerning false witnesses

(69) When the accused will not confess following the proof

(168) Concerning the stealing of wood or its chopping in forbidden manner
(169) Punishment of those who steal fish
(170) Punishment of those who deal faithlessly with entrusted or pledged goods
(171) Theft of holy or sacred things from sacred or nonsacred precincts
(172–175) Concerning punishment of the aforesaid thefts
(176) Concerning punishment or detention of persons of whom crime and evil must, upon manifest ground, be anticipated
(177) Concerning punishment for aiding, abetting, and assisting the criminal
(178) Punishment of attempted crime
(179) Concerning criminals who, owing to youth or other reasons, lack understanding
(180) When a gaolkeeper of criminals helps one escape
(181–189) Concerning a general account of how the court scribes shall completely and properly transcribe the criminal court proceedings, following in the next and several subsequent articles
(190–191) A regulation and account how court scribes shall formulate the final death sentence
(192) Opening part of every sentence of death or perpetual imprisonment
(193) Concerning dragging
(194) Concerning tearing with glowing tongs
(195) The formulation of the sentence to confine a dangerous man in gaol
(196) Concerning corporal punishment in which [the criminal] is to be condemned neither to death nor imprisonment, as above
(197) Opening part of the sentences aforementioned concerning corporal punishment short of death
(198) Cutting out the tongue, chopping off the fingers, ears cut off, with rods flogged
(199–203) Concerning the form of sentence for freeing an accused person
(204) Concerning the court costs in criminal courts
(205) That the judges shall accept no special payment for the punishment of criminals
(206) What shall be done with the property of the fugitive criminal
(207–214) Concerning stolen or robbed goods which come into the court
(215–217) To what extent the craftsmen are obligated to build and to repair the necessary gallows in the criminal courts
(218) Concerning abuses and evil senseless customs practiced in some places and locations
(219) Clarification from whom and in which places advice shall be sought

The Carolina

Preamble

We, Charles V, by grace of God Roman Emperor, Augustus *(merer)* of the Empire for all time, King in Germany, to Castile, to Aragon, to Leon, both Sicilys, to Jerusalem, to Hungary, to Dalmatia, to Croatia, Navarre, to Granada, to Toledo, to Valencia, to Galicia, Majorca, Seville, Sardinia, Cordoba, Corsica, Murcia, Jaen, the Algarves, Algeciras, to Gibraltar, and of the Canary Islands, also the islands of the Indies and of the continents of the high seas, etc.; Archduke to Austria, Duke to Burgundy, to Lotharingia, to Brabant, to Styria, Carinthia, to Caeniola, Limbourg, Gelderland, Wurtemberg, Calabria, Athens, Neopatria; Count to Hapsburg, to Flanders, to Tyrol, to Görtz, Barcelona, to Artois, to Burgundy, in the County Palatine of Hainaut, to Holland, to Zealand, to Ferette, to Kyburg, to Namur, to Rossilion, to Cerdoña, and to Zutphen; Landgrave in Alsace, Margrave to Burgau, to Oristano, to Gothia; and of the Holy Roman Empire sovereign to Swabia, to Catalonia, to Asturia, etc.; Lord in Frisia, on the Windic Marches, to Pordenone, to Biscay, to Molina, to Salins, to Tripoli, and to Mechlin--we do publicly declare, that whereas according to old custom and tradition of the Roman Empire of the German Nation as carefully confided to us through our and the holy Empire's Electors, Princes, and other Estates, most criminal courts are staffed with persons who have not studied, had experience with, or exercised our Imperial law. And that therefore in many places proceedings are often contrary to law and reason, and either the innocent are punished and killed or the guilty reprieved, dismissed and set free through irregular, deceitful, and protracted proceeding with great disadvantage to criminal complainants and to the common weal. [A]nd that, according to long-established usage in German territory in these matters, the criminal courts in many places cannot be staffed with legally knowledgeable (*rechtverstendigen*), experienced and practiced persons.

Therefore we, together with our Electors, Princes, and Estates have deigned to command several learned, thoroughly experienced persons to make a summary, assembled in a form which we have ordered to have printed, of how and in what manner judicial proceedings in criminal cases ought best to be conducted according to law and equity; in order that from henceforth all and each of our and the Empire's subjects can in penal matters—in consideration of the enormity and hazardousness of the same—follow the above-mentioned summary, in accord with the common law *(gemeynen rechten)*, equity, and honored customary usage, as any man would doubtless be inclined to do in his own interest, and also in the hope of receiving reward from the Almighty. However, we deign by this ordinance to have taken away from the Electors, Princes, and Estates nothing of their old, well-established, lawful, and equitable usages.

Of judges, judgment-givers, and court personnel

(1) First: we decree, ordain, and will that all criminal courts shall be staffed and provided with judges, judgment-givers and court scribes—persons of piety, honor, knowledge, and experience—the best and most upright to be got and had according to the circumstances of each place. Moreover, nobles and professionals *(gelerten)* may also be used. In these matters every authority shall exert all appropriate diligence to see that the criminal courts are ordered

to the best, and that injustice be done to no one; both proficiency and surpassing concern are essential to these great cases—which concern human honor, body, life, and property—in order that nobody be able to excuse his negligence and remiss in such transgression with legally proper and sufficient reason, but rather be justly punished according to this our ordinance[.] To that end shall every authority holding penal courts stand solemnly cautioned.

And because for some time in some places some nobles and others who are entitled to sit in such courts by virtue of personal inheritance, by virtue of office, or otherwise, have refused to sit in such courts, being unwilling to do so on account of their noble estate, evildoing has often times gone unpunished. Because such court-sitting neither can or shall work any disadvantage whatsoever to their dignity or rank, indeed to the contrary, through the furthering of justice and the punishing of the wicked, serve and redound to the honor of the noble and the officer, they may therefore sit in person in such criminal courts as judge and as judgment-giver so often and so much as is thought good and necessary according to the circumstances, and therein deal and proceed as appropriate to and in conformance with this our ordinance. Where, however, following old tradition some nobles and others have up to now been sitting in such courts, it is our will that they shall continue to sit without future refusal, and that this tradition and usage remain in full force and effect.

Concerning those who hold court by virtue of property

(2) Those persons who are obligated on account of their property to hold criminal courts, and are unable either to hold or to administer them due to weakness and infirmity of body or mind, or on account of youth, age, or other incapacity, shall, as often as the need arises, name and ordain other capable persons to hold the criminal courts in their stead—with the knowledge and approval of the proper chief judge *(oberrichter)*.

The oath of a judge who judges capital matters

(3) I *N.* do swear that I shall and will in criminal cases allow the law to take its course, and that I shall judge and sentence the poor like the rich, not wavering through affection, enmity, bribe, gift, or anything else. And especially will I faithfully adhere to and apply Emperor Charles V's and the holy Empire's criminal courts ordinance, all to the best of my understanding, faithfully and undeceitfully, so help me God and the holy Gospels.

Oath of the Schöffe or judgment-speaker

(4) Each Schöffe or judgment-speaker of a criminal court shall solemnly swear and vow to the judge of the court as hereafter follows, which obligation shall be read out to the Schöffe, and he shall thereafter repeat.

I *N.* do swear that I shall and will give lawful judgment in criminal cases, judging the poor like the rich, not wavering through affection, enmity, bribe, gift, or anything else. And especially will I faithfully adhere to and apply Emperor Charles V's and the holy Empire's criminal courts ordinance, all to the best of my understanding, faithfully and undeceitfully, so help me God and the holy Gospels.

Scribe's oath

(5) I *N.* do swear that I shall and will in cases which concern the criminal court pay diligent attention to complaint and answer; indicia, suspicion, or evidence; also the confession of the accused; and faithfully record, preserve, and if necessary read out what is dealt with. Also therein to use or to attempt no deceit. And especially will I faithfully advance and adhere to Emperor Charles V's and the holy Empire's criminal courts ordinance and all matters thereunto pertaining to the extent that they concern me, so help me God and the holy Gospels.

Proceeding against the alleged wrongdoer by the authorities ex officio

(6) When someone is suspected of a crime through common repute, or is notorious on account of other credible indication, and consequently has been arrested by the authorities acting ex officio, he shall at first not be examined under torture unless there is credibly established legally sufficient *(redlich)* and consequently suitable indication connecting him to the said crime. Further, every judge in these serious cases, before investigation by torture, shall to the extent feasible and according to the character and circumstances of each case, make inquiry and diligently investigate as to whether the crime of which the accused is suspected and made notorious happened or not, as will be hereafter further expounded in this our ordinance.

(7) When the aforementioned judgment-givers are in doubt about the decision whether, in a particular case, the adduced suspicion is or is not sufficient for examination by torture, they shall in consequence seek advice from the authorities—from the local authorities directly in charge of the penal jurisdiction, or from those places cited at the end of this our ordinance; and moreover, they shall accurately report in writing to the said authorities in such advice-seeking all the details and circumstances of suspicion known to them.

(8) When the crime obviously merits the death penalty, or when legally sufficient indication (as before mentioned) is produced in such a case, it shall be examined into—under torture, if useful to establish the truth—and the judicial proceedings shall be held upon the culprit's confession in the manner below prescribed and ordered for those who are brought before the court upon private complaint.

(9) When, however, such an accused refuses to confess to the suspected crime without or despite examination by torture, and when he may nonetheless be convicted of it, the same proofs and procedure shall apply as when capital matters are raised by a complainant, as hereafter plainly set forth.

(10) When, however, on account of a sufficiently undoubted crime, someone is convicted and found guilty and is finally to be punished on body or limb according to this our and the holy Empire's ordinance by the authorities acting ex officio; that is, when the said penalty comprises neither death nor perpetual

imprisonment, the sentencing to this penalty shall be in accord with Article 196; and the same applies when someone has been caught in the act.

Concerning proceeding against an alleged criminal when the complainant demands his right

(11) When a complainant demands of the authorities or the judge that, on account of a serious matter of penal law, someone be gaoled, the said complainant shall report the crime and the legally sufficient suspicion which points to criminality, and this is to be done at once, without regard to whether the complainant has demanded (as is his right) the gaoling of the accused, or whether the complainant has sought to arrange a settlement with the accused. And when the complainant does that, the accused shall be put in gaol and the complainant's statement shall be accurately written down; and it is particularly to be noticed in this connection that the gaols should be erected and established for the custody of the prisoner and not intentionally to intensify his suffering. And when there is more than one prisoner, they should be kept apart from one another to the extent that the gaol cells are available, in order that they may not plot false testimony with one another or discuss how they can explain away their deed.

Concerning detention of the complainant until he has provided surety

(12) As soon as the accused is gaoled, the complainant or his representative shall be taken into physical custody until he has provided surety *(bürgen, Caution, bestandt, und sicherung)* which the judge and four Schöffen together determine to be adequate, in view of the circumstances of the case and with regard to the two parties, as hereafter follows. To wit: when he the complainant fails to carry through with the criminal action or to proceed according to the law, or fails to prove the crime complained of, or fails within the time allotted to him by the judge to prove legally sufficient and adequate indicia as decided by the judge and the court or the majority of them, or when the proceeding otherwise miscarries for legal cause, he bears the costs thereby arising, and compensates the accused for the indignity and damage inflicted upon him, all according to the judgment of the civil (*burgerlicher*) law. And in order that the said gaoled accused may recover compensation for the costs, indignity, and damage suffered all the quicker and all the more fully, the option shall be provided him to sue the complainant for the costs and for indignity and damage before the same competent judge or in the same criminal court in which the judicial proceeding and judgment took place; and this proceeding shall be summary and treated without the formality of legal procedure, and the judgment shall be executed without further appeal or review; however, apart from these cases, and from any previously existing, the said criminal court shall have no civil jurisdiction or authority.

Concerning the surety of the complainant where the accused has confessed the deed, but produces legally sufficient exculpation to the deed

(13) When the culprit does not deny the deed, but brings forward a legally sufficient excuse, which would free him from penal sanction were he

to prove it; yet, however, the complainant does not concede to him the cause and excuse pleaded; then the complainant in such a case shall provide surety as necessary—according to the circumstances of the person and the case and the decision of the judge together with four court persons or Schöffen—obligating him (in the sort of case in which the accused establishes an excuse such that he would suffer no penal sanction on account of the deed complained of) to compensate the accused, according to the judgment of the very same court, for the confinement, indignity, and damage according to the civil law (as previously set out); and beyond that, to make good all court damage; and following the provision of surety, a proceeding shall be conducted to determine exculpation as is set out hereafter in Article 151 ("When someone has admitted an act, etc."); and in this case, examination by torture shall not be employed before this proceeding has been conducted and specifically decided.

How there shall be countercustody when the complainant has been unable to give surety

(14) During and as long as the complainant has been unable to make the aforementioned surety, yet nevertheless wishes to prosecute for serious crime, he shall be held in the gaol with the accused, or kept in custody, according to the circumstances of the person and case, until the legal proceeding referred to above is completed; and it shall be permitted to the complainant—also to one who wishes to establish his exculpation—that the people who stand to his surety or who will be his witnesses (as set out above) can have access to and from him. Further, in the case in which the complaint issues on behalf of a prince, an ecclesiastic, a body corporate, or some other person of high status against someone of a lesser class, another person may be gaoled or put in custody along with the accused in place of the complainant, but certainly not someone of lesser rank than the accused. And if this gaoled person wishes otherwise to give surety, as is detailed above, then that person shall be freed from his confinement.

Concerning another surety when the complainant has proven the suspicion of the crime or the crime is otherwise admitted

(15) When the complainant has proven the suspicion or the crime complained of is otherwise undeniable, and the culprit cannot produce sufficient exculpation (as dealt with above), the complainant shall give surety of compliance with the law in serious criminal matters through which the accused has been arrested, as this our and the Empire's ordinance prescribes, but in such a case he shall not be bound to make further surety; and all that is dealt with through the arrest of the accused—the complaint, answer, surety, questioning, investigation, proof, and other, also what is thereafter given in judgment—all such the court scribe shall properly and clearly write down, according to the general model and form of such an account hereafter provided in Article 181 ("Every court scribe shall, etc.") and to be found in several pages thereafter.

Concerning undoubted crimes

(16) It is especially to be noted by judges and judgment-givers, where a

crime is or has been openly and undoubtedly committed without lawful and urgent occasion (apart from legally sufficient cause which properly exculpates from criminal penalty)—for example, when someone has been a wanton public enemy or enemy of the peace *(friedbrecher)*; or when someone has actually been caught in the act of committing a crime; or when such a person knowingly has the robbed or stolen property with him and cannot on any ground explain it away or legally justify it or deny it, in the manner hereafter to be found with regard to the said crimes when there is exculpation: In these and similar obvious and undoubted crimes, when the culprit brazenly denies the obvious and undoubted crime, the judge shall examine him under severe torture to induce him to confess the truth, in order that the ultimate judgment and penalty as regards such obvious and undoubted crimes be proceeded to and executed at the least possible cost.

Concerning how the complainant shall not depart following the gaoling of the accused until he has first supplied the name of a place where the court may summon him

(17) The complainant shall also, following the incarceration of the accused, not take leave of the judge until he has named a distinct house at an easy-to-reach, secure, and nondangerous place or location, where the judge may thereafter send him all necessary summons; and the complainant shall be bound and obligated to pay an appropriate delivery charge, according to the common custom of each land, to the person who brings him such summons, for each mile that that person must travel out to him from the court; and the court scribe shall enter in the court records the place named by the complainant.

Concerning the cases in which a legally sufficient indication of a crime shall be made out

(18) In this our and the holy Empire's criminal courts ordinance, conforming to the common law *(gemeynem rechten)*, the arrest and confinement, and also the examination by torture of one who is accused and suspected as the criminal and has not confessed, is based upon legally sufficient indication, sign, and suspicion of the wrongdoing (as dealt with above and below); yet it is not possible to set forth all of these matters or signs which suffice for legally sufficient indication or suspicion. Nonetheless, however, in order that the officials, judges, and judgment-givers, who are otherwise uninstructed in these matters, may be the better informed as to what establishes a legally sufficient indication or suspicion, the following examples of legally sufficient indication or suspicion are hereafter set forth in a manner that everyone, to the extent of his German, can identify or distinguish.

Concerning the meaning of the word "indication" *(anzeygung)*

(19) Where hereafter we discuss "legally sufficient indication" *(redlich anzeygen)*, we intend thereby also to have consistently meant legally sufficient signs, suspicion, and presumption, and therefore we drop the residual words.

That no one shall be examined under torture without legally sufficient indication

(20) When legally sufficient indication of the crime which it is desired to investigate has not been produced and proven beforehand, then no one shall be examined; and should, however, the crime be confessed under torture, it shall not be believed nor shall anyone be condemned upon that basis. When, notwithstanding, some of the authorities or the judge proceed in this way, then they shall be bound to make appropriate compensation to the person who was tortured in this illegal way without the proven indication for his injury, pain, costs, and damage.

Furthermore, no authority or judge in this situation shall support, protect, or uphold any recognizance *(urphede)* such that the tortured person cannot legally recover for his injury, pain, costs, and damage—quite excluding his own wrongful acts.

Concerning indication produced by those who dare to soothsay with sorcery

(21) No one shall be gaoled or examined under torture upon indication of those who purport to be able to soothsay through sorcery or other artifice. Rather these pretended soothsayers and complainants shall in consequence be punished. If, however, the judge should nonetheless continue to proceed upon such soothsayers' denunciation, then he shall be obliged to compensate the tortured person for costs, pain, injuria *(injurien)*, and damage, as set out in the previous article.

That upon indication of a crime only examination under torture, and not further penal sanction, shall be ordered

(22) It is further to be noticed that no one shall be definitely sentenced to penal sanction on the basis of any indication of a suspicious sign or upon suspicion, rather on that basis there may only be examination under torture; when the indications are sufficient (as will be found below), then the person shall be finally condemned to penal sanction; however, that must take place upon the basis of his own confession or a witness proof procedure (*beweisung*) (as will be found plainly elsewhere in this ordinance), and not on the basis of presumption or indication.

Concerning how the sufficient indication of a crime shall be proven

(23) Every sufficient indication upon which it is sought to examine under torture shall be proven with two good witnesses, as described below in several articles concerning sufficient proof. When, however, the essential element of the crime is proven with one good witness, then this, as a half proof, serves as sufficient indication, as set out below in Article 30 ("a half proof, as when someone is caught in [*sic*] the essential element, etc.").

That an analogy may be inferred from the indications following below for unnamed and herein unexpounded suspicions of crime

(24) From these articles below following treating suspicion and indication of crime, an analogy shall be drawn in cases not named in these articles. For it is not possible to set forth all cases and circumstances which raise suspicion.

Concerning general suspicion and indications which relate to all crimes

(25) To begin with[:] concerning matters which raise suspicion, with explanation following, how and when these suffice as legally sufficient indication.

[And as a second purpose of this article:] When the indication does not appear among those described in numerous following articles and regulating sufficiency for examination under torture, investigation shall correspond to the following and to similar circumstances of suspicion, because not all can be set forth.

First: When the accused is an insolent and wanton person of bad repute and regard, so that the crime could be credibly ascribed to him, or when the same person shall have dared to perform a similar crime previously or shall have been accused of having done so. However, this bad repute shall not be adduced from enemies or wanton people, rather from impartial and upright people.

Second: When the suspected person has been caught or found at a place suspicious in the context of the deed.

Third: When a culprit has been seen in the deed or while on the way to or from it; in the case when he has not been recognized, attention shall be paid to whether the suspect has such a figure, such clothes, weapon, horse, or whatnot corresponding to what the above-mentioned culprit was seen to have.

Fourth: When the suspected person lives with or associates with such people who commit similar crimes.

Fifth: In cases of damage to property or person, attention shall be paid to whether the suspected person could have been motivated to the present crime out of envy, enmity, former threat, or in the expectation of some advantage.

Sixth: When a victim injured in person or property himself accuses someone of the crime on various grounds, and thereafter dies or affirms it with his oath.

Seventh: When someone flees on account of a crime.

Eighth:

(26) When someone is in litigation with another concerning substantial property, which thereby constitutes the larger part of his support, goods, and possessions, he will be regarded as a grudge-holder and great enemy of his opponent; should the opponent be secretly murdered, a presumption arises against the other party that he committed this murder; and when this person is otherwise inherently suspect of having done the murder, he may be gaoled and examined under torture, when he has in the matter no legally sufficient excuse.

A rule concerning when the above-mentioned matters of suspicion together or singly suffice as adequate indications for examination under torture

(27) In the last article[s] above are found eight matters of suspicion concerning indication for examination under torture; none of these matters of

suspicion alone suffices as legally sufficient indication upon which basis torture may be employed. When, however, more than one of these matters of suspicion concerning someone are found together, then those persons who are responsible for ordering and conducting examination under torture shall decide whether the aforementioned or corresponding matters of suspicion established really provide as much legally sufficient indication of the suspected crime as in the following articles (concerning that which singly constitutes legally sufficient indication for examination under torture).

Another rule in the above-mentioned matters

(28) In addition, it is to be borne in mind when someone is suspected of a crime on the basis of more than one matter of suspicion (as above), that two things must always and invariably be observed[:] First, the suspicions uncovered; second, what favors the suspected person—that which could exculpate him of the crime. And when in consequence it is decided that the weight of suspicion is greater than the weight of exculpation, then torture may be employed. When, however, the grounds of exculpation have higher regard and attention than some lesser suspicions which have been made out, then examination under torture shall not be employed. And when something is doubtful in these matters, those responsible for ordering and conducting examination under torture shall seek advice from the legally knowledgeable and at those places and locations set out at the end of this our ordinance.

General indications each of which singly suffices for examination under torture

(29) When someone in the committing of the crime loses something or lets it fall or be left behind, so that it can afterwards be found and determined to have belonged to the criminal, examination under torture is appropriate in order to discover who had the thing immediately before it was lost—unless he interposes something to the contrary, and were it to turn out or be established, the said suspicion would thereby be resolved, in which case this excuse shall first be investigated, before any examination under torture.

(30) A half proof, as when someone thoroughly proves the essential element of the crime with a lone good and upright witness (as discussed below concerning good witnesses and witness proof proceedings)—that is and is called a half proof, and such a half proof also constitutes a legally sufficient indication of suspicion of the crime. When, however, someone wants to prove sundry circumstances, signs, indication, or suspicion, he shall do it with at least two good upright and unimpeachable witnesses.

(31) When a proven criminal who has had accomplices in his crime informs while gaoled against someone who helped him with the crime he committed and was detected at, that is a ground of suspicion against the person so denounced, insofar as there are found and observed in connection with such denunciation the following matters and circumstances.

First: That the informer has not been asked after the denounced person by name under torture, hence has not been particularly examined or tortured with reference to just this person; rather that he have named and himself revealed the denounced person in the course of general examination regarding who helped him with his crime.

Second: It is pertinent that the said informer be particularly questioned as to how, where, and when the denounced person helped him and what relationship he had to him; and in such situations the informer shall be questioned about all possible and necessary details which can, according to the circumstances and character of each individual instance, best serve the subsequent discovery of the truth; and which can not all be described here, but which, however, every diligent and knowledgeable person can himself upon reflection work out.

Third: It is pertinent to inquire whether there is particular enmity, conflict, or ill will between the informer and the person he accuses. Because, were such enmity, conflict, or ill will obvious or revealed, then such accusation against the denounced person would not be believed from the informer, unless he otherwise credibly indicated adequate basis and signs, which would then hold up when investigated and constitute legally sufficient indication.

Fourth: That the person denounced be so suspicious that the accused crime can be believed of him.

Fifth: Where the informer has held to his denunciation, some priest-confessors nonetheless practice the abuse of instructing the miserable fellows in confession eventually to recant upon their truthful statement[s]; to the extent possible the priest-confessors shall be prevented from that, for no one is authorized to help criminals conceal their evil, which can disadvantage innocent people and the common weal. When, however, the informer in the end repudiates his denunciation or statement, which he himself has earlier made with great detail; and when it is thought that he wishes thereby to abet his accomplices, or that he was perhaps instructed to it by his father-confessor as above discussed; then the informer's statement and the other investigated circumstances must be considered and it must be thereupon decided whether or not the denunciation is adequate as legally sufficient indication. And in such a case it must be noticed and inquired, what sort of good or evil standing or reputation the denounced person has, and what sort of association or relationship he has had with the informer.

(32) When someone is sufficiently convicted, as has been previously mentioned concerning a complete witness proof proceeding, through things he himself has needlessly said out of conceit or otherwise—that he committed the alleged or suspected crime or that he threatened to do such a crime before this one happened and the crime actually thereupon followed within a short time—and he is also the sort of person of whom such a deed could be believed, that can also be taken as legally sufficient indication of the crime upon which to examine under torture.

Concerning indications relative to particular crimes; and each article is enough for legally sufficient indication of that crime and therefore for examination under torture

Concerning sufficient indication of a murder committed clandestinely

(33) When the person suspected and accused of the murder was seen in

a suspicious manner at the time the murder occurred with bloody clothes or weapon; or when he has taken, sold, given away, or still retained property of the murder victim; that may be deemed legally sufficient indication upon which examination under torture may be employed, unless he can contradict such suspicion with credible indication or proof (which shall be heard before any examination under torture).

Concerning sufficient indication of publicly committed homicides happening in brawls or riots among many people, and which no one admits to having done

(34) A homicide which occurred in a public brawl or riot, which no one will admit[:] When the suspected person who was at the brawl has also been an enemy of the deceased, and when he has taken his knife and slashed, hacked, or otherwise maliciously struck at the deceased, that is, as regards the crime committed, a legally sufficient indication for examination under torture; and it is yet more suspicious of such a suspect should his weapon be seen bloody. When, however, such or similar is not present, and particularly when he was present at the event in a harmless manner, then he shall not be examined under torture.

Concerning sufficient indication of the clandestine having of children and their killing by their mothers

(35) When a girl, purportedly a maiden, comes under suspicion of having secretly had and killed a child, it shall be especially inquired, whether she was seen with a large and unusual body, and further, whether the body then became smaller and she was then pale and weak. When such and similar is discovered, and where this girl is a person of whom such a suspected crime could be believed, then she shall be inspected by knowledgeable women in an enclosed place, so far as that facilitates further inquiry; and if the suspicion is there confirmed, and nonetheless she will not confess the deed, she may be examined under torture.

(36) When, however, the baby was killed only such a short time before that the milk in the breasts of the mother has not yet gone away, then she may be milked in her breasts; and when mother's milk is found in the breasts, there is in consequence a strong presumption for the use of examination under torture. Since, however, some physicians say that for several natural reasons a woman who has not borne a child may have milk in the breasts, when, therefore, a girl exculpates herself in this way, she shall be further investigated by the midwife or other.

Concerning sufficient indication of secret poisoning

(37) When it is found that the suspect bought or otherwise dealt with poison, and the suspect had quarreled with the poisoned person or could have anticipated gain or advantage from his death or was otherwise a wanton person of whom the crime could be believed, that then suffices for legally sufficient indication of the crime unless he can produce credible indication that he used or wanted to use the said poison for other noncriminal ends.

Further: when someone buys poison and denies it to the authorities, and then the purchase is nonetheless proven, then this constitutes a sufficient ground for examining him as to why he used or wanted to use this poison.

Further: all authorities shall everywhere put the apothecaries and others who sell or deal in poison under vow and oath that they shall not sell any poison to anyone, nor allow him to get it, without indication, prior knowledge, and permission of these authorities.

Concerning sufficient indication of the suspicion of being a robber

(38) When it is discovered that someone has with him goods that have been robbed; has sold, passed on, or otherwise dealt with them in a suspicious way; and he refuses to identify the person who sold or supplied him; he has raised against himself a legally sufficient indication, unless he demonstrates that he did not know that these goods were robbed and that he took them upon himself in good faith.

(39) When horse soldiers or foot soldiers regularly tarry and eat and drink in inns and cannot demonstrate the sort of honest service relation, trade, or income on hand from which they could suitably defray their expenses, they are suspected of many evil deeds, and in particular of robbery, as especially to be understood from our and the Empire's common *Landfrieden*, wherein it is provided that such villains shall not be tolerated, rather proceeded against and rigorously examined and severely punished for their crimes; likewise shall every authority pay diligent regard to suspicious beggars and vagrants.

Concerning sufficient suspicion of those who aid robbers or thieves

(40) When someone knowingly and maliciously takes robbed or stolen goods or loot, or shares therein; or when someone knowingly and maliciously gives the culprits food or drink, or knowingly takes in, conceals, or harbors the culprits or takes in, conceals, harbors, sells, or disperses the said illegal goods in whole or in part; or when someone otherwise in some similar way maliciously furnishes the culprits with help, advice, or assistance or had improper association with them in their crime, that is also an indication upon which to examine under torture.

Further: when someone has concealed prisoners, who leave him and then reveal where they were; further, when a suspect who is rather distrusted in the matter, but who feels good reason to be partial and on the side of the culprit, makes a contract of composition without telling the gaoling authorities, and does compose it or go surety therein—all these things in both the above articles are collectively and singly signs which constitute legally sufficient indication of criminal complicity and may be examined under torture.

Concerning sufficient indication of clandestine arson

(41) When someone is suspected or accused of a covertly committed act of arson, and when this person is otherwise a fellow to be suspicious of, and it can be discovered that shortly before the fire he was in a stealthy and suspicious manner concerned with unusual and suspicious incendiary materials

of the sort typically used to set fires clandestinely, that provides legally sufficient indication of the crime unless he can show with good, credible basis that he used or wanted to use them to noncriminal ends.

Concerning sufficient indication of treason

(42) When the suspect has been seen behaving stealthily, unusually, and insidiously with those he is suspected of having betrayed, and when he pretends that he is afraid of them, and when he is a sort of person of whom such a crime can be believed, this is an indication for examination under torture.

Concerning sufficient suspicion of theft

(43) When the stolen property is found with the suspect, or when it is discovered that it was, in whole or in part, possessed, sold, dispersed, or squandered by him, and he refuses to name his seller or supplier, he has raised a legally sufficient indication of the crime against himself, so long as he does not establish that he brought the said property upon himself in an undeceitful, noncriminal manner in good faith.

Further: when the theft was accomplished with special lock opening or breaking tools, then when the suspect has been at the very place dealing with such insidious lock opening or breaking tools with which the theft was committed, and the suspect is a sort of person of whom the crime can be believed, examination under torture is to be employed.

Further: when a particularly large theft occurs and there is suspected of it someone who, after the crime, is found to be more effusive with his spending than could be within his means apart from the crime; and when the suspect cannot show other good ground, where he got the indicated suspect wealth, and he is a sort of person of whom the crime could be believed, then there is present against him legally sufficient indication of the crime.

Concerning sufficient indication of sorcery

(44) When someone offers to impart sorcery to other people, or threatens to bewitch someone and such befalls the threatened person, and the aforesaid person otherwise has associated with men or women sorcerers, or has employed suspicious things, gestures, words, and signs such as characterize sorcery, and when, further, the said person has a bad reputation of similar sort, then that constitutes a legally sufficient indication of sorcery and is adequate basis upon which to examine under torture.

Concerning examination under torture

(45) When the suspicion of a crime complained of and denied is established as above provided, and taken or recognized as proved, then a day for examination by torture shall be notified to the complainant upon his demand.

(46) When it is desired to examine the prisoner under torture, either ex officio or upon demand of the complainant, then the said prisoner shall first, in the presence of the judge and of two of the court and of the court scribe,

be diligently exhorted to speak up, with words (appropriate to the circumstances of the person and case) best serving to further understanding of the crime or the suspicion; and he shall be interrogated under threat of torture, whether or not he confesses to the alleged crime and what he knows about the said crime; and what he then confesses or denies shall be transcribed.

Regarding demonstration of innocence before threatened torture, and further proceeding thereupon

(47) When, in the case now being discussed, the accused denies the crime under consideration, then it shall be assiduously inquired of him whether he can show that he is innocent of the alleged crime, and the prisoner shall in particular be asked to remember whether he can prove and establish that at the time the crime under consideration was committed he was with people or at a place or location whereby it can be recognized that he cannot have done the crime of which he is suspected. And such exhortation is thus needed because many a person out of simpleness or fright, even when he is quite innocent, does not know how he should proceed to exculpate himself of the thing. And when the prisoner in this manner or in like-serving way indicates his innocence, then the judge shall as quickly as possible investigate the exculpation proffered at the cost of the accused or his friends; moreover, when, with the approval of the judge, the witnesses which the prisoner or his friends wish in proper manner to proffer—as hereafter set forth concerning witness proof proceeding in Article 62 ("Where the accused will not confess, etc.") and in several subsequent articles—want on their own request to be examined, then the aforementioned hearing of the witnesses, also of the prisoner and of his friends on their demand, shall not be denied or disallowed without good and lawful ground. When, however, on account of poverty, the accused or his friends cannot bear or suffer such aforementioned costs, then nevertheless, in order that evil be punished while the innocent be not unlawfully taken advantage of, the authorities or the court shall put up the costs and the judge shall proceed with the case.

Further: when in the investigation now under discussion the innocence of the accused is not established, then he shall be examined under torture concerning the aforementioned, established legally sufficient suspicion in the presence of the judge and of at least two of the court and of the court scribe; and that which is revealed in the confession or in his admission and in all [subsequent verifying] investigation shall be particularly transcribed, and insofar as it concerns the accusor, disclosed to him, and at his request a copy shall be given to him without any intentional procrastination or delay.

How those who confess a crime when examined under torture shall be questioned subsequently without torture for further information

First, concerning murder

(48) When the person examined confesses the crime under consideration through torture (as above) and his confession is transcribed, those persons who examine him on account of his confession shall diligently question him with great care to the extent that it serves the discovery of the truth (as will

be further treated to some extent hereafter); and indeed, when he has confessed to a murder, he shall be asked the reason he did the crime, on which day, at what hour, and at what place, whether anyone helped him to it and who; also where he buried or put the dead man, with what weapons the said murder was committed, how and what sort of blows or wounds he gave or inflicted upon the dead man, or how otherwise he killed him, what the murdered person had upon him by way of money or other things, and what he took from him, where he put this, or sold, dispersed, parted with, or hid it; and such questions as in many respects apply just as well to a robber or thief.

When the examined person confesses treason

(49) When the prisoner confesses treason, he shall be asked who put him up to it and what he got for it, also where, how, and when this happened, and what motivated him to it.

Upon confession of poisoning

(50) When the person examined confesses that he poisoned or wanted to poison someone, he shall also be asked about all the reasons and circumstances (as above), and moreover, what motivated him to it, also wherewith and how he employed or meant to employ the poison, and where he got the said poison, and who helped him or advised him to it.

When the person examined confesses arson

(51) When the person examined confesses a fire, he shall be particularly questioned as to the reason, time, and company (as above), and furthermore, with what incendiary materials he set the fire and from whom, how, or where he procured the said incendiary materials or the corresponding tools.

When the person examined confesses sorcery

(52) When someone confesses sorcery, he shall also be questioned about the causes and circumstances (as above), and moreover, with what, how, and when the sorcery occurred—with what words or deeds. Further, when the person examined states that he hid or held on to something which allegedly facilitated the said sorcery, then afterwards there shall be an attempt to find it; when, however, the said sorcery was committed with other things through word or deed, then they too shall be investigated to see whether they are infected with sorcery. The person shall also be asked from whom he learned such sorcery, and how it came about; whether he also employed such sorcery against more people, and against whom, and what damage thus occurred.

Concerning general, unparticularized questions regarding a confession secured under torture

(53) From the brief instructions above any knowledgeable person can well gather what should be further and additionally inquired about concerning the confessed crime of the person examined, according to the circumstances

of each case—what serves to the discovery of the truth, although it is all too long to be described. Any knowledgeable person can surely deduce from the above exposition how he should handle such additional questioning in other cases in order that one who has confessed a crime can be questioned about those signs and circumstances which no innocent person can know or discuss, and it shall be carefully transcribed how the person questioned explains the details.

Concerning the checking out and investigating of the incriminating circumstances confessed

(54) When there is employed the aforementioned questioning of a confession secured with or without torture, the judge shall send to the places and shall (with all diligence appropriate to the circumstances which the person examined told of in confessing the crime to the extent useful to precise knowledge of the truth) have it inquired whether the confession of the aforementioned circumstances is or is not true; because when someone declares the extent and mode of a crime as explicated in part above, and when just these circumstances are discovered, then it can be firmly established that the person committed the crime confessed, particularly then when he discloses such circumstances as occurred in the event and which no innocent person can know.

Where investigation reveals the circumstances confessed to be untrue

(55) When it is determined in the aforementioned investigation that the circumstances confessed were untrue, this falsehood shall be put to the prisoner, who shall in consequence be verbally severely chastised, and he may then be brought to examination under torture a second time, in order that he declare the above-mentioned circumstances truly and properly, because sometimes the guilty falsely declare the circumstances of a crime and believe that they can thereby make themselves appear innocent when the investigation discloses the untruth.

That the circumstances of the crime not be told to any prisoner beforehand, rather that they be told entirely by him alone

(56) In the previous articles it is plainly set forth how someone who confesses under torture or threat of torture to an unsolved crime shall be questioned about all the circumstances of the said crime and how on that basis subsequent investigation shall take place, in order thus to get at the truth thoroughly, etc.; that would, however, probably be frustrated when the said circumstances of the crime were previously told to the prisoner upon arrest or examination and he thereupon examined. For that reason we want judges to take precautions against such happening; instead we want nothing to be put to the accused before or during examination other than according to the manner plainly written out in the articles just concluded.

Further: the prisoner shall also, at minimum two or more days after the torture and his confession (as set by the judge), be brought before the competent judge and two Schöffen in the guard room or in another room and his confession read to him by the court scribe, after which he shall be asked a second time whether his confession is true, and what he says to that shall also be transcribed.

When the prisoner retracts the confession

(57) When the prisoner denies the previously confessed crime, and the suspicion is nonetheless manifest (as above), then he shall be returned to the gaol and again examined under torture, in addition to there being a thoroughly diligent investigation of the circumstances (as above) to the extent the examination under torture turns upon them—unless the prisoner adduces such reason for his denial that the judge is persuaded that the prisoner made the confession in error, in which case the judge may allow the said prisoner to detail and prove such error.

Concerning the extent of torture

(58) Torturing shall be conducted according to the circumstances of the suspicion regarding the person—much, often or seldom, hard or lenient—according to the discretion of a good, sensible judge; and what the tortured person says shall not be taken down or transcribed while he is being tortured, rather he shall make his statement when he is released from the torture.

When the miserable fellow to be examined has serious wounds

(59) When the accused has serious wounds or other injury to his body, examination under torture against him shall be conducted so that he is as little as possible hurt in these wounds or injury.

Establishing when the confession arising from examination under torture is ultimately to be believed

(60) When, upon the making out of legally sufficient indication of a crime, examination under torture is conducted (as all that is plainly set out in the articles just concluded) and all possible subsequent investigation and interrogation has taken place and the sort of truth is revealed respecting the said confessed crime that no innocent person can tell or know, then this confession is soundly and undoubtedly credible; and upon it, according to the nature of the case, penal sanction is to be pronounced, as hereafter set forth in Article 104 ("When, according to our common written law, someone, etc.") and to be found in several articles following concerning penal sanctions.

When the prisoner has been put to examination under torture upon legally sufficient suspicion and not found guilty or the guilt not proven

(61) When the accused on the basis of such a suspicion as is deemed sufficient for examination under torture (as above) has been gaoled and examined under torture and nonetheless is not convicted through his own confession or through proof of the alleged crime, then the judge and complainant have notwithstanding incurred no penalty on account of the aforementioned legal and proper examination under torture, because the incriminating indica-

tions made out gave reason and excuse for the examination which took place; for the law says that one should keep oneself not only from the committing of crime, but also from all appearance of evil, of the sort that can cause ill repute or indication of crime, and he who does not do that has himself in this way caused his own complaint. And in this case the complainant shall bear his own costs; and the accused shall bear his own support [while in gaol], since he supplied ground for his being suspected; and the authorities shall themselves bear the remaining court costs, for example, for the executioner and other court and gaol attendants. When, however, such examination under torture was employed in violation of this and the holy Empire's lawful ordinance, then the said judges,* as causes of such unjust examination under torture, are subject to punishment, and they shall in consequence suffer punishment and make recompense according to the law corresponding to the nature and circumstances of the violation, and further, shall be brought to account before their next appropriate authorities.

Concerning proving the crime

(62) Where the accused will not confess, and the complainant wishes to prove the crime complained of, he shall be allowed that according to the law.

Concerning unknown witnesses

(63) Unknown witnesses shall not be allowed when challenged by the opposing party unless he who proffers the witnesses proves in essence that they are upright and without evil repute.

Concerning paid witnesses

(64) Paid witnesses are also to be rejected and disallowed and criminally punished.

How witnesses shall testify

(65) Witnesses shall testify from their own true knowledge, declaring the detailed grounds of their knowledge. When they would testify to hearsay, however, that shall be treated as inadequate.

Concerning adequate witnesses

(66) Adequate witnesses are those who are without evil repute and who otherwise are unchallengeable for any legal ground.

Concerning acceptable evidence

(67) When a crime is proved with at least two or three credible good witnesses, who testify from a true knowledge, then there shall be process and judgment of penal law according to the nature of the case.

* The change to the plural without apparent reason is original to the text.

Concerning false witnesses

(68) When witnesses are discovered and convicted of having brought or having intended to bring criminal sanction upon an innocent person through false and wicked testimony, they have incurred the penalty which they wanted to bring upon the innocent person through their testimony as above.

When the accused will not confess following the proof

(69) When the accused still will not confess after sufficient proof, it shall be declared to him that the crime is proven of him, in order that his confession can be secured that much easier; and when, notwithstanding, he persists in not confessing, although (as above) it has been sufficiently proved of him, then he shall nonetheless be condemned on account of the proven crime without any examination under torture.

Concerning designating and interrogating of witnesses

(70) Since, however, it is necessary that the testimony upon which someone shall be condemned to penal sanction be wholly reliable and lawful, where the accused's crime was covert and is not confessed on examination (as above), and nevertheless the complainant wishes to prove the alleged and denied crime, and is permitted, then we want the complainant to have his articles that he wishes to prove by witnesses *(weisen)* properly written up and transmitted to the judge, along with the witnesses' names and addresses, in order that thereafter witness-testimony *(kundtschafft)* be taken in necessary and appropriate manner by several of the judgment-givers or by other proper delegates *(Commissarien)*, as plainly set forth hereafter.

Concerning those among the court who take witness-testimony [examiners]

(71) When the said criminal court is staffed with persons who are knowledgeable enough and capable enough to take such witness-testimony in a lawful manner, then the judge, together with two of the said fitting persons and with the court scribe, shall diligently take the indicated witness-testimony according to law and shall pay particular attention to whether the witness is found inconsistent and shifting in his testimony; and he shall transcribe such circumstances, and how he observes the demeanor of the witness in the proceeding.

Concerning examiners from outside the court

(72) However, [it can happen that] a criminal court (as is found in many places in the Empire) is not staffed with such above-described knowledgeable persons, although nonetheless, according to the common law (*gemeyner rechten*) in criminal matters, persons outside the said court are not to be given duties as examiners or delegates. Yet much depends upon knowledgeable examiners in order that no abridgment occur on account of the ineptness of these examiners. We therefore will and ordain that, should the aforesaid deficiency appear, the drafted articles for witness-proving previously discussed

shall be sent through the judge and four Schöffen (however, without disadvantage or cost to the parties) to the aforementioned next authorities, and that the circumstances and nature of the case, to the extent disclosed, be declared to them, in order that the said authorities can arrange knowledgeable examiners, even though they will not belong to the court at whose request the witness-testimony is to be heard; and when necessity requires or when it is demanded, letters of compulsory summons and safe conduct shall be given, in order that the witnesses be thereby brought to appropriate testimony. And correspondingly, the said authorities shall (to the extent that it concerns them) do all things diligently; and as to what they themselves do not understand, they shall seek advice of the legally knowledgeable (*rechtverstendigen*), in order that such witness-testimony be taken according to law and also without expense and disadvantage to the parties.

Concerning the taking of witness-testimony

(73) When such witness-testimony is to be heard, then the taking of it shall be thus, to wit: when the testimony-taking is to be before several members from a criminal court who are knowledgeable in these matters, the judge shall set a day for the convening of the said testimony-taking, and written objection and defense shall be permitted in proper form as hereafter follows.

Where, however, owing to lack of knowledgeable persons among the court, testimony-taking is conducted as above discussed by delegates from outside the court; or when the Schöffen of the said criminal court have not met, so that further expenses and delay would be occasioned by having them meet, and when their meeting is neither useful nor necessary to such a proceeding, and consequently, expenses and delay of process would be prevented, then we will and ordain in that case that the delegates and examiners shall proceed as afterwards follows.

At the outset, the said delegates and examiners shall set a day to the parties for the taking of witness-testimony, and upon such fixed day upon payment of the appropriate fees give written copies to both sides and set an appropriate period which they hold and regard as necessary according to the circumstances of the case, in order that such copies can be brought to the attorneys and in particular the prisoner; and the counselors of the prisoner shall in this case be allowed to him; and what then each party wants to say about or in the said witness-testimony-taking, that he shall adduce to the above-said examiners in writing in duplicate upon a fixed day set him by the examiners within a period appropriate to the circumstances of the case. Furthermore, one copy shall be kept by the examiners, and the second handed on to the other party, in order that he can make his written rejoinder (if he wishes).

When, however, the parties wish to write further in the matter, that shall all be written in duplicate and take place within the period set for it by the examiners; and, however, neither side shall be allowed to make more than two writings on account of one testimony-taking (in which they shall bring forward and conclude all their pleas and requirements), unless the examiner* finds due to particular, cogent, and compelling reasons that this absolutely cannot

* The change to the singular follows the original.

be managed, whereupon he shall allow each party one further writing and not more, and within an appropriately expedited period. When, therefore, the witness-testimony has been taken and disclosed, and the pleas and objections of both parties have been adduced and completed, then the examiner or delegate shall as promptly as possible forward all this to the authorities who authorized him to conduct the said hearing, which authorities shall then send their proposed judgment to the judge before whom the said proceeding is pending, concerning what shall be decided in the said case.

Concerning witness-testimony of the accused to his exculpation

(74) When an accused wants to proffer witness-testimony and witness proof to exculpate himself from his alleged crime, and when the judge deems such proffered witness proof relevant, then the same shall be carried out as above regulated, and additionally concerning such representation of innocence, as set forth in Article 151 ("When someone has admitted a deed, etc.") and still more plainly in several articles thereafter.

Concerning the expenses of the witnesses

(75) When someone proffers witness-testimony in criminal matters, he shall give every witness who is a common man and pedestrian eight Kreuzer (or the equivalent amount in the coin of each territory) for his expenses for each day he spends in such testifying. However, with other and various persons this matter shall be handled according to the discretion of the examiners.

That no witnesses be given safe-conduct for the legal proceedings

(76) Neither party nor witness shall be given safe-conduct before the judges or delegates for the criminal proceeding. However, against coercion the parties and witnesses may be given safe-conduct to the court.

That justice be done rapidly

(77) In order to prevent expense we ordain and establish that justice be rapidly done in all criminal cases—rapidly proceeded with and not intentionally protracted.

Concerning the setting of a final *Rechttag*

(78) When the complainant moves for a final Rechttag upon the basis of the accused's confession or of witness-testimony presented and adduced and completed (as above), then this shall be set for him without delay. When, however, the complainant does not want to move for a final Rechttag, then the said final Rechttag shall also be set upon the motion of the accused.

That the Rechttag be notified to the accused

(79) He whom it is sought to punish upon the motion of the complainant with final criminal proceedings shall be notified of this three days before, in

order that he may have time to consider, lament, and confess his sins; and if he asks to receive the Holy Sacrament, it is mandatory that he be given it without refusal; and also following such a [religious] confession, as is the custom, there shall be sent to the accused in gaol such persons as will admonish him to good salutory things and thereby help him; however, too much to drink shall not be given him lest his understanding be impaired.

Proclaiming court

(80) Court shall be proclaimed as in each place is appropriate to good customary tradition.

The conference of the judgment-givers before the Rechttag

(81) Before the Rechttag all that has been gone into shall be read out before the judge and judgment-givers; everything shall be properly written out (as hereafter set forth in Article 181) and brought before the judge and judgment-givers. On that basis judge and judgment-givers can discuss among themselves and decide what judgment they wish to speak. And where they are in doubt they shall seek further advice from the legally knowledgeable—in such places and locations as are indicated at the end of this our ordinance; they shall then have the concluded judgment written down for the other court proceeding, according to the forms hereafter set out in Article 190 ("When corresponding to this our and the holy Empire's ordinance, etc., is found"), in order that the said judgment can subsequently be issued without delay at the final Rechttag, as is hereafter set out concerning the issuing of such a judgment.

Concerning the sitting and the ceremonial bell-ringing of the final court

(82) On the day of court at the arrival of the customary time of day, the criminal court shall be called to session with the customary bell-ringing, and judge and judgment-givers shall proceed to the court place where it is regular for the court to sit according to good custom, and the judge shall have the judgment-givers be seated and he shall also sit, having his staff or his bared sword in hand, according to the territorial tradition of each place, and he shall remain seated in a dignified manner until the end of the proceeding.

That this our and the holy Empire's ordinance be kept present, and that there not be denied to the parties what they need therein

(83) At all criminal proceedings judge and Schöffen shall have present this our ordinance and decree and shall proceed accordingly and shall also give directions from this our ordinance to the parties upon their request to the extent necessary to their case, in order that they know how to keep to it, hence that they not be denied their due or endangered through ignorance thereof. The parties shall also be given written copies of the articles they need from this our ordinance upon their request with appropriate payment.

Concerning the judge's question whether the court is properly staffed

(84) When the court has thus seated itself, then the judge shall ask each of the Schöffen individually: "*N.*, I ask you whether the final court is properly staffed for criminal proceedings." When the said court is staffed with not less than seven or eight Schöffen, then each Schöffe shall answer: "Lord judge, the final criminal court is properly staffed according to Emperor Charles V's and the holy Empire's ordinance."

When the accused shall be publicly put in the stock, pillory, or iron collar

(85) When the sentence to penal sanction is finally decided against the accused, then before or after there shall be maintained (where it is customary) the practice of putting the culprit publicly in the market or square for some time in stock, pillory, or iron collar.

Leading the accused before the court

(86) Afterwards the judge shall command that the accused be brought before the court by the executioner and court attendant, well guarded.

Concerning the ceremonial denunciation of the accused

(87) The ceremonial denunciation *(beschreien)* of the accused at this stage in the presence of the complainant and upon his demand shall be retained according to the good custom of each court. When, however, the accused is held innocent because the complainant does not want to carry on with the judicial proceeding, and nonetheless the accused demands the proceeding, then this ceremonial denunciation is not requisite to it.

Concerning orators *(fürsprechen)*

(88) Complainants and respondents shall each upon their demand be allowed an orator from among the court, and these shall by their oaths promote justice, truth, and the system of this our statute and in no harmful way knowingly or wilfully hinder or misrepresent it—this shall be commanded of them by the judge upon their obligation; moreover, the said Schöffe who has thus been the orator of the complainant shall abstain from the concluding of the judgment, although the remaining judge and Schöffen shall continue. Indeed, it shall be left to the wishes of the complainant and accused to take their speakers from among the Schöffen or from elsewhere or to speak each for himself; however, when someone takes a speaker from outside the sworn Schöffen of the court, the said speaker shall beforehand swear to the judge so to conduct his speech as is set forth above in this article concerning orators taken from among the Schöffen.

Further: in the next following article concerning the complaint, the orator shall insert in the first place the name of the complainant where an "*A*" appears, and for "*B*" the name of the accused; further he shall for "*C*" indicate the crime in the briefest fashion, be it murder, robbery, theft, arson, or other, in the way each crime is named. And it is to be plainly noticed when a complaint is made ex officio that invariably in such a complaint there shall be said in place of the name of the complainant: "Complaint of the authorities ex officio."

Prayer of the orator who complains ex officio or otherwise

(89) "My Lord (name of judge): *A*, the complainant, complains against *B*, the culprit who presently stands before the court on account of the crime of *C* which he committed; whereas the said complaint has already been brought before you, the complainant prays that the said complaint might be earnestly judged with regard to all the proceedings and to the writings produced, this all having previously sufficiently happened according to the estimable and lawful criminal courts ordinance of Emperor Charles V and of the holy Empire; and that thereupon the accused be appropriately punished for the proven crime with final sentence, in a manner suitable to law and to the ordinance of this court."

Further: when the orator cannot make the said complaint and motion orally he may submit it to the court in writing and say the following: "Lord judge: I ask that you might let your scribe publicly read out the complainant's complaint and plea from the sheet of paper submitted."

What and how the accused may plead through his orator

(90) When the accused has previously confessed the crime in an incontrovertible manner, or it has been sufficiently proved of him (as plainly set forth previously concerning sufficient proving and such incontrovertible confession), then he may do nothing other than plead for mercy or let it be pleaded for him; when, however, he does not confess or when he admits the alleged deed but brings forward thereto the sort of grounds by which he hopes to be exculpated from penal sanction, then he shall have pleaded through his orator as hereafter follows.

Further: where in the now following article a "*B*" stands, the accused shall be succinctly named and understood; where "*A*," the complainant; and where "*C*," the crime complained of.

"Lord judge: *B*, the accused, responds to the alleged crime of *C*, which it has been alleged through *A* as complainant that he is said to have committed, in every detail as he has previously responded and as sufficiently adduced. And he prays that you earnestly judge all the proceedings and writings relative to the said complaint and relative to the response in the manner in which all that has heretofore been sufficiently brought out and brought forward in the estimable and lawful criminal courts ordinance of Emperor Charles V and of the holy Empire; and he prays that on the basis of his revealed innocence he be declared innocent with final judgment and law, together with reimbursement of the court costs incurred, and that the complainant, in accord with this imperial criminal courts ordinance, be bound to final process before the court (as above indicated) regarding punishment and compensation."

Further: when the designated orator cannot make this aforementioned response and plea orally, he may submit it to the judge in writing and say the following: "Lord judge: I pray you, let your scribe read out the response and plea of the accused from this sheet of paper submitted." Upon such a prayer the judge shall command the scribe to read out the said submitted sheet.

Concerning the denial of a crime which has been previously confessed

(91) Should the accused at the final Rechttag deny the crime which he has in fact previously confessed properly and incontrovertibly; and further, when the judge on the basis of this confession has discovered so many different circumstances that such a denial is only to be taken as obstructive of justice (as is found above in Article 56 and in several articles afterwards through to Article 62, concerning incontrovertible confession), then the judge shall inquire on oath of the two commissioned Schöffen who with him heard the said confession read out whether they heard the confession read out. And when they say "yes" ["no"?] to that, the judge shall always seek advice of the legally knowledgeable or others at those places as are hereafter indicated; and because such Schöffen in this case act not as witnesses but as cojudges, they shall not therefore be excluded from the court or from the judgment.

How the judge and Schöffen or judgment-givers, following the submissions of both sides and everything else and also following final decision, shall formulate the judgment; and how also the Schöffen or judgment-givers shall be questioned by the judge

(92) After both sides have made their submissions, and after everything else has been brought up, and after these matters are finally decided, then the judge, Schöffen, and judgment-givers shall take up with diligent consideration and deliberation everything which was submitted to and done before the court, and shall thence (upon their best understanding of this our criminal courts ordinance and according to the circumstances of each individual case) have formulated in writing the most appropriate and even-handed judgment; and when the judgment has been so formulated, the judge shall thereupon ask: "N., I ask you the law."

Whereupon the Schöffen and judgment-givers shall forthwith answer in this way

(93) "Lord judge: It is my judgment which has been formulated in writing as judgment, upon the ground of all which has been brought before the court and dealt with there (lawfully according to the court ordinance) and upon the ground of sufficient consideration of all that which has been asserted."

How the judge shall announce the judgment

(94) Upon the above-discussed decision of the Schöffen and judgment-givers the judge shall have the final judgment which has been formulated in writing publicly read out by the sworn court scribe to both parties; and where penal sanction has been decided upon, it shall be properly announced how and to what extent this shall occur to body or life, as is found and set forth below concerning penal sanctions in Article 104 and in several pages thereafter. And how the scribe shall formulate and transcribe such judgments which it is appropriate to proclaim and read out (as above set out), that is to be found below in Article 190.

(95) The speech just regulated, which is to take place in court, is framed

in terms of a complainant and a respondent. But it is particularly to be noticed where more than one complainant or one respondent stand before the court, the same words shall be used with concern to the way several people are spoken of.

When the judge shall break his staff

(96) As the accused is being finally condemned to penal sanction, the judge shall break his staff (in those places where it is custom), and he shall turn over the miserable fellow to the executioner, and command the executioner by his oath faithfully to carry out the judgment delivered; then he shall rise from the court and see to it that the executioner carries out the sentence pronounced under adequate security conditions.

Concerning the proclaiming of the executioner's peace

(97) When the judge has broken his staff after the final judgment, and when, further, the executioner has brought the miserable fellow to the place of execution, the judge shall have publicly proclaimed and announced—and ordered by the authorities on pain of body and property—that the executioner is under no circumstances to be hindered, likewise that no hand is to be laid upon him should he bungle.

Question and answer following execution of the judgment

(98) When the executioner asks whether he has carried out the judgment properly, the said judge shall reply to the question in this manner: "Because you have executed as judgment and law provided, I now put the matter to rest."

When the accused is lawfully found innocent

(99) Should, however, the accused be found innocent by judgment and law, then to the extent that that happens and the judgment is declared, it shall be suitably followed and complied with. As concerns compensation, however, should the person held innocent demand it as complainant, in that case the parties shall be remitted to final civil process before the court as heretofore thereof set forth and established.

Concerning unnecessary, useless, and malicious questions which occur in court

(100) Since we have also learned that in the past in some criminal courts many superfluous questions and motions have been used, which are unnecessary to the discovery of the truth or to justice, but which only hinder and protract the law, we desire that such and other unseemly bad usages, which unnecessarily delay or hinder, or which endanger the people, be hereby discontinued and abolished. And where the authorities learn that something to the contrary is practiced, they shall vigorously abolish it and punish for it, as often as it wrongfully appears.

Concerning corporal punishments which are not sentences to death or perpetual imprisonment, and which are undertaken ex officio

(101) Concerning how there are to be pronounced by the judge punishments upon body or limb which are not to death or perpetual imprisonment, and which are undertaken as a public matter ex officio, the form of judgment therefore is found set forth below in Article 196 ("When a person . . .").

Concerning [religious] confession and admonition after the condemnation

(102) After the condemnation of the miserable fellow to death, he shall be allowed [religious] confession a second time, and there shall also be at least one or two priests alongside when he is led out or dragged out, who shall admonish him to the love of God, to proper faith and trust in God and in the sacrifice of Christ our Saviour, and also to the repentance of his sins. Further, a crucifix may always be carried in front of him when he is led before the court and led out to death.

That the fathers-confessor shall not instruct the miserable fellows to deny admitted truth

(103) The fathers-confessor shall not instruct the culprits to deny again what they have truthfully admitted relative to themselves or other persons; because it is inappropriate for anyone to help criminals to conceal with falsehood their wickedness against the common good and to the disadvantage of pious people, and to help fortify further evil, as stated in Article 31 ("When a proven criminal . . .").

A preamble concerning how crime shall be punished

(104) When, according to our common written law *(gemeynen geschriben rechten)*, someone has forfeited his life on account of a crime, he shall be condemned and executed in the form and manner appropriate to good usage or to the disposition of a good, legally knowledgeable judge who can rule upon circumstances and seriousness of the crime. But in those cases (or similar ones) in which our imperial law does not provide or authorize someone to be sentenced with death, we have also in this our and the Empire's ordinance imposed no death penalty, but instead, for some crimes we have authorized the law to punish upon body or member such that the person punished nonetheless remains alive. Such penalty may also be imposed and employed, according to the good custom of each territory, or moreover, in the discretion of a good knowledgeable judge, as is above said of death penalties, if our imperial law imposes some punishments which are inopportune according to the circumstances of the time and of the territory and to some extent cannot be well employed according to the letter; further, when this same law does not declare the form and extent of every punishment, rather enjoins resort to good custom or to the decision of a wise judge and provides for his discretion, the penalty is to be set and handled according to the circumstances and seriousness of the crime, from esteem of justice and for the sake of the common weal. But it is especially to be noticed that, in those (or similar) cases where

our imperial law inflicts or provides absolutely no punishment to life, honor, body, or member, judge and judgment-givers are to punish no one in a contrary manner, by death or otherwise. And in order that judges and judgment-givers who are not learned in such law may, in deciding upon such punishment, act that much less against the said law or against good and permissible custom, there is below set out regarding some punishments when and how the said law shall operate in accord with good custom and reason.

Concerning criminal cases and punishments not particularly explicated

(105) It is further to be noticed that in those criminal cases or complaints as to which punishment is not provided or made sufficiently plain or understandable in the following articles, judge and judgment-givers (when guilt is apparent) shall seek advice how such odd and incomprehensible cases shall be best judged and dealt with according to our Imperial law and to this our ordinance, and they shall give judgment accordingly. For not every conceivable sentence and punishment can be sufficiently set forth in this our ordinance.

How those who defame God or take his name in vain shall be punished

(106) . . .

Punishment of those who perjuriously swear a solemn oath before judge and court

(107) . . .

Punishment of one who breaks a sworn recognizance

(108) . . .

Punishment of sorcery

(109) . . .

Punishment of unlawful criminal libel

(110) . . .

Punishment of counterfeiters of coin and also of those who coin without having privilege

(111) . . .

Punishment of those who falsely make a seal, letter, real estate title document, deed, or interest books or register

(112) . . .

Punishment of someone who falsifies weights, measures, and goods

(113) . . .

Punishment of those who falsely and fraudulently disturb boundary sign, field boundary, monument, or marker

(114) . . .

Punishment of attorneys who deal against the interest of their clients, intentionally and maliciously to disadvantage them

(115) . . .

Punishment of immoral sexual relations against the order of nature

(116) . . .

Punishment of immoral sexual relations with nearly related partners

(117) . . .

Punishment of those who kidnap wives or maidens

(118) . . .

Punishment of rape

(119) . . .

Punishment of adultery

(120) . . .

Punishment of the evil of the sort incident to bigamous marriage

(121) . . .

Punishment of those who, for wicked gain, sell their wives or children into immoral sexual traffic

(122) . . .

Punishment of pimping and facilitating adultery

(123) . . .

Punishment of treason

(124) . . .

Punishment of arsonists

(125) . . .

Punishment of robbers

(126) . . .

Punishment of those who agitate the populace

(127) . . .

Punishment of those who wickedly live outside the law

(128) . . .

Punishment of those who wickedly feud against people

(129) . . .

Hereafter follow several evil homicides; and concerning the punishment of their authors

First, concerning the punishment of one who clandestinely administers poison or toxin

(130) . . .

Punishment of women who kill their children

(131) . . .

Punishment of women who, in order to be rid of their children, abandon them to danger—the children, however, being found and saved

(132) . . .

Punishment of those who abort the children *[sic]* of pregnant women

(133) . . .

Punishment of a doctor who kills by his doctoring

(134) . . .

Punishment of suicide

(135) . . .

When someone has a harmful animal which kills someone else

(136) . . .

Punishment of murderers and killers who can have no adequate excuse

(137) . . .

Concerning undisputed killings which occur in circumstances such that the punishment is excused

(138) . . .

First, concerning genuine self-defense, since it exculpates

(139) . . .

What genuine self-defense is

(140) . . .

That the self-defense shall be proven

(141) . . .

When and how in self-defense cases, the burden of proof shifts to the complainant

(142) . . .

Concerning killings seen by no one else, and to which self-defense is pleaded

(143) . . .

Concerning asserted self-defense against a woman

(144) . . .

When someone, in genuine self-defense, kills an innocent person against his—the actor's—will

(145) . . .

Concerning accidental homicide which happens against the actor's will, apart from self-defense

(146) . . .

When someone is struck and dies, and it is mooted whether he died of the wounds

(147) . . .

Punishment of those who intentionally or unintentionally assist others with murder in fights and brawls

(148) . . .

Concerning inspecting a deceased before the burial

(149) . . .

Hereafter explicated generally are several sorts of homicide, which may also be subject to exculpation, in order that they may be properly handled

(150) . . .

How the grounds which tend to exculpate a conceded deed shall be adduced

(151) . . .

When the articles of proof submitted by the culprit are not persuasive

(152) . . .

Concerning who shall bear the costs of [room and board] in the aforesaid process

(153) . . .

Concerning when one who wishes to proceed in the aforesaid manner is very poor

(154) . . .

When someone who was [observed] in the act of murder is gaoled and wishes to adduce his innocence

(155) . . .

Concerning proceedings on the alleged criminal transgression before the accused is gaoled

(156) . . .

Hereafter follow several articles concerning theft

Concerning a first offender's trifling clandestine theft

(157) . . .

Concerning a first offender's publicly committed theft, for which he is denounced, it being more serious

(158) . . .

Concerning a first offender's malicious theft committed by climbing or breaking in, that being still more serious

(159) . . .

Concerning a first offender's theft, in amount of five gulden or more, yet otherwise without aggravating circumstances: here advice shall be taken

(160) . . .

Concerning a second theft

(161) . . .

Concerning theft a third time

(162) . . .

Where more than a single ground of aggravation is attached to the theft

(163) . . .

Concerning young thieves

(164) . . .

When someone takes something clandestinely from goods as to which he is a next heir

(165) . . .

Stealing in genuine distress of hunger

(166) . . .

Concerning the fruits and profits of the field, how and when theft thereof is to be defined

(167) . . .

Concerning the stealing of wood or its chopping in forbidden manner

(168) . . .

Punishment of those who steal fish

(169) . . .

Punishment of those who deal faithlessly with entrusted or pledged goods

(170) . . .

Theft of holy or sacred things from sacred or nonsacred precincts

(171) . . .

Concerning punishment of the aforesaid thefts

(172) . . .
(173) . . .
(174) . . .
(175) . . .

Concerning punishment or detention of persons of whom crime and evil must, upon manifest ground, be anticipated

(176) . . .

Concerning punishment for aiding, abetting, and assisting the criminal

(177) . . .

Punishment of attempted crime

(178) . . .

Concerning criminals who, owing to youth or other reasons, lack understanding

(179) . . .

When a gaolkeeper of criminals helps one escape

(180) . . .

Concerning a general account of how the court scribes shall completely and properly transcribe the criminal court proceedings, following in the next and several subsequent articles

(181) Every court scribe shall transcribe in criminal cases upon his oath all proceedings which take place on account of the criminal complaint and response, in a manner thoroughly accurate, distinct, and orderly. And indeed, the complaint of the complainant shall be transcribed before he gives surety regarding the accused; or always beforehand when the complainant cannot give surety and is in consequence taken into custody in gaol along with the accused, hence before examination under torture or criminal process is employed against the accused. And this shall all take place before, at minimum, the judge or his official representative and two of the court, and the said transcription shall be made by the court scribe of the said court properly and distinctly; and thereafter shall be written down whether and how the complainant has lawfully given surety respecting his claim, according to this our ordinance, or where he has not made surety, whether and how he had himself gaoled on account of the carrying out of the lawsuit.

(182) Further, what the accused replies to the said complaint when he is urged to do so at the outset without torture—that shall be transcribed following the said complaint; and the scribe shall always record the year, day, and hour upon which occurred every event before or after mentioned, also who was present each time; and he, the scribe, to show that he himself heard and transcribed this, shall also sign with his own Christian name and surname.

(183) When, however, the accused denies the complaint in his response, and the complainant may adduce legally sufficient indication concerning the alleged crime (as previously set forth concerning such legally sufficient indication), then what the complainant adduces concerning the said indication or suspicion before the court or the delegated Schöffen, also what is proven by the said adduced indication according to this ordinance, shall all be accurately transcribed as aforesaid.

(184) The legally sufficient indication and suspicion of the crime deemed proven according to this our and the holy Empire's ordinance; and in addition (since according to this our ordinance the prisoner shall at first be urged without torture and only upon the threat of it, and also exhorted to explaining his innocence) what he is asked and urged, and what he finally answers, also everything thereupon subsequently investigated and discovered—that shall all be transcribed as aforesaid.

(185) And when it comes to examination under torture, what then the accused thereby confesses, also what details he gives of the confessed crime which are useful and beneficial to the truth (as above set forth in this our ordinance); and further, what is also (in accord with this our ordinance) discovered and dealt with as a result of this search for the truth—all that and every detail the court scribe shall properly, distinctly, and sequentially transcribe.

(186) When, however, the accused persists in denying the complaint and the complainant wishes to prove with witnesses the essential element of the crime according to this our ordinance, then, to the extent the said court is suited to conduct such proceedings, the court scribe shall also, as aforementioned, diligently transcribe them. When, however, for this purpose the aforesaid authorities appoint delegates, they shall have transcribed in its entirety and suitably that which is dealt with before them.

(187) When, however, the accused admits the crime, yet alleges the sort of grounds which would exculpate him from the crime, these together with all proofs, witness-testimony, witness proof, subsequent investigation and results therefrom, and whatever else (to the extent the said court is suited to conduct such proceedings)—these shall be transcribed as aforesaid.

(188) Where, however, the complaint issues ex officio and not from particular complainants, then there shall be transcribed how the complaint came to the judge, also what the accused responded to it, and what thereafter occurred in all stages of the proceedings in accord with this our ordinance as is above provided in the other instance where there is a complaint.

(189) And the transcription of all the above-treated proceedings, whether occurring ex officio or through a complainant, shall be written out by every

criminal court's court scribe in the aforementioned manner thoroughly, diligently, and distinctly, sequentially and in the form of a file; and there shall always be reported for every proceeding the year, day, and hour it transpired; in addition the scribe shall affirm in the manner aforementioned that he heard and transcribed everything, in order that upon the basis of a thorough transcript done in this way judgment may be firmly and surely given, or where it is necessary, that advice may be sought thereupon as to proposed judgment as need be; in all these matters every court scribe shall upon his oath as aforesaid act with all possible diligence, shall keep secret what has been dealt with, and shall be bound to do all this according to his oath. And the said court book or file shall always be closed and kept in custody at the end of each court day.

A regulation and account how court scribes shall formulate the final death sentence

(190) When, corresponding to this our and the holy Empire's ordinance, a crime is proven or found true, and when, consequently, the stage is reached that a final sentence of death has been decided upon (in the manner aforesaid corresponding to this and the holy Empire's ordinance), then the court scribe shall transcribe the judgment, and the script shall be formulated in the following manner, in order that he can upon the command of the judge publicly read it out at the final Rechttag as is set forth in Article 94 ("Upon the above-discussed . . .") concerning the proclamation of such final judgments.

(191) Where in the next following article a "*B*" stands, the court scribe shall, in formulating and transcribing the judgment, insert the name of the criminal; for "*C*" he shall briefly account the crime.

Opening part of every sentence of death or perpetual imprisonment

(192) "Upon the ground of complaint, response, and everything which was brought before the court, and also upon the ground of the necessary investigation and inquiry into the truth, which has all occurred according to Emperor Charles V's and the holy Empire's ordinance, it is finally adjudged by the judgment-givers and Schöffen of the said court that *B*, who presently stands before this court, on account of the crime of *C* which he has committed . . ."

Note the following concluding part of every sentence[:]

To fire

". . . shall be put to death by burning."

To the sword

". . . shall be put to death with the sword."

To quartering

". . . shall be cut into four pieces through his entire body, and thus put to death, and the four pieces shall be hung out and displayed upon four common roads."

To the wheel

"... shall be executed upon the wheel by the crushing of his members, and further, shall be publicly left upon it."

To the gallows

"... shall be executed upon the gallows with rope or chain."

To drowning

"... shall be put to death with water."

To burial alive

"... shall be buried alive and impaled."

Concerning dragging

(193) When someone has been sentenced to death by the aforementioned final sentence, and it has been decided that the criminal shall be dragged to the place of execution, then the following few words shall be appended to the other sentence (as above) as follows: "And he shall in addition be dragged to the place of execution by dumb animals."

Concerning tearing with glowing tongs

(194) When, moreover, it is decided that the condemned person should be torn with glowing tongs before the execution, the following words shall in addition stand in the judgment, viz: "And he shall in addition before the final execution be publicly driven around upon a wagon up to the place of execution, and the body torn with glowing tongs, specifically with *N.* strokes."

The formulation of the sentence to confine a dangerous man in gaol

(195) "Upon investigation and the finding as true of sufficient indication of bad intention regarding future criminal harm, it is adjudged that *B*, who presently stands before the court, shall be confined until he provides sufficient and suitable surety, in order that land and folk be assured of him."

Concerning corporal punishment in which [the criminal] is to be condemned neither to death nor to imprisonment, as above

(196) When upon the basis of convincing proof (had in accord with this our ordinance) a person is to be punished on body or member, yet in such a manner that he nonetheless remains alive, that sentence the judge shall determine, but not otherwise than with the previous advice or upon the command of his authorities and the legally knowledgeable, at minimum with four of the judgment-givers or Schöffen, whom he regards as the most virtuous, and who shall also follow him therein; and he shall issue the sentence in court, ex officio, and it shall be publicly read out by the court scribe. The judge shall also see to it in the aforementioned cases that the executioner executes his judgment, which said judgment shall be formulated by the scribe in the script below following.

In formulating the sentence next set out, the court scribe shall insert the accused's name where a "*B*" stands, and where "*C*" appears, he shall account the crime as briefly as possible.

Opening part of the sentences aforementioned concerning corporal punishment short of death

(197) "After diligent inquiry into the truth, which has taken place in accord with Emperor Charles V's and the holy Empire's ordinance, it is adjudged that *B*, who presently stands before the judge, on account of the criminally reprehensible deed of *C* which he committed . . ."

Note the following concluding part of every sentence[:]

Cutting out the tongue

(198) ". . . shall be publicly placed in pillory or neck collar, the tongue cut out, and in addition be banished from the territory until publicly permitted by the authorities."

Chopping off the fingers

". . . shall be publicly placed in pillory and then the two right fingers—with which he committed the crime and sin—cut off; and further, be banished from the territory until publicly permitted by the authorities."

Ears cut off

". . . shall be publicly placed in pillory, both ears cut off, and be banished from the territory until publicly permitted by the authorities."

With rods flogged

". . . shall be publicly placed in pillory, and further, flogged with rods, and be banished from the territory until publicly permitted by the authorities."

Note that when it is adjudged that a criminal, in addition to a corporal penalty lawfully imposed upon him, restore to someone that person's property, or instead, give to someone something from his own property, as previously in this connection set forth in several punishments, viz: perjury in Article 107 ("He who, before judge or court . . ."), also on account of the immoral sexual relations practiced by a married man with a single girl as in Article 120 ("When a married man another . . ."), further, upon the criminal business of bigamy as in Article 121 ("When a married man another wife . . ."), likewise in several cases of theft as above set out, or otherwise in unnamed cases when it is lawfully decided to do something similar—then the manner in which this restitution or giving over of property shall occur shall be appended to the sentence with plain words, transcribed and proclaimed.

Concerning the form of sentence for freeing an accused person

(199) Where, however, corresponding to this our and the holy Empire's ordinance it is determined that a person, who was detained and accused on account of a criminal matter, is to be declared innocent with judgment and law, then this judgment shall be transcribed as follows and publicly read out upon the command of the judge at the final Rechttag, as previously set forth in Article 99 ("Should, however, the accused . . .").

(200) In the next-set-out article concerning the opening part of a judgment the court scribe shall insert in the transcript of such a judgment the name of the complainant instead of "*A*"; for "*B*" the name of the accused; and where "*C*" stands, the alleged crime shall be accounted.

(201) "Upon the ground of the complaint of *C* which was brought on behalf of *A* against *B*, who now stands before this court, also upon the ground of the accused's response and of all the necessary completed investigation and inquiry, thorough and diligent, all of which occurred according to Emperor Charles V's and the Empire's ordinance, the said accused is found innocent of all crime by final judgment and law"; and when it is the case that the complainant had lawful cause for his complaint, the judge for honestly founded legal cause may be thereby induced to compensate and compromise the costs and damage. What the parties beyond that intend to complain of in the way of damage or compensation against each other, that they shall litigate, as prescribed in the aforesaid ordinance, with final civil law before the same court; or when the complaint has been made ex officio, before the next regular authorities of those who complained ex officio.

(202) Every court proceeding and every sentence (as previously detailed concerning the transcription of all of this) shall, further, following the conclusion of the legal proceedings be fully retained in the court and stored away by the court in a special container, in order that (should it in the future be necessary) such a court proceeding can be found there.

(203) A court scribe who cannot gather a sufficient understanding from the foregoing exposition as to how he should formulate any complete court proceeding or sentence shall first seek guidance of his authorities as aforesaid; when, however, the said authorities have also insufficient understanding of it, they shall seek the advice of other knowledgeable persons.

Concerning the court costs in criminal courts

(204) The authorities of every criminal court shall produce an appropriate and uniform ordinance concerning the costs and the maintenance of the said court, in order that thereby no one be excessively burdened and in order that the guilty criminal be brought all the easier to appropriate punishment and in order that law and justice not be hindered for fear of unfair costs. And in particular a complainant shall not be required to pay to the gaoler more than seven Kreuzer per day and night for the maintenance and custody of the accused. Where, however, it is the custom in such cases to take less, then it shall remain so; as for the remaining court costs and other costs accrued for the staffing of the court—the expense money of the Schöffen or judgment-givers, also of the court scribes, gaolers, doorkeeper, executioner and his assistant—shall be paid by the court or by the authorities of the said court without disadvantage to the complainant.

That the judges shall accept no special payment for the punishment of the criminals

(205) We have been informed that in some places the abuse prevails by

which the judges request and receive special payment from the complainant on account of every criminal who is punished, which practice is wholly contrary to the office and dignity of a judge and contrary to the law and to all equity, because such a judge, when he gets his reward from every job, could well be compared with the executioner. Therefore, we will that henceforth all these judges shall neither request nor receive payment from the complainants.

What shall be done with the property of the fugitive criminal

(206) When a criminal flees, then the judge shall collect two or three friends of the said fugitive; and in their presence and that of two Schöffen of the court who are disinterested in the case he shall have the sworn court scribe record and describe all the fugitive's goods and property lying within the court; and he shall let the criminal succeed to none of it. But those goods which are perishable and cannot be stored the judge with two of the court and the aforementioned friends shall sell, and the proceeds therefrom shall be made note of and the revenue together with the list consigned to the court where it can best be kept safe for wife and children or for his other next heirs. If, however, the friends of the fugitive wish themselves to take this recorded property before it is consigned to the court or indeed afterwards, and provide the necessary surety for the keeping of the said property in their custody and for the withholding of it from the fugitive for so long as he has not yet made peace or the case is not settled, that shall be allowed them; indeed, the said recipients of the property concerned shall provide the criminal's wife and children (if he has such) with the necessary sustenance from the said property, and shall do all this with the knowledge and advice of the judge and of the said authorities; furthermore, the judge and the authorities shall take absolutely nothing from the goods of fugitives for their own benefit.

Concerning stolen or robbed goods which come into the court

(207) . . .
(208) . . .
(209) . . .
(210) . . .
(211) . . .
(212) . . .
(213) . . .
(214) . . .

To what extent the craftsmen are obligated to build and to repair the necessary gallows in the criminal courts

(215) . . .
(216) . . .
(217) . . .

Concerning abuses and evil senseless customs practiced in some places and locations

(218) Whereas[:] it is custom and practice in some places when a criminal is caught with stolen or robbed property and gaoled, that this stolen or robbed property is not restored to the person from whom it was stolen or robbed, rather confiscated by the local authorities. Similar is the abuse in many places that when a sailor has lost his way with his ship and is shipwrecked, that he shall be forefeited to the authorities of the said place with ship, body, and goods. Further, that when a wagoner overturns his wagon and thereby inadvertently kills someone, the said wagoner shall also be forfeited to the authorities with wagon, horses, and goods. Also found connected to many criminal courts and their [authorities] are several abuses, for example, that the gaols are contrived more to torture than to keep custody of the prisoners and persons confined. Further, that occasionally through the authorities' carelessness, honorable persons are seized, without previous denunciation, ill repute, and other sufficient indication, and brought into gaol, and that in the said seizure there is occasionally hasty and thoughtless conduct by the authorities, through which the person seized suffers detriment to his honor. Further, that the sentence is pronounced and proclaimed by the executioner rather than the judge or judgment-givers. Further, in some places, apart from the traitor to our Majesty or otherwise in other cases where the criminal has not forfeited body and property, when a criminal is punished with death, wife and children are reduced to begging and the property confiscated to the lord. Concerning these and similar customs we desire that each of the authorities abolish them and pay attention that they be not practiced, used, or maintained in the future; hence we now by imperial authority hereby abolish, nullify, and do away with them; and they shall in the future not be introduced.

Clarification from whom and in which places advice shall be sought

(219) Since in many places previously in this our and the holy Empire's criminal courts ordinance the seeking of advice has been spoken of, it is therefore required that all criminal courts, when they find themselves in doubt as to their criminal procedure, court practices, and sentences, be obliged to seek advice of their superior courts (*Oberhöfe*), those from whom they have previously been advised according to ancient usage. Those, however, which have no superior court shall, in cases in which the court proceeding has been carried out upon the demand of a criminal law complainant, seek advice of their authorities who are empowered to conduct the said criminal court ex officio and without intervention. When, however, the authorities ex officio bring criminal complaint or proceedings against a criminal, the judges (where they find themselves in doubt) are obliged to seek advice from the nearest universities (*hohen schulen*), cities, free cities, or others legally knowledgeable there where they think the information is obtainable at the least cost. And it is particularly to be noticed that in all doubtful cases not merely Schöffen and judgment-givers themselves, but also anyone who is supposed to deal with and to advise such authorities in criminal matters, shall take the advice of the legally knowledgeable without cost to the parties. When, however, a penal complainant has petitioned the judge to seek the advice of the legally knowledgeable in the particular criminal proceeding and practice, it shall take place at the cost of the petitioning side. When, however, the master, friend, or counselor of the prisoner requests for his benefit similar advice-seeking of the

judge, he shall oblige at the cost of the friends or counselor of the prisoner. Where, however, the friends of the said prisoner are unable, on account or poverty, to bear the aforesaid costs, then the said judge shall be bound to pursue this advice at the cost of the authorities; but only to the extent he has not observed that the advice-seeking is occurring intentionally to the protraction of matters or in order to create more costs (which the aforementioned friends and counselors shall also affirm upon their oaths); thus shall no conceivable effort be spared, lest otherwise denial of justice happen to anyone; for to these great matters great effort is appropriate, because regarding such transgressions, ignorance on the part of those who ought in fact to know will not excuse—concerning which judges, Schöffen, and the said authorities shall be hereby cautioned.

End of the criminal courts [ordinance].

APPENDIX C. THE ORDINANCE OF VILLERS-COTTERETS

Preface to the Translation

The following translation of the Preamble and Articles 139–167 of the ordinance is based on the French text in Isambert, Decrusy, and Jourdan, *Recueil général des anciennes lois françaises depuis l'an 420 jusqu'à la révolution de 1789* (Paris, 1823–1833), XII (pt. 2) 600–601, 629–635. I have had the collaboration of Mr. Courtland Fransella of Bristol, England, and Mrs. Sheila Shinn of Chicago. Many of these paragraphs are translated in whole or in part in A. Esmein, *A History of Continental Criminal Procedure with Special Reference to France*, J. Simpson, trans. (Boston, 1913), 148–163, reference to which has occasionally been helpful.

Ordinance on the subject of the legal system.
Villers-Cotterets, August 1539

[PREAMBLE] Francis, etc.: We make known to all men living and to those yet unborn, that in order to provide in some measure for the good of our legal system *(justice)*, for the shortening of proceedings, and for the relief of our subjects, we have by perpetual and irrevocable edict established and decreed, and we do establish and decree, the following things. . . .

(139) We enjoin all our judges diligently to attend to the expedition of criminal proceedings and cases, previously and before all other things, on pain of suspension, of deprivation of their offices, and of other penalties within our discretion, should they do the contrary: with which we charge the honor and conscience of our said sovereign courts.

[(140)] To whom similarly we enjoin to proceed at criminal sessions to the dispatch of prisoners and criminals, without being able to attend to the judgment of any other proceeding where there be question of civil interest, even if it should depend upon criminality, until all the prisoners and criminals have been disposed of.

(141) And because a number of lesser judges, ours as well as those of others, have hitherto made a number of mistakes and errors in the conduct of criminal proceedings, which have several times caused our superior courts to give interlocutory judgments for the correction of the said mistakes, from which great delay has resulted in expediting the said proceedings and in punishing the crimes.

(142) That judges who shall be found to have made serious mistakes in expediting the said criminal proceedings shall be condemned to [pay] substantial fines to us upon the first occasion, and upon the second occasion shall be suspended from their offices for a year, and upon the third occasion deprived of their said offices and declared ineligible to hold royal office.

(143) And moreover [to them] shall be charged all the damages and interest of the parties, which shall be determined and regulated as above, according to the nature of the case.

(144) And in order that the lesser judges shall not hereafter fall into such great errors, we will that all criminal proceedings, including examinations, reexaminations, and confrontations or other acts and phases of the said criminal proceedings, be conducted by the proper *(leur)* judges or lieutenants, and assessors, and not by our procureurs and avocats, the clerks or their deputed clerks, and this on pain of suspension from their offices, and of deprivation of the same, or of greater punishment and fine if they have habitually offended.

(145) And as soon as complaint of the said crimes, transgressions, and wrongdoings shall have been made, or that they [the criminal courts] shall otherwise have been advised of them, they shall investigate or see to it that a proper and diligent preliminary inquiry is made, in order to advise our said procureur of the inquiry as soon as it is made, and in view of his *conclusions* (which he must promptly enter on the bottom of the said inquiries, without

taking any payment for so doing) [there shall] be ordered by the judge such legal disposition as he finds appropriate to the circumstances of the case.

(146) The said delinquents, those who are imprisoned as well as those summoned to appear in person, shall immediately be properly and diligently examined, and their examinations reiterated and repeated according to the legal form of our former ordinances, and according to the quality of the persons and of the cases, in order to find out the truth about the said crimes, lesser offenses, and transgressions from the mouth[s] of the accused persons if possible.

(147) And after the said examinations have been finished and completed and put in form, they shall be immediately shown and communicated to our procureur, who, with the advice of his avocat, shall inspect them in all diligence in order to make the appropriate *conclusions.*

(148) And if the confessions of the accused are found to be sufficient, and the nature of the case to be such that law may and should be taken upon them [that is, final judgment demanded], the said confessions shall be communicated to the private party, if there be any, to see whether he likewise wishes to take law upon them, for which purpose the written *conclusions* both of the royal or seignorial procureur and of the party to their respective ends shall be communicated to the accused, in order that he may reply to them by way of extenuation only.

(149) And if they or one of them wishes to take law upon the said confessions, it shall immediately be ordered that the witnesses shall be summoned for reexamination and confrontation with the said accused within a period of time which shall be legally fixed, according to the distance of the places and the nature of the case and of the parties.

(150) Unless the case be of so little importance that after the parties have been heard it should be ordered that they be received in ordinary procedure, and have fixed a period to investigate their sides, and meanwhile the accused to be released on bail established according to the nature of the transgression and of the offense, under obligation to appear prepared on the day of the *enquête.*

(151) And if within the period granted for summoning witnesses and having them confronted, or for investigating as [described] above, [these matters] shall not have been satisfied and furnished by the respective parties, the case shall be judged in the state in which it shall be found after the said period has expired, and upon the *conclusions* which shall promptly be taken upon this and submitted in writing by both sides, each to its ends, unless for some great and urgent reason a second period be granted to do as above: after expiry of which no extension can be made, by dispensation or otherwise.

(152) In cases subject to confrontation the accused shall not be released during the period provided for bringing about the said confrontation.

(153) When the witnesses appear in order to be confronted, they shall immediately have their depositions read over to them by the judges, and upon oath, in the absence of the accused; and those who insist on what is charged

against the accused shall immediately be confronted with him separately and apart, and one after the other.

(154) And in order to bring about the confrontation, both the accused and the witness shall appear before the judge, who, in the presence of both of them, shall swear them to tell the truth: and after this has been done, and before reading the deposition of the witness in the presence of the accused, he [the accused] shall be asked if he has any objections to the witness there present, and enjoined to utter them promptly: which we will him to be bound to do: otherwise they shall not afterwards be received, of which he shall be well and expressly warned by the judge.

(155) And if he raises no objection, and declares no wish to do so, wishing to proceed to the depositions of the witnesses, or requesting delay in order to submit the said objections in writing, or after having set in writing those which he shall have seen fit promptly to raise, the reading of the deposition of the said witness shall be proceeded to, as confrontation, after which the accused shall not be admitted to say nor to raise any objections to the said witness.

(156) When the confrontations are done and finished, the dossier shall immediately be put in the hands of our procureur, who shall examine it well and diligently to see what *conclusions* he should make, be they definitive or peremptory, and he shall submit them promptly in writing.

(157) And if he finds that the accused has raised any peremptory facts inclining to his exculpation, or his innocence, or any facts [raising] legitimate and admissible objections, our said procureur shall require that the accused promptly name the witnesses by whom he proposes to prove the said facts, be they [the defenses] of justification or of objection, or otherwise he [the procureur] shall make definitive *conclusions.*

(158) And upon the said *conclusions,* the judge shall diligently examine the dossier, and shall extract the admissible facts, if there are any, in favor of the accused, be they of justification or of objection: which he shall present to the said accused, and shall order him to name promptly the witnesses by whom he proposes to investigate the said facts, which he [the accused] must do, otherwise they shall cease to be admissible.

(159) And we will that the witnesses who shall thus be named by the said accused shall be heard and examined, ex officio, by the judges or by their appointees or deputies, at the expense of the said accused, who shall be obliged to deposit in the registry the amount which shall be ordered of him for this, if he can afford it, or otherwise at the expense of the partie civile, if there be such, otherwise at our expense, if there is no other partie civile who can do it.

(160) And to this end shall be taken a sufficient and reasonable amount of money, as shall be decided and fixed by our local officers, from the collector of our domain, to whom the said amount, reported with the order of our said officers, shall be approved as an expense in his accounts, and the receipt for the handing over (which he shall have made) of the said money.

(161) The rest of the costs of criminal proceedings shall be charged to

the parties civiles, if there be any, who might recover at the end of the case, and if there be none, or they manifestly cannot bear the expense, then to the funds of our ordinary receipts, as above.

(162) In criminal matters the parties shall in no wise be heard through counsel or the agency of anyone else, but they shall answer the charges of which they are accused through their own mouths, and shall be heard and examined as above, separately, secretly, and apart, excising and abolishing all practices *(styles)*, usages, or customs by which the accused have been wont to be heard in hearings *(jugemens)*, in order to ascertain whether they should be accused, and to that end to have discovery of the facts and articles concerning the crimes and offenses of which they were accused, and all other things contrary to what is contained above.

(163) If upon examination of the dossier the case is found to be subject to torture, or *question extraordinaire*, we will that the sentence to such torture be pronounced to the prisoner immediately, in order to be promptly executed if he does not appeal. If there is an appeal, [we will that] it be taken at once into our local supreme court *(cour souveraine du lieu)* where we wish all appeals in criminal cases to be brought immediately and without intermediary stage, on whatever [grounds] the said criminal matters be appealed.

(164) And if through interrogation or torture nothing can be gained against the accused, so that there is no basis for condemning him: we wish that he, upon being absolved, be done justice as regards the partie civile for reparation of the calumnious accusation: and to that end the parties shall have a hearing of their *conclusions*, the one against the other, and to be disposed of in ordinary procedure, if need be, and if the judges consider it appropriate to the case.

(165) That as for fugitive and contumacious delinquents who have refused to obey the law, credit shall be given to the depositions of the witnesses contained in the *informations* made against them, and verified by legal authority, just as if they [the accused persons] had been confronted, and without prejudice to their objections: and that [shall also apply when] witnesses shall have died, or other[wise] shall not have been able to be confronted by the time the said delinquents do make legal appearance.

(166) That there shall be no ground of immunity for debts nor for other civil matters . . . .

(167) The rest of our and our predecessors' ordinances heretofore made on the subject of the said criminal cases remain in their force and effect, insofar as they are not found to conflict with or prejudice the contents of these present.

INDEX

Bei Fragen zur Produktsicherheit wenden Sie sich bitte an:
If you have any questions regarding product safety,
please contact:

Walter de Gruyter GmbH
Genthiner Straße 13
10785 Berlin
productsafety@degruyterbrill.com